WHEN THE WORK'S ALL DONE THIS FALL

ALSO BY DAVE MCINTOSH

Terror in the Starboard Seat

The Seasons of My Youth

The Collectors

Ottawa Unbuttoned

VOICES OF EARLY CANADA

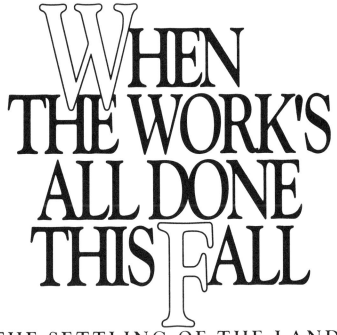

WHEN THE WORK'S ALL DONE THIS FALL

THE SETTLING OF THE LAND

DAVE McINTOSH

Stoddart

First published in 1989 by
Stoddart Publishing Co. Limited
34 Lesmill Road
Toronto, Canada
M3B 2T6

CANADIAN CATALOGUING IN PUBLICATION DATA

McIntosh, Dave
        When the work's all done this fall

ISBN 0-7737-2323-4

1.   Frontier and pioneer life — Canada. 2.   Canada — Description and
travel. 3.   Pioneers — Canada.
I.   Title

| FC162.M25 | 1989 | 971 | C89-094425-3 |
| F1026.M25 | 1989 | | |

Design: ArtPlus Limited / Brant Cowie

Printed and bound in the United States of America

All photographs are from the National Archives of Canada.

For Jean, especially now

CONTENTS

INTRODUCTION

IN THE EVENING, when the grass between the chicken-wire sweetpea trellis and the farmhouse became cool and damp on our bare feet, my cousin John fetched his accordion, and his brother Herb his fiddle, and they sat on the verandah and played and sang, among other favorites, "When the Work's All Done This Fall."

We all knew the words by heart long before we ever saw them in print in *The Family Herald and Weekly Star*. The song is western, but my cousins rendered it on a farm in New Brunswick's St. John River Valley with as much feeling as that of any prairie cowboy beside his campfire.

The yearning in the song then (the early 1930s) came from the knowledge that the wish expressed was unattainable: work on the farm is never concluded, in the fall, or in any other season.

James Inches, a Scottish traveller in Canada, put it this way in 1836: "There is no such thing as the work ever being *finished* — it is always, in every case, *behind*."

Farming is plain damned hard work. Animals demand as much attention as babies and, just like babies, on weekends and holidays, too. Soil yields decent crops only after it has been tenderly bathed and fed. Discouragement has always driven farmers off the land and into jobs with roofs and artificial light.

Canada sprang mainly from agriculture, once the quick-rich attractions of the fishery, fur trade, lumbering and gold strikes were put aside. Up to my generation (I was born in 1921), the bulk of the population was still on the farm, and many urban Canadians today, though city-born, feel some attachment for the land. My high-finance brother, Rob, maintains that public farm policy is driven by the fact that nearly all of us came from farms not more than two or three generations ago. My city-bred daughter-in-law Sandy made her first visit, with her toddlers, to a sugar bush in the spring of 1988; she loved the day and found, to her amazement, that maple syrup doesn't flow directly from trees into retail receptacles. And I read just recently that a new danger — death by choking — faces cattle: condoms discarded by AIDS–conscious lovers in barn mows, haystacks and open pastures.

I believe that the way to tell farm history, and in the process the history of this country, is in the words of those who cleared and tended the land or who, at least, were in attendance as witnesses to farm life. In the past several years, I have been collecting hundreds of excerpts from eighteenth- and nineteenth-century writings that in any way touch on Canadian agriculture. The scope of this book is pre-1900 and all of Canada. There are three sections — Atlantic provinces, the Canadas (i.e., Ontario and Quebec) and the west, with a bibliography for each. The bibliographies cover only the sources of the excerpts and not scores of other writings whose crashing dullness has persuaded me not to cite them. The excerpts are in chronological order, as they should be, apart from several instances, especially in the western section, where some close relationships in subject matter dictated assembly. All the splendid authors of the Peterborough district are gathered together, for example.

The cover painting and six other illustrations are by William George Richardson Hind (1833-1889), whose travels included the Winnipeg-Victoria journey with the Overlanders in 1862. He was the brother of Henry Youle Hind, also represented in this book, who was geologist and naturalist with the expeditions to the Red River, Assiniboine and Saskatchewan countries in 1857 and 1858. Six sketches are by Rev. Jacques Frédéric Doudiet (1802-1867), a Huguenot minister whose attempts to convert Roman Catholics in Lower Canada fell on pretty stony ground. His sketchbook was bought at auction in London in 1985 by the National Archives of Canada, and this publication is believed to be the first to reproduce his work. The National Archives supplied all the illustrations here except for the cattle brands, which appear courtesy of the Glenbow Museum, Calgary.

This book is for the land lover, layman or otherwise, and not for the agricultural scientist, statistician, footnoting historian or economist (though we thank the Canadian economist John Kenneth Galbraith for recording the saying, "When the horse dies on the street the oats no longer pass through for the sparrows").

Of the hundreds of writers quoted here, a few were long-time farmers, some were writers who took up farming, some were leisurely travellers, mainly from Britain, who rolled up their sleeves and pitched into farm work, and a few made observations, usually unflattering, about agricultural resources from the vantage point of a cushy seat in boat, stagecoach or train.

The settler's battle in the earliest days was against the "universal forest," George Henry maintained in 1835. Basil Hall wrote in 1829 that farms were cut out of the wilderness "as stones are hewn out of quarries." And Anna Brownell Jameson said, "A Canadian settler *hates* a tree, regards it as his natural enemy, as something to be destroyed, eradicated, annihilated by all and any means." M. C. S. London, on the banks of the Tobique River in New Brunswick, noted in his journal for October 28, 1851: "Chop-chop-chop."

To the first settlers in Newfoundland, Nova Scotia and the St. Lawrence River Valley, the land bore an aspect of hostility: where there was not rock and cliff, the forest ran down to the shoreline. Even this, probably, was a relief after the terrible voyages in cramped, odious, vomit-slippery holds of the overcrowded immigrant ships. Nearly a tenth of the 189 Highlanders aboard the *Hector* in 1773 died before she reached Pictou harbor, two and a half months after leaving Lochbroom in Scotland. The debilitated survivors received an aftershock: they did not see the open farmland they expected but, instead, wilderness to the water's edge. That dismaying scene was repeated in a variety of circumstances. A destitute family would arrive at the port of Quebec only to find it had another five hundred miles to go to reach an acreage that didn't have a clearing large enough for a garden.

By the 1820s, emigration from Britain and Ireland (the word *emigration* generally covered immigration as well) was being used to rid the country of its pauper (or "redundant") population, which knew little or nothing of farming. Farmers themselves came to Canada because agricultural production was being modernized in England by enclosing land into larger units with higher rents (much as in Canada today).

There were two distinct classes in agriculture: the farmer, or self-described gentleman-farmer, who possessed capital and thereby had some substance, usually small, but sometimes great; and the rest, comprising yeomen, husbandmen, planters, tenants, farm laborers, dairy maids, herdsmen, gardeners, ploughmen, wagoners, and drovers. Only the gentlemen farmers, and by no means all of them, tried to adapt to Canadian climate and soil conditions to improve agricultural methods and yields. Scientific farming was known as "book farming" and largely disdained. This was particularly the case in New France. Norman methods had been good enough for grandfather; they were adequate now.

Book farming gradually won out, more or less. But it took generations. First, the land had to be rid of its trees, big and small. The only useful weapons in this continuous war were the ax and the hoe. It was years before stumps and roots could be removed (by natural rot, mostly) to allow ploughs and harrows to manoeuvre. The literature abounds in descriptions of land clearing; they are exhausting just to read. Little wonder that, right from the start, it was difficult to keep them down on the farm. Anything but agriculture was the customary reaction of farm sons; the fur trade, fishing, lumbering, hunting, sealing, mining were all more attractive than tillage. The voyageur and coureur des bois were the true ancestors of the farm son or daughter who went to the city for a twelve-, ten- or eight-hour job (compared with twenty-four at home). The farmer who had (and could retain) a large family had a built-in workforce. An early rhyme went:

Of all the crops a man can raise,
Or stock that he employs,
None yields such profit and such praise
As a crop of Girls and Boys.

Out on the frontier, there was, as T. R. Preston wrote in 1840, "surpassing loneliness." Clearings were far apart; even when they were not, dense woods separated neighbors. There were appalling accidents caused by ax or falling tree. Cholera and ague (malaria) were prevalent. Medical help was never close at hand, if available at all. Burials were in family farm plots, usually under a favorite tree. Cooperative endeavours (bees) for log burning, barn raising, and the like often turned into drunken brawls, and settlers died in fights or in falls from high rafters. People continually became lost and starved or froze to death. On the prairies, there was not the same extensive forest to contend with, but there were enormous distances to cover on horseback or by Red River cart, a fiendishly squeaky conveyance, and a climate that often killed wheat and other crops before they could ripen — by rust, drought, locust or frost.

Agricultural societies in Canada date from the late 1700s. The first ones were social clubs (like the early temperance societies, but with substitutes for tea) but by the 1850s were, as J. Sheridan Hogan wrote in 1855, "admirable contrivances to make men ashamed of being behind the age, and honoured by keeping pace with it."

There is an enormous body of writing on scientific agriculture in Canada; a favorite subject was fertilizer, possibly because the early farmers didn't use manure. Indeed, they shunned it, moving barns rather than the encircling manure piles. Farmers in the Red River settlement in Manitoba chucked their manure into the Red.

Cheap land often prevented farm improvements. When unmanured land was played out, the farmer simply started another clearing, unloading his exhausted acres on unsuspecting immigrants attracted by the presence of farm buildings and the absence of stumps. Philip Kelland wrote in 1858 that he saw land so used up that the weeds looked half starved.

I have largely avoided the technical literature, apart from machinery and tools and the development of Red Fife and Marquis wheat. The federal government and the provinces (and before them the separate colonies of British North America) produced mounds of pamphlets not only to boost agricultural immigration but to provide instruction on every aspect of farming, from ploughing a section of land to raising hogs or raspberries. We have used a lot of immigration material (it was translated into European languages as early as 1859); one of the delights in reading it today is the variety of euphemisms for forest wilderness ("nature unadorned" is one from a British Columbia pamphlet of 1891). Advice for immigrants poured off Canadian, British and other presses. A lot of it was contradictory. Most of the early travellers praised Canada's agricultural prospects, some blinking at the hard work involved, but there are notable exceptions. The critical authors are, of course, generally the most readable.

Some of the writers were farmers and teachers dedicated to improvements: John Young in Nova Scotia, James F. W. Johnston in New Brunswick, Charles

Grece, William Evans and J. Perrault in Lower Canada, James Anderson and George Buckland in Upper Canada and John Macoun in the West. All pleaded for recognition by public and government of the importance of agriculture to the nation. Evans wrote in 1842:

> It is amazing that other classes, whose interests are fenced in on every side by protecting laws, should take immediate alarm if the Agricultural Class should ask for encouragement and protection. They instantly cry out against them that they want to secure a monopoly, and extravagantly high prices. I never would wish to see extravagantly high prices, but I would wish *remunerating* prices in order to secure the advance of improvement, by the safe and profitable investment of capital in clearing and properly cultivating the wilds of British America.

I wish to acknowledge, with gratitude, the assistance unstintingly given me by a lively group of bibliophiles at the National Archives and National Library. I speak specifically of Liana Van der Bellen, Joyce Banks, Linda Hoad, Claude LeMoine and Peter Rochon of the Library's Rare Book Room, Gilles Desormeaux of the Archives' Manuscript Division, and Gilbert Gignac of the Archives' Photography Collection. I also wish to thank Erik J. Spicer, Parliamentary Librarian, and his staff for their unfailing co-operation, and Lindsay Moir of the Glenbow Museum Library (again) for her generous help.

THE ATLANTIC PROVINCES

NEWFOUNDLAND

CAPT. RICHARD WHITBOURNE was one of Queen Elizabeth's gallant captains who broke the Spanish Armada. He spent forty years trading to Newfoundland. He writes:

> The land of Newfoundland is large, temperate, and fruitful. . . . Then have you there fair strawberries red and white, and as fair raspberries and gooseberries as there be in England, as also multitudes of bilberries, which are called by some whortes, and many other delicate berries in great abundance.
>
> Here also are many other fruits, as small pears, cherries, filberds, etc. And of these berries and fruits, the store is there so great that the mariners of my ship have often gathered at once more than half an hogshead would hold; of which divers eating their fill, I never heard of any man whose health was thereby any way impaired.
>
> There are also herbs for salads and broth, as parsley, alexander, sorrell, etc. And also flowers, as the red and white damaske rose. . . .
>
> This being the natural fruitfulness of the earth, producing such varieties of things, for food, without the labour of man, I might in reason hence infer, that if some were manured, and husbanded in some places, as our grounds are, it would be apt to bear corn, and no less fertile than the English soil.
>
> But I need not confine myself to probabilities, seeing our men that have wintered there divers years, did for a trial and experiment thereof sow some small quantity of corn, which I saw growing very fair; and they found the increase to be great, and the grain very good; and it is well known to me, and divers that trade there yearly, how that cabbage, carrots, turnips, lettuce, parsley, and such like prove well there. Capt. Richard Whitbourne. *A Discourse and Discovery of Newfoundland.* London, 1622.

Whitbourne was not widely believed. Even if he had been, it would likely have made no difference because Britain used Newfoundland strictly as a base for its cod-fishing fleet. Settlement and agriculture were not only discouraged but also outlawed. William Knox told a British parliamentary committee in 1793: "The Island of Newfoundland had been considered in all former times as a great English ship, moored near the Banks during the fishing season, for the convenience of the English fishermen. The Governor was considered as the ship's captain, and all those concerned in the fishery business as his crew, and subject to naval discipline." Thus was coined the famous Newfoundland term, "fishing admirals."

The anti-settlement policy meant that the agricultural possibilities of the interior valleys of Newfoundland were not explored for some 150 years. Such policies were not confined to Newfoundland. The Hudson's Bay Company discouraged agricultural development in the Red River Valley and elsewhere in Rupert's Land on the premise that any kind of permanent settlement on the land interfered with the nomadic fur trade.

John Oldmixon wrote on Newfoundland in the early eighteenth century:

> There is no trusting to the Relations of the first Adventurers. Their hearts were set upon a Settlement, and they made use of their Imaginations in the Description of the Country, to invite the English to follow them thither, and there settle; for the Land and its Product is very different in their Accounts of it, and those that are now given of it.

Early Newfoundland settlers cleared land by burning the forests in winter, but the townspeople had to pay to have them cut down for firewood:

> They built themselves Cabins, and burnt up all that part of the Woods where they sat down. The following Winter they did the same in another Place, and so cleared the Woods as they went. The People of St. John's Town, who did not remove, were put to great Streights for Firing. Wood indeed there was more than enough; but the felling and fetching was very chargeable. Capt. Francis, who commanded there, and was there in the Winter Season, told me, it was the greatest Part of the Profits of the smaller Officers in the Garrison to let out their men to cut and fetch Wood at very good Rates. John Oldmixon. *The British Empire in America.* 2d ed., 2 vols. London, 1741.

Ephraim W. Tucker, an American, explained to the inhabitants of Bonne Bay, where he had landed, that his fellow countrymen set aside a day of public thanksgiving for a bountiful harvest.

> They coolly replied, that they were not under such an obligation; for it was evident to them that the all wise Disposer of events had more favored the Americans by giving them a rich and fertile soil, adapted to cultivation, while he had allotted to the islanders scarcely the means of raising a patch of good potatoes.

On Labrador, Tucker wrote that "the prevailing aspect of the whole region is a heap of bare and frightful rocks." There was not even enough soil to provide decent burials:

I was told that in some instances the dead have been carried miles, in order to find some little hollow in which the earth was deeper, or where a thicker covering could be scraped together to form the resting place of the departed. Ephraim W. Tucker. *Five Months in Labrador and Newfoundland.* Concord, 1839.

Sir Richard Henry Bonnycastle in his chapter on the agricultural resources of Newfoundland quotes Captain Hayes, second in command to Sir Humphrey Gilbert on his voyage to Newfoundland in 1583:

The soil along the coast is not deep of earth, bringing forth abundantly peas small, yet good feeding for cattle. Roses, passing sweet, raspberries, good and wholesome to eat. The grass and herbs fatten sheep in very short space, proved by English merchants who have carried sheep thither for fresh victuals and had them raised exceeding fat in less than three weeks.

The only part of Newfoundland cleared and cultivated was immediately around the main settlements: St. John's, Harbour Grace, Carbonear, Brigus, Conception Bay, and so on. The first agricultural society had only just been formed at St. John's in 1842.

The principal objects of agricultural industry are potatoes, oats, barley, hay, straw, turnips, and cabbages, with the common garden esculent vegetables, which all thrive well, excepting onions, and they are imported cheaper than they could be reared at present, for want of proper manure. . . .

Wheat is growing now within a mile of the house I am writing in [at St. John's]; it was sown in the fall of the year, and in this month, April, has survived all the severe alternations of the winter. Winter wheat, in fact, is better adapted to the climate than any other, as this grain, if sown in the spring, is apt to rot before it shoots, and the short summer will not allow of a sufficient time for its growth. . . .

The great drawback to agricultural pursuit is, however, the want of adequate manure and of roads. If there were roads, of course the miserable half-starved dogs which now draw the small farmer's supplies of wood would give way to horses, and horse-manure would be obtainable. . . .

Of all the ill-used animals in creation, none are worse treated by capricious man than these patient and forbearing [Newfoundland dogs], which, in winter, may be seen toiling harnessed in pairs, or with two and a leader, to low sledges called catamarans, from before day-break until the evening sets in, hauling fire-wood and fence-pickets, at the mercy of boys, and the very lowest class of the population, beaten, jaded, ill-fed, and occasionally wounded and

killed when their over-exerted strength forbids their further progress.
Sir Richard Henry Bonnycastle. *Newfoundland in 1842.* 2 vols. London, 1842.

J.B. Jukes, Newfoundland's geological surveyor, was shown over a farm at St. Mary's, on the southeast coast, by "Father D." The subsoil was generally gravel but better for agriculture than the land around St. John's:

> In two years Father D. has cleared and reduced to a tolerable state of cultivation a considerable space of ground, probably twenty acres, and he intends to grow oats, barley, and turnips. He has several cows, horses, pigs, and sheep, all very fine of their kind. His sheep were certainly the fattest and best-looking and had the most wool of any I had seen in the country. It was now shearing time, and the wool appeared very fine, and was used by my entertainer for his own dress, such as stockings, etc. At present all his cattle ramble about loose in the woods; and in the winter are sometimes harassed and destroyed by the wolves. He hopes to have a complete farm cleared and fenced in a few years, but told me he thought it would require ten years before he could realize the money expended, and begin to gain a profit.

Jukes concluded:

> The country is generally entirely destitute of vegetable mould, and can never, therefore, under any circumstances, become an extensively agricultural one. . . . Were roads opened between the richer and more populous districts (as between the different bays of Avalon and St. John's) quite enough beef, mutton and vegetables might be produced to supply the wants of the population. J. B. Jukes. *Excursions in and about Newfoundland during the years 1839 and 1840.* 2 vols. London, 1842.

Joseph Hatton and Rev. Moses Harvey found that cods' heads provided manure.

> A large portion of the manure used by the farmers is a compost made by mixing cods'-heads and fish offal of all kinds with earth and peat. After standing for a year a fertilising compound, equal to guano, is thus produced. . . .
>
> The growth of agriculture . . . has been very slow. The census of 1836 gave 11,062 acres as the quantity under cultivation. That of 1845 gave 29,656 acres; that of 1855, 41,108 acres; that of 1869, 38,134 acres; that of 1874, 34,293 acres. On these points, however, the censuses are not to be relied on as entirely accurate. As the returns stand they show a decline since 1855 instead of an advance in the quantity of land under cultivation. The want of all facility of access to the fertile districts, and of every encouragement to settle in the interior, is sufficient to account for this stagnation. Joseph Hatton

and Rev. M. Harvey. *Newfoundland: The Oldest British Colony, Its History, Its Present Condition, and Its Prospects in the Future*. London, 1883.

Harvey, in a later guidebook, cites the observations of a Prince Edward Island farmer who spent a winter in the valleys of the Great and Little Codroy Rivers in the southwestern corner of Newfoundland:

> You may judge of the richness of these Codroy lands by the fact that at the homestead where I passed the winter, a farm of not more than fifteen acres of roughly cultivated land, supported a stock of twenty head of cattle and thirty-five sheep wholly upon hay. Along the "intervals" I passed over rich fields where clover had been grown luxuriantly for more than thirty years, without manure, and with no sign of decay or loss of the soil. . . . Indeed, the manure-heaps are considered an encumbrance by farmers there. Observing large and unsightly heaps of stable manure, which had been accumulating for thirty years, as I was told, I asked one of the farmers why he did not turn the manure to account. He replied that their hay-fields had no need of manure, and as for their potato lands, any manure on them would choke the potatoes with clover. Moses Harvey. *Hand-Book of Newfoundland*. Boston, 1886.

NOVA SCOTIA

THOMAS PICHON WAS POSTED to Louisbourg in 1751 as secretary to the French governor, Jean-Louis de Raymond, and travelled widely in Cape Breton and St. John (Prince Edward Island). He was captured when Louisbourg fell to the English in 1758. He retired in England because he had done some spying for the English while at Fort Beausejour in 1753. His book was published in French and English in 1760.

> The surface of almost the whole country [Cape Breton] is extremely disagreeable, being nothing else but a light kind of moss and water. The great humidity of the ground is productive of continual vapours. . . . Being quite uncultivated, and almost uninhabited, it is covered on the one hand with frozen lakes during the space of several months; and on the other, the woods are so thick as not to admit the rays of the sun. . . . Hitherto they have been able to reap no sort of grain; but they have a vast deal of meadow-lands in some parts of the woods, on mossy grounds, and on the banks of rivers, which produces excellent pasture. . . . In some places they have begun to sow wheat and rye; but never could bring them to proper maturity. I believe that oats would grow here, if the small quantity the island is able to produce was worth sowing. . . . They have no manner of fruit except raspberries in the woods, with strawberries and blue-bottles in the plains. . . .
>
> The inhabitants [of St. Peter on the island of St. John] should attend to the essential part, namely to agriculture and pasturage, for the breeding and maintaining of all sorts of cattle, and especially sheep. By keeping them together in folds, the upper lands might be improved, and meadows and corn-fields laid out; from whence the inhabitants would reap a plentiful harvest of all kinds of grain. . . . The white cedar distils a kind of incense. The Acadian women are accustomed to chew this incense, which preserves their teeth, and makes them look exceeding white. Thomas Pichon. *Genuine Letters and Memoirs Relating to the Natural, Civil, and Commercial History of the Islands of Cape Breton and Saint John.* London, 1760.

An anonymous account described Nova Scotia this way:

> . . . it [Nova Scotia] is subject to severe Colds, and thick Fogs; but it would certainly grow better and better every Day, in Proportion as

the Woods are cut down, and the Country cleared and improved. . . . A wholsesome Climate, well agreeing with a British constitution, abounding with all Necessaries of Life, the Seas and Rivers with Stores of excellent Fish, and the Woods with Plenty of winged Creatures and Quadrupeds fit for the Table: The Soil very capable of Improvement, insomuch that the Husbandman and the Fisherman may well vie with one another for Success in their respective Vocations, and set their Industry in Competition, to attain a grateful Retreat for the Decline of Life. *A Genuine Account of Nova Scotia: containing, A Description of its Situation, Air, Climate, Soil and its Produce; also Rivers, Bays, Harbours, and Fish, with which they abound in very great Plenty. To which is Added, His Majesty's PROPOSALS, as an Encouragement to those who are willing to settle there.* London, 1750.

Britain was about to colonize Nova Scotia (Halifax was founded in 1749), and land grants were based on the ranks of discharged soldiers and sailors: fifty acres for a private, eighty acres for a noncommissioned officer, 200 for an ensign, 300 for a lieutenant, 400 for a captain, and 600 above captain. Similar grants applied for certain tradesmen: carpenters, shipwrights, smiths, masons, joiners, brickmakers, bricklayers, and other artificers in building or husbandry. The French traveller Charlevoix is quoted:

One single Grain of Wheat produced 150 pretty Ears of Corn, and each of them so loaded with grain that they were forced to inclose all the Ears in a Ring of Iron, and support them by a Pole.

Robert Rogers observed:

The soil of this province [Nova Scotia] is various, being in some parts very rough and barren; in others exceeding pleasant and fertile, as it is in particular round the Bay of Fundy, and on the rivers which fall into it, where are large tracts of marsh that extend on the sides of these rivers for fifty or sixty miles into the country, and several miles from the bay which, being dyked, is improved to great advantage. Robert Rogers. *A Concise Account of North America.* London, 1765.

John Mitchell was less optimistic:

In Canada and Nova Scotia the snow lies six feet deep for six months in the year and as they have hard frosts and snows for a month or six weeks before this severe season, which they call winter, their winters are eight or nine months long; they have little or no spring or autumn season; the spring does not begin before the month of June; and even in that month our people who resided at Oswego, in the most southern part of all Canada, [Oswego, N.Y., on Lake Ontario was a British garrison] observed hard frosts which destroyed every thing at that time of year; and the like frosts in the month of June are sometimes felt on the warmer sea coasts of New England to the southward of that. These frosts continued all over Canada during the whole summer. . . .

When they have not these frosts, they are subject to more pernicious cold winter fogs, which destroy the fruits of the earth, in the middle of summer, particularly about the great lakes, and in Nova Scotia. . . . Hence they can neither plow, sow, nor reap, in the proper season for either, but are obliged to plow their lands in August or September, and cannot sow them till the month of May the next year, when they must be very unfit to receive seed. John Mitchell. *The Present State of Great Britain and North America, with regard to Agriculture, Population, Trade, and Manufactures.* London, 1767.

Capt. Samuel Holland completed his survey in 1767.

On the South side of the Entrance of St. Andrew's Channel or Petite Bras d'Or, & on the opposite Side to St. George's Island, Monsr. Boulandrie had a convenient Habitation with a fine Farm, which produced Grain of all Sorts, equal to any in Canada; this House was burned by us after the taking of Louisburg, but the Orchard, which was very good, remains, with all Sorts of Fruit Trees; by this it appears that many Parts of Cape Britain are as capable of Improvements in Agriculture as Canada. Public Archives of Nova Scotia. *Holland's Description of Cape Breton Island.* Compiled by D. C. Harvey. Halifax, 1935.

The two Yorkshire farmers John Robinson and Thomas Rispin didn't think much of former soldiers near Annapolis Royal as agriculturalists:

They plough here a little, and there a little, and sow it with the same grain, without ever a fallow, till it will grow nothing but twitch grass; then they cast it aside and go to a fresh place. . . . They are obliged to buy Indian corn, rye and wheat, which they would have no occasion to do would they but properly cultivate their own lands, leave off the use of rum, which they drink in common, even before breakfast. By the growth of a sufficient quantity of barley, which by a little industry they might accomplish, and the brewing of malt liquor, the many fatal disorders which are the consequence of too liberal use of rum would not be known amongst them.

Like nearly all visitors to British North America, Robinson and Rispin had a comment on a summer affliction:

The moschettoes, small flies, resembling gnats, are exceedingly troublesome here. Their bite is venemous, and occasions blisters to rise, something like the small pox.

The two farmers were impressed by Nova Scotia's dikes:

Here [at Windsor] is large marsh, all diked in, called the King's Meadow: Part of it is plowed out, and grows good wheat, barley, oats and peas. . . . This town is situated on a fine navigable river, where they can export or import goods to any part of Europe.

Other observations:

Their method of rearing calves is somewhat singular; as soon as they go to milk, they turn out their calves which suck one side of the cows, as the women milk on the other. . . . They never hopple their cows, but milk them into a pail [and] it turns sower in six or eight hours. . . . The milk is so very sower and stiff that it turns out of the bowl like a cake of flummery: they say the sowerer it is they get the more cream or butter. . . .

The women are very industrious house-wives, and spin the flax, the growth of their own farms, and weave both their linen and woolen cloth; they also bleach their linen and dye their yarn themselves. . . . The candles, soap and starch, which are used in their families, are of their own manufacturing. They also make their own yeast, and make a kind of liquor, by boiling the branches of the spruce trees, to which they add molasses, and cause it to ferment in the manner we do treacle beer in England. . . .

Great numbers of the inhabitants employ much of their [winter] time hunting in the woods, where they will frequently continue for a week, taking a quantity of provisions with them. . . . At night they make large fires near which they wrap themselves up in blankets, and lay down to sleep with as much composure as if they were in their own houses. . . . When the snows are very deep, they have what they call snow shoes to walk on, which keep them from sinking. John Robinson and Thomas Rispin. *Journey through Nova Scotia, containing a particular Account of the Country and its Inhabitants*. York, 1774.

On the Acadians of Nova Scotia, Abbé Raynal wrote:

Agriculture [was] begun in the marshes and lowlands, by repelling the sea and rivers which covered these plains with dikes. These grounds at first yielded fifty times as much as before, and afterwards twenty times as much at least. Wheat and oats succeeded best in them, but they likewise produced rye, barley, and maize. There were also potatoes in great plenty, the use of which was become common.

At the same time they had immense meadows, with numerous flocks. Sixty thousand head of horned cattle were computed there, and most of the families had several horses, though the tillage was carried on by oxen.

The habitations, built chiefly of wood, were extremely convenient, and furnished as neatly as a substantial farmer's house in Europe. The people bred a great deal of poultry of all kinds, which made a variety in their food, and which was, in general, wholesome and plentiful. Their common drink was beer and cider, to which they sometimes added rum.

Their usual clothing was, in general, the produce of their own flax and hemp, or the fleeces of their own sheep; with these they made common linens and coarse cloths. . . . If any of them had any inclination for articles of greater luxury, they procured them from Annapolis or Louisburg, and gave in exchange corn, cattle, or furs. . . .

Real misery was entirely unknown, and benevolence prevented the demands of poverty. Every misfortune was relieved before it was felt, and good was universally dispensed without ostentation on the part of the giver, and without humiliating the person who received. . . .

There never was an instance in this society of an unlawful commerce between the two sexes. This evil was prevented by early marriages; for no one passed his youth in a state of celibacy. As soon as a young man came to the proper age, the community built him a house, broke up the lands about it, sowed them, and supplied him with all the necessaries of life for a twelvemonth. Here he received the partner whom he had chosen, and who brought him her portion of flocks. Abbé Raynal. *A Philosophical and Political History of the Settlements and Trade of the Europeans in the East and West Indies.* 8 vols. London, 1783.

This idyll was short-lived. The British expelled the Acadians from Nova Scotia, fearing a fifth column, in much the same way and for almost the same reason Canadians interned Japanese Canadians during the Second World War.

Never choose a farm in winter, S. Hollingsworth said in 1787:

Port Matoon [has] very few inhabitants. The soil, for several miles round, is full of rocks and stones; and the most barren of any in the province, producing scanty vegetation, and appearing incapable of ever being cultivated. One of the regiments . . . began a settlement here, and built a town in the autumn of the year 1783, which, unfortunately for them, being somewhat too late, and the ground consequently covered with snow, prevented their observing the nature of the soil until the following spring. Their town, at this time, consisted of 300 houses, and the number of people was something more than 800; they, seeing the sterile appearance of their lands, and all their hopes, of course, frustrated, were meditating on the best means of getting away to other places, when an accidental fire, which entirely consumed their town to ashes, with all their live stock, furniture, and wearing apparel, filled up the measure of their calamities, and rendered them perfectly miserable. . . . Those persons who suffered by the conflagration have mostly removed to Chedabucto Bay, in the easternmost extremity of the province.

The island of St. John, commonly called St. John's in the Gulf . . . contains about 6,000 inhabitants who are making rapid advances in the cultivation of their lands, which are esteemed the best of any in the Gulf of St. Lawrence, and produce very large crops of excellent wheat. A considerable portion of the island has been cleared of its woods. The soil is a light sand, and, in some places, a deep, rich, black mould. The heat of the sun in summer is very violent, as this island is not so much elevated above the surface of the sea as the neighbouring countries. S. Hollingsworth. *The Present State of Nova Scotia: with a Brief Account of Canada and the British Islands on the Coast of North America.* 2d ed. Edinburgh, 1787.

Letters and Papers on Agriculture extracted from the correspondence of a Society instituted at Halifax for Promoting Agriculture in the province of Nova-Scotia, a 142-page collection of papers, is the first book on agriculture published in Canada. There were earlier pamphlets (i.e., fewer than 100 pages), including the sixty-eight-page bilingual *Papers and Letters on Agriculture* printed at Quebec in 1790. John Howe, the Halifax publisher of this book, is believed to have printed a 1789 pamphlet on the proceedings of the Halifax Agricultural Society, but no copy has apparently survived.

The first agricultural societies were established about the 1790s in Nova Scotia, New Brunswick (at Saint John in 1790), Quebec and Ontario. The very first may have been the King and Hants Society in Nova Scotia, founded in 1789 a few months before the Halifax Society. But long before this, in 1765, prizes were offered for the best cattle, horses, sheep, butter and cheese exhibited at the agricultural fair in Windsor, N.S. The fair was mainly the creation of Halifax gentry.

The Halifax *Papers* start off in praise of Nova Scotia soil:

Our soil is adapted to every kind of vegetable, and is such as the most judicious Husbandmen prefer. It is in general a sound, friable, crumbling loam; very little clay, or even stiff loam is found, except in our dyked lands. On the southern sea coast, the land in many places is stoney for some distance from the shore, which is a continued range of granite, or coarse slate rock; but large tracts in the interior parts, consisting of a light, sandy loam, are wholly without stones. Properly speaking, we have no mountains, at least none that are high; and a circumstance peculiar to Nova-Scotia is that the highest ridges of land generally have the best soil. No soil produces more luxuriant herbage and crops of grass. With tillage that is any way tolerable, it yields from 20 to 30 bushels of wheat per acre, and the wheat is remarkably heavy — upon accurate trials, it has weighed 64 lb. and even 64 1/2 lb. per bushel. No country produces better potatoes, turneps or carrots, or a greater quantity of each per acre. Flax, hemp, buck-wheat, and indian corn succeed well; and the cyder made in Nova-Scotia is not inferior to any in North-America.

These are notorious facts, too well known to admit of any doubt; the plain inference from them is, that if we are obliged to have recourse to strangers for provisions, it is not owing either to our soil or climate. . . .

The first paper ended with an exhortation — "be industrious, be frugal, be virtuous; and then, be prosperous and happy" — and these recommendations:

Keeping your fields in good heart by manure, and in good tilth by frequent plowing, and clearing them entirely of weeds; the culture of Grasses, Turneps, Potatoes and Carrots to feed and fatten Cattle; a judicious course of crops; and attention in chusing good seed, and frequently changing it. Vol. I, Halifax, 1791.

A Description of the Island of Cape Breton in North America . . . by a Gentleman who has Resided Many Years in the British Colonies (London, n.d. [ca. 1818]) gave this account:

During this [winter] season the settlers are occupied in feeding their cattle, providing their fuel, building vessels or boats, preparing timber for exportation, or catching peltry for sale. In March the ice begins to thaw, and flow out of the harbours, and navigation opens. It is at this time the French fishermen venture on the most hazardous voyage among the icebergs, in pursuit of seals . . . having for this purpose followed the floating ice clear off the coast; they return, to render their oil, and prepare for the cod fishery.

John Young ranks in the forefront of Canadian pioneer-writers in early agriculture. He had a great and quick impact on farm development. At his urging, for instance, fourteen agricultural societies were formed in Nova Scotia less than a year after he had begun his letters in the *Acadian Recorder* of Halifax. His background certainly didn't point in this direction.

Born in Scotland in 1773, Young wanted to become a doctor. His father wanted him to be a Presbyterian minister. The unhappy compromise was business. Young arrived in Halifax in 1814 and failed miserably as a merchant, even when he smuggled goods.

But he had had a keen interest in agriculture since youth, a wide knowledge of scientific farming and a good deal of practical knowledge, as well. He advertised in the *Recorder* in 1818 for a copy of Jethro Tull's *Horse-hoeing Husbandry*, saying he had not read the book for fourteen years. Young wrote thirty-eight letters for the *Recorder*, beginning July 13, 1818, and they were later gathered in this book. His introduction and first letter on the state of agriculture in Nova Scotia in the early 1800s were scorchers:

The contempt in which rustic labour was held originated partly in poverty, meanness and abject fortunes of the emigrants and settlers who were peopling the wilderness, and struggling hard for subsistence with the natural obstructions in the soil. Wherever any of these were so successful or so parsimonious as to amass a little wealth, they were sure to escape from the plough and betake themselves to something else.

The keeper of a tavern or tippling-house, the retailer of rum, sugar and tea, the travelling chapman, the constable of the district, were far more important personages, whether in their own estimation or that of the public, than the farmer who cultivated his own lands. He was of the lowest caste in society, and gave place to others who, according to the European standard of rank and consequence, are confessedly his inferiors. This sense of degradation was perceptible among husbandmen themselves. Such of them as were under the necessity of working set about it with great reluctance and always under a mortifying sensation of shame. They would blush to be caught at the plough by their genteeler acquaintance, as much as if surprised in the commission of crime: and if they saw them approaching, many would skulk from the field, and plunge into the neighbouring thicket. The children were easily infected with this humbling sense of inferiority; and the labours of the farm were to the young men objects of aversion, as those of the dairy were to the women. . . .

When such views were predominant among a people, it is easy to infer the state of their agriculture. The principles of vegetation were so grossly misconceived, that few even of the farmers imagined that plants, like animals, stood in need of food; and manures of all kinds were either disregarded, or shamefully wasted and thrown away. The dung by many was suffered to accumulate about the barns till it became a question of expediency whether it was less expensive to shift the site of the building, or to remove such an intolerable nuisance; and several instances are on record where the former alternative was preferred. . . .

Further, the agricultural machinery in use betrayed the same visible tokens of the degradation of the art. The ploughs were of unskilful construction; fans were rare; and a threshing-mill did not exist in the province. A machine for sowing turnips in rows, a weeding plough with moveable mouldboards or bent coulters to cut up and destroy whatever grew in the intervals of the drills, a cultivator, or a grubber were implements of which the names had hardly crossed the Atlantic. Even a common roller was a wonder, and there were counties that could not furnish one of them. . . .

Agriculture is not an art which may be acquired, like other mechanic trades, by patient drudgery and plodding dullness. The ignorant and unlettered boor is not more capable of being an enterprising and successful farmer than the team which he drives. His ill-directed and unenlightened efforts may fell the forest and burn the timber, and in this way obtain a stunted and ungenerous crop: but he wants the talents and address to court vegetative nature in her coyer moods, to draw forth her latent beauties, and induce her to display the full luxuriance of her charms.

Young held that the "first great duty" in promoting scientific agriculture was liberal public and private patronage protection. He gave the example of "gentlemen farmers" in Britain who gave generously of their private funds to improve farming methods and machinery. No country could flourish, he said, unless it could at least feed itself.

He devoted twelve of his letters to manure, lime, peat and other fertilizers, and five to machinery. His explanation of the purpose of the plough (a "moveable wedge," he called it) and harrow can benefit the layman today:

The only effect of ploughs in subdividing the soil is to cut it lengthways into furrows varying from six to ten inches, according to the pleasure of the workman. They are contrived not so much to produce pulverization as to reverse the surface, to overwhelm the weeds and the remains of the pre-existing crop, and turn up a fresh mould for the reception of the seed. A field of strong clay, after it is laid up into regular ridges by the action of the share and the mouldboard, is almost as little subdued in its tenacity as before the operation. It has only been pierced one way, and ranged into unbroken and unpulverized strips, placed alongside of each other. The former roots maintain firm possession, the earth is little stirred or shaken from them, and without the aid of some other instrument the work is ineffectual and incomplete. Hence the harrow is of as ancient date as the plough, and of as prime necessity. The one inverts the glebe, and the other reduces it to powder; the one buries the weeds, and the other tears out their roots; the one brings up the fresh mould, and the other breaks the clods and overcomes their cohesion. John Young. *The Letters of Agricola on the Principles of Vegetation and Tillage, written for Nova Scotia*. Halifax, 1822.

Young's articles in the *Acadian Recorder* were attributed to Agricola and delegates to the founding meeting of the central board of agriculture in 1819 did not know that it was Young's pen name until after Agricola, sight unseen, had been elected the board's first secretary.

His work continued to have a wide influence on Nova Scotia agriculture for the next quarter century at least. Travellers and historians referring to the agriculture industry simply cited Young. In his 1832 two-volume history, *British America*, John McGregor wrote that the attention of the Nova Scotia government and inhabitants had been directed to improved cultivation with great spirit, vigor and ability by Young, resulting in "extraordinary excitement which gave birth to a new train of ideas on the subject of agriculture."

Thomas C. Haliburton wrote in *A General Description of Nova Scotia*. (Halifax, 1825):

Nova Scotia has been settled for 220 years, but the attention of the French, who occupied it for a century and a half, was devoted almost exclusively to the fisheries and fur trade; and their agriculture was confined to the diked marshes, which each successive year yielded a crop of grain without manure. . . .

It was not until 1783-4, when the great emigration took place from New England, that Nova Scotia could be said to possess an agricultural population. It is therefore probable that persons adverting to the length of time this country has been inhabited, (four years before Canada) would attribute the backward state of its agriculture, rather to sterility of soil or inclemency of climate, than to a studied neglect by both the early French and English planters, who pursued other objects of more immediate gain. . . .

On the side towards the Bay of Fundy, the soil is very rich and free from stone, and contains many thousand acres of diked marsh land. This is alluvial land, and is made by the deposit of the tides, a sediment composed of the finer particles of soil, brought away by the rivers and torrents in their course to the Bay of Fundy, of putrescent matter, salt, etc. This land called marsh, after it has attained a suitable height is diked, and the waters of the rivers excluded. Nothing can exceed its fertility. In many places, particularly around Windsor and Truro, it yields three tons of hay per acre, and has continued to do so without manure for fifty years past. There is a difference in its quality. Where the tide which overflows it is not much enriched, by a long course through the country, it is thin and of inferior quality, and on the other hand, that which is partly marsh and partly intervale, that is, composed as well by the sediment of salt water, as that of fresh water, it exceeds in luxuriance any land in the Province. The quantity of these dikes is very great. At the head of the Bay of Fundy there are seventy thousand acres in one connected body. . . .

The French seldom made use of manure, but continued from year to year to plough the land and sow it with grain. Few soils can bear those repeated drafts upon their bounty without failure in the end, but the diked land, which they inclosed, was too rich to be exhausted in their time, and has descended to their successors not much injured by this hard treatment. . . .

Horticulture is greatly neglected by the farmers. A stranger is much surprised at the total want of good kitchen gardens, so essential to the economy and comfort of a farmer. He is also astonished to see a lavish expenditure in the erection of large farm houses, handsomely painted, and neatly fenced with ornamental railings and pallisades, while the interior of the building is not infrequently cold and unfinished.

In a later work, *The Old Judge*, Haliburton gave this description of the Aylesford sand plain in the Annapolis Valley:

The plain is given up to the geese, who are so wretched poor that the foxes won't eat them, they hurt their teeth so bad.

Frederick Fitzgerald De Roos, *Personal Narrative of Travels in the United States and Canada in 1826* (London, 1827) warned:

Some attempts at cultivation [near Windsor] were visible here and there; but. . . . so striking was the sterility of the scene that a gentleman who accompanied me stopped the carriage and recommended one poor man, an emigrant, who was at work, to leave this unproductive country and remove to Canada, where the soil would repay his labour. . . .

It is to her forests, her fisheries, and her gypsum that her [Nova Scotia's] inhabitants must look for subsistence; the corn-field and the orchard are not for them.

W. Moorsom, an officer in the 52nd Light Infantry, toured Nova Scotia to make military observations, but he observed a great deal else as well. He also had a sense of humor. He notes that farmers instead of confining their cattle at night allowed them to lie out in the woods or along the road; as a result, he often stumbled over a "cow couchant" while travelling at night. He says an English tax collector would have been flabbergasted at the number of windows in new frame farmhouses; in England there was an excise tax on windows.

Moorsom tells us that he liked Nova Scotia country inns, nearly all operated as a sideline by farmers, but warned fellow Englishmen not to bring their fancy airs to such hostelries:

> The last crack of the [stagecoach] whip which, in England, places, as if by magic, a stable-boy at the head of each leader [horse], and a waiter at the door, here dies away unheeded in echo among the woods. He looks round with surprise — surmises that he may have mistaken the house — descends to inquire. By this time, a countryman makes his appearance from the field, announces that the host will "be here after fixing the next load," and cooly begins to unharness. *Milord Anglais* may walk in if he pleases — for though there is no one to invite, there is no one to forbid his entrance: a neat little parlour will then receive him; perhaps even the "mistress" will be sufficiently on the alert to perform the office of introduction in person.
>
> Woe betide him if any symptoms of dissatisfaction or *hauteur* express themselves! If he has the address to conceal his impatience — to open the heart of the good lady by a few civil inquiries — all will be well; his wishes will be attended to with all the ability in her power; but if the costume of the hayfield shock his sensibility; if his pride take offence at the nonchalance and the familiar style of conversation opened by his host in the shape of question and answer, adieu to his expectations of attention and speedy refreshment; he must submit to the convenience of both master and mistress, for they will not put themselves out of the way for him.
>
> This may present no very favourable picture, when contrasted with the corresponding establishments at home; yet I confess myself a great admirer of these little inns. There is a style of simplicity, of primitiveness about them, which has not yet yielded to the calculating habits of commoner intercourse. A few fair words aptly employed will ensure an attention and good-will far beyond those of more splendid establishments, if we estimate each by its motives. Their cleanliness would match that of a Dutch housekeeper; and if the larder be not so well supplied, nor the cookery so piquant, as in England, the best that the farm, the poultry-yard, and dairy afford, seasoned with the best exertions and modest excuses of a pretty hostess, may at least be graciously accepted as a reasonable compensation. Capt. W. Moorsom. *Letters from Nova Scotia.* London, 1830.

E.T. Coke was travelling by stagecoach from Windsor, N.S., to Halifax when he came across a farm owned by T. N. Jeffery, collector of Customs at Halifax and son-in-law of Richard Uniacke, the former attorney-general of Nova Scotia who owned the adjacent farm. Jeffery's farm was quite a treat to a traveller who had been so long accustomed to see nothing but a most slovenly system of agriculture. It displayed much better management than that of his near neighbour [Uniacke] whose farm and house were erected upon such a barren spot, and so much money had been expended upon the estate, that, to use a fellow-passenger's expression, "for every stone he had picked up he had laid down a dollar. . . ." The adjoining clearings produced a crop of oats, above which the innumerable stumps appeared thick and crowded as men upon a chess-board, and a few miserable wooden shantys completed the scene. E. T. Coke. *A Subaltern's Furlough: Descriptive of Scenes in Various Parts of the United States, Upper and Lower Canada, New-Brunswick, and Nova Scotia.* 2 vols. New York, 1833.

When R. Montgomery Martin wrote of Sable Island, 100 miles east of Halifax, a Mr. Hodgson had been superintendent there since 1804. A supply ship called once a year to take in provisions for him and his large family and to take off any shipwrecked sailors. On the island was eighteen-mile-long Lake Wallace:

About the centre of the north side of the lake is the house of Mr. Hodgson, which is one storey in height, and forty feet in length by twenty in breadth, near which stand the stores and a large barn. . . . Two small kitchen gardens are attached to the house, and one place has been found where cabbages can be reared. Rye, oats, and Indian corn have been frequently sowed, but they have never arrived at maturity. The stock of cattle consists of four domesticated horses, a few cows and oxen, and some hogs and poultry. But though the attempt to raise sheep has been often made with every possible care, it has hitherto failed, the climate or the food not being congenial to them. Besides the barn adjoining the house, there is another at the east end of the lake which is filled with hay made of the beach grass. The family are supplied with firewood by drift timber on the south end of the island, which is hauled to the lake and there formed into a raft, and towed to the dwelling house, for which purpose they are furnished with two excellent whaleboats. R. Montgomery Martin. *History of Nova Scotia, Cape Breton, the Sable Islands, New Brunswick, Prince Edward Island, the Bermudas, Newfoundland, etc.* London, 1837.

The Colonial Farmer, a sixteen-page journal edited by Titus Smith, was the first of its kind to attempt to cover the interests of more than one province. By 1843 it was publishing twice a month, but didn't last much longer. Its name was revived in an 1863-1878 paper published at Fredericton.

Pick up all the apples that fall from your trees, carefully, and let them be boiled with potatoes for the pigs. They make a very nourishing food for swine; but the most important reason for the practice is this: These apples all contain worms or eggs of insects, and if they are allowed to decay upon the ground, not a few of them will become insects, who will again next Spring deposit their eggs in the blossoms, and produce another crop of wormy fruit. It has often been observed that less fruit falls from trees which stand in yards where pigs and poultry are kept, than from those in the Orchard, which makes it probable that these creatures deposit their eggs generally in the flowers of the tree upon which they were bred.

The May 16, 1843, issue of *The Colonial Farmer* carried this advertisement for a Nova Scotian, custom-built threshing machine:

Blaikie's Portable Threshing Machine.
Worked with two, three, or four horses at pleasure.
The Subscriber begs to intimate to the Agricultural community throughout Nova Scotia, and the adjoining Colonies, that he is prepared to receive orders for making Threshing Machines, either portable or stationary. He believes that he is justified in stating that his machines are equal in speed, if not superior, to any now in use in the Colonies, or in the United States. With two horses, his machine will thresh 25 bushels of wheat per hour, and a fourth more for every additional horse, when the grain is in fair working condition. With two horses it will thresh 45 bushels of oats per hour, and a fourth more for every additional horse. The horses move in a circle of 25 feet in diameter, at the rate of 2 1/2 to 3 miles per hour, and can work during the full day without fatigue. The portable machines can be removed from one barn to another with ease — are easily erected and put in operation, and are rarely subject to get out of order. From the low price at which they are made, and the rapid sale they have already received, wherever they have been tried, he has reason to believe that they only require to be known to come into extensive use.
Letters addressed (post paid or free) to the manufacturer, or to the editor of *The Mechanic & Farmer*, will receive every attention.
Thomas Blaikie. Green Hill, West River, February 1. *The Colonial Farmer, devoted to the agricultural interests of Nova-Scotia, New-Brunswick, and Prince Edward's Island.* Vol. 1, no. 2 Halifax, N.S., August 1841.

No price was given. *The Mechanic and Farmer* was cited because it was published at Pictou, N.S., near Green Hill, which became famous (and it still is) for its spectacular look-off.

The Mechanic and Farmer was the longest lived (at least five years) of the earliest farm journals in Canada. It was devoted almost exclusively to agriculture, though shipping intelligence was well represented because Pictou was a major port.

We often hear people who set out trees declare that they are planting for posterity, and cannot expect to reap the fruit of their own labors; but posterity will not be under any great obligation to them for setting trees as many do. It ought to be universally known that apple trees well set, in land that is rich enough to produce good corn, and cultivated in a proper manner, will yield enough in the fourth or fifth year to pay the interest of the first year's outlay. One acre of trees well set will supply any common family with an abundance of fruit by the fourth or fifth year. And it is our own folly to suffer posterity to be the only generation which will reap the fruit of our labors. *The Mechanic and Farmer.* Vol. IV, no. 2 Pictou, N.S., May 26, 1841.

Joseph Outram maintained in *Nova Scotia, Its Condition and Resources* (Edinburgh and London, 1850), that Nova Scotia was occasionally stigmatized by "superficial observers" who looked at the rocky coast and never visited the interior "where there are large tracts of very superior soil, some of which cannot be surpassed by any country that I have seen." Natives of Nova Scotia who had been induced to move to the Canadas or the United States bitterly regretted the change. Nova Scotia was surrounded by magnificent natural harbors, a great advantage to farmers in conveyance of their produce to market compared with the "long, expensive, land, canal and river carriages" of Canadian farmers.

Agriculture had been "strangely neglected" in Nova Scotia, not a little from the unfortunate idea that cultivation of the soil was a degrading employment. Moreover, there was a disposition by the country people to engage in fisheries and the "restless practice" of lumbering.

J.H. Crosskill was the reporter to the House of Assembly of Nova Scotia. He gave the following description of a Halifax agricultural exhibition:

On nearing the Horticultural Gardens the sight was inspiring. The day was delightful, balmy and fresh, with glorious sunshine. On a strip of Common near the Gardens were numerous horses gaily decked, champing and pawing impatiently round their grooms. Flags floated cheerily from various points. Carriages were driving to and fro, or were drawn up along the road. In front of the Garden fence were picketed the more steady horses whose fire did not require them to be constantly led about.

On entering the grounds, we found an animated scene there. The band of the 72nd Regiment was playing sweet music. Gaily dressed groups strolled about, varied by the sturdy and plain forms of the farmers, and the jolly weatherburnt faces of the country dames and lasses. The Garden Hall was devoted to the exhibition of fruit, thumping big apples, giant bunches of luscious looking grapes, peaches almost as lovely as a maiden's blushing cheek, plums as big as a Shanghai hen's egg.

Behind the hall was run out a canvas tent, or rather roof, under which was a fine display of vegetables. There were specimens of mangel-wurzel looking like a bushel of beets run mad — ears of corn half a yard long — turnips as big as a man's head feels after a "jolly night," and squashes, one of which weighed 130 lbs. The hothouse [greenhouse] was besieged by a crowd in search of the beautiful. Behind the hothouse were arrayed in coops the much talked of Shanghai fowls, gallinaceous giants, a kick from one of whom would send a tolerably sized boy into the middle of next week.

We then found our way to the Cattle, picketed and folded in the rear of the Garden, and along the edge of the Common bordering on the main road. Here we beheld fine bulls, some looking cross, some benevolent, and some roguish — clean white-wooled sheep, and pigs of all sorts and sizes, and ages. We wound up with climbing a wheel and looking down into a countryman's cart where we saw the largest pig we ever saw in our lives. He was said to weigh 900 pounds. J. H. Crosskill. *Agricultural Exhibition of Nova-Scotia held at Halifax Wednesday and Thursday, Oct. 5th and 6th, 1853, Halifax, N.S.* Printed at the office of *The British North American.*

Crosskill reported that the dinner, with mutton and excellent wines, began at 4:30 p.m. in the Masonic Hall. The band of the squadron's flagship played. There were twelve formal toasts and a speech by Sir Gaspard LeMarchant, lieutenant-governor of Nova Scotia. The seventh toast was proposed by Hon. John E. Fairbanks, chairman of the Central Board of Agriculture, to "the Agriculture of the Province, our independence and strength, all success attend it." The band played the air "Speed the Plough" and there were "cheers galore."

At 4:00 p.m. the second day, Sir Gaspard presented the prizes and Crosskill reported: "After the Prizes were awarded, His Excellency addressed a few words to the Farmers, which gradually became more lengthy, as His Excellency was cheered on by the hearty plaudits of the multitude. As a speech of any length was unexpected, we found ourselves unprovided with material to take notes." However, Crosskill reconstructed the speech "as well as possible from memory."

William Chambers attended the same Halifax agricultural exhibition described by Crosskill and wrote:

Wandering about the field, enjoying the sight of the eager competitors, and also the graceful spectacle of ladies on horseback and in carriages, and the elite of the provincial government surveying the proceedings, I derived an additional gratification in knowing that the spot was in some sort classic ground. It formed part of the experimental farm of the late John Young, an enthusiastic Scotch agriculturist who, writing in the local press under the name of *Agricola*, was the first to stimulate a spirit of improvement in the province, and lived to see the principles and practice of East Lothian husbandry naturalized in this part of America. Men not very aged remember the time when the only vegetables consumed in Halifax were imported from Boston, and when butter, pork, and other edibles came from Ireland. All this has been changed, and not a little of the progress in various branches of culture is due to John Young, whose son, the Hon. William Young, Speaker of the House of Assembly, very appropriately opened the proceedings on the present occasion. William Chambers. *Things as They Are in America*. London and Edinburgh, 1854.

Rev. Robert Everest had a less exalted impression of Halifax:

The houses appear slovenly kept and dirty; nor even in the suburbs did I see a trace of the neat little flower-gardens I should have expected from people of English descent. . . . The newspapers complain grievously of the quantity of drunkenness and prostitution. . . . The soil is poor and rocky in the country round. Rev. Robert Everest. *A Journey through the United States and part of Canada*. London, 1855.

J. W. Dawson's *Contributions toward the Improvement of Agriculture in Nova Scotia* (Halifax, 1856) suggests:

It is not however very generally known that the straw of wheat, if cut sufficiently early, and chopped with a straw cutter, is highly nutritive food for cattle and horses, and is much relished by them. In this country, wheat is generally cut too late, and thus the grain is thick in the husk and inferior in flouring qualities, and the straw is comparatively worthless. By cutting immediately after the grain is filled, and before the straw is wholly dead, both would be much more valuable and nutritious. . . .

The extended culture of [buckwheat] cannot be considered as an indication of improved or prosperous agriculture, since this grain is generally a substitute for others, or a refuge from the want caused by impoverishment of the ground. Buckwheat, however, is a grain of some value and, if properly used, need have no connection with bad farming.

James Fergusson was one of those travellers who gained their knowledge through a train window:

We left Halifax yesterday at 6:30 a.m. by train. . . . The railway carriages are of the American model, enormously large open saloons: I don't like them; and they are so cheap that men in working clothes go first class. . . .

The line [to Truro] ran all the way through fir forest, only here and there cleared by the rude plan of setting it on fire, which leaves for miles blackened stumps, and a wreck of great stumps; by degrees patches round the wooden huts are cleared and brought into cultivation. James Fergusson. *Notes of a Tour in North America in 1861.* Edinburgh, 1861.

H. Reid relates that "unlucky negroes" abound in Halifax and vicinity:

During the last war with the United States some of our ships captured a number of slaves, and took them to Halifax, to be free, to be frozen, and to starve. In them Nova Scotia truly caught a Tartar.

They have a settlement a few miles from Dartmouth, where they cultivate a little land and carry on a few simple branches of industry, such as making brooms, casks, etc., and they may often be met in the Dartmouth boat, bringing their produce to market [in Halifax], or returning with their little purchases. With all their industry, they are in but a poor way, scarcely able to make the two ends meet. With their inferior organization and the universal prejudice against them (as strong in Nova Scotia as in in the Northern United States), they cannot compete with the intelligent and energetic Caucasian, and mostly sink to the very bottom of the social scale. H. Reid. *Sketches in North America; with some account of Congress and of The Slavery Question.* London, 1861.

Andrew Learmont Spedon recorded his enthusiasm for the "dyked marshes" he saw on his tour through Nova Scotia and New Brunswick:

The richest lands are the "dyked marshes" of Albert and Westmorland near the Bay of Fundy, and also on the alluvium deposited along the banks and islands of the rivers. . . . The marine alluviums are carried inward by the rapid tides of the Bay of Fundy, and are spread along its estuaries, where in the course of time they become grass-bearing marshes, and are then rescued from the sea by embankments built for the purpose. These "dyked marshes" possess extraordinary and enduring fertility. One of the "dyked marshes" divided between New Brunswick and Nova Scotia contains over 250,000 acres. . . .

By dyking, or building a dense wall across the front of these marshes when the tide is out, so as to exclude the sea-water from overflowing the land, a soil is thus reclaimed, capable of producing crops for an indefinite period without manure.

Spedon said only 700,000 of 6,000,000 acres in New Brunswick granted by the crown had been cultivated because many of the principal purchases had been made on speculation. There was a trivial tax, or none at all, on land thus held.

> The attention of the government should be directed to this matter, and legislation should be had for the purpose of making land held in this way productive in some degree to the province. . . .
>
> Agriculture is deserving of more consideration at the hands of the government, and hence a liberal policy should be pursued toward it.

Agriculture had been largely neglected, or even excluded, because of concentration on lumbering and shipping of timber. Farmers deserted their homes in winter to cut lumber and "in the spring when they should be clearing and preparing their land, they are engaged in floating their timber down the rivers, to the neglect of farming operations."

Spedon found agriculture in Nova Scotia in a "transition state":

> It is to be found in all stages of advancement — from the rude attempts of the half lumberer half farmer to the productive results of more formal and scientific husbandry. The deficiency then in agricultural products may be ascribed, in a great measure, to the want of a more advanced and intellectual system of culture, and the injudicious impoverishment of the soil: another great evil is, that as a general thing, too much land is brought under half tillage. Were the labor which is spread over so wide a surface confined to fewer acres with more systematic and thorough cultivation, the operations of farming would be carried on with incalculably greater profit. Such will apply also to both New Brunswick and Canada. Andrew Learmont Spedon. *Rambles among the Blue-Noses; or, Reminiscences of a Tour through New Brunswick and Nova Scotia during the summer of 1862*. Montreal, 1863.

Richard Lewes Dashwood was an officer of the fifteenth Regiment garrisoned at Fredericton. He was a keen hunter and fisherman who travelled widely through the Maritimes and Newfoundland. On the trip described here, he was in the Margaree Valley of Cape Breton Island where the settlers did more than farming:

> The poaching on the Margaree is far worse than in any other river in North America, the settlers spearing and netting the pools nightly, in open defiance of the law. We were much annoyed by their spearing the pool opposite our camp, and reported it to the chief warden, who was afraid to do anything, and as the settlers came in gangs of over twenty, with blackened faces, we could not identify them, and so were powerless.
>
> I was informed that the late chief fish-warden was a plucky fellow, who did his duty and prevented poaching to a great extent, but his

politics not suiting the Hon. Member for the District, he was turned out to make way for the present useless individual.

I cared less for the Margaree than any river I had ever visited in North America. It was too civilised, and you were apt to have your camp surrounded, especially on Sundays, by a crowd of loafers and gaping natives. One afternoon, whilst making flies in camp and resting the river for the evening cast, I was horrified at the sight of two tourists in canoes splashing about in the middle of our best pool. Richard Lewes Dashwood. *Chiploquorgan; or, Life by the Camp Fire.* Dublin, 1871.

The Nova Scotia Farmer and Bridgewater Times, January 4, 1871, contained this report:

At a farmers' [meeting] a farmer said that no talking should be allowed while milking was going on. He said he discharged one of his servants who persisted in talking during milking time, and that in three days the increase of milk was equal to the man's weekly wages.

We fear an increase to such an extent must have been due to other causes besides the one assigned. If the enlarged yield followed solely from the dismissal of the man, we suspect his presence affected the supply of milk in some way apart from his loquacity.

We have frequently found a change of servants prove beneficial. It may be that talking prevents hens from laying also. We know we have often experienced a vast increase in the number of eggs brought into the house after the removal of a too officious individual from our employ. Besides, some poor cows have sometimes improved in produce by the same means, but we generally attribute it to cleaner milking by fresh and more industrious hands.

It is, however, well known that cows are peculiarly sensitive to sights and sounds during the time they are milked. Unless they are at perfect ease, they will not give their milk freely. They should be daily milked, under the same conditions. Cows that are fed at milking time require their usual meal, or they become restless and dissatisfied, and put a stop to their bounty. Many of them will allow only some special favourite to milk them. In those parts of the country where women are solely employed to milk, we frequently find one or two tuneful lassies singing at their work, and many cows become so pleased with the rustic harmony as to show evident signs of their approval by giving their milk only by being sung to. Everything that distracts the attention of the cow and disturbs her placidity should be avoided when she is called upon to yield her milk. Her nervous system should not be excited by strange noises, unwelcome objects or rough treatment or the affect will be apparent in diminished supply in the milk pail. Vol. 4, no. 46. Bridgewater, Nova Scotia.

The Nova Scotia Farmer and Annapolis County Times offered advice on horses:

A horse will endure severe cold weather without much inconvenience so long as he is furnished with a dry stable. But require him to stand on a wet foul floor and his health will soon begin to fail. Horses often suffer from cold feet and legs, and many stables have damp and wet floors. . . .

Much time is spent in the morning in rubbing and brushing and smoothing the hair on the sides and hips, but at no time are the feet examined and properly cared for. The feet of a horse require more care than the body. They need ten times as much, for in one respect they are almost the entire horse.

All the grooming that can be done won't avail anything if the horse is forced to stand where his feet will be filthy. The feet will become disordered; and then the legs will get badly out of fix; and with bad feet and bad legs there is not much else of the horse fit for anything. Stable prisons generally are very severe on the feet and legs of horses; and unless the buildings can afford a dry room, where a horse can walk around, lie down, or roll over, they are not half so healthy or comfortable as in the pasture, and should be avoided by all good hostlers in the country. *The Nova Scotia Farmer and Annapolis County Times*. Vol. 7, no. 46. Annapolis Royal, Thursday, January 22, 1874.

Herbert Crosskill speculated on the commercial possibilities of peat:

In many parts of the Province there are large tracts of peat lands or bogs. . . . Peat is not required for fuel in Nova Scotia, because, at present, there is plenty of coal and wood. The celebrated Caribou Bog, in King's County, is about a square mile of as fine peat as can be found in the Emerald Isle itself. . . . In a few years, as wood for fuel becomes scarce, such districts as the Caribou Bog will be considerably enhanced in value. Even now I believe it would pay well to cut the peat for fuel. . . . There are probably over one million cords of peat in the Caribou Bog alone. Herbert Crosskill. *Nova Scotia: Its Climate, Resources, and Advantages*. Halifax, 1874.

One benefit of keeping cattle was enlarged on in this piece from the *Acadian Orchardist*:

Clover and commercial fertilizers, while good in their place, cannot wholly supply the lack of barnyard manure. Cattle are needed on every farm in order to give a complete solution to the fertilizing problem, if for no other purpose. . . .

A good manure-saving barnyard may be made without roofing it. Scoop out the earth so as to form a basin or dish, and pave it with stone to avoid mud, and make it water tight. The extra value of the manure saved will amply repay the expense. *Acadian Orchardist.* Vol. 1 no. 12. Kentville, N.S., Tuesday, May 2, 1893.

PRINCE EDWARD ISLAND

THE EARL OF SELKIRK CONDUCTED 800 Highland Scots to Wood Island, P.E.I., in three ships in 1803:

> The settlers had spread themselves along the shore for the distance of about half a mile, upon the site of an old French village, which had been destroyed and abandoned after the capture of the island by the British forces in 1758. The land, which had been overgrown with wood, was overgrown again with thickets of young trees, interspersed with grassy glades. . . .
>
> I arrived at the place late in the evening, and it had then a very striking appearance. Each family had kindled a large fire near their wigwams, and round these were assembled groups of figures, whose peculiar national dress added to the singularity of the surrounding scene; confused heaps of baggage were everywhere piled together beside their wild habitations; and by the number of fires, the whole woods were illuminated. At the end of the line of encampment I pitched my own tent, and was surrounded in the morning by a numerous assemblage of people, whose behaviour indicated that they looked to nothing less than a restoration of the happy days of Clanship. These hardy people thought little of the inconvenience they felt from the slightness of the shelter they put up for themselves.

The settlers had land under cultivation by the time Selkirk left about a month later, in September. He returned at the end of September the following year:

> It was with the utmost satisfaction I then found that my plans had been followed up with attention and judgment. . . . I found the settlers engaged in securing the harvest which their industry had produced. . . . There were three or four families who had not gathered a crop adequate to their own supply; but many others had a considerable superabundance. . . .
>
> To obviate the terrors which the woods were calculated to inspire, the settlement was not dispersed over a large tract of country, but concentrated within a moderate space. The lots were laid out in such a manner that there were generally four or five families, and

sometimes more, who built their houses in a little knot together. The distance between the adjacent hamlets seldom exceeded a mile. Earl of Selkirk. *Observations on the Present State of the Highlands of Scotland, with a view of the Causes and Probable Consequences of Emigration.* London, 1805.

John Stewart, a long-time resident-farmer of the island, wrote that at the start of settlement there had been too great a propensity to engage in the cod fishery, to the neglect of cultivation. But at time of his writing, some attention was being paid to agriculture, he said.

Potatoes are raised in great abundance, and in no other country better. I have had three hundred bushels an acre with cultivation. They grow very well in the forest lands, when first cleared, and though not so large a crop, they are in such situations more delicate and much finer flavoured than any I ever saw elsewhere.

Turnips are universally raised as winter food for cattle and sheep. . . . They are a fine crop though never hoed. . . . The practice is to cow-pen and fold sheep upon the lands intended for turnips; the effects of even a slight dressing of this kind are very great, tolerably done it communicates a fertility that is very evident for several years, under what in England would justly be thought the most abominable management, as three crops of grain, each with a single ploughing, are often taken without rest. . . .

A great many old apple trees left by the French are still alive and bearing. . . .

The horses are in general small, but strong, active, and hardy, and being seldom subject to any complaints, live to a great age; it is a common thing to take them off the grass, and ride them thirty or forty miles, during which they have to swim three or four times perhaps across broad creeks or arms of the sea, and after performing such a journey with great spirit without being once fed on the way they are turned out to grass at the end of it, and probably perform such another journey the next day equally well, and without appearing to be hurt by such hard usage. . . . In some parts of the island they are allowed to run out all winter, when they are not used, and maintain themselves by scraping away the snow with their hoofs till they come to the grass, on which they live, and keep in tolerable order till spring. . . .

Oxen are used in agriculture and for drawing timber out of the woods more than horses. John Stewart. *An Account of Prince Edward Island in the Gulph of St. Laurence.* London, 1806.

Abraham Pryor, an American surgeon, said "the practice of medicine in the Provinces is not very respectable."

I shall mention now a most fearful circumstance belonging to this island [Prince Edward Island] which British subjects have concealed. About once in seven years the island is visited with swarms of mice which, like the locusts of Egypt, leave neither earing or harvest.

The inhabitants are more subject to cancers than any other people in the world.

Pryor visited the Maritime provinces and Lower Canada and found on his 280-mile land trip from the St. John River to the St. Lawrence that so many travellers had perished in this "fearful desert" that the government had installed army veterans on farms twenty miles apart not to farm but to succor weary travellers. Pryor's conclusion of his visit:

> Notwithstanding all that can be truly said in favour of the Provinces and their government, they compose a poor, distressed and starved country in comparison with the United States. Abraham Pryor. *An Interesting Description of British America, from personal knowledge and observation*. Providence, 1819.

Walter Johnstone was an itinerant preacher who walked across Prince Edward Island establishing Sunday schools where he could. The only aspect of life that seemed to concern him was the religious. Thus:

> On Wednesday, the 12th July [1821], I left Charlotte Town for the west end of the island. The road was rough, and in many parts very solitary, often six miles or more without a human habitation. On the Friday, I reached the settlement of Tryon, about twenty-six miles west of Charlotte Town. Before I got into the open settlement, I met a gentleman, a farmer there, who kindly invited me to his house. There is one comfort in that country, if one has long and solitary walks sometimes in the woods, they are always sure of a hearty welcome to such cheer as the people have to give when they once find a house; and there is very few of the old settlers who have not plenty of the common supports of life. I lodged the first night in the house of a Baptist. His conversation was of the most pious and sensible kind; and his prayers were both fluent, fervent and refreshing. Walter Johnstone. *Travels in Prince Edward Island*. Edinburgh, 1823.

John McGregor wrote his observations on farming conditions in Prince Edward Island:

> The prevailing colour of both soil and stone is red. . . . The soil is friable and easily tilled, and there is scarcely a stone on the surface of the island that will impede the progress of the plough. . . . One observes, now and then, a solitary block of granite on the surface of

the ground but two stones of this description are seldom found within a mile of each other. . . .

Potatoes of a kind and quality equal to the produce of any country are raised in great quantities, and are exported to the neighbouring provinces, and sometimes to the West Indies. . . . Potatoes and turnips are left undug until the middle or end of October; the first are generally ploughed up, except in new land where the hoe is altogether used. . . . Potatoes are planted in round hollows, scooped three or four inches deep, and fifteen to twenty inches broad; three or five sets are planted in each of these and covered over; the hoe alone is used. . . .

The general system of cultivating the farms all over the island is so careless and slovenly that it appears astonishing that many of the settlers raise a sufficiency to support their families. Composts are rarely known, and different manures that would fertilize the soil are also disregarded.

McGregor says young men "of steady habits" from Prince Edward Island sometimes spent the winters lumbering in New Brunswick and had saved enough to buy farms on the island. Others were not as lucky:

To stimulate the organs, in order to sustain the cold, these men swallow immoderate quantities of ardent spirits, and habits of drunkenness are the usual consequence. Their moral character, with few exceptions, is dishonest and worthless . . . shuffling and rascally. Premature old age, and shortness of days, form the inevitable fate of a lumberer. Should he even save a little money, which is very seldom the case, and be enabled for the last few years of life to exist without incessant labour, he becomes the victim of rheumatisms and all the miseries of a broken constitution. John McGregor. *Historical and Descriptive Sketches of the Maritime Colonies of British America.* London, 1828.

J. L. Lewellin was a progressive farmer who arrived in Prince Edward Island in 1824 about the time the legislature and colonial government were making some preliminary moves to aid agriculture, afflicted since the British conquest by absentee landlordship over land grants of 20,000 acres each. Lewellin's informative, twenty-nine-page pamphlet was written to attract farmer-immigrants and the author's friends, and other "very respectable gentlemen" — twenty-two in all — subscribed for twenty copies each to help out the cause. Lewellin is listed in the appendix with ten others as importers of livestock to improve horse, cattle, sheep and pig breeds. Lewellin's pamphlet was republished in London in 1834.

The general mode of conducting a Farm is slovenly, often wretched. Cattle, sheep and pigs are turned into the woods, or on the shore, to get their own living during Summer; and, frequently, as much time is lost in seeking the stock, as would clear enough land to support them in good pasture.

Few farms have any subdivision fences. A patch is ploughed here for wheat, another there for barley, the intervening spots are mown for hay; and yet, under all this want of judicious arrangement, it is astonishing what returns are obtained. But there are many meritorious exceptions to this cobbling sort of system. Many farmers display in their management an accurate and intimate knowledge of their difficult calling; these are developing the powers of the Island soil; and their example, in connection with the exertions of the Agricultural Society, are operating a great and satisfactory change. . .

It is the common practice to pen all the neat cattle on some border of the cleared ground every night during Summer, and this, with the manure obtained from the byres or beast-houses and the stables, is all some farmers depend on. J. L. Lewellin. *Emigration. Prince Edward Island: A Brief But Faithful Account Of This Fine Colony*. Charlotte-Town, 1832.

Lewellin advised the use of kelp, seaweed and eelgrass for manure, as well as mussel mud, which he spelled, not inappropriately, "muscle-mud." He said many settlers lived mostly on fish (herring, mackerel, cod, lobsters and so on), potatoes, oatmeal porridge and milk. There was a "miserable deficiency" of winnowing machines, chaff cutters, and other labour-saving implements.

There are no manufactures carried on in the Colony, except domestic ones for the use of the farmer's family. The settlers generally make of their wool a very useful cloth, called homespun, which serves the men for jackets and trowsers, whilst a finer sort supplies the females with gowns for winter use; they also manufacture blankets, stockings or socks, and mittins. The wool is simply died with indigo. Some families make the greater part of their table, bed, and personal linen from flax, often using with it cotton warp of American manufacture. Leather is tanned by most settlers from their own hides; and there is need of it, shoes being very expensive to purchase. The Colonists make a great part of the soap and candles they use, but the greater number burn fish oil for light.

A twenty-six-page foolscap manuscript history was written by the son of a Prince Edward Island pioneer to deliver as a lecture. It collects much information from early documents and newspapers. The author devotes considerable attention to imported thoroughbreds, including stallion Roncesvalles and mare Roulette, both imported by Colonel Ready, the lieutenant-governor, in 1826. But no horse ever made "a better name for himself" than Columbus, named after the ship that brought him from Britain in 1839. The horse was selected by Professor Dick and Mr. Low of the Edinburgh College of Veterinary Surgeons, and Mr. Low here describes Columbus in a letter to the Central Agricultural Society, the purchaser (for £160):

> The Clydesdale stallion I have procured by the assistance of Professor Dick who examined a considerable number before making a selection. Clydesdale horses are chiefly valued for their steadiness and usefulness in draught. The one sent is free from vice and possesses that docility of temper which form the characteristics of the breed.

On statutory labor by farmers for road making:

> Road making in those days was a very arduous job and overseers were required by their appointments to be much more exacting with their men than now. In 1820 and for many years since, each man was required to work 6 entire days; the time for meals and travelling to and from the place of Statute Labor was not to be computed, but every person was to work his full time, but not to exceed 12 hours in any one day, and not a minute allowed but the actual time he was working.
>
> A clause in the act forbids the improper practice of placing ropes across the roads during the performance of Statute Labor, and illegally stopping travellers to obtain Rum from them and must on no account whatever be permitted. A History of early Prince Edward Island, by Mr. Gardiner of Charlottetown. [Manuscript] N.p., n.d. National Archives of Canada, MG 55/30 #139.

S. S. Hill, the author of another account, found island horses to be "sociable":

> The most sagacious, when bred at a distance from the populous settlements, will, in the summer time, if far from home, follow you for miles in the woods in spite of every obstruction. They dread being alone in the forest at any time.
>
> When you travel in the winter behind a young horse, and are for some time silent, the animal will begin to fear he is alone: he will first stop and attempt to look round, but being prevented seeing by his blinkers, he will run and stop again; and after attempting to turn, which he cannot do on account of the snow on each side of the narrow sleigh road, he will start off again, with the action and speed of a scared deer. But the instant you speak, the affrighted animal will stand still, and then resume his ordinary pace. . . . It appears to be the love of society, and the sense of dependence, that gives the horse so strong a distaste for the solitude of the woods.

The author said the island life brought health and longevity:

> The intermittent fevers of Upper Canada and the United States, with several other diseases incident to the latter, are of very rare occurrence, or entirely unknown in the island: nor does any endemic disorder whatever here exist.
>
> There is no country where the peasantry enjoy better health, or where more instances of longevity occur. . . . More people in this island attain the age of a hundred than in any other part of America.

P.E.I. wild raspberries were abundant and not inferior to the cultivated ones of Britain:

> Where the woods have been burnt, or the land cleared and left uncultivated, they are found in great quantities; and they are common in all parts of the island by the road side.
>
> Besides these, there are wild cherries, blue-berries or whortle berries, and currants and gooseberries. The wild cherries have, as a medicine, powerful astringent qualities. S. S. Hill. *A Short Account of Prince Edward Island, designed chiefly for the information of agriculturists and other emigrants of small capital.* London, 1839.

Lord Durham had described Prince Edward Island as having a "poor and unenterprising population of 40,000" when it had the agricultural resources to support ten times that number. This was absurd, commented an unnamed, large land-owner. If one man cleared twenty acres a year, it would take 1,000 men seventy years to clear the island's cultivable 1.4 million acres.

About Nova Scotia, Durham had written that half the farmhouses ("tenements," he called them) were abandoned "and lands everywhere falling into decay." A colonist (also anonymous) replied:

> A grosser misstatement it has never been my lot to peruse. . . . It is not merely untrue, but there is not a word of truth in it. . . . In the first settlement of a farm, a rude and temporary building, constructed of logs of timber, is erected for the use of the family, which, as the proprietor's means increase and his arable lands are enlarged, is abandoned for a larger and more commodious framed house; and it sometimes occurs that this pleasing evidence of prosperity is found on the same property in the existence of both houses at the same time, though on sites at some distance from each other. A Proprietor. *Remarks upon that Portion of the Earl of Durham's Report relating to Prince Edward Island.* London, 1839; A Colonist. *A Reply to the Report of the Earl of Durham.* London, 1839.

The Prince Edward Island Royal Agricultural Society's *Annual Report for the year 1845* (Charlottetown, 1846), deplores the potato rot plaguing farmers:

Your Committee regret that for the first time for many years their report of the staple crop of the farmer, the potato, is of an unfavourable nature. In common with the greater part of the agricultural world, the potato fields of this Island were, during the past season, visited by a disease generally known as *taint*, or *rot*, to an extent that has caused serious fears in the minds of many as to whether that there will be a sufficient quantity preserved out of that portion of the crop which has been cellared, sound enough to serve for seed for the ensuing season. From recent inquiries made by your Committee, the loss sustained in many districts fully confirms the report, but they venture to hope that it will not, in every instance, turn out as bad as it has been represented, as they are led to believe that where the potatoes were not dug too early, and where care has been taken in sorting them before housing, the disease has not since spread to any great extent. So much has appeared upon the subject in the newspapers published on both sides of the Atlantic, that your Committee feel it to be unnecessary for them to dwell any longer upon it, particularly as they are unable to throw any satisfactory light upon so mysterious a subject as the disease in question appears to be.

They would, however, suggest to their brother farmers the propriety of taking particular care to preserve out of their stock, by frequently turning over and separating the good from the bad, some portion, however small, to serve them for seed.

James H. Peters was a judge as well as a farmer, and some of his advice sounded judicial:

Nature has been bountiful in giving great fertility to the virgin soil, but you cannot abuse her gifts with impunity; if you exhaust the ground by the reckless system of taking crop after crop, without manuring, be assured you and your children will suffer for it in after years. . . .

If you are industrious in clearing, and raise turnips, you will be able to keep a cow and pig the second year; place a good lot of earth in the shed under the cow, it will catch the urine; keep adding fresh earth to the sty where the pig is kept in the autumn, and have a good quantity of it under him all winter. In many places fern grows plentifully by the road side and through the woods; it is very valuable as manure. Make it a rule, that each child every day in summer gather an arm full and throw in the pig sty or cow house, in autumn, when the leaves fall, gather as many as you can, and throw in the cow house; every spring, turn all out of the cow house and pig sty, and make it into a heap. Every little helps, and in a year or two, by the time you want manure, you will have a respectable pile. James H. Peters. *Hints to the Farmers of Prince Edward Island.* Charlottetown, 1851.

As an army officer, C. M. Sleigh saw a good deal of the Maritimes and the Canadas. Here he comments on Prince Edward Island, which he reached in March 1852 by crossing the Icy Straits (Northumberland Strait) in an ice boat:

> The winter sets in early in December, and continues in intensity until the following June; nay, snow is often to be found in the woods as late as July. When once the season of more genial warmth commences, the rapidity of vegetation exceeds belief . . . and the ploughman is quickly followed by the reaper. The fertility of the soil is not to be found equalled in any other portion of North America: the whole island, to the water's edge, is capable of cultivation; the land is easily cleared of the forest, and its prolific nature grants to the husbandman the means of subsistence. But this happy state of existence has barely three months' duration, within which period are to be reckoned the Spring, the Summer, and the Autumn of this evanescent climate. The expense of supplying fodder for the seven dreary months of winter bears heavily upon the farmer, and in countless instances cattle are actually destroyed in preference to keeping them. The result is, the people of the Island are decidedly the poorest, as far as pecuniary means are concerned, to be found in the British Provinces. It is a well-known though vulgar saying in the Island, that "the sight of a shilling acts as an onion on a farmer's eyes." C. M. Sleigh. *Pine Forests and Hackmatack Clearings; or, Travel, Life and Adventure in the British North American Provinces.* 2d ed. London, 1853.

C. Birch Bagster spoke with feeling on the subject of farming in Prince Edward Island:

> To farm in Prince Edward Island is no sinecure. A man must bring as much intelligence into the business as to any other branch of industry — must keep up as good fences in Prince Edward Island as in England — must be as careful to provide food for stock, as stock for food. . . . The soil is light, and therefore hungry; is fertile, and therefore requiring to be kept clean; is brief of season, obliging foresight, and early preparation, and having crops specially adapted to the soil and climate, such as barley, oats and turnips. . . .
>
> Potatoes can be grown at an average of 250 bushels to the acre . . . but of all crops the turnip crop is the grand crop of the Island . . . and it takes the lead of ALL THE WORLD, with produce figures that *begin* at 500 bushels [per acre] and often reach a round thousand. C. Birch Bagster. *The Progress and Prospects of Prince Edward Island.* Charlottetown, 1861.

On the other hand, Alex Rivington related:

A story runs that a traveller, once visiting the island [Prince Edward Island], asked an Irishman why he lived in such an out-of-the-way spot, and he replied that he had never yet been able to earn enough money to enable him to get out of it. Alex Rivington. *In the Track of Our Emigrants.* London, 1872.

Donald Ferguson, the provincial secretary of Prince Edward Island, was a strong advocate of scientific farming:

The thinking farmer finds himself confronted every day of his life with questions which he is wholly unable to answer. The peculiarities of soils, the causes of differences in crops, the insects that destroy them, the diseases of his stock, the unproductiveness of his orchard; these and similar things attract his attention, and give rise to questions which he cannot answer. In his mind will be found a latent feeling that it is possible that his son may be so taught as to know many things which are beyond his own comprehension. But the large majority of farmers do not belong to the thinking class, at least in the sense now referred to. They see, for instance, the productiveness of their soil becoming less every year through excessive cropping; and yet they do not adopt an ameliorative system, although they may see its beneficial effects demonstrated in their own neighbourhood. They find their dairies and cattle stalls yield them scarcely any profit; and yet they make no efforts to acquire new methods or improve their breeds. Men of this class will generally laugh at the advocates of scientific farming, and are content to continue to work by the rule of thumb. Such men offer the greatest obstacles to well-considered improvement in their profession, and many of them will never improve until the mortgages on their farms are foreclosed, or they pay the debt of nature. Donald Ferguson. *Agricultural Education.* Charlottetown, 1884.

Thomas J. Dillon was brought from Ontario to Prince Edward Island in 1892 to establish and manage a cheese factory at New Perth. John Hamilton describes what happened:

The establishment of these [milk pickup] routes was a service of some difficulty. The prospects of supply were exceedingly doubtful all through the month of May and first weeks in June. Cattle were lean and the pastures backward, and farmers generally seemed to have little confidence in the undertaking. The Superintendent had to travel over the district in company with one or other of the directors, hold meetings, and almost literally beg for patronage. The milk had to be collected from a wider area than was at first anticipated, and special arrangements made with carriers who had the longest routes to travel. At length, when the persevering energy of the manager had brought matters into something like working order, a meeting was convened at the station, and the drawing of supply on the several routes sold at auction to the lowest bidder per hundred pounds. . . . The carrier was required to keep his milk wagon clean and free from all bad smells. John Hamilton. *Experimental Dairy Station at New Perth*. Charlottetown, 1893.

The longest route was twelve miles, which brought the carrier (horse and wagon) $1.50 a trip. The first deliveries on June 22 totalled 4,300 pounds of milk but quickly rose in a few days to 9,000. The total of 696,247 pounds of milk produced 66,089 pounds of cheese.

NEW BRUNSWICK

Howard Trueman's forbears were Chignecto settlers. In *The Chignecto Isthmus And Its First Settlers* he quotes a letter of Mrs. Sarah Patterson, daughter of Robert Trueman, about how her father built his home in 1818:

> When my father first came to live in the place now called Truemanville it was a dense forest. In summer the only road was a bridle path. In winter, when the snow was on the ground, they could drive a pair of oxen and a sled along the road.
>
> The winter my father was married, as soon as there was enough snow and frost, he and one of his brothers and another man set out to build a house. They loaded a sled with boards, doors and windows, and provided themselves with bedding and provisions to last till the house was finished. They then hitched the oxen to the sled and started on their twenty-mile journey and most of the way on a trackless path.
>
> When they arrived at their journey's end, they erected a rude hut to live in and commenced building a house. They did not have far to go for timber — it was standing all around the site chosen for the house. They built a very nice log house, 15 feet by 18 feet. Their greatest trouble was, the stones were so frosty they could not split them. They had to kindle a huge fire of brushwood and warm the stones through, when they split finely.
>
> After they had built the house they returned home, having been absent about three weeks. My father and mother then moved to their new home, and father began to build a saw mill and grist mill. Their nearest neighbors were one and a half miles distant, unless we count the bears and foxes, and they were far too sociable for anything like comfort. Sheep and cattle had to be folded every night for some years.

Mrs. Patterson related that hogs were driven into the woods in fall to feast and fatten on fallen beechnuts. Sometimes the pigs were caught by bears.

> Once ominous squeals were heard from the woods. The men armed themselves with pitchforks and ran to the rescue. What should they meet but one of my uncles coming with an ox-cart. The wooden

axles had got very dry on the long, rough road, and as they neared my father's the sound as the wheels turning resembled very closely that made by a hog under the paws of bruin.

In his book on early Maritimes agriculture, Trueman gives us a description of how Prince Edward Island farmers harvested mussel mud from bays and inlets to use as fertilizer:

A number of farmers would join together and construct or buy a mud-digger. This piece of machinery was constructed on very much the same principle as a harbor dredge, but with this difference that instead of floating on the water it was set as firmly as possible on the ice and horse power was used instead of steam to move it forward when required and to hoist the shovel filled with mud. When the team arrived on the ice the sled was placed where the mud from the shovel could best drop into it, and the horses were hitched onto the windlass. A few shovels full would fill the sled, and the horses would be hitched up again and the mud taken wherever it was wanted and another sled put in its place. It was a cold place to work, especially on a windy day. A long piece of ice had to be cut out to give the shovel a chance to do its work, and there was always some danger of getting wet, but this did not seem to hinder the work in the least so long as the mud was to be found. . . .

Mussel mud is an estuarine silt containing great quantities of oyster, mussel, and clam shells, the first usually predominating, which occurs in the bogs and estuaries around Northumberland Strait and at the mouth of the Bay des Chaleur. The mussel beds are often deep and furnish an almost inexhaustible supply of this valuable fertilizer. Its chief value for agricultural purposes is owing to the quantity of lime it contains. The fertilizing value is increased when it is composted with barn-yard manure, peat, swamp muck, etc. Howard Trueman. *The Chignecto Isthmus And Its First Settlers.* Toronto, 1902; *Early Agriculture in the Atlantic Provinces.* Moncton, 1907.

Peter Fisher noted the special circumstances of black settlers in New Brunswick.

The last class [of inhabitants] that I shall notice are the people of Colour, or Negroes. These are found in considerable numbers in different parts of the Province. In some parts a number of families are settled together as farmers; but they do not make good settlers, being of a volatile disposition, much addicted to dissipation; they are impatient of labour, and in general fitter for performing menial offices about houses as domestics, than the more important, but laborious, duties of farmers.

The New Brunswick Historical Society reprinted Fisher's book in 1921 with some additional material, including an account by the author's mother, Mary, about arrival of settlers at St. Ann's (Fredericton) in the fall of 1782:

> Sometimes a part of the family had to remain up during the night to keep the fires burning, so as to keep the rest from freezing. Some destitute people made use of boards, which the older ones kept heating before the fire and applied by turns to the smaller children to keep them warm. . . .
>
> For years there were no teams, and our people had to work hard to get their provisions. Potatoes were planted among the black stumps and turned out well. Pigeons used to come in great numbers and were shot or caught by the score in nets. We found in their crops some small round beans, which we planted; they grew very well and made excellent green beans, which we ate during the summer. An Inhabitant of the Province [Peter Fisher]. *Sketches of New Brunswick*. Saint John, 1825.

John Mann arrived at Saint John, N.B., November 22, 1816, from Scotland as an eighteen-year-old laborer. In the fall of 1819 he was at Magegadavic Settlement in southwestern New Brunswick:

> The season being excessively dry, the farmers embraced the opportunity of setting fire to all the old stumps in the fields. The wind blew extremely high, so that the different fires communicated together, and the conflagration spread all around, consuming the woods and fences, to the no small danger of several houses in the neighbourhood. The sparks were carried by the wind to the distance of half a mile. One of these struck upon the end of the house in which I lodged, and fell down among some shingles lying at the end of the house. We immediately removed the shingles; but fearing that the house would immediately catch fire, we took all the furniture, and carried it into the middle of the field, and watched it till about midnight, when the wind and the fire abated.
>
> An unfortunate man, being the worse of liquor, was travelling through the woods, and insensible of danger, rushed into the fire and smoke. He was found next morning by the road-side, as black as a burnt root, lying on his back, all his clothes being burnt on his body, and his shoes on his feet. His arms, legs, and every part of his body were completely scorched and burnt. As he was so disfigured that he could not be put into a proper coffin, we nailed a few boards together, in that form in which he was lying. We wrapped him in a sheet, and buried him in his own orchard, as is customary in that quarter. John Mann. *Travels in North America: particularly in the Provinces of Upper & Lower Canada, and New Brunswick*. Glasgow, 1824.

Stud horses imported from Britain were prize possessions in the North American colonies. Surely no immigrant, animal or human, was more pampered than Young Cannon Ball, the stallion brought to Fredericton from England by the New Brunswick Agricultural and Emigrant Society in 1825.

The early 188-page handwritten record of the society is preserved in the National Archives of Canada (MG 24 L6 Vol. 3) and makes it possible to trace, sometimes month by month, the coddling of Young Cannon Ball.

The society was formally established March 5, 1825, at the instigation of Lieutenant-Governor Sir Howard Douglas and comprised the members of the legislature "and other respectable Gentlemen from all Parts of the Province." Its first piece of business was "that the thanks of this Society be given to His Honor The Chief Justice [John Saunders] . . . for the trouble that he has taken to carry into effect the Grant of the Legislature made for the purchase of two entire horses for the use of the Province." An asterisk guides one to this amendment:

> That notwithstanding the active endeavours of His Honor The Chief Justice and Col. Shore to carry into effect the grant of the Legislature, made for the purchase of two entire horses, great difficulties had arisen, but through the agency and active exertions of Capt. Thomas Smith, late of the 2nd Lifeguards (a brother in law of Col. Shore's) in England, the [society] had been enabled to obtain the purchase of one valuable seed horse for the use of the Province, which is to come out early in the Spring.

Here are several subsequent entries, starting May 3, 1825:

> The Chief Justice reports that the Horse expected for the Society has arrived in St. John, and would be in Fredericton by the first steam boat, when the members present undertook to make inquiries for a suitable Groom to take charge of the Horse and a Stable to receive him in, and report the result on Friday next at a meeting to be held at 12 o'clock on that day.

May 6, 1825:

> It appearing to the Board that William Payne now residing in the house of Mr. Clopper below the Town will undertake the care of the Society's Horse, Ordered — That it be left to the President, and vice-president Mr. Baillie, to make an engagement with Payne, for that purpose, and to fix upon a stable for the reception of the Horse, and to do what is necessary for putting the same in proper state of equipment for that purpose.

May 16, 1825:

> Mr. Baillie reports — "that he has agreed with Payne that the Society shall give him £48 for the taking charge of the Horse as Groom for one year and for the use of the stable, he (Payne) agreeing to devote his whole time and attention to the Horse for that period," and also, "that he (Mr. Baillie) had employed a carpenter at the expense of the Society to fit up a stall in the same stable in a way to make it suitable for the reception of the Horse."
>
> Ordered — that the Horse do remain while in Saint John under the care of George Hazen, Esquire, subject to the direction of the Board of Directors of the Saint John Society, and that Mr. Baillie be requested to make arrangements with Major McNair for securing, if possible, the services of Boswell, the present groom, for six months.
>
> Ordered — that the Horse be not allowed to cover more than ten mares this season and that those be mares of the most approved description.
>
> Ordered — that the Horse be allowed to remain in Saint John until he is in a condition to cover and that he then be allowed to cover four mares at Saint John to be approved by the Director of the Saint John Society, and immediately after be brought to Fredericton.
>
> Ordered — that the price for covering by the Horse for this season be five pounds each mare and the colt insured.

June 13, 1825:

> The Society's Horse "Young Cannon Ball" imported from England reported to the Board as having arrived safe in Fredericton in good condition and fit for covering,
>
> Read a letter from Captain Smith to Colonel Shore detailing the steps he had taken in respect to obtaining the Horse, and inclosing his account of the Expenses amounting to one hundred and eighty four pounds two shillings and one penny halfpenny sterling. The price of the Horse £126 sterling. . . . The Secretary produces the account of John Boswell who had the care of the Horse in Saint John amounting to thirteen pounds, seven shillings and ten pence for his services as groom and supplies which is passed and ordered to be paid.

Sept. 2, 1825:

> The Secretary presents an account of William Payne for clearing rocks out of the stable yard where the Society's Horse is kept, amounting to £1-2-6.

Sept. 19, 1825:

> The Secretary reports that he had made enquiry for another groom for the Horse, that Matthew Corbett had agreed to take the charge of the

Horse if the Society would pay him £4 per month wages and find a stable and all food and supplies, that a stable could not be got under 20 shillings per month, Whereupon Mr. Baillie, the vice-president, offers to take charge of the Horse for the present in his own stable, and will charge the Society only with the actual expenses incurred for his food and other supplies, the Society making a reasonable compensation to Mr. Baillie's groom for his extra trouble.

Wherepon ordered — that Mr. Baillie's offer be accepted with the thanks of the Committee.

Oct. 21, 1825:

The Secretary presents to the Board an account of Mr. Hazen's for expenses incurred in the importation of the Horse "Young Cannon Ball" amounting to £31-6-8, which account is passed and ordered to be paid. And it is further ordered that the thanks of the Board be given to Mr. Hazen for his liberality in making no charge for the passage of the Horse from England in his ship. The Secretary presents an account of Kendall's the carpenter for fitting up the stable and yard for the Horse, amounting to £9-15-0.

Feb. 7, 1826:

Read the Honble. Thomas Baillie's account for keeping the Horse Young Cannon Ball from 20th Sept., 1825, to 7th Feby, 1826, for his Groom's attendance for that period and for a Saddle, Bridle, Headstall etc. amounting in the whole to £46-11-6, which account was approved and ordered to be paid. Mr. Baillie made the three following proposals to the Board with regard to the Horse Young Cannon Ball: 1st that he would give £120 for the Horse and would keep him in the Province for the purpose for which he was imported. 2d that if the Society were not inclined to sell, he would keep the Horse for £100 a year, and, 3d, that he would keep the Horse without any other remuneration than the sums that might be received during the time he remained in his charge for his services as a covering Horse, and that he would take his chance of profit or loss if this last proposal were accepted.

General meeting, Feb. 8, 1826:

It was resolved that the said Horse be sold by public auction at the Market House in Fredericton on Wednesday, the eighth day of March next at noon, the purchaser to enter into a bond with two sufficient sureties in the sum of five hundred pounds, to the Secretary of the General Society, upon condition that the Horse be kept for the purpose of covering within the Province for the term of five years, and the time and place, and the above condition of sale be immediately advertised by the Secretary in the several newspapers in the Province, payments to be made one half in six months and one half in twelve months from the day of sale.

Young Cannon Ball realized £200 at auction. The money spent on the stallion (oddly, there is no description of it, not even the color, in the society's records) far exceeded the crown grant for the New Brunswick Agricultural and Emigrant Society, which, in 1825, amounted to £175 spread among its seven county associations. Lieutenant-Governor Douglas raised the grant to £ 300 in 1826.

The society began importing from England Ayrshire cattle and shorthorn Durhams ("very large, of fine figures"), South Down and Dishley sheep and other livestock, and from the United States hogs and farm implements, including a threshing machine from which parts were missing, and various ploughs. And it imported two more horses: Buzzard, which cost £298-14-8 including transportation and keep, and sold for £ 167, and Eclipse, which cost £254-11-4 and sold for £99-13-10. The society took the losses in stride, considering them a reasonable price for improvement of the breed. Its third annual report, delivered March 1, 1828, said in part:

> The promising appearance of Cannon Ball's colts, the valuable points and pedigree of that Horse, and of two others imported by the Society, afford us good reason to believe that the breed of Horses will be greatly improved, although the qualities of their offspring, and their adaptation to the climate, pasturage and work of the country, cannot be exactly ascertained until some years shall have elapsed after their arrival.
>
> Cannon Ball is kept in the County of York; Buzzard in Sunbury; and Eclipse was purchased for Judge Botsford and some other Gentlemen in Westmorland. Another well bred Horse might be advantageously introduced into the northeastern parts of the Province where the inhabitants are desirous of improving their breed of Horses. At present, on the Gulf Shore, and at Chaleur Bay, nearly all are of the Canadian breed.

On Aug. 9, 1828, the society approved expenditure of £250 for a stallion and Dishley sheep to be landed at Miramichi.

Thomas Baillie, commissioner and surveyor-general of crown lands in New Brunswick, could hardly have been more discouraging. He advised the new arrival to take a job with a farmer the first year to acquire first-hand information on cultivation. He would earn part of the crop to take with him to his small acreage.

> Our emigrant, his wife and children, by repeated journeys through the woods, commonly without any road, and with no other guide

than a line of blazed or marked trees, carry off a portion of their produce sufficient for present consumption to their chosen abode. Having by the assistance of their old neighbours erected the shell of a log hut, they will commence building their chimney with rough stone cemented with loam, filling the interstices of the outside logs with moss, forming a floor with poles rendered flat by the axe or adze, and making other preparations for the winter, which is now rapidly approaching. The man will next proceed to make a path to the nearest settlement, in order to allow a pair of oxen to draw the remainder of his necessities to his new habitation, and when he has laid in his little stock of provisions for the winter, consisting of salt fish, potatoes, and bread stuff, another difficulty assails him in the want of warm clothing and bedding. To pay for articles of so indispensable a description, he is compelled to labour as a timber cutter for about two months during the severity of the winter, at which time he could do but little in clearing up his land on account of the depth of the snow. He will then direct his attention to the clearance of his land, which he sets about without delay.

As soon as the land be sufficiently dry, he will set fire to his little chopping, which will probably consist of about four or five acres; and as this will not consume more than the brush and light boughs scattered around, he will then roll together what logs are not too heavy for himself, assisted by his wife and children, into piles.

When these are sufficiently dry, fire is again communicated; which process must be repeated until the whole be consumed, leaving the stumps only for the hand of time to destroy.

His wheat is sown about the middle or latter end of May, which he covers with a harrow drawn by oxen, or, which is by far the most usual, entirely by manual labour with the hoe. The latter implement is the only one which he can use in planting his potatoes, for the plough can never be inserted until a considerable part of the stumps be extracted, and the roots which are interlaced in the soil decayed.

The stumps, roots, and unevenness of the surface in its natural state form an obstruction to good husbandry, so serious in its consequences that a farmer can never expect to receive more than one-third of the produce which would be obtained by the same system of husbandry as is practised in England, for an acre of land seldom produces here more than twenty bushels of wheat, or more than 150 bushels of potatoes.

The stumps occupy one-third of the land, and by preventing animal labour, they render the application of manure next to impossible, superinduce a slovenly system of husbandry, liable to be perpetuated, and effect a gradual deterioration in the productiveness of the soil. Thomas Baillie. *An Account of the Province of New Brunswick; with Advice to Emigrants*. London, 1832.

The Saint John Agricultural and Horticultural Society went ahead with establishment of a twenty-four-page journal, *The New-Brunswick Agriculturist,* despite rejection by the colonial government — after approval by the legislature — of a £150 grant. It was edited (i.e., largely written) by Dr. R. Bayard. It contained a surprising amount of local material and fewer reprints from British and American farm journals than was usual for such papers at the time.

> If the farmers throughout the provinces are really desirous to promote their own interests, they should form Agricultural Societies, and co-operate with the Press for the improvement of husbandry. A society should be formed in each county; meetings should be held four times a year; agricultural subjects should be discussed; defective systems exposed and relinquished; improvements urged, and experiments suggested; theory and practice should be directed by science and experience; error and apathy should give way to truth and energy. The societies should communicate with the Editors of the respective agricultural papers — they should send the results of their experiments for publication, when they are calculated to diffuse useful information, or to expose any prevailing error; and when they require information upon any particular subject, they should submit their questions, that answers, extracted from the most approved agricultural authorities, may be returned through the different agricultural Periodicals for the benefit of all. In this manner, zeal will be kindled and sustained. Farmers will appreciate the importance of their employment, and one of the most rational and delightful pursuits in life will be elevated to its proper dignity in the provinces.
>
> We are aware that societies have been formed in many counties; that they have had an ephemeral existence, and have withered away, leaving little or no record of their utility. The failure was attributable to the want of support. The best efforts of the Few will be ineffectual if the Many do not advance in support of them. Indifference will perpetuate ignorance. *The New-Brunswick Agriculturist*. Vol. 1, no. 1. Saint John, May 1841.

In his account of the area around Fredericton, Edmund Ward complained about the disastrous economic conditions that prevailed in the new settlement:

> Altho' there is abundance of cultivated land in the neighbourhood of the town [Fredericton], and settlements are springing up continually at no great distance, above and around it, yet the supplies of garden-

stuff and other vegetables is extremely limited; and owing to this cause and the truck and barter system, against which public opinion should be arrayed, the price demanded for all the necessaries of life is extravagantly high for an inland country; and flour, meal and salted provisions are brought up from St. John during the summer; while such is the neglected state of agriculture, and so inferior is the mode of husbandry throughout the Province, that large quantities of oats are imported from Europe, although they may be sown here without the risk of failure. Owing to the lumbering pursuits in which the people on this River as well as elsewhere have engaged, and to which toilsome and semi-savage life they are unaccountably prone, a large amount of property is under mortgage to the supplying merchants, who have to secure themselves in this way for provisions and other articles advanced to enable parties to pursue an occupation attended with very great risk. Edmund Ward. *An Account of the River St. John, with its Tributary Rivers and Lakes*. Fredericton, 1841.

James S. Buckingham embarked at Windsor, N.S., for Saint John, N.B., and did his laudatory agricultural assessment from aboard ship:

We started at half-past two o'clock, and proceeded down the river Avon, both banks of which were lined with beautiful farms.

Later, he stopped overnight at Woodstock, N.B.:

The inn was so dirty, and the hostess so unaccommodating, that we preferred sitting up rather than going to bed; and the night being excessively cold, we had great difficulty in procuring sufficient fire-wood to keep us warm. We had met with nothing more disagreeable than this in any of the back settlements of America, and we hoped the time would soon come when more settlers, and of a higher and better class, would be poured into this region, to fill it with those who would have means and taste to surround themselves with greater comforts, and be able and willing to furnish them to others. James S. Buckingham. *Canada, Nova Scotia, New Brunswick, and the other British Provinces in North America*. London, 1843.

C. W. Atkinson gives one of the first descriptions of a grain cradle:

The operation of cutting the grain is much facilitated by the use of a "cradle," which is a machine of American invention. It is composed of a scythe, and its handle, with the addition of a few light bars of wood, placed parallel with the blade; the straw is severed with this instrument, and as it falls behind the scythe, is received by the frame. The mower, by a dexterous movement, which alone can be obtained by practice, disencumbers the cradle of the grain, and deposits it at his feet, as regularly, and much more expeditiously, than if it were reaped.

Atkinson advised settlers to take these basic articles into the woods: ax, hand saw, auger, pickax, spade, hammer, iron wedge, kettle, frying pan, iron pan, iron pot, two gimlets, three hoes, nails and a small portable hand mill for grinding grain. He added one other not usually found in emigrant guidebooks:

> A pocket compass will be of great service to you. There are many instances of persons getting lost, and wandering for days and weeks in the woods of America. If you lose yourself in the woods, select a course, and follow it, turn neither to the right nor the left, till you come to a road — without a compass you cannot be sure of proceeding a straight course. C. W. Atkinson. *A Historical and Statistical Account of New-Brunswick, British North America.* 3d ed., Edinburgh, 1844.

Some early customs were recounted by Mrs. F. Beavan:

> By the accustomed sun-mark on the floor, which Sybel prefers to the clock, she sees 'tis now the hungry hour of noon, and blows the horn for Lank to come to dinner. This horn is a conk shell, bored at one end, and its sound is heard at a great distance. At the hours of meal-time it may be heard from house to house, and, ringing through the echoing woods from distant settlements, telling us, amid their loneliness, of happy meetings at the household board; but it comes, too, at times when its sounds are heralds of trouble and dismay. I have heard it burst upon the ear at the silent hour of midnight, and, starting from sleep, seen the sky all crimsoned with the flames of some far off dwelling, whose inmates thus called for assistance. I have also heard it when some member of the family has been lost in the woods, and the horn is blown to guide him homewards. . . .
>
> In the days of the early settling of the country, marriages were attended with a ceremony called stumping. This was a local way of publishing the banns, the names of the parties and the announcement of the event to take place being written on a slip of paper, and inserted on the numerous stumps bordering the corduroy road, that all who ran might read, though perchance none might scan it save some bewildered fox or wandering bear; the squire read the ceremony from the prayer-book, received his dollar, and further form for wedlock was required not. Mrs. F. Beavan. *Sketches and Tales Illustrative of Life in the Backwoods of New Brunswick.* London, 1845.

The glamor of other trades — particularly lumbering — lured many settlers away from farming:

Owing to the great repute of the Timber Trade, Ship Building, and other pursuits, too many of the active and enterprising inhabitants of the Province have neglected Agriculture, and more have neglected to study it as a science, but enough is practised to convince the observing that this country is capable of producing all the necessaries of life. . . .

The idea of accumulating [timber] property by hundreds and thousands throws the slow profits of the farmer in the shade, and he leaves his farm and takes his team to the forest . . . although the last twenty years have produced ten successful farmers to one independent timber maker. C. L. Hatheway. *The History of New Brunswick from its First Settlement*. Fredericton, 1846.

Abraham Gesner was a strong advocate of manuring, whether by wood ashes, limestone or marsh mud. But he opposed the use of fish:

In Nova Scotia . . . herring are sometimes taken upon the coast in such quantities that the fishermen are unable to preserve the whole catch, and with smelts and caplin, they are taken for the sole purpose of supplying manure. The taking of fish for this object is very reprehensible, and should be prevented by law, for it tends to destroy the young fry and the bait that allures the deep sea fish to the shores.

Herrings, smelts, or caplin, are taken up the shores of New Brunwick and coast of Gaspe in great quantities and carted into the fields. This unprepared manure produces a few good crops, but by its constant application the soil loses many of its natural properties, and finally becomes very meagre.

Gesner said seaweed was particularly valuable as manure because the salt in it "destroys foul weeds." The benefits of animal manure were often lost because the barn was usually built "upon some small eminence, and the most valuable fertilizing substances are swept away by every shower into brooks and swamps." He was disappointed that guano didn't provide an abundance of manure; "the climate, heavy rains, frosts and snows, prevent the accumulation of that kind of manure in North America."

Gesner wrote about agricultural subjects other than manure. On farm implements:

Several machines have been proposed for extracting the stumps from the earth before they are rotten, but none of them have been successful . . . The stump machine of Sir Henry Vere Huntley, late Governor of Prince Edward Island, promised to extract stumps in the manner the dentist dislodges teeth, but it failed in practice. . . . Until very lately, the farming utensils used were very imperfect. The old German plough, with a wooden roller under the beam, is still adhered to by many farmers of the County of Lunenburg. The ploughs of the Acadians are of equally antique model. The harrows are also of ancient stamp.

Gesner uses an old piece of doggerel to make his point that six kernels should go into each hill of corn:

One for the cut-worm,
One for the crow,
One for the grub,
And three for to grow.

Abraham Gesner. *New Brunswick, with Notes for Emigrants.* London, 1847; *The Industrial Resources of Nova Scotia.* Halifax, 1849

James F. W. Johnston, a teacher at Durham University in England, was hired by the New Brunswick government to survey the province for its agricultural, forestry and mineral resources. His resulting work became widely known and was quoted for decades by other travellers. Johnston visited every district of New Brunswick and declined to condemn farmers for supposedly outmoded methods. He was on the side of the farmer, as we see in this observation made at Jacksontown, in the St. John River Valley, some seventy miles north of Fredericton:

Old Country agriculturists, or those who, without being farmers themselves, condemn every practice which differs from what they have been in the habit of hearing commended at home, cannot fairly appreciate the circumstances of the occupier of new land in a country like this. For ten years — for eight, or twelve, or twenty years in other localities — this new land requires no manure to make it yield good crops. On the contrary, the addition of manure makes the grain or grass crops at first so rank that they fall over, or lodge, and are seriously injured. Thus, to a settler on new land, which he clears from the wilderness, manure is not only unnecessary, but it is a nuisance; and hence he not only neglects the preparation of it, but is anxious to rid himself in the easiest way of any that may be made about his house or barns.

Careless and improvident farming habits were no doubt thus introduced, so that, when at last the land became exhausted, the occupiers were ignorant of the means of renovating it. Old habits were to be overcome, new practices to be adopted, and a system of painstaking care to which they had been previously unaccustomed. Hence, no doubt, the reason why I was almost everywhere told that it was cheaper and more profitable to clear and crop new land than to renovate the old.

Still, because of these future evils, we are not justified in speaking contemptuously of present holders of new land, who, being desirous of making the most of it with the means at their command, waste none of their attention upon unnecessary manures. These men form that body of pioneers in American agriculture, who, having done their work in clearing and superficially exhausting one tract of land, move off westward to do the same with another, selling off each farm in succession to men possessed of more knowledge than themselves; whose skill and industry must bring back the fertility which had disappeared under the treatment of their predecessors, and who have no temptation to fall off into negligent modes of farming.

According to this view, the emigration of this class of wilderness-clearing and new land-exhausting farmers, is a kind of necessity in the rural progress of a new country. It is a thing to rejoice in rather than to regret.

On threshing:

Portable thrashing-machines travel the country at this season of the year, and are hired by the day to the farmers. The machine is driven by the horses of the person who hires, and is worked by the two owners who accompany it. The county Agricultural Societies have exerted themselves to introduce these machines, and where labour is scarce they are very useful; though the expense incurred by the farmer in hiring them still makes the thrashing a comparatively costly operation. James F. W. Johnston. *Notes on North America, Agricultural, Economical and Social.* 2 vols. Edinburgh and London, 1851.

Johnston had a telling phrase for unproductive land: "thin and cold." He applied it, for example, to poor clay-slate soils between Halifax and Windsor, N.S., an area that still has few farms.

M. C. S. London got fed up cutting firewood, and noted in his diary:

October 28th — Chop-chop-chop. This chopping of fuel has become to me like the money-gathering of the miser; even as he is tormented by the constant fear of want and starvation in the winter of his years, so have I ever in my mind the dread of the winter before me. So I [be]grudge every bit of wood I put on the fire, and only cease chopping when I can barely raise my hand for the blow. M. C. S. London. *Two Months on the Tobique, New Brunswick; An Emigrant's Journal, 1851.* London, 1866.

The *Journal of the New Brunswick Society for the encouragement of Agriculture, Home Manufactures, and Commerce,* founded in 1849, presented the individual reports of the county agricultural societies throughout the province, with their resolutions to government and legislature.

Farmers in most countries have a proverbial dislike for book farming, but this prejudice gives way as general enlightenment proceeds, and the results of practices different from their own can be fairly examined: this Society then should . . . urge most strenuously upon the Legislature to strike at the root of this degrading ignorance: Agricultural reading should be provided for every school in the country, and an Agricultural education should be provided for a population which has come expressly to get their living by and from the soil. The want of an Agricultural element in the education of a country like this would argue that our rulers were as averse to book farming as the farmers of the old schools themselves. We hope yet to see the day when the elements of Agriculture will form more or less a part of the teaching of every common School, Grammar School and College supported by public money in New Brunswick. Special Agricultural schools and model farms should also have early and liberal encouragement. . . . The strong, the great and paramount interest of this country must ever be the Agricultural interest. Part II, Fredericton, 1851.

The society was one of the very first groups in the province to recognize New Brunswick's bilingual nature. In 1851, it published and distributed 7,000 copies in English and 1,000 in French of a pamphlet entitled *For The Back Settlements. On General Management of a Farm; showing how an exhausted soil may be rendered perfectly fertile, without the aid of capital.*

The pamphlet was written originally by a Montreal district farmer and so pleased Lord Elgin, the governor-general of the United Province of Canada, that he had it distributed as a New Year's gift to the farmers of Lower Canada. It was, however, a very rudimentary work, and its advice on dairy products was:

The Canadian women are industrious and cleanly, consequently they are well fitted to make good butter and cheese.

Orchardists struggling to protect their crops from thieves were advised to give as good as they got:

One objection, perhaps the only one which can be urged against growing fruit in this country, is the difficulty of preserving it during the period of ripening from the young pilferers who infest the place every fall. The same objection will apply with equal truth to the growing of any kind of fruit, turnips, pease, etc, and the cause of the annoyance is easily traced to two sources, viz. loose discipline on the part of the parents or guardians of such boys, and the lax manner in which our Laws are enforced. Perhaps the most effectual method of protecting Gardens and Orchards against such depredations, would be to erect (while the fruit is in the process of ripening) a comfortable tent in each, and let one or two persons, accompanied by a trusty dog and not less trusty revolver, take up their abode in it nightly till the fruit be pulled. A little experience after this fashion might convince such worthies that after all honesty is the best policy, and a few reports from the revolver might prove that British Subjects will not for ever tamely submit to have their properties pilfered with impunity while a mode of redress, however repugnant, is within their reach. *The Gleaner and Northumberland, Kent, Gloucester and Restigouche Commercial and Agricultural Journal. Vol. XIII.* [Chatham-Miramichi, N.B.], Saturday Evening, February 4, 1854.

The harsh winters, surprisingly, could benefit the crops:

The severe frosts in winter generally penetrate so deep into the ground, especially when it is not covered with grass, as to raise up and separate the particles from each other, to a considerable depth; so that when the thaw comes, it is already so loose and open as scarcely to require ploughing at all, or if ploughed, to be done with little force and great speed. . . .

The manner in which all root-crops thrive in the Province is really remarkable, and the frost is one of the agents by which the large product is brought about, by opening and pulverizing the soil. M. H. Perley. *A Hand Book of Information for Emigrants to New-Brunswick.* Saint John, 1854.

Alexander Monro reported a rare criticism of the agricultural societies:

The only forcible objections we have yet heard urged against these societies are that they sometimes appropriate large sums in introducing horses better adapted for the race course than for the plough or for general purposes; and the awarding premiums to a few only of the best stock, to the exclusion of the many. It is contended that the rich only take these premiums, as the poorer portion of the society are not able to compete for them, and if they do make the attempt, it is only by over-feeding part of their stock, to the injury of the remainder. We think that these objections, which are frequently made, are much over-balanced by the examples afforded of improved cultivation, the introduction of seeds and stock, which ultimately find their ways to all, and other benefits which, directly or indirectly, have been found to result from these societies. Alexander Monro. *New Brunswick; with a brief outline of Nova Scotia, and Prince Edward Island.* Halifax, 1855

James Robb, professor of chemistry at King's College, Fredericton, wrote a sixty-four-page pamphlet for the New Brunswick Society for the Encouragement of Agriculture, Home Manufactures and Commerce.

In this Province, there are probably not more than a dozen mowing machines as yet, but in the United States the demand is ahead of the supply; and no wonder, for with two horses one will mow at least twelve acres a day. The horse drill in the same way will sow seven or eight acres a day and save half the horse work.

The progress of agriculture may be measured by the desire shown by the cultivators of the land for improved implements and agricultural machinery. . . .

The sub-soil and trench-plough, the mole-plough, the cultivator, clod-crusher and scarifier, the drill-harrow and the horse-hoe, manure-distributor and drain-tile machine, the horse-drill, the hay, straw and root-cutter, the grain-crusher, the root-grater, the thrashing machine, the reaper and mower, the horse-rake, the potato-washer, the corn-sheller, the hay-press — all these are implements of comparatively modern invention. There ought to be an Agricultural Depot or Museum in this country where such implements should be always open to public examination. James Robb. *Agricultural Progress*. Fredericton, 1856.

James Brown, the surveyor-general of the province when he wrote his twenty-one-page pamphlet, is one of the very few such essayists to include personal (and pertinent) information.

I was nineteen years of age when I arrived in New Brunswick, a stranger and alone. I was not destitute, for I was under the protection of Divine Providence — had excellent health — two suits of clothes — seven dollars in cash, and a smattering of spelling, reading, writing and arithmetic, which I had learned at a Parish School.

Thus qualified, I went to work with a farmer for my board and lodging, and began to learn to drive oxen and cut down trees. I was very kindly used, and through the haying and harvest season, had half a dollar a day as wages. I afterwards was employed at cellar and well digging, and when the winter came on, joined another Emigrant, and went from farm to farm threshing out the grain. In the latter part of winter, I hired with a lumberer — camped out, and wrought in the forest as a swamper.

Next season I was chiefly employed in digging cellars and wells, and joined another young man in the purchase of a small lot of wilderness land, of which we cleared three acres, on which we sowed three bushels of wheat the following spring; from which we reaped and threshed seventy five bushels of excellent grain. Next year we cleared up three acres more, and sowed four bushels of wheat thereon, which produced eighty bushels; after which I sold my share

J.S. Meres, *Farms at Placentia, Newfoundland*, 1786.

A.C. Mercer, *Farmland on the Dutch Village Road, Halifax*, 1840.

W.G.R. Hind, *Cutting Wood in the Forest*.

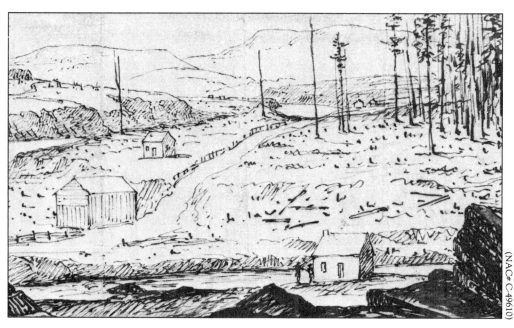

P.J. Bainbrigge, *River St. John from the Forks of the Madawaska, 1839*.

of the little farm. By this time I could readily obtain a dollar a day for haying, and the same for reaping. I was one of five who engaged to reap a field of new land wheat, of twelve acres. We had fine weather, and cut it all down, bound and set it up in stooks, in six days. It produced twenty three bushels to the acre. One generation has passed away since that time, and last year, "as there I walk'd with careless steps and slow," I saw on the one side a productive orchard, and on the other a crop of hay cocked up, about three-quarters of a ton to the acre. That side of the field has never been either plowed or manured, and has produced a crop of hay every year since we did the reaping. . . .

I saved £155 which I paid for one hundred acres of wilderness, in a very convenient situation, and had enough left to build thereon a small framed house and shed, and there commenced house keeping, with property worth about £225, the savings of seven years. I raised sixty bushels of wheat the first year. I have camped out thirteen winters and parts of winters as a lumberer; and wrought twelve springs at river driving; have cleared up many acres of the wilderness, and so had opportunities of becoming practically acquainted with the whole process of clearing and settling the forest lands.

My own case resembles that of hundreds who have come at different periods from the British Islands, and are now scattered over all parts of the Province. James Brown. *New Brunswick as a Home for Emigrants.* Saint John, N.B., 1860.

Arthur Hamilton Gordon, the lieutenant-governor, was happy hiking and canoeing through remote parts of New Brunswick. On this tramp in the upper Nashwaak valley, he reached the farm of a Mr. Johnson about 6:15 p.m.:

The farm had every appearance of being as prosperous as any I had seen in the province. Fine cows were roaming about; the tinkling bells, which are always suspended to their necks to prevent their being lost by straying into the forest, sounding pleasantly in the twilight. A large amount of land had been cleared, a substantial, whitewashed house, with a verandah, erected, and the whole place wore an air of progress and comfort. Mr. Johnson was at work in a field, in which he was still chopping at tree-stumps, and was just concluding his day's work when we approached, and asked him if he could let us sup and sleep at his house. His reply was characteristic of the country: "No man, white or black, is ever turned away by me." In the evening I sat long with him on the edge of the verandah, discussing the working of the common school system, and watching the fire-flies, or as they are styled by the people, with more descriptive accuracy than poetical elegance — lightning bugs. We slept on the floor of one of Mr. Johnson's rooms, and at five the following morning started in earnest on our forest walk. Arthur Hamilton Gordon. *Wilderness Journeys in New Brunswick in 1862-63*. Saint John, 1864.

At first sight, reported Samuel Watts, the assigned lot of forest trees might appear daunting, but bulky, tall and dense trees denoted strong, rich, and deep soil.

He has hard blows and many to deal; days of toil to pass before he can put in his first crop. But a gracious and generous reward for his toil awaits him. The character of the labor before him if it is heavy will be found healthy; it will develope his muscle and strengthen his lungs. The crash of every tree he falls will tell him of his constant march toward the reward he seeks. Samuel Watts. *Facts for the Information of Intending Emmigrants about the Province of New Brunswick*. Woodstock, N.B., 1870.

A good ax was "the grand instrument of all his future success."

Another writer found the appearance of the people formidable.

To one just arrived from Northern Europe there is assuredly something disappointing in the outer aspects of the middle aged of both sexes inhabiting the remoter districts of New Brunswick. Where he expected to meet burly, well-nourished farmers, sallow, weather-beaten countenances and spare, sinewy frames predominate among men of forty, while the pallid faces of the women indicate often ten years in advance of their real ages. . . .

As the intense cold invites crowding around the fire, it is a usual custom for the whole family to pass days in the dry, stove-heated atmosphere of their small cottages, so that in spring they look pale and shrivelled. A. Leith Adams. *Field and Forest Rambles*. London, 1873.

J. W. Robertson had grown up on a farm and was an agricultural scientist.

We sometimes think that because a cow will eat almost any kind of plant, therefore everything is adapted to the cow. That is not the fact. By feeding expensive food we increase the cost of production and therefore the cow consumes more value than she produces and thus becomes unprofitable. It does not pay to feed a cow on strawberries. I tried that one time myself. While I was talking to a young lady one evening a cow ate two baskets of strawberries out of my wagon, and yet she did not give any more milk or produce better butter. . . .

In feeding and fattening little pigs, they should have the trough room in length, not in depth. Many of the hog troughs I see around the country seem to have been constructed with the object of affording bath accommodation for the pigs, so deep and wide are they that the pigs take headers right into them. J. W. Robertson. *Lectures on Agriculture*. Fredericton, 1890.

THE CANADAS

LOWER CANADA

CHAMPLAIN IN HIS EXPLORATION of the Ottawa River in 1613 observed Indian agriculture at Muskrat Lake:

> They showed me their gardens and the fields, where they had maize. Their soil is sandy, for which reason they devote themselves more to hunting than to tillage, unlike the Ochateguins [Hurons]. When they wish to make a piece of land arable, they burn down the trees, which is very easily done, as they are all pines, and filled with resin. The trees having been burned, they dig up the ground a little, and plant their maize kernel by kernel, like those in Florida. At the time I was there it was only four fingers high.

Later, Champlain reached the Algonquins on Allumette Island in the Ottawa River and observed:

> I went out walking in their gardens, which were filled with squashes, beans, and our peas, which they are beginning to cultivate. *The Voyages of Samuel de Champlain.* C. P. Otis translation in the Prince Society edition, Boston, 1882.

Earlier, when he founded Quebec in 1608, Champlain had noted varieties of wild fruit trees in the area and remarked that if the land were cultivated it would bear as well as French soil. In 1617, he invited Louis Hébert, already Canada's first white farmer, to come to Quebec. Hébert arrived that year with his wife, Marie Rollet, and three children, after a voyage of thirteen weeks from Honfleur, France, and cleared seven acres at the top of the cliff to plant Indian corn and peas.

Hébert had been to Canada twice before. In 1604, he accompanied Champlain, de Monts, de Poutrincourt and de Pont-Gravé to Acadia and St. Croix Island (now called Dochet) in the St. Croix River (the modern border between New Brunswick and Maine). An apothecary, he sailed as the ship's doctor and was appointed chief gardener of the island settlement. He experimented with the roots, herbs and vines he collected.

Marc Lescarbot wrote in his account of the expedition that Hébert "took great pleasure in working the soil." The next summer, the disease-decimated settlement moved to Port Royal (now Annapolis Royal, N.S.), where Hébert began cultivating a new garden. In 1606, de Monts lost his fur-trading charter and returned to France, Hébert with him.

In 1610, de Poutrincourt returned to Port Royal, accompanied by Hébert and Hébert's wife. They lived there until 1613 when the British razed the settlement. Hébert went back to France and, with his wife, ran a chemist's shop in Paris for the next four years, until the call from Champlain. Hébert built a stone house on his small holding at Quebec where he farmed until his death in 1627 after a fall.

The Jesuit missionaries in New France frequently commented on Indian agriculture. But in *The Jesuit Relation* for 1663 there is an observation on farming carried on by the white settlers. It is quoted by N. H. Bowen in *An Historical Sketch of the Isle of Orleans*, published in Quebec in 1860:

> The Isle of Orleans . . . abounds in grain which grows there of every description and with such facility that the farmer has only to scrape the land which yields him all that he can desire: and this, during 14 or 15 consecutive years without any repose.

The early farmers faced a "troublesome and disagreeable" problem: the Iroquois kept them closely confined, as Pierre Boucher wrote:

> We cannot go to hunt or fish without danger of being killed or taken prisoners; and we cannot even plough our fields, much less make hay, without continued risk: They lie in ambush on all sides, and any little thicket suffices for six or seven of these barbarians to put themselves under cover in, or more correctly speaking, in an ambush, from which they throw themselves upon you suddenly when you are at your work, or going to it or coming from it.

Boucher reports that wheat grew very well in New France, giving bread "as fine and as white as any in France." Also grown were rye, barley, oats, millet, buckwheat, peas, lentils, vetch, broad beans, hemp, flax, turnips, radishes, beetroots, carrots, parsnips, salsify, cabbages, sorrel, chard, asparagus, spinach, lettuce, parsley, endive, onions, leeks, garlic, chives, melons, cucumbers and watermelons.

Boucher says he was asked in Paris why vineyards were not planted in New France.

> To this I answer that eating is more necessary than drinking, and therefore the raising of wheat has to be attended to before the planting of vineyards; one can do better without wine than without bread. It has been as much as we could do to clear land and raise wheat, without doing any thing else. . . .
>
> What is the ordinary beverage?
>
> Wine in the best houses. Beer in some others; there is another beverage called *bouillon* that is in common use in all the houses; the

poorest people drink water which is very good and very common in this country. Pierre Boucher. *True and Genuine Description of New France, commonly called Canada.* Paris, 1664.

Thomas D'Arcy McGee was then minister of agriculture, immigration and statistics. His 1864 report included a short memorandum from his deputy minister, J. C. Taché, "on the vine question":

There is at this moment a beginning of experimental proof of the practicability of getting good wine from the vine in Upper and in Lower Canada: — *Firstly*, in the recorded fact that pure wine has been made out of the wild grape of Canada for sacred purposes, by the first missionaries in the time of the primary occupation of the country by Europeans; — *Secondly*, in the facts ascertained by a Committee of the last Session of the Legislative Assembly, showing that the wild vine of Canada, after a few years of cultivation, has yielded comparatively fine crops of grapes, from which good *vin ordinaire* has been manufactured. . . .

There could be no doubt that the success of vine-growing in Canada would be of great public advantage, both in a moral, intellectual and material point of view; for it is a fact, historically ascertained through ages, that in countries where the wine is a common article of food, drunkenness is less frequent and less detrimental in its character than in countries where beer or ardent spirits (even when they are pure) are used for that stimulation which is likely to be sought for by all populations, in spite of all efforts to the contrary. Province of Canada. *Report of the Minister of Agriculture for the year 1864.* Quebec, 1865.

J. Perrault, secretary treasurer of the board, was the French-language counterpart to William Evans in promoting better farming methods in Lower Canada. In this issue of the bilingual *Journal*, he printed a "Historical Review of the Agriculture of Canada," including the following two ordinances:

Decree of the Conseil Superieur of New France, 20th of June 1667
On the information of the Procureur General that experience has shown that the principal cause that a large portion of the lands of the country are infested and destroyed with thistles, arises from the neglect at the outset from having attended to this matter; that this evil will infallibly spread over all the deserts of the country if not prevented, because the thistles coming to seed and the seed to ripen, the wind will carry this seed a large distance and spread it around everywhere, even to places the most distant; that in order to prevent this evil from increasing excessively, it will be proper to oblige those whose lands are infested with thistles to prevent their coming to seed.

The Conseil therefore ordains that those whose lands are infested with thistles shall be bound to cut them down perfectly every year between the 1st and the end of July, so that there shall remain none uncut, even in the roads which pass through their lands, under the penalty of thirty sols on demand, for every arpent of ground which shall be overgrown with them, and those who may not have to the extent of an arpent, shall nevertheless be bound to pay for an arpent.

Ordinance, 20th April 1749:

According to the account which has been rendered to us, the considerable works done on account of the King for some years have attracted to this city [Montreal] a number of habitans married in the country, who have abandoned their lands, either to become carters, or laborers, or to keep taverns, which has caused considerable loss to the colony, the lands lying uncultivated and not producing as they might; that the habitans thus established find seasons in the year when they can scarcely support their families; and that there is just fear that in the future they may become dependent on mendicancy, which may subject a portion of them to troublesome consequences, and may throw them on the public for support; and seeing that it is of the first importance for the public weal of the colony to extend the culture of the soil;

We expressly inhibit and forbid all habitans who have land in the country from coming to establish themselves in the city, on whatever pretext, without our permission, on pain the said contravenors of being driven from the city, and sent back upon their lands, their moveables and effects confiscated, and, besides, fifty livres damages being payable on the spot, all to be applied to the support of the hospital, and in order to be enabled to recognize all the habitans who may come clandestinely to establish themselves therein;

We decree that at the census of the 1st of May next, all the individuals of the city and suburbs who shall lease for the future houses or chambers to parties whose condition is unknown to them, or whom they suspect to be habitans from the country, shall be held bound to declare before the Lieutenant General of Police three days after granting leases, the names, surnames, and professions of those to whom they have let the said houses and chambers, on pain against the individual contravenor, of a hundred livres fine, payable without delay, and applicable as above. J. Perrault, ed. *Journal of the Transactions of the Board of Agriculture of Lower Canada*. Montreal, 1859.

Keeping them down on the farm was serious business in New France.

Baron de Lahontan in a letter dated at Beaupré, New France, May 2, 1684, wrote of the seigneuries dotting the banks of the St. Lawrence River:

> The poorest of them have four arpents of ground in front, and thirty or forty in depth: the whole country being a continued forrest of lofty trees, the stumps of which must be grubbed up, before they can make use of the plough. 'Tis true this is a troublesome and chargeable task at first; but in a short time after they make up their losses; for when the virgin ground is capable of receiving seed, it yields an increase to the rate of an hundredfold. Corn is there sown in May, and reaped about the middle of September. Instead of threshing the sheaves in the field, they convey 'em to barns, where they lie till the coldest season of the winter, at which time the grain is more easily disengaged from the ear. In this country they likewise sow pease, which are much esteemed in France. All sorts of grain are very cheap here, as well as butchers meat and fowl. . . .
>
> Most of the inhabitants are a free sort of people that removed hither from France, and brought with 'em but little money to set up withal. The rest are those who were soldiers about thirty or forty years ago, at which time the Regiment of Carignan was broke, and they exchanged a military post for the trade of agriculture. Neither the one nor the other paid anything for the grounds they possess, no more than the officers of these troops, who marked out to themselves certain portions of unmanured and woody lands. Baron de Lahontan. *New Voyages to North-America.* 2 vols. London, 1703.

In an introduction to a 1932 edition of Lahontan's *Voyages,* Stephen Leacock wrote that the trade in beaver skins and not agriculture governed the life and destiny of New France. As the English were to show, "the real secret of the domination of the continent lay in emigration and settlement, the occupation of the land, the substitution of the pioneer for the bush-ranger (coureur des bois), the farmstead for the trail." And historian Donald Creighton wrote later, "The expansion of the French westward was penetration, not occupation; travel, not home-building; commerce, not agriculture."

There was no printing press in New France and consequently any treatises were handwritten. A thirty-eight-page anonymous manuscript, *Outline on Means to increase Cultivation and Production of lands in Canada and avoid famines without cost to King or Colony,* dated simply Canada, 1753, is the only such document on the subject of agriculture we have been able to find. It is in the National Archives in Ottawa. Printed material circulated in New France, of course, but it was printed in France; there are no imprints from New France on any subject.

This French-language memoir (the author's name for it) makes the point that was to be made often in the next century and a half: agriculture in Lower Canada (Quebec) was in a sorry state because its practitioners refused to modernize or pay the slightest attention to scientific farming, which meant using manure and rotating crops.

The treatise advocates radical change: establishment of a board of agriculture with powers to draft soldiers for farm work, make a census of all agricultural land and report cases of neglect or abandonment, order the types of crops to be grown and to direct produce at fixed prices to local use or export. A modern parallel would be a Soviet collective.

The author takes a very harsh view of city dwellers: parasites living off the hard work of poor farmers and other "idlers and vagabonds." The "courtiers" of Quebec were unscrupulous, if not criminal. He recommends parish contributions to help new settlers for three or four years with food, tools and animals. Funds could also come from taxes on liquor, cuts in royal pensions to the clergy and special assessments on the landowners. It is not difficult to guess that none of these recommendations was ever carried out.

One of the novel aspects of the memoir was the assertion that the army in New France could learn a great deal from farmers and thus improve defence of the colony against the English.

The farmers knew a lot more than the soldiers about guerrilla warfare and survival by use of snowshoes, living off the land by hunting and fishing, finding their way through the forests, sleeping outdoors and transportation by canoe and portage. Soldiers housed on farms throughout the countryside would pick up such skills — and acquire a taste for farming in their post-army days. And they would be well away from the taverns in the towns and debauchery.

Pierre Charlevoix chronicled his arrival in Lower Canada at the Isle of Orleans:

> On Sunday the 22d [of September, 1720], we came to an anchor in the traverse of the Isle of Orleans, where we went ashore whilst we waited the return of the tide. I found the country here pleasant, the lands good, and the planters in tolerable good circumstances. . . . It produces good wheat and excellent fruits. They begin also to cultivate tobacco on it, which is far from being bad.

In his fourth letter, dated February 15, 1721, at Quebec, Charlevoix regretted the quick-rich attractions of the fur trade for settlers occupying fertile, productive soil:

> Thus one part of our youth is continually rambling and roving about . . . with a habit of libertinism of which they never entirely get rid; at least, it gives them a distaste for labour, it exhausts their strength, they become incapable of the least constraint, and when they are no

longer unable to undergo the fatigues of travelling, which soon happens for these fatigues are excessive, they remain without the least resource, and are no longer good for anything. Hence it comes to pass that arts [of husbandry] have been a long time neglected, a great quantity of good land remains still uncultivated, and the country is but very indifferently peopled. Pierre Charlevoix. *Journal of a Voyage to North-America*. London, 1761.

Abbé Raynal described the conditions he observed in Lower Canada in 1779:

The truly fertile fields began only near the capital, and they grew better as one drew nearer to Montreal. Nothing can be more beautiful to the eye than the rich borders of that long and broad canal [St. Lawrence River]. Woods scattered here and there which decorated the tops of the grassy mountains, meadows covered with flocks, fields crowned with ripening corn, small streams of water flowing down to the river, churches and castles seen at intervals through the trees, exhibited a succession of the most enchanting prospects. These would have been still more delightful, if the edict of 1745 had been observed, which forbade the colonist from dividing his plantations, unless they were an acre and a half in front, and thirty or forty acres in depth. Indolent heirs would not then have torn in pieces the inheritance of their fathers. They would have been compelled to form new plantations; and vast spaces of fallow land would no longer have separated rich and cultivated plains.

Nature herself directed the labours of the husbandman, and taught him to avoid watery and sandy grounds, and all those where the pine, the fir-tree, and the cedar grew solitary; but wherever he found a soil covered with maple, oak, beech, horn-beam, and small cherry trees, there he might reasonably expect an increase of twenty to one in his wheat, and thirty to one in Indian corn, without the trouble of manuring. All the plantations, though of different extents, were sufficient for the wants of their respective owners. . . . Most of the inhabitants had a score of sheep where wool was very valuable to them, ten or a dozen milch-cows, and five or six oxen for the plough. The cattle was small, but their flesh was excellent, and these people lived much better than our country people do in Europe.

With this kind of affluence, they could afford to keep a good number of horses. They were not fine, indeed; but able to go through a great deal of hard work, and to run a prodigious way upon the snow.

Such was the situation of the 83,000 French dispersed or collected on the banks of the River St. Lawrence. *Philosophical and Political History of the British Settlements and Trade in North America*, from the French of Abbé Raynal, Edinburgh, 1779.

The first farm pamphlet published in Canada of which any known copies survive, is a bilingual publication — English and French on facing pages — titled *Papers and Letters on Agriculture, Recommended to the attention of the Canadian Farmers, by The Agricultural Society in Canada* (Quebec, 1790). It served mainly to promote the Society for the Improvement of Agriculture in Canada, formed in 1789 under the auspices of the governor, Lord Dorchester. The introduction says:

> The present publication, from the infancy of the Society, will rather serve to shew the zeal of the Members than add to the stock of agricultural knowledge in the Province: But as it is the intention of the Society to publish annually such communications as shall be thought worthy of notice, it is humbly presumed that its future publications will prove more important, and of course more likely to promote the laudable views of the Right Honorable Patron [Dorchester], and the benevolent designs of the Society at large.
>
> As the importance of Agriculture to every community must at all times have forcibly struck mankind, it will at present be unnecessary to enlarge on the advantages that may be derived from a Judicious cultivation of the Earth. It will perhaps be sufficient to express our regret that either the want of knowledge to improve the Ancient practice, or the want of courage to attempt innovations, have hitherto retarded the improvement which the science of Agriculture is capable of receiving.

The chief article dealt with the cultivation of hemp, used in the manufacture of rope, especially for the British navy.

Isaac Weld noted some characteristic Lower Canadian practices in driving and caring for horses:

> The calash, or marche-donc, is a carriage very generally used in Lower Canada; there is scarcely a farmer indeed in the country who does not possess one; it is a sort of a one horse chaise, capable of holding two people besides the driver, who sits on a kind of box placed over the foot board, expressly for his accommodation. The body of the calash is hung upon broad straps of leather, round iron rollers that are placed behind, by means of which they are shortened and lengthened. On each side of the carriage is a little door about two feet high, whereby you enter it, and which is useful when shut, in preventing anything from slipping out. The harness is extremely heavy, studded with brass nails and to particular parts of it are attached small bells, of no use that I could ever discover but to annoy the passenger. . . .
>
> It is surprising to see how well the Canadian horses support the cold; after standing for hours together in the open air at a time

when spirits will freeze, they set off as alertly as if it were summer. The French Canadians make no scruple to leave their horses standing at the door of a house, without any covering, in the coldest weather, while they are themselves taking their pleasure. None of the other domestic animals are as indifferent to the cold as the horses. During winter all the domestic animals, not excepting the poultry, are lodged together in one large stable, that they may keep each other warm; but in order to avoid the expense of feeding many through the winter, as soon as the frost sets in they generally kill cattle and poultry sufficient to last them till the return of spring. The carcasses are buried in the ground, and covered with a heap of snow, and as they are wanted they are dug up; vegetables are laid up in the same manner, and they continue very good throughout the whole winter. The markets in the towns are always supplied best at this season, and provisions are then also the cheapest; for the farmers having nothing else to engage them, and having a quantity of meat on hand, flock to their towns in their carioles in great numbers. Isaac Weld. *Travels through the States of North America and the Provinces of Upper and Lower Canada during the Years 1795, 1796 and 1797.* London, 1799.

Farmers could have their ice in summer too, as J. C. Ogden observed:

A luxury is enjoyed very generally in ice, during the summer, which is easily preserved in houses of a very simple construction. These are small cellars, about twelve feet square, formed in gardens, or on the north side of their houses. They are secured by hewn timber instead of stone, and covered with plank or slabs, which are supported by a pole which rests on two standards. Upon these planks earth is cast, and the whole covered with green sods. Small bushes, such as the rose and goose-berry, are set in this layer of earth, and trees are planted around the whole to increase the shade. The ice is taken in winter from the lakes and rivers, and cast into these houses, where it is broken into as small pieces as possible, and water poured in, which is congealed by the frost, and forms a solid mass. J.C. Ogden: *A Tour through Upper and Lower Canada.* Litchfield, 1799.

George Heriot wrote of the Gaspé in *Travels Through the Canadas* (London, 1807):

Agriculture is uncommonly neglected, and in an entire state of infancy. It has of late years been somewhat more attended to than formerly, because the want of salt, an article ever scarce in those parts in time of war, and other causes, gave to the fisheries a temporary check, and obliged the inhabitants to secure the means of subsisting their families by tillage and husbandry. But, it is probable they will, as

Rev. Jacques Frédéric Doudiet, *The Little Child's Tomb*, 1845.

Rev. Jacques Frédéric Doudiet, *In the Countryside*, 1844.

E.J. Massicotte, *Boiling Maple Sap*.

they have ever done, resume the hook and line as soon as they have a prospect of encouragement in that their favourite pursuit. . . .

Many of the women are handsome when young, but as they partake of the labours of the field, and expose themselves upon all occasions to the influence of the weather, they soon become of sallow hue, and of masculine form. George Heriot. *Travels Through the Canadas.* London, 1807.

As surveyor-general, Joseph Bouchette was widely travelled in the Canadas. Here is his description of sugar-making:

In the spring, when the sap begins to rise in the [maple] trees, the habitants repair to the woods, furnished with kettles, troughs, and all the necessary apparatus for carrying on the manufacture, where they form a temporary encampment; the mode of collecting the sap is by making an incision in the tree, into which is inserted a thin bit of stick to serve as a conductor, from whence, an hour or two after sunrise, the sap begins to trickle down into a trough placed to receive it; when a sufficient quantity of this liquor is obtained from several trees, it is put into an iron kettle and boiled, until it comes to the consistence of a thick syrup; it is then cooled, and afterwards subjected to another process of boiling and clarifying. When this is sufficiently performed in proportion to the degree of purity they intend to give it, it is put into vessels of different sizes to harden, containing from half a pound to eight or ten pounds. Its colour is of all shades between a dark and a light brown, according to the care that is taken in clarifying it; indeed, by a repetition of the process it may be rendered as white as common refined sugar. Being considered very wholesome, the use of it is general among the country people for all purposes, and the consumption of it is considerable in families of respectability for ordinary occasions; the price of it varies from three pence halfpenny to six-pence per pound. It is constantly to be had in the market of Quebec. Joseph Bouchette. *A Topographical Description of the Province of Lower Canada with Remarks upon Upper Canada.* London, 1815.

John Lambert gave the following sketch of the habitants:

Parts of the market-place [in Quebec City] are occupied from five o'clock in the morning till twelve, by the Habitans (country people), who bring the production of their farms to market in carts during the summer, and in sleighs in the winter. They generally bring their wives and daughters with them, who often remain exposed all the morning to the piercing cold of winter, or the burning sun of summer, disposing of their provisions, while their husbands or fathers are getting drunk in the spirit-shops and taverns. . . .

The Canadians at the commencement of winter kill the greatest part of their stock, which they carry to market in a frozen state. The inhabitants of the towns then supply themselves with a sufficient quantity of poultry and vegetables till spring, and keep them in garrets or cellars. As long as they remain frozen, they preserve their goodness, but they will not keep long after they have thawed. I have eaten turkeys in April which have been kept in this manner all the winter, and found them remarkably good. Before the frozen provisions are dressed, they are always laid for some hours in cold water, which extracts the ice; otherwise, by a sudden immersion in hot water, they would be spoiled. . . .

The Habitans are as poor gardeners as they are farmers. . . . The high lands with good management would yield very tolerable crops, but the Canadians are miserable farmers. They seldom or never manure their land, and plough so very slight and careless that they continue, year after year, to turn over the same clods which lie at the surface, without penetrating an inch deeper into the soil. Hence their grounds become exhausted, over-run with weeds, and yield but very scanty crops. The fields of wheat which I have seen in different parts of the country were often much choked with weeds, and appeared to be stinted in their growth. When cut down, the straw was seldom more than 18 or 20 inches long, the ears small, the wheat itself discoloured, and little more than two-thirds of the size of our English wheat. . . . The French Canadians sow only summer wheat, though I should think that winter wheat might be sown in autumn with success. Peas, oats, rye, and barley are sown more or less by every farmer. . . . The Canadians sow small quantities of maize, or Indian corn; they, however, do not make such general use of it as the people of the United States who feed their cattle upon it, and make hominy and bread of it for themselves. The Canadians cultivate it more as an article of luxury than of necessity. They are extravagantly fond of the corn cobs boiled or roasted, and rubbed over with a little butter and salt. . . . Culinary vegetables are raised in tolerable plenty. The favourite roots are onions, garlic, and leeks; of these they eat largely, and consequently smell abominably. The disagreeable effects of these strong esculents are, however, somewhat checked by the fumes of the tobacco plant, which they are smoking from morning to night.

The French Canadians are not possessed of any agricultural enterprise or spirit. They are a perfect contrast to the inhabitants of the United States, who wander from forest to forest, extending cultivation to the remotest regions; while the Canadians have settled for upwards of two centuries upon the banks of the St.

Lawrence without attempting to remove from the spot, or explore the recesses of the forest which surrounds them. This close association of the first settlers was no doubt occasioned by a variety of circumstances. Exposed at an early period to repeated attacks from the Indians, their safety depended on numbers which a scattered settlement could not furnish in proper time. Their religion exacted from them numerous ceremonials which required a strict and frequent observance. No situation could therefore be so well adapted for settlement as the shores of a large and noble river which, besides the richness of the soil and inviting prospects, afforded them a ready communication with each other, and, what was of equal importance, the means of observing certain religious formalities, and providing subsistence at a time when their lands were yet uncultivated. . . .

The view which this extensive chain of farms exhibits along the lofty shores of the St. Lawrence, for more than 400 miles, is beautifully picturesque, and carries with it the appearance of one immense town: corn-fields, pasture and meadowlands, embellished at intervals with clumps of trees, snow-white cottages, and neatly adorned churches alternately present themselves to the eye. . . . The interior of the country, from the settlements on the north shore of the River St. Lawrence to the confines of Hudson's Bay, is entirely uncultivated, and uninhabited except by the fur traders and some few Indian tribes and Esquimaux. No roads, no villages, nor towns enliven that dreary and immense waste. The woodsman's axe is never heard. . . .

The furniture of the Habitans is plain and simple, and most commonly of their own workmanship. A few wooden chairs with twig or rush bottoms, and two or three deal tables, are placed in each room, and are seldom very ornamental; they however suffice, with a proper number of wooden bowls, trenchers and spoons for the use of the family at meals. A press, and two or three large chests, contain their wearing apparel and other property. A buffet in one corner contains their small display of cups, saucers, glasses, and teapots, while a few broken sets may grace the mantlepiece. A large clock is often found in their best apartment, and the sides of the room are ornamented with little pictures of the holy virgin and her Son, or waxen images of saints and crucifixes. An iron stove is generally placed in the largest apartment, with a pipe passing through the others into the chimney. The kitchen displays very little more than kettles of soup, tureens of milk, a table, a dresser, and a few chairs. The fireplace is wide, and large logs of wood are placed on old-fashioned iron dogs. A wooden crane supports the large kettle of soup, which is for ever over the fire. Their chief article of food is pork, as fat as they can procure it. They all keep a great number of swine, which they fatten to their liking. Pea-soup, with a small quantity of pork boiled in it, constitutes their breakfast, dinner and supper, day after day, with very little alteration, except what is occasioned by a few sausages, and puddings made of the entrails when a hog is killed. . . .

The Canadian country people bake their own bread, which is made of wheat-flour and rye-meal; but for the want of yeast it has a sour taste, and is coarse and heavy. The ovens are built of wicker-work, plastered inside and out with a thick coating of clay or mortar. Some are built of bricks or stones. They are situated at a short distance from the house to prevent accidents from fire. John Lambert. *Travels through Canada and the United States of North America in the Years 1806, 1807 and 1808. London, 1816.*

Joseph Sansom was harsher:

Most of those who cultivate the soil can neither read nor write, of course they know nothing of the advantages of composts, or the rotation of crops, by which the means of life are so cheaply multiplied by intelligent agriculturists. And before Quebec was taken by the English, all the manure produced in its stables was regularly thrown into the river. Joseph Sansom. *Sketches of Lower Canada.* New York, 1817.

Charles Frederick Grece's *Essays on Practical Husbandry addressed to the Canadian Farmers* (Montreal, 1817) is almost certainly the first Canadian book on agriculture by a named author, as opposed to the collection of papers on the subject printed in book form in Halifax in 1791. It was followed two years later by a London imprint, *Facts and Observations respecting Canada and the United States of America: Affording a Comparative View of the Inducements of Emigration presented in those Countries*; this latter book included much from *Essays* quoted here.

Grece came to Canada about 1803 and settled on the island of Montreal. After 1807, he engaged in experimental agriculture. Between June 1816 and October 1817, he wrote a monthly report on the "state of the crops in the district of Montreal" for *The Montreal Herald*. These reports are included in the 143-page *Essays* published by William Gray, Montreal.

Grece said in his preface that the voluminous European writings on agriculture were adapted to climates very different to that of Lower Canada, "where the season for labour in the field is so short, and the pursuits of the Husbandman so limited, that it is impossible to assimilate the one with the other." Thus the requirement for advice on agriculture adapted to Canadian needs.

The errors they [Canadian farmers] commit arise from the first settlers of the colony, following the Norman practice of the last century: that is, dividing their farms into two equal parts, ploughing one half annually and feeding their animals on the wild growth of the former year's cropped land. . . .

The general opinion amongst the Farmers that their lands are worn out has created an apathy, and no one has courage enough to step out of his old path, but acts like those who, bewildered in the forest, give themselves up for lost. Let them examine the cause of the sterility of their land; it is no other than having been too avaricious — too frequently cropping with grain. They have not considered that the earth requires rest and nourishment, otherwise it soon becomes exhausted. The soil being thus reduced, demands a different management, to bring it back to its primitive strength. Land that has due nourishment and repose cannot be worn out, as is supposed, but will produce to the end of time. . . .

The quality of the soil may be judged by the growth of trees; where they are large, it is a sign of good land; where there is plenty of beech, maple and butter nut, that land is good. Where elm, white ash, white and red oak grow, the soil is generally strong. Where pine, hemlock, birch, and spruce grow, the soil is sandy, the worst that there is. Cedar swamps, though often composed of good soil, are not desirable to take, unless easy to drain. Ash and soft maple swamps are mostly on a clay or marl; if easy to drain, they are good for meadows. White birch and poplar denote very poor light loam, or white clay.

The spot being chosen, which ought to be near a constant supply of good water, trees are cut to build a log house; if a saw mill is not near, to get boards to cover it, the bark of ash becomes a substitute for them. It is best not to lay out money at first to build a fine house, because when the land is cleared, if often happens, more advantageous spots are discovered to build on. A good large cellar must be made under the house for the vegetables. Log stables and a barn ought to be erected, and care taken to make them shade the cattle from the north and north-west winds — they are the coldest in this country. . . .

The cows that feed in the woods give very poor milk: hence arises the bad flavour of the greater part of the American butter and cheese. The leading cow will require a good toned bell, buckled to her neck, because cows are often too idle to return home; by which means they are easier found: salt should be given them every week, to entice them to the house. But with this care, they sometimes absent themselves, and if not looked after, they soon become dry, which is a serious loss.

Grece said most tools were available in Lower Canada but advised settlers to bring with them a hand saw, a six-foot cross-cut saw, a hammer, adze, howel (hollow adze), augers, socket chisels, small gimblets and a thirty-pound iron crowbar to help dig up stumps. He had sound words about not getting lost:

It will sometimes happen that people lose themselves in the woods. This is found by returning several times to the same spot.

Cloudy weather operates to deceive, but the sun will always direct by observing its rising and setting from the dwelling place, which Europeans ought strictly to attend to on their first beginning in the forest.

Swamps are the most difficult, from the thickness of the green timber: in such a case, let the person avoid flurrying himself, because fear is the first thing that agitates the mind, and leads to frenzy. If fatigued, sit down, and examine the trees; the north side of large trees is covered with moss; the branches are longest on the south and south-east sides: these will form a compass.

Should you fall on a river or brook, its course will lead to some settlement. The brooks, many of which are little rivers in the spring at the melting of the snow, become dry in summer; but their course may be discovered by observing the way that the wild growth of herbs, grass, and roots of trees lay: their heads will point to the out-let of such water; the stones will be cleaner on the side next the source, than that next the out-let.

Sometimes cattle are met with miles from home; by starting them, they run from a stranger, and generally go home: that will lead the lost person to a settlement. There being little to fear from wild beasts, food is a primary object. As berries are not always to be had any more than nuts, herbs become a consideration. The coltsfoot, called by the Americans snake root, has a leaf formed like the foot of a colt; it is of a deep green colour; the roots run horizontally and are of the thickness of a tobacco pipe; they taste like lemon peel.

Grece was keen on wild growth as substitute fodder. From his monthly report to *The Montreal Herald* for July 1816:

When a review is taken of the present state of Crops in general, and the probability that a deficiency will arise in the article of Fodder during the ensuing winter, it may not be improper to point out to the industrious farmer substitutes for the usual food given to horses, horned cattle, and sheep during that season, and which might be collected from the wild growth on almost every farm, viz., Mugwort, called by the Canadian peasantry Herb St. Jean, Thistles, Wild Tares, and Hop Clover, to be given to horses. For horned cattle and sheep, the Cotonier, or Milk Weed, Panet or Wild Parsnips, Wild

Endive, or Chiccoree, the young growth of Raspberries, the Fern and the Wood or Bouquet Jaune.

The Rev. Charles Stewart noticed a better crop than fodder:

In some of the Townships large quantities of potatoes are raised, from which a pretty good whisky is distilled. Rev. Charles Stewart. A *Short View of the Present State of the Eastern Townships in the Province of Lower Canada.* London, 1817.

Francis Hall wrote of arriving in Canada from the United States in March, near St. Johns in Lower Canada:

Nothing could be more Siberian than the aspect of the Canadian frontier: a narrow road, choked with snow, led through a wood, in which patches were occasionally cleared, on either side, to admit the construction of a few log huts, round which a brood of ragged children, a starved pig, and a few half-broken rustic implements, formed an accompaniment more suited to an Irish landscape than to the thriving scenes we had just quitted. Francis Hall. *Travels in Canada and the United States in 1816 and 1817.* 2d ed. London, 1819.

The rations often left something to be desired, as John Talbot complained:

The beef of Canada is in general poor and tough. The Canadians have not a proper method of fattening their cattle, which are for the most part lean and ill fed. . . . Butter is generally of a cheesy or sour flavor, owing to the cream being kept so long before it is churned. . . . Maple sugar is very hard and requires to be scraped with a knife when used for tea, otherwise the lumps would be a considerable time dissolving. John Talbot. *History of North America.* 2 vols. Leeds, 1820.

Benjamin Silliman was more favorably impressed:

Almost every moment we met the cheerful looking peasants, driving their little carts (charrettes) drawn by horses of a diminutive size. The men were generally standing up in the body of the cart, with their lighted pipes in their mouths, and wore red or blue sashes and long conical woollen caps of various colours. These carts were furnished with high rails, and occasionally with seats, occupied by females and children; they appeared, (like our one-horse waggons), to furnish the most common accommodation for transporting both commodities and persons. . . .

The barns, frequently of a large size, were usually built in the same manner [hewn logs]; but the want of good frame work was very obvious in their frequently distorted appearance. . . .

We found a man and boy ploughing. The oxen were yoked, not as with us [Americans], by the shoulders and neck, but *by the horns*. A kind of yoke lay upon their necks, and was fastened, by leather straps, to the horns; but no bow, or other contrivance, passed around the neck; thus the oxen draw entirely by their horns; and I am told that the French farmers cannot be induced to adopt our method, although it is obvious that the animal is thus sadly embarrassed, and can exert very little power. I saw, however, one yoke in another field, harnessed in our way. . . .

The agricultural productions of the country are very fine. . . . The only article which we have found generally bad has been bread. The best which we have seen has been only tolerable, and most of it has been so sour, dark coloured, and bitter, that it took some time to reconcile us to it in any degree. . . . The sour bread also appears to have its share in producing a derangement of the stomach. Benjamin Silliman. *Remarks Made on a Short Tour between Hartford and Quebec in the Autumn of 1819.* New Haven, 1820.

Andrew Oliver, on the other hand, had only praise for the abundantly stocked markets:

Let us now view the [Montreal] markets, which are said to excel any in America. These hold on Monday and Friday, but the latter is the principal day. The two squares in which they hold are called the upper and lower market place. In the first of these are sold fire-wood, hay, etc. The wood which meets the readiest purchaser is maple, ash, elm, and oak, with several other kinds of hard wood; no person will purchase fir for fuel. The body or trunk of the tree is cut into lengths of two feet, and split. For a cart-load they commonly ask 5s, but the price depends much upon the present demand. . . .

Before you can reach the centre of the lower market, by St. Paul street, you must press through between two long ranges of carts, loaded with the production of the country. Wheat, flour, Indian corn, potatoes, pork, mutton, live sheep, geese, turkies, ducks, chickens, etc., with a nameless variety of articles of country manufacture, amongst these rush-bottomed chairs, for which they charge 5s for half-a-dozen, and plaster laths, of which I saw a cart-load sold at 2s 6d per thousand.

Approaching the square, the next scene is the vegetable market. Here are cabbages, melons, cucumbers, fruits in their seasons, apples, pears, currants, cherries, etc. Around the square the butchers retail their meat in open sheds. . . .

On the east, toward the river, is the fish market, but salmon and trout are rarely to be met with. Amongst the various other kinds of fish which come here in plenty, the shad claims the preference. It resembles the salmon, and in June and July, which are the only months it is to be caught, is remarkably cheap. A fish weighing six, seven, or eight pounds may be bought for 3d; it is excellent eating, and many barrels of them are put up for winter. They are caught in nets in the river, and are brought in by the country people in carts, covered with green branches. . . .

The leather merchants and shoemakers from the country stand by the wharf. The shoes are mostly of the light kind, and are sold about 4s a pair. Mogozeens, which are only worn by Canadians, are cheap. Besides these, the Indians furnish a superior kind, beautifully indented with porcupine quills. They also bring to market a variety of birch vessels, of curious workmanship. . . .

In winter, milk is brought to market in small ice cakes, packed in baskets or boxes; in purchasing 2d worth, you are complimented with a little straw to keep it from slipping through your fingers. . . .

The taverns contiguous to the market are generally crowded; the chief drink is grog. Rum is sold in the shops at 15d, and wine, called black strap, at 10d per bottle. Brandy and gin are dearer, ale 6d, cider 3d, and spruce beer 1 1/2d per bottle.

Canadian sugar, which is drawn from maple trees, is brought to the market in cakes, and sold at 5d and 6d the pound. Tobacco sold in the leaf, but twisted like ropes of straw, and coiled up, may be purchased very low. I saw a coil, weighing eight pounds, for 6s; but that which is manufactured in Britain is preferable. Andrew Oliver. A *View of Lower Canada, interspersed with Canadian Tales and Anecdotes, and Interesting Information to Intending Emigrants*. Edinburgh, 1821.

Philemon Wright, the American founder of Hull, wrote the account for the House of Assembly committee studying settlement of crown lands. It was published by the Assembly and appeared subsequently in various publications containing advice for settlers. In mid-February 1800, Wright led five families in seven sleighs, with fourteen horses and eight oxen, from Montreal to Hull, the last eighty miles without road or track. He and his men were laboriously hacking a road through the bush when an Indian volunteered — "without the promise of fee or reward" — to guide the party over the river ice.

With his small axe, trying the ice at every step he went, as if he had been the proper guide or owner of the property. We passed on until we found night coming on, and the banks of the river being so high, say about twenty feet, and that it was impossible to ascend them with our sleighs, we then left our sleighs upon the ice, and ascended the banks of the river, cleared away the snow, cut down large trees as usual to make a fire, carefully observing that no stooping or dead trees could fall upon us. After cooking our supper and getting our regular refreshments, we then brought up our bedding and spread round the fire, and made ourselves as comfortable as possible, having nothing over us but large trees and the canopy of the heavens. Before daylight in the morning, we cooked our breakfast and provisions for the day, and, as soon as daylight appeared, we were ready to proceed on our march. I must observe that our Indian behaved with uncommon civility during the night, taking his regular refreshments with us, and proceeded to the head of the company, as he had done the preceding day, with uncommon agility. Philemon Wright. *An Account of the First Settlement of the Township of Hull, on the Ottawa River, Lower Canada.* Quebec, 1821.

Adam Hodgson outlines the shock experienced by uninformed settlers arriving in Canada:

There is not one emigrant in five hundred who does not feel bitterly disappointed on his arrival at Quebec. Instead of finding himself, as his confused ideas of geography had led him to expect, on the very borders of his little estate, he learns with astonishment that he is still five hundred miles from his transatlantic acres; and, if he has no money in his pocket, he may probably have to encounter, in reaching them, more severe distress than he ever felt at home. . . .

I can hardly conceive any thing more distressing than his sensations when, arriving on his new estate, with an axe in his hand and all his worldly goods in his wallet, he finds himself in the midst of a thick forest whose lofty trees are to be displaced by a labour almost Herculean, before he can erect the most humble shelter, or cultivate the smallest patch. And if at such time he has further to anticipate the rigours of a long Canadian winter, his situation must be deplorable in the extreme. Adam Hodgson. *Remarks during a Journey Through North America in the Years 1819, 1820, and 1821 in a Series of Letters.* New York, 1823.

P. Finan visited Lower Canada to look over a piece of land he had bought sight unseen on the south shore of the St. Lawrence:

In the afternoon we walked down to Mr. L — 's farm, which is situated in a back concession. I took a gun with me; and on our way I saw a fine looking bird on a branch, at a good distance from me; but, being remarkably near sighted, I could not discern of what kind it was. I fired, and it fell, and when I reached it, it proved to be a robin. The discovery afforded me regret; though robins, in this county, are very good eating, and it is quite common to shoot them for that purpose.

Every farmer has a good, comfortable house, commodious offices [barns] capable of containing all his crop . . . a sufficient stock of

cattle of every description, a handsome light cart or calash for the accommodation of his family during the summer, and a cariole for winter. . . . They have no heavy burden of rent to groan under, no harsh and cruel tyrant of an agent or land lord to seize their crop or stock or drive them from the humble, but cherished, cottage of their ancestors, no bailiff or constable to torment them for [taxes], no unwelcome visitor from the excise office to exact money from them.
P. Finan. *Journal of a Voyage to Quebec in the Year 1825*. Newry, England, 1828.

Godfrey T. Vigne wrote approvingly of the habitants:

The Canadian peasantry may be said to be smoke-dried, being seldom without a pipe in their mouths, and in winter they shut themselves up in their cottages, and breathe an atmosphere of tobacco fumes. . . . Nevertheless the French Canadians are a brave, hardy, independent race, and happier, I should imagine, than any peasantry in the world. They pay no taxes, or just sufficient to keep the roads in repair. . . . In general, the Canadian farmers when old and unable to work make over their property by a notarial writing to one of their sons, on condition of his paying a certain sum of money to his other children; a custom which has the effect of preventing too great a division of real property. In the deed, which is rather curious, it is stipulated that the old man is to be supported by his son; that he is to receive from him a certain quantity of tea, sugar, and tobacco; he is to be furnished if necessary with a horse to ride to chapel on Sundays and festivals; and when dead a certain number of masses are to be said for his soul.
Godfrey T. Vigne. *Six Months in America*. 2 vols. London, 1832

The houses of the habitants were sometimes of stone but generally of wood, always one storey:

The walls outside are whitewashed, which imparts to them, particularly in summer, when almost every thing else is green, a most lively and clean-looking appearance. Each contains a large kitchen, one good sittingroom, and as many sleeping or bedrooms as may be judged requisite. The garret is generally used for lumber, and seldom for bed-places. Some of the houses have verandas, and an orchard and garden is often attached; near the house there is always a clay-built bake-oven, and a well; from the latter the water is drawn by means of a lever. . . . The sittingroom or parlour, and bedrooms, are lined with smoothly planed boards, and painted with blue, red, green, yellow, etc., and, according to our ideas, in very bad taste, but according to Jean Baptiste's fancy, very fine and *bien joli*; and why not, if he be happy in the idea? Wax and brass images of the virgin and child, or of the crucifixion, and pictures of grim saints, the madonna and child, etc., all of the cheapest and most common kind, are hung round the room; and one middle-sized and several common looking-glasses, and a common clock, are seldom wanting. Sometimes we observe a looking-glass and picture which, from their curious wrought frames, must be from one to two hundred years old. There is also one or more cupboards, or *boufettes*, in the room, which exhibit common glasses, decanters, cups and saucers, etc., and generally a large punch-bowl, for the purpose usually of making egg-nog, or milk punch. The geese raised on their farms afford sufficient feathers for beds. Their sheets and blankets are rather coarse, but manufactured by themselves of the fleeces of their sheep, and of the flax they cultivate.

The barns and cattle-houses are plain oblong buildings. The farms run parallel with each other; pole fences occasionally separate them, and from ten to fifty arpents of each are cleared and cultivated. The post-road runs across them all, and each habitant keeps his own portion in repair. . . .

There is not probably in the world a more contented or happy people than the habitants or peasantry of Lower Canada. They are with few exceptions in easy circumstances; and they are fondly attached to the seignorial mode of holding their farms. In all the settlements, the church forms the point around which the inhabitants born in the parish like to dwell; and farther from it than they can hear the ringing of its bell, none of them can be reconciled to settle. They are not anxious to become rich, but they possess the necessary comforts, and many of the luxuries of life. . . .

Their mode of agriculture is clumsy and tardy; yet the soil, with the most negligent culture, yields abundance for domestic consumption, and something over the tythes to sell for the purchase of articles of convenience and luxury. . . .

We discover among the Canadians the customs and manners that prevailed among the peasantry of France during the age of Louis the Fourteenth; and to this day the most rigid adherence to national customs is maintained among them. Contented to tread in the path beaten by their forefathers, they in the same manner till the ground; commit in the like way the same kind of seeds to the earth; and in a similar mode do they gather their harvests, feed their cattle, and prepare and cook their victuals. . . . They are fond of soups, which are seldom, even in Lent, of meagre quality. Bread, butter, cheese, with eggs, tea, poultry, fish, and flesh, constitute nearly all the other articles of their food. They have their *jours gras*, or feasting days, before and after Lent, on which they gourmandize vast quantities of pork and beef, and indulge in drinking; but on other occasions they are temperate. John McGregor. *British America.* 2 vols. Edinburgh and London, 1832.

The *Quebec Gazette* offered useful tips:

> Orchard trees may be defended against insects by sprinkling them frequently with soap-suds, salt and water, lime-water, or water impregnated with sulphur, and by dusting them with hot lime. . . .
>
> Steeping the seed of wheat in a solution of arsenic is certain to give clean crops from smutty seed. . . .
>
> Pigs make the best manure on the farm. Young pigs require warm meat to make them grow. . . .
>
> Horses fed on turnips will eat barn chaff and other dry food, have a good appetite, and will work without oats. . . .
>
> Pumpkins form a fattening food for horses. With a little salt at first on them, they will soon eat them without, and get very fond of them. Quebec Gazette. *The Lower Canada Farmers' and Mechanics' Almanack for the Year 1834.* Quebec, 1834.

Henry Tudor described Lower Canada as a little utopia filled with virtuous inhabitants.

> Uncorrupted as the French-Canadians are by the vices of a highly artificial state of society, as that which exists in Europe; blessed with a happy competency that supplies their few and unexaggerated wants, and removed by their comparative seclusion from the seductive and fatal influence of fashion and extravagance, they live in a state of pastoral and partriarchal purity of manners, sedulously attending to all the ordinances of their religion, that strongly engage in their favour the feelings and regard of all those who come in contact with them. Henry Tudor. *Narrative of a Tour in North America.* 2 vols. London, 1834.

William Evans, a practical farmer and secretary of the Montreal Agricultural Society, and later the Lower Canada Society, was probably the most prolific writer on farming in the nineteenth century. He could be pontifical and repetitious at times, but he assembled a mass of useful information in his books and periodicals. He constantly urged scientific farming and its dissemination through model (experimental) farms.

He writes in his introduction to *A Treatise on Agriculture*:

> It is agriculture, and agriculture alone, that can support the inhabitants of such a country as this in plenty and real dignity. If our lands are covered with corn and cattle — corn and cattle will always purchase what manufactures and delicacies we may require from other countries. William Evans. A *Treatise on the Theory and Practice of Agriculture, adapted to the cultivation and economy of the animal and vegetable productions of agriculture in Canada.* Montreal, 1835.

And in his book on agricultural education, he says:

> Agriculture must be the main source of the wealth and prosperity of Canada, and if it is not maintained in a healthy and prosperous state, every other profession, trade, and business must inevitably languish. *Agricultural Improvement by the Education of those who are engaged in it as a profession; addressed very respectfully to the Farmers of Canada*. Montreal, 1837.

What follow are random samplings of his other works (see Bibliography):

> The winters are as much in favour of the farmer as otherwise. . . .
> The severe frost and snow fertilizes to a great degree the ploughed soil, and prepares it in the best manner to receive the seed in spring. Without a rigorous winter in the North American provinces, farmers at a great distance could not bring their produce to market: a thin population scattered over a wide extent of country would, for many years to come, be unable to incur the expense of making roads sufficiently good to travel on in winter. Snow and ice give roads and bridges, without any cost, the greatest perfection, almost equal to railroads. . . .
>
> Mowers should begin their work as early as there is light in order that they may take rest in the middle of the day, when the heat is very great, and work again until a late hour in the evening. All the grass mown before twelve o'clock at noon may be tedded on the same day, strewing it evenly over all the ground. This should be done before dinner. By this regular method of tedding grass for hay, the hay will be of a more valuable quality. When the grass is suffered to lie in the swath, the upper surface is dried by the sun and winds, and the interior part is not dried, but withered, and is of different colour. In fine weather, in this climate, the hay tedded in the forenoon should, in the afternoon, be carefully turned, and about three or five o'clock gathered and raked into rows, and put up into well made grass cocks.

In the first issue of his *Canadian Quarterly Agricultural & Industrial Magazine* in 1838, Evans was writing at a time of rebellion in Lower Canada:

> The whole population of the Canadas are now perfectly peaceable, and certainly have no temptation to be otherwise. Agriculture cannot be neglected with us, without incurring the risk of a famine next year. In the spring we shall have a sufficient military force here that will relieve farmers from the necessity of being constantly armed, and enable them to give due attention to the business of husbandry, so necessary for our very existence, and that of the whole community.
>
> The number of persons usually employed in agriculture are not sufficient for the judicious management of the soil already in

cultivation; consequently it must be extremely injurious to withdraw any of them from that employment in the seasons of spring, summer, and harvest, if it were possible to avoid it. If you can in the spring safely lay aside your arms for a season, you will not be less ready and willing to resume them again at a moment's warning, should enemies threaten you from any quarter. . . . We would be giving too much consequence to the enemies of the peace and prosperity of Canada, were we to be constantly occupied in preparation to resist their foolish and wicked designs. We can carefully observe their proceedings — be prepared against any surprise — and at the same time plough, sow, and plant, and with the blessing of Providence, gather in the harvest — and eat the fruits thereof — notwithstanding all that our enemies would or could do to prevent us.

Evans became secretary of the Lower Canada Agricultural Society when it was formed in 1847 and less than a year later was publishing the society's monthly journal in French and English — between 2,000 and 3,000 copies in French and about 1,000 in English.

We are still of opinion that wheat ought to be the staple produce of Canada for exportation — provided we can produce it in good quality, and in sufficient quantity per acre to be profitable. We shall not be able to raise any other produce to the same extent we could wheat, that will be so suitable for exportation and be always sure to find a market at a remunerating price, which we consider five shillings the bushel to be. We may grow peas and beans for exportation, but both these crops are often as uncertain as wheat, and will not pay the farmers so well.

Evans lost his temper with some farmers. The greatest barrier to agriculture advancement was

a rooted and grounded conviction in the breasts of certain farmers around us that because they know how to plough, harrow and sow, they have nothing to learn; they are perfect farmers; and acting upon this belief, they despise Agricultural Societies and every other mean or method of becoming wiser.

Evans did not often stray onto a subject like this:

Beer, in moderation, might be very properly supplied to agricultural labourers while at work constantly in the fields, often employed in the cultivation and management of those crops from which beer is manufactured, and one of those crops — hops — would be useless for any other purpose. We consider beer as a part of the subsistence that should be allowed to farm labourers, without producing any

injury to them — any more than the other portions of their food. . . .
The moderate use of beer is neither sinful nor "contrary to the best
interests of society." We have no desire to bind men with fetters that
our Creator has not imposed upon them, nor do we pretend to
restrict people from the moderate use of what our laws grant a
licence for manufacturing.

In a later issue, Evans said on the same subject:

It is said that the Temperance movement in Canada will prevent
much barley being sown this year. Although it might not be
manufactured into beer, it is an excellent grain to employ for feeding
beef and pork, and we would recommend farmers not to give up its
cultivation, as it is a suitable grain for our soil and climate.

From the *British American Cultivator* of April 1842 (of which Evans was editor):

The farmer ought to rise early, and see that others do so. In the
winter season, breakfast should be taken by candle light, for by this
means an hour is gained, which many farmers indolently lose,
though six hours so lost are nearly equal to the working part of a
winter day.

George Henry set out for prospective or new emigrants some hard facts on the
Canadian winter:

The extreme severity of the frost in Canada in the winter is almost
incredible, for it frequently freezes the nose and ears. . . . I have sat
by the fire-side when, while the sap has been oozing out of the ends
of the wood then burning on the fire, it has instantly frozen hard. In
taking tea, the cups, and saucers, tea-pot and all, frequently freeze to
the table. . . .
   In January the ice begins to be of a proper thickness to bear a load
with safety. The method adopted here, in order to ascertain if it be
of a proper thickness to bear a horse with sleigh and load, is to take a
good sharp axe and to strike it into the ice with all your might at
one single blow, and if you penetrate to the water, it is considered
not safe enough to travel on with a load, but if no water gushes out,
it might then be trusted. . . .
   It is a custom in the winter to make, or rather plant roads on the
ice; it is done when the ice first takes by collecting a quantity of
green brush, the branches of the fir and cedar trees, making holes in
the ice, and planting this brush in groves across the ice to any given
place; it thus serves for a road all the winter. At different places,
both on the St. Lawrence and on the Ottawa, you will see these
roads continuing for miles, and are of the greatest utility.

Henry advised prudence by farmers to keep out of debt to merchants or innkeepers:

It is too often the case with the young farmer to obtain goods upon the faith of his forth-coming crop. This is a system of thraldom that frequently keeps him in debt for years, for while he gets his supplies upon credit, there is not the same providential management over his out goings. But when a man takes no credit, but pays for his goods as he gets them, he will feel the necessity of keeping within due bounds, besides the consideration that at the end of seven years he will be a considerable gainer. For where he buys for the ready cash, he will purchase considerably cheaper. George Henry. *The Emigrant's Guide, or, Canada As It Is.* Quebec, n.d. [ca. 1835].

William F. Buchan also had advice about winter:

The continuance of *hard snow* on the ground for several weeks . . . becomes a matter of great moment. The greater part of the farmer's productions are, at this period, to be transported for sale; his supplies for summer or winter consumption, and his implements, are to be brought back; his timber-logs are to be removed (if by land) to the saw-mill, his firewood to be drawn home from the uncleared land, and lastly the socialities of the season require him to be moving about among his friends: for all these objects, a good, even, hard road is an indispensable requisite, not only as a matter of comfort, but as a means of saving an immensity of animal labour.

Buchan maintained that winter in Lower Canada was superior to Upper Canada's. In the former, the snow

freezes, and offers until the very end of winter a hard smooth surface, over which vehicles (sleighs) loaded heavily with produce, etc., are drawn with great facility . . . while in the Upper Province thaws are frequent, so that the good road, or sleighing ground of to-day, is a mass of mud and puddle in a day or two after. William F. Buchan. *Remarks on Emigration: More Particularly Applicable to the Eastern Townships, Lower Canada*, 2nd ed. Devonport and London, n.d. [ca. 1835].

It is difficult to say when the first Canadian farm journal was published, mainly because few, if any, copies of the earliest newspapers survive, and many publications lasted no more than a handful of issues.

The Farmers' Journal and Welland Canal Intelligencer was probably published at St. Catharines in 1826, and *The Farmers' Gazette* at Markham, Upper Canada, in 1826 or 1827. *The Farmers' Journal* amalgamated with another paper in 1834 but resumed under its original name in 1835, a good indication of the uncertainty of publishing at that time.

The Patriot and Farmers' Monitor was published at Kingston, U.C., in 1828, and moved to York in 1832. *The Plow and Anvil* was issued at St. Stephen, N.B., in 1835. *The Bytown Independent* and *Farmers' Advocate* appeared in Ottawa in 1836, *The Mechanic and Farmer* at Pictou, N.S., in 1837, and *The Western Herald and Farmers' Magazine* at Sandwich, U.C., in 1838, the same year that saw William Evans begin publication of *The Canadian Quarterly Agricultural & Industrial Magazine* at Montreal.

Some researchers have judged *Le Glaneur* the first farm publication, possibly because it lasted ten months and copies of the first issue have survived. However, it was mainly a literary magazine — only two pages of its first sixteen-page issue were devoted to agriculture. There was a discussion of cheese making, and another on the use of salt to keep down insects and spur the growth of vegetables. (Vol. I, No. 1, St. Charles, Que., 1836)

By issue number three, the farm section had expanded to three pages and contained a plea for a return to the good old days when every farmer made his own clothes, sugar, soap, candles and beer. City taverns were corrupting Lower Canada's youth, who were exhorted to stay home among religious and honest people.

The Earl of Durham's most-quoted finding was "two nations warring in the bosom of a single state." The struggle, he said, was not political but racial. And the greatest hostility was between the French habitants and the new English settlers.

Lord Durham said New France's system of seigneuries had inured the habitants "to the incessant labour of rude and unskilled agriculture." The British had provided none of the institutions that would have "elevated them in freedom and civilization."

By degrees, large portions of land were occupied by them [English settlers]; nor did they confine themselves to the unsettled and distant country of the townships. The wealthy capitalists invested money in the purchase of seignorial properties; and it is estimated that at the present moment full half of the more valuable seignories are actually owned by English proprietors. . . .

But an irritation greater than that occasioned by the transfer of the large properties was caused by the competition of the English with the French farmer. The English farmer carried with him the experience and habits of the most improved agriculture in the world. He settled himself in the townships bordering on the seignories, and brought a fresh soil and improved cultivation to compete with the worn-out and slovenly farm of the habitant. He often took the very farm which the Canadian settler had abandoned, and by superior management made that a source of profit which had only impoverished his predecessor. . . . The most profitable and flourishing farms are now in the hands of this numerical minority of the population. . . .

The French could not but feel the superiority of English enterprise; they could not shut their eyes to their success in every undertaking in which they came into contact, and to the constant superiority which they were acquiring. They looked upon their rivals with alarm, jealousy, and finally with hatred. The English repaid them with scorn, which soon also assumed the same form of hatred. . . .

The entire mistrust which the two races have thus learned to conceive of each other's intentions induces them to put the worst construction on the most innocent conduct; to judge every word, every act, and every intention unfairly; to attribute the most odious designs, and reject every overture of kindness or fairness, as covering secret designs of treachery and malignity. . . .

The difference of language produces misconceptions yet more fatal even than those which it occasions with respect to opinions; it aggravates the national animosities, by representing all the events of the day in utterly different lights. This political misrepresentation of facts is one of the incidents of a free press in every free country . . . they [Lower Canadians] thus live in a world of misconceptions, in which every party is set against the other not only by diversity of feelings and opinions, but by an actual belief in an utterly different set of facts. Earl of Durham. *Report on the Affairs of British North America.* Montreal, 1839.

Canadians today, especially farmers, might find it difficult to accept Durham's assertion that our French-English problems stem from the introduction by British settlers of a better system of agriculture in Quebec in the early nineteenth century.

The Rev. Joseph Abbott was a farmer as well as clergyman who arrived in Canada in 1818. His articles on farming first appeared in *The Quebec Mercury* and then in a book entitled *The Emigrant to North America*, published in Montreal in 1842. A second edition appeared in 1843 and a much larger third edition in 1844, published in London and Edinburgh. Much of the same material was produced in different form in the book quoted here. Abbott's eldest son, Sir John Abbott, was prime minister of Canada in 1891-92. When this book was published, Abbott was living at Grenville, Canada East.

In the summer of the second year of my residence we were visited by a long and very severe drought. Many of the springs and wells were dried up, and so were several rivulets which never had been known to fail before. In some settlements the inhabitants suffered much from want of water. In one, which was within a few miles of me, they had to drive their cattle several miles for this necessity of life, until they had deepened their wells or dug new ones. The depth to which the influence of the drought extended was very surprising. I had a well, forty-two feet deep, which was quite dry, and I had to sink it six feet lower before I recovered the water.

But these annoyances were mere trifles compared with a great calamity which befell our own settlement in consequence of it. Every thing was so dry, that people were careful not to set fire to the woods. One settler, however, who had a slash which he was very anxious to burn, imprudently set fire to it. But it was more easily lighted than extinguished; for, to the terror and dismay of the inhabitants, who all hurried to the spot the instant they saw the smoke rolling upwards in heavy black masses, it did not stop when its intended work was done, but literally ran along the ground, extending its ravages far and wide. At length it reached a farm-yard, when the barn and other outbuildings immediately caught fire and were consumed. They were all built of wood, and as dry as tinder. In spite of the united efforts of the whole settlement to stop it or turn it aside, the fire reached the dwelling-house hard by. Here it blazed up with renewed vigour. This house was hardly half consumed when the cry of fire was heard from the affrighted occupants of the next farm-house, which met with a similar fate; and then the next, and the next. In short, nothing could stay its fury. It destroyed every farm-stead, house, and fence on one side of the settlement; and then went off again into the woods, where its desolating path could be discerned, for several days, by the dark cloud of smoke by day, and by the bright streak in the heavens above it by night. Four dwelling-houses and five barns, with a number of inferior outbuildings, were totally consumed. And nothing was insured. . . .

It is my painful task to record another calamity which came upon our secluded community during this eventful summer. And although what I allude to was nothing more than the measles, yet, whether from bad nursing, or from improper treatment (we had no doctor within many miles of us), or that the disease had assumed a more virulent type than usual, it was indeed a calamity, and to my family and to many others a fatal one. We lost our youngest child, a lovely little boy nine months old. This was the first time the King of Terrors had ever crossed our threshold, and we felt our bereavement acutely. Rev. Joseph Abbott. *Philip Musgrave; or Memoirs of a Church of England Missionary in the North American Colonies.* London, 1846.

The Lower Canada Agricultural Society was incorporated by an act of the Provincial Parliament in July 1847, though individual county agricultural associations had existed for many years in both Lower and Upper Canada.

First object: To promote the interest of all classes dependent on agriculture by improving the state of cultivated land generally, by better draining, by more judicious cultivation and manuring of the soil for whatever crop, by encouraging the cultivation of such new plants as it may be considered advantageous to introduce, by encouraging the selection and improvement of suitable breeds of neat cattle, and sheep, and good pasturing for their keep, so that they may yield large and profitable returns to the farmer, in beef, mutton, wool and dairy produce, to encourage domestic manufactures, and useful inventions applicable to agriculture, and to the domestic purposes of the agriculturists. Lower Canada Agricultural Society. *Prospectus.* Montreal, 1847.

The society listed five other aims: establishment of an agricultural museum to display the latest farm machines, formation of agricultural libraries, establishment of an agricultural college, co-operation among county farm associations, and gathering correct statistics on agriculture.

The annual report of the society (Alfred Pinsoneault, president, William Evans, secretary) in 1851 said the rural population of Lower Canada was industrious and intelligent but that the land did not yield more than one-third of what it was capable of producing. The chief defects of the agricultural system were an absence of judicious rotation of crops, improper application of manures, careless raising of cattle, poor drainage and a scarcity of improved farm implements.

But the English-dominated Agricultural Society of the County of Beauharnois (L. G. Brown, president) had another reason: too many Roman Catholic holidays. It said in its 1851 report, published as part of the report of a special legislative committee on Lower Canada agriculture in 1852, that there were two fundamental causes for the "inferiority of French Canadian Agriculture." One was lack of education and the second was

Absorption of so large a portion of the farmer's valuable time in week-day devotion, and the drain of his pecuniary means for the requirements of his Church. It is a moderate calculation that abstracts thirty such days from his own productive industry, and that of his family, not unfrequently at the most precious season of the year. Such a consumption of time may be for high and salutiferous purposes, but it is clearly inconsistent with the efficient cultivation of his farm. . . . It is impossible he can elevate his condition, far less enter into competition with his similarly uncumbered Protestant fellow-farmers.

The special committee reproached the Beauharnois association for being "unreasonable."

Dr. Stratton, who practised at the Grosse Isle quarantine station and the Quebec City emigrant hospital, said that one in five immigrants to Canada died before reaching their destinations. Of 65,353 immigrants in 1847, 13,365 had died by the time they reached Montreal: 5,293 during sea passage; 3,452 at the Grosse Isle quarantine hospital; 1,041 in the Quebec emigrant hospital and 3, 579 in the Montreal emigrant hospital. Thousands more died on the way to destinations in Upper Canada — for example, 707 in the Kingston emigrant hospital, 757 in Toronto. Dr. Stratton wrote in his treatise seeking better conditions, especially on shipboard:

> In the ships where there was so much mortality (in some vessels one third, and in others three-fifths, of the passengers died), there was, of course, among the passengers a great amount of sickness, weakening them for one, two or three months, and incapacitating them for labour on their arrival in America.
>
> The sickness and mortality were almost entirely from fever (typhus fever, and that variety of it called ship-fever), and dysentery [arising] sometimes from improper and imperfectly cooked food. . . .
>
> The spreading of these diseases would have been much less if it had not been aided by want of medical advice, an overcrowded state of the ship, an absence of due cleanliness, want of exercise on deck, and of proper cooking of the food. . . .
>
> In some ships . . . the passengers often did not cook their provisions at all. In others, in obeying the calls of nature, they invariably did so into the hold, and sometimes would not even leave their sleeping-berths [being] too weak to move or even to be moved.

Stratton recommended that all passenger ships carry a surgeon; more space be provided between decks and berths; better provisions and that the number of passengers be limited.

> I heard of a ship that cleared with the full number of passengers, and then dropped a few miles down the river, and in the dusk a number of carpenters came on board with wood, and in an hour or two put up rows of berths in places where there was properly no room for them; then about 100, or more, emigrants came on board, and the ship sailed.
>
> The *Richard Watson*, with 170 passengers from Sligo, arrived at Quebec on the 7th November, a date much too late. There were several deaths from cold, some of the children having no clothing whatever, and their relatives not being able to spare them any of their own. T. Stratton, M.D. *Remarks on the Sickness and Mortality among the Emigrants to Canada in 1847*. Montreal, 1848.

A committee of the Legislative Assembly of Lower Canada estimated that 20,000, out of a population of some 800,000, had gone to the U.S. in five years, two-thirds farmers and one-third "working class." The reasons were difficulties obtaining land, high debt, bad roads, the 1837-38 rebellion, and destruction of crops by the wheat-fly.

Some farmers, who having left their country for political reasons, had reached the States of Michigan, Ohio, and Illinois, which were then, and are still, cultivated with so much activity and success, struck with the fertility of these lands, sent to their friends and relations whom they had left in Canada, exaggerated descriptions of the prosperity which awaited them there, and spared no means to induce these friends to join them. . . . Many Canadian farmers, discouraged by the want of roads, the vexations of the large land-holders, and sometimes through their own fault and want of perseverance, abandon the lands they have begun to open, and go hire themselves as labourers to the American farmers. Province of Canada. Legislative Assembly of Lower Canada. *Report of the Select Committee into the Causes and Importance of the Emigration which has taken place annually from Lower Canada to the United States.* Montreal, 1849.

William H. G. Kingston wrote:

Children are sent out here every day to walk even in the coldest weather. Infants in arms wear fur caps, and have thick veils thrown over their heads when they meet the wind. If they cry while they are out, they are apt to come back with the tears frozen to their eyelashes, or on their cheeks; but I never heard that they suffer from it. Indeed, children seem to flourish better in winter than in summer, and all we saw were pictures of health. . . .

The great amusement of the Canadian winter for all classes and both sexes is sleighing. Everybody . . . has a sleigh of one description or another; and pleasant conveyances they are, with their cheery, tinkling bells and the gay trappings of their steeds. There is a great variety of them, and the ingenuity of builders is constantly taxed to invent new shapes. There are however, only two distinct species — the Upper-Province sleigh, which is a modern Anglo-Saxon invention, and the French-Canadian cariole.

The difference consists in the form and material of the runners. The sleigh has iron runners, with a light iron framework, which lifts the body some way from the ground, and allows the snow to pass freely under it. The cariole, on the contrary, is placed on low runners of wood so that the front part of the body almost touches the ground; and when it meets with any slight impediment in the shape of a heap of snow, it drives it onward till a ridge is formed, over which it has to mount; when coming down on the other side it forms a corresponding hollow. Thus it progresses, covering the whole road with ridges and hollows like the waves of the sea, which gradually increase in size as other carioles pass over them. These hollows are called "cahots," and they and their cause are justly held in abhorrence by all Canadian travellers in winter. The cariole, however, from being close to the ground, is supposed to be the safer of the two. . . .

Some of the sleighs are placed on very high runners, and require proportionately careful driving to avoid upsetting. There is no object in having them so high, except that the inmates may look down on the rest of the sleighing world, which must, of course, be a great satisfaction; while, however, they run the usual risk of those placed in exalted positions of being liable to a fall. William H.G. Kingston. *Western Wanderings or a Pleasure Tour in The Canadas.* 2 vols. London, 1856.

The widely travelled Amelia M. Murray wrote:

[Governor-general] Lord Elgin took me to the great Agricultural and Industrial Exhibition of Quebec, held in a fine situation overlooking the river. I saw some interesting things; one useful little instrument, not much larger than a hoe, a kind of earth-boring screw with which you can dig to the depth of two or three feet in as many minutes. . . . The sheep were scanty and poor. I did not much admire the pigs, though some were thought good; but there was a fine show of Ayrshire cattle, and very good cart-horses.

Also at Quebec, the traveller met Col. Tulloch, in charge of land grants for military pensioners:

He has been very successful in improving their condition, and land is not — as it used to be — a misfortune, rather than a blessing, to the pensioned soldier. . . . The grant consists of three or four acres instead of one hundred, as was formerly the case, when the occupant, unfit to clear and bring into cultivation so large a portion, was ruined by it. Now, the smaller allotments are cultivated garden fashion; and one individual made fifty pounds last year from his three acres, principally by growing vegetables for the Toronto market.

In case of the death of an occupant, his widow is left in possession on condition that she remarries with no one but a soldier; and no widow has ever yet (Col. Tulloch declares) remained two months without a husband. Such is the anxiety for a housewife that men of fifty marry widows fifteen years older than themselves rather than remain bachelors. What a chance for antiquated spinsters wishing to change their state!

The entry for Sept. 23, 1854, at Quebec says:

> The Governor-General went in state today to give his assent to the Reciprocity Bill; and that glorious measure is now all settled, happily for both countries. Amelia M. Murray. *Letters from the United States, Cuba and Canada.* New York, 1856.

Letters from Canada (Tenth ed. Quebec, 1862) quotes the diary of a farmer which appeared in an 1843 work called *The Emigrant to British North America.* This is the entry from Sept. 27:

> Some years, when the nuts in the woods are plentiful, the squirrels are so numerous as to do great damage to the Indian corn, when a conspiracy like the following is entered into, for the destruction of them, as well as of all enemies that may be met with, whose depredations are chiefly confined to this valuable crop. All the men, young and old, for miles round, form themselves into two bands, each under a captain, and whichever gets the least quantity of game, has to pay for a ball and supper, at the village tavern, for the whole — each kind of animal being reckoned according to its importance, thus the right paw of a bear counts for 400 — of a raccoon 100 — squirrel one — right claw of a crow, woodpecker, or blue jay, one, &c. — By daylight of the morning of the muster, the woods were all alive with the eager hunters, and in the after-part of the day, the fields were swarming with groups of women and children, with provisions and ammunition for their several partizans, and to disburthen them of their spoils — it was truly a season of merry and joyous holiday, in which all business and work was suspended; many a small party spent sleepless nights watching for bears and raccoons, for it is only then they come out — this lasted for three days, when we all met at the tavern to count up our spoils, in trembling anxiety for the award of two judges appointed to decide upon the claim for victory — the party I belonged to had 2 bears, counting 800 — 4 racoons, 400 — 473 squirrels — 27 crows — 105 blue jays and woodpeckers — counting altogether 1,835, and yet we lost, as the other party had nearly the same, besides one bear more.

The Lower Canada Agriculturist, a thirty-two-page monthly farm magazine, was the Lower Canada counterpart to Upper Canada's *Canadian Agriculturist.* It was published in Montreal under the direction of M. J. Perrault and spoke for the agricultural board and its member societies. It was issued in French and English. The issue for October 1863 contained this report:

> The Exhibition of the Lower Canada Agricultural Society was held on the 15th, 16th, 17th and 18th September [at Montreal] in an

enclosure on the left of Peel Street. On two sides of this enclosure, substantial wooden sheds had been erected, containing two hundred stalls. Along the fence bounding on Sherbrooke Street, a large open shed had been constructed, also divided into stalls. A few hundred feet distance from the same fence, three open sheds had been put up. These sheds measure together 800 feet. Very large hay sheds were also provided. On the upper portion of the enclosure, a building, 20 x 50 feet, was erected for a refreshment room, near which a band stand was also erected. There were, likewise, buildings for the Agricultural Association, the Local Committee, police station, and ticket offices. The site of the Prince of Wales Ball Room was levelled, and enclosed with ropes, for showing and exercising the horses. Horned cattle were entered from Sherbrooke Street, while horses were admitted from Stanley Street, thus preventing accidents which might arise from collision. The heavy agricultural implements, such as threshing and mowing machines, were in the enclosure, while the lighter ones were allotted a space in the Crystal Palace. . . .

The judges, who, it is to be regretted, were not all practical men, had a very onerous duty to perform. They met and organized at ten o'clock in the morning, and were then furnished with the committee books containing the numbers of entries in each class. In addition to the premiums offered for articles enumerated in the list, they had power to award discretionary premiums for such articles, not enumerated, as they might consider worthy; and though no one doubted their desire to do justice, still their awards were very much questioned.

At the Lower Canada exhibition of 1858, held at Pointe St. Charles, some breeders declined to enter competition on the grounds that they would be risking their sheep to wolves in the district.

Not every settler had to cut down the forest. Cyrus Thomas wrote of the St. Armand district on the border of Vermont:

When the first settlers came to St. Armand the streams were in several places obstructed by beaver dams. Owing to this, much of the land was free from timber and overflowed with water. A great benefit was thus, providentially, conferred on the pioneers. They tore down the dams constructed by the industrious beavers, and the grass, springing up in luxuriance on the land recently covered with water, furnished abundant sustenance for the animals. Cyrus Thomas. *Contributions to the History of the Eastern Townships.* Montreal, 1866.

Mrs. C. M. Day discussed the evils of drink, and the difficulty in getting a doctor, in the settlements.

Spiritous liquors were considered essential as a beverage, and no doubt the stimulant went far toward promoting the general enjoyment and hilarity on their festive occasions. . . . A most astonishing quantity of whiskey was manufactured and consumed by these early people. As their land was new and generally very productive, after the first few years the farmers raised a large surplus of grain which, till a market was available, was mostly converted into whiskey and taken as a beverage. Distilleries became exceedingly numerous, the making and selling of this article being pursued and recognized as a respectable and legitimate employment. After the introduction of taverns, selling whiskey became the most lucrative and of course the most important branch of the industry. Although this whiskey was not then adulterated and drugged as at the present day, its effects on those who became slaves to their appetites were in most respects the same. The way was thus gradually but too surely prepared for drunkenness, poverty, and the various forms of vice which often culminated in crime and its fearful penalties. . . . Many of the more remote settlements were without a resident physician for years, and if sudden sickness or severe casualties occurred, much suffering often ensued for want of proper medical or surgical aid. When sent for to attend patients at a distance, the doctor was often obliged to find his way through the woods guided by marked trees; perhaps to walk on snow-shoes over the drifts; or to go up or down the river or lake in bark canoes. After the opening of lines of road, these distant visits were usually made on horseback. When infectious diseases prevailed, many were carried off, or were beyond help, before a doctor could be got to them. Mrs. C. M. Day. *History of the Eastern Townships*. Montreal, 1869.

Mrs. Davenport's two-week ride from Quebec to Lake St. John was the first such journey by a white woman, and Mrs. Davenport confessed she would never have started out if she'd realized that a so-called road of more than 100 miles petered out altogether after twenty.

We all looked perfectly hideous from fly bites, besides feeling great pain, my head and neck were so swollen that I could not lie down, but had to remain in a sitting position, and Malcolm was stone deaf, the blood running from his face and ears; my habit was in rags, but fortunately I had brought needle and thread, so, tired as I was, I managed to stitch it together. The night was cold, but we had our tent, and a roaring fire, which was generally kept up all night. [Next day] we walked for several hours through swamps, high grass and underwood. I had to walk with outstretched arms to keep my face from being torn by the branches of the trees. Mrs. Davenport. *Journal of a Fourteen Days' Ride Through the Bush from Quebec to Lake St. John*. Quebec, 1872.

After that, the going got rough.

The first grange was organized Dec. 4, 1867, in the United States as a means of advancing farmers' interests. The U.S. National Grange began organizing in Quebec in 1872, its first local being at Stanstead, on the Vermont border, and therefore called International. By 1874, there were only ten locals in Canada, all members of the American ogranization. Not until Sept. 22, 1874, at a meeting in Toronto, was the independent Dominion Grange formed. Its 1876 brochure outlined the background:

> The isolation of farmers is proverbial. Living as they necessarily must at greater distances apart than the inhabitants of cities and towns, friendly intercourse is not so convenient, and although their interests conflict less than do those of any other business, and though their aims are exactly alike, they rarely make their plans in unison, but each lays out and executes his work by his own light, without advice or counsel from his neighbours. Various means have been tried for overcoming this evil. Dominion Grange. *History of the Grange in Canada.* Toronto, May, 1876

J. C. Langelier wrote of the Gaspé:

> Both as regards soil and climate, Gaspesia is beyond doubt one of the finest, if not the finest, portion of the Province of Quebec, to say nothing of the fact that the sea supplies the farmers of this region with inexhaustible quantities of the richest fertilizers. Kelp is found in abundance on the shore and in addition to fish offal immense quantities of inferior kinds of fish can be taken which are not required either for local consumption or for export. The mud from the beach and the seaweed are also excellent fertilizers which are of great benefit to laborious and intelligent husbandmen. All these exist in abundance in Gaspesia, chiefly on the shores of the Baie des Chaleurs. After each tide, especially when the water has been agitated by the wind, quantities of kelp and seaweed are heaped upon the shore. This accumulation is continually renewed; the farmer has a constant supply of good fertilizers to spread over his land or increase the yield and quality of the grain which he raises. It costs him nothing beyond the trouble of carting it and spreading it on his fields. It improves instead of injuring pasture lands because cattle prefer the grass to which the seaweed has given a slightly salty taste. Mussels, star-fish and sea urchins can be used as the basis of an excellent compost, which can be improved by the addition of mud and shells from the beach. J. C. Langelier. *Notes on Gaspesia.* 3d ed. Ottawa, 1886.

A. M. Pope travelled to the Magdalen Islands and reported:

Here one finds a distinct peasantry — a hardy, self-reliant race, that keep to their own customs of dress and speech as handed down from their Basque and Breton ancestry. No faded flounced and tawdry flowers or meretricious jewelry incommode these women in their daily toil. Short, full, homespun gowns, generally of some dark, rich color, surmounted by a loose, light, print jacket; their glossy black heads covered by large sunbonnets of snowy whiteness, furnished with a deep cape; their shapely feet and well-turned ankles encased in gaily-striped stockings and strong leather shoes — such is their week-day attire. They are very tenacious about these same shoes and stockings, and would be terribly scandalized at being caught going barefooted. A. M. Pope. *In and Around the Magdalen Islands*. New York, 1884.

UPPER CANADA

In EARLY UPPER CANADA, there was a tendency to form societies of all kinds, chiefly temperance and agriculture. The first agricultural society was formed in 1792 at Niagara and was mainly social. The first agricultural fair was held there a year earlier. Frontenac County had a society and fair at Kingston in 1825. In the following years, the societies flourished, especially with £100 grants from the provincial parliament. The objectives were improvement of stock, better farm management, good fences, ploughing, buildings and implements and encouragement for farmhands to stay with their employers. (The Bathurst society offered a £5 prize to the best servant who had remained with one employer the longest time). A province-wide organization was formed in 1846. Some agricultural fairs lasted four days: first day, exhibition of stock and presentation of prizes (at an inn after dinner); second, sale of horses; third, sale of cattle, sheep and pigs; fourth, sale of domestic manufactures such as flannel and cheese. The fair ended with a horse race.

The manuscript of an anonymous British traveller was first printed in 1912, more than a century after it was written. It contains a reference to the first agricultural society in Upper Canada:

> They had monthly meetings at Newark [Niagara-on-the-Lake] at a house called "Freemasons' Hall," where they dined together. It is not supposed in such an infant settlement many essays would be produced on the theory of farming, or that much time would be taken up with deep deliberation. Every good purpose was answered by the opportunity it afforded of chatting in parties after dinner on the state of crop, tillage, etc. Two stewards were in rotation for each meeting, who regulated for the day. The table was abundantly supplied with the produce of their farms and plantations. Many of the merchants and others, unconnected with country business, were also members of this society. All had permission to introduce a visitor. The Governor [Simcoe] directed ten guineas to be presented to this body for the purchase of books — a countenance honourable to himself, and to the Society.

This early traveller observed that labor was so scarce that "as soon as a child can walk, he becomes useful in some shape or other." His backwoods journeys brought these comments:

The roads through the woods are every where difficult, and would be in many places impassable, were it not for trunks of trees, which, at bad steps, afford firm footing. . . .

Moist grounds and swamps are every where to be found, which, corrupting the air, tend to render the days of man brief and languishing. The trees are in many places so thick, that the sun cannot penetrate the shady gloom. Even in the middle of summer, I have travelled through roads where, at almost every step, the horse sank above his fetlocks, in many places to his belly. Hence, the ague, with slow but certain progress, undermines the life of the husbandman, unstrings his nerves, prostrates him on the couch of sickness. His wife, his children are debilitated by the tainted breeze. The song of rural cheerfulness is exchanged for the small, slender voice of sympathetic wailing. All labor is suspended, and the little savings of industrious exertion, exultingly laid by to increase the stock of the farm, waste away by the frequent necessity of purchasing expensive remedies to check the progress of disease.

The writer cheered up occasionally:

It is to be remarked of this part of the country [Glengarry, in today's eastern Ontario] that scarce a twig was cut in it till the year 1784. To a philosophical mind, no prospect can be so grateful as to the progress of culture. A small patch of waving grain, a little eddy of smoke scarce surmounting the tops of the trees and announcing a human habitation, the cheerful crowing of a cock, all gratify when unexpectedly encountered.

But he is happiest describing winter:

Winter is universally through Canada the season of festivity. Cut off from communication with the rest of the world, the good people find resources within themselves to mitigate the severity of the climate. About the close of October, all the ships have departed for Europe. Business is then at an end, and pleasure becomes the general object. The common amusement of the morning is what they call carrioling or driving a chaise, with one horse over the ice or snow. This carriage has no wheels but glides along on iron bound shafts. . . . The rapidity of the motion excites a flowing satisfaction of the most grateful nature. The gallantry of the young men is displayed in the fancy of the cariole, and the excellence of the horse and his trappings, who is further distinguished by bells. Races are run, and emulative happiness is everywhere visible. Balls, concerts and moderate plays occupy their evenings. Their entertainments are furnished with a profusion of whatever constitutes good cheer, and contributes to the pleasures of the table. This is the unvarying round, and thus passes the Canadian winter, till the arrival of the first ship from Europe awakes them to the active pursuit of business. "Description of a Tour thro' the Provinces of Lower and Upper Canada in the course of the years 1792 and '93." *The Canadian Antiquarian and Numismatic Journal.* Vol. IX, nos. 3 & 4. Montreal, 1912.

Communications were not wholly cut off by winter, as another writer observed:

Travelling here is so habitual, that a farmer and his wife think it nothing extraordinary to make an excursion of six or seven hundred miles in the winter to see their friends; neither does such a trip incur much expense; for they usually carry with them, in their sleigh, provisions for their journey, as well as grain for the horses. D'Arcy Boulton. *Sketch of His Majesty's Province of Upper Canada.* London, 1805.

Michael Smith analyzed the good health he observed among settlers in the London area:

The inhabitants of this district [London] enjoy a greater degree of health than is common to observe in most places [because]:

1st. The inhabitants are from their prosperous situation exempt from the necessity of labouring too hard.

2d. The most of the people were poor when they first came to the province [and] retain a wise moderation in eating and drinking.

3rd. The climate is quite temperate. . . . The winter commences gradually, and goes off in like manner.

4th. All the water in this district is clear from any foreign body.

5th. The soil being of a sandy quality naturally produces sound and sweet grain, and vegetables.

6th. The people of this Canadian paradise are more contented in their situation of life, than is common to observe in most places. Michael Smith. *A Geographical View of the Province of Upper Canada.* 3d ed. Philadelphia, 1813.

David William Smyth was surveyor-general of Upper Canada and wrote this account for Governor Simcoe. Near Sandwich, on the bank of the Detroit River,

There are several windmills and an orchard adjoining almost every house. The settlers are numerous, and the improvements handsome and extensive. When the fruit trees are in blossom, the prospect . . . is perhaps as delightful as any in the world. David William Smyth. *A Short Topographical Description of His Majesty's Province of Upper Canada, in North America.* 2d ed. London, 1813.

Charles Stuart was a justice of the peace in western Upper Canada from 1817 to 1819.

> The settler has to go to the forest, and select for himself, from its damp and gloomy shades, the immediate scene of his exertions. With toil, and subject to privation, that is, with but poor shelter, and poor diet, and destitute of almost every convenience, he must open for himself a place of shelter, and, under mercy, of future comfort and independence.
>
> He must clear away the underwood; he must cut down the thick and lofty trees; he must deprive them, after they are fallen, of their branches; of these, he must separate the more massy from the smaller parts; he must pile together in compact heaps whatever he can lift; he must divide the formidable trunks into moderate lengths (generally of twelve or fourteen feet); he must toilfully burn those heaps after they are sufficiently dry for that purpose; he must get hauled together, by the help of his neighbours and of cattle, the massy logs which remain; he must have them heaped and burn them. . . .
>
> To clear a spot and build a cabin, and to clear, prepare, and cultivate, a few acres in this manner, must obviously be, in the first place, a discouraging and an oppressive toil. It daunts many a heart. . . .
>
> The alleviations are that the original settlers . . . are extremely hospitable and kind. They are as willing to yield as to receive assistance; and an industrious, sober, and good-tempered stranger may, under mercy, depend upon the most friendly furtherance from them in his efforts after independence. This disposition in his neighbours affords the new-comer a vast facility, and is often the means of crowning with success efforts that were otherwise useless.
> Charles Stuart. *The Emigrant's Guide to Upper Canada*. London, 1820.

Burning trees produced a profitable sideline for farmers:

> Pot and pearl ash have now become of great importance in Europe, and are used for a variety of purposes, particularly in bleaching, soap manufacture, dyeing, etc., and the clearing of land thus becomes a profitable concern.
>
> The process of making potash is as follows: the trees are cut down and burnt, and ashes are mixed with lime, and put into several large vats which stand in rows on a platform; water is then poured into them, and after filtering through the lime and ashes it dribbles out of a spicket into a long trough placed in front of the vat for that purpose. The water thus drained becomes a strong lye of a dark brown colour, though it gives the buckets which are continually

dipped into it a yellowish tinge; the lye is then put into large iron boilers, or as they are generally called, potash kettles, fires are made underneath, and the lye is kept boiling for many hours, till it approach a fine claret color, after which it is taken out, left to cool, and becomes a solid body like grey stone, and is called potash. The manufacture of pearl-ashes differs but little from the other, except that they are done with more care, and afterwards calcinated in an oven. The harder and better woods afford the most alkali. 1000 lbs. of Maple ashes will make 110 lbs. of potash, Oak 111 lbs., Elm 166 lbs., Hickory 180 lbs., Beech 219 lbs. William Kingdom, Jun.: *America and the British Colonies*. London, 1820.

John Duncan was dubious about the prospects for settlers in the new land.

The backwoodsman who buries himself in the pathless savannas or drearier forests of the western country, a hundred miles from a surgeon, and two or three hundred miles from a church, with his thousand acres of land untenanted by a human being but those in his own hut, is surely an object of pity to the poorest inmate of an hospital or a work-house. . . .

Should he not fall a victim to copperheads, bears, broken limbs, or swamp fevers, what has he that the poorest need covet? He may manage to raise as much wheat and Indian corn as will satisfy the cravings of hunger, and perhaps procure him once a-year clothes for himself and his family; he may shoot wild animals to make cords of their sinews, candles of their fat, and shoes of their skins — but he is absolutely excluded from human society, and a stranger to all the relations, duties, and comforts which are connected with it. His children grow up without instruction, ignorant of their duty to God and to man. In the monotonous sameness with which time passes, he loses reckoning of the days of the week, or should he remember the return of the First Day, in all probability he disregards it; he has scarcely a single motive for action superior to those which impel the inferior animals, nor is he animated by any hope beyond the anticipations of the merest physical gratifications. The hog that burrows beside him for acorns has scarcely a less intellectual existence. John M. Duncan. *Travels through part of the United States and Canada in 1818 and 1819*. 2 vols. Glasgow, 1823.

William Dalton hired a wagon and driver to traverse woods near Chippawa in the Niagara district. The road was so bad that it would have been considered impassable elsewhere:

Our charioteer conducted us over all these places in safety, and even when trees, blown down by the wind or by the ravages of time, lay across our road, we went directly over them. Marvellous shocks did we often receive when going over these, or over the stumps of others which had been carelessly felled. We were often obliged to stop to mend our vehicle, which was frequently disjointed by the roughness of this road. The docility and activity of these horses is very remarkable. Upon one occasion, the road seemed completely blocked up by several trees which lay entirely across the road, from side to side. There was no alternative, and we drove over them. And it was worth enduring all the shocks to see these animals step over trees nearly breast high without any hesitation or even making a plunge or a false step. William Dalton. *Travels in the United States of America and Part of Upper Canada*. Appleby, England, 1821.

John Howison was probably the most acerbic of all the early residents of Upper Canada:

The houses of the Canadian farmers are almost all formed of wood. The proprietors display no taste whatever in selecting sites for their dwellings, which are as often placed in a swamp as on a dry eminence. . . .

A very great majority of the houses [in the Glengarry Settlement] are built of logs, and contain only one apartment; and the possessors display no inclination to improve their mode of life, being dirty, ignorant, and obstinate. . . .

They [farmers of the Niagara district] are still the same untutored incorrigible beings that they probably were when, the ruffian remnant of a disbanded regiment, or the outlawed refuse of some European nation, they sought refuge in the wilds of Upper Canada, aware that they would neither find means of subsistence nor be countenanced in any civilized country. Their original depravity has been confirmed and increased by circumstances in which they are now placed. Possessing farms which render them independent of the better class of society, they can, within certain limits, be as bold, unconstrained, and obtrusive as they please in their behaviour towards their superiors; for they neither look to them for subsistence, nor for anything else. They now consider themselves on an equality with those to whom, in former times, the hope of gain would have made them crouch like slaves, and tacitly avow their contempt of the better part of society by avoiding the slightest approximation towards them, so far as regards habits, appearance, or mode of life.

The excessive obstinacy of these people forms one great barrier to their improvement, but a greater still is created by their absurd and boundless vanity. . . .

It is indeed lamentable to think that most of the improved part of this beautiful and magnificent Province has fallen into such "hangmen's hands"; and to feel convinced that the country will retrograde in everything that is truly great and desirable, or remain detestable to persons of liberal ideas, as long as these boors continue to be the principal tenants of it. . . .

The Canadian peasantry, feeling no religious constraint, are profligate, unamiable, and dishonest.

Howison lived for eight months in the Talbot Settlement on the north shore of Lake Erie. At first view, it was a grand place, the forests "vanishing away before the industry of man."

But a deliberate inspection will destroy all those Arcadian ideas and agreeable impressions. He who examines a new settlement in detail will find most of its inhabitants sunk low in degradation, ignorance, and profligacy, and altogether insensible of the advantages which distinguish their condition. A lawless and unprincipled rabble, consisting of the refuse of mankind, recently emancipated from the subordination that exists in an advanced state of society, and all equal in point of right and possession, compose, of course, a democracy of the most revolting kind. No individual possesses more influence than another; and were any one, whose qualifications and pretensions entitled him to take the lead, to assume a superiority, or make any attempt at improvement, he would be strenuously opposed by all the others. Thus, the whole inhabitants of a new settlement march sluggishly forward at the same pace, and if one advances in the least degree before the others, he is immediately pulled back to the ranks. . . . Most of the settlers might live much more comfortably than they do at present if they exerted themselves, or had any ideas of neatness or propriety; but they follow the habits and customs of the peasantry of the United States and of Scotland and, consequently, are offensively dirty, gross, and indolent, in all their domestic arrangements. . . .

Great numbers of emigrants from the Highlands of Scotland have lately taken lands in the upper part of the Talbot Settlement. These people, with the clannishness so peculiar to them, keep together as much as possible, and, at one time, they actually proposed, among themselves, to petition the governor to set apart a township into which none but Scotch were to be admitted. Were this arrangement to take place, it would be difficult to say which party was the gainer, the habits of both being equally uncouth and obnoxious.

Among those whom Howison advised not to come to Canada were retired military men:

The idle and inactive life to which they have been accustomed while in the army, particularly during these "piping times of peace," totally incapacitates them for making good settlers in the backwoods. A lounger, unless independent, has no business in Canada. . . . Lawyers are not wanted; Canada swarms with them. . . . Too many young men, and generally those of respectable families, die of delirium tremens. It is well known to be a fatal complaint, particularly to the officers.

Howison's unkindest cut was at women:

They lose their teeth and good looks eight or ten years sooner then the females of Europe; but I am unable to account for this early constitutional failure. John Howison. *Sketches of Upper Canada*. London, 1821.

Robert Gourlay was another outspoken critic.

The present very unprofitable and comfortless condition of Upper Canada must be traced back to the first operations of [Governor John Graves] Simcoe. With all his honesty, and energy, and zeal for settling the province, he had really no sound views on the subject, and he was infinitely too lavish in disposing of the land — infinitely too much hurried in all his proceedings.

In giving away land to individuals, no doubt he thought he would give these individuals an interest in the improvement of the country — an inducement to settle in it, and draw to it settlers; but he did not consider the character and condition of most of his favourites; many of them officers in the army, whose habits did not accord with business, and less still with solitude and the wilderness; whose hearts were in England, and whose wishes were intent on retirement thither. Most of them did retire from Upper Canada, and considering, as was really the case, their land grants of little value, forgot and neglected them.

This was attended by many bad consequences. Their lands became bars to improvement: as owners they were not known; could not be heard of; could not be applied to, or consulted with, about any measure for public advantage. Their promises under the Governor's hand, their land board certificates, their deeds, were flung about and neglected.

But mischief greater than all this arose, is, and will be, from the badness of surveys. Such was the haste to get land given away, that ignorant and careless men were employed to measure it out, and such a mess did they make of their land-measuring, that one of the present surveyors informed me that in running new lines over a great extent of the province, he found spare room for a whole township in the midst of those laid out at an early period. It may readily be conceived, upon consideration of this fact, what blundering has been committed, and what mistakes stand for correction.

Boundary lines in the wilderness are marked by blazing, as it is called, that is, chopping off with an axe a little bark from such trees as stand nearest to the line. Careless surveyors can readily be supposed to depart wide of the truth with this blazing: their measuring chains cannot run very straight, and their compass needles, where these are called in aid, may be greatly diverted from the right direction by ferruginous substances in the neighbourhood.

In short, numerous mistakes and errors of survey have been made and discovered: much dispute has arisen therefrom; and I have been told infinite mischief is still in store. It occurred to me, while in Canada . . . to have pressed on the notice of the government that a complete new survey and map of the province should be executed; and at the same time a book, after the manner of Doomsday-book, written out and published, setting forth all the original grants, and describing briefly but surely all property both public and private. I would yet most seriously recommend such to be set about. It might be expensive now; but would assuredly save, in time to come, a pound for every penny of its cost. To proprietors of Canadian lands who reside in Britain, I would more particularly advise the forwarding of this necessary measure, for they may depend upon it that blazing may be out-blazed, and absentees ousted by roguish residents. How easy, even for a single axeman in the lone and remote wood, to cut down the originally blazed timber, and blaze afresh in a very different direction. The lawyers of Upper Canada will have an abundant harvest before them if nothing is done to cure this evil. Robert Gourlay. *Statistical Account of Upper Canada Compiled With a View to a Grand System of Emigration*. 2 vols. London, 1822.

Gourlay wrote this book soon after he was banished from Upper Canada in 1819 for sedition. A reformer as well as a successful farmer, he held views on land use that were much too radical for the ruling Family Compact. His exile was rescinded in 1839, and he returned briefly to Upper Canada in 1856.

He was right about the survey in Simcoe's time. To this day, some Ontario counties have odd-size leftovers usually called bastard townships.

The 236-page book *Hints to Emigrants* was one of the very best guides for emigrants as well as an entertaining account of everyday pioneer life. Its author, William Bell, was a farmer as well as a clergyman — a common combination of vocations at the time — who arrived in the village of Perth in Lanark County in June 1817. Perth's population was 1,890, made up mainly of discharged soldiers and their families. Perth was a semimilitary outpost designed to help defend Upper Canada against any further American incursions. Bell informs us:

The implements granted to each settler were as follows: a spade, an adze, a felling axe, a brush-hook [or bushwhack], a bill-hook, a scythe, a reaping-hook, a pitch-fork, a pick-axe, nine harrow teeth, two hoes, a hammer, a plane, a chisel, an auger, a hand saw, two gimblets, two files, one pair of hinges, one door, lock and key, nine panes of glass, one pound of putty, fourteen pounds of nails, a camp-kettle, a frying-pan, a blanket for each man or woman, and one for every two children. Besides these there were concession tools, which a number of settlers in the same neighbourhood had in common: such as a pit-saw, a cross-cut saw, a grindstone, a crow-bar, a sledge hammer, etc.

An officer's allowance was just the above list doubled. But, indeed, the supply that any one received depended on how he stood with the secretary [to the governor]. Those who enjoyed his good graces obtained more, and those who had incurred his displeasure less. . . .

The clearing of land is done in the following manner: In the first place, the underbrush, and all the small trees less than four or five inches thick, are cut close by the ground, cut into pieces and thrown into heaps. There is always a great quantity of timber lying on the ground, which has been blown down by the wind, and which must be cut up. The next step is to cut down the large trees, which is done by making a cut half through the tree, about three feet from the ground on the side to which it leans, and then cutting it on the other side till it falls. It should be so cut as to fall clear through between the other trees, for if it should lodge upon another, it will be dangerous cutting that one down for fear of the other one falling. People who are very careless often get themselves hurt, and some are even killed this way. As soon as a tree is cut down, it is cut into logs twelve feet long, and its branches are thrown into heaps. In this manner, the whole of the piece intended to be cleared is gone over, and not a tree must be left. Some have recommended cutting only the underbrush and girding large trees, that is, cutting a notch all round them so that they die, as the best way for new settlers to do; as the way that they will get most crop in, and which will cost them least labour. But this is a very bad plan, because the trees in this country, from being so closely crowded together, grow to an immense height, and, of course, when they are left exposed to the wind, and are notched in a piece at the root, they are apt to be blown down, and besides spoiling the crop, they may, in their fall, kill cattle, or perhaps people themselves. The crop is much inferior, both in quantity and quality, to that raised in an open clearing; and then, after all, the trees will have to be cut some time or other.

Those of the logs that are most easily split, generally basswood, are split into rails and drawn off. The remainder of the wood, when sufficiently dry, is set fire to. All the brush and small stuff is clean burnt off, and the large logs are then rolled together, or drawn together with oxen, and piled up in heaps and burnt. The decayed leaves, and the remaining rubbish, is raked into heaps and clean burnt off. A fence between five and six feet high is put up about the field, and it is then ready for crop.

A good workman will cut down and prepare for burning the timber upon an acre in a week, but most new settlers, when they first come, take a month. Taking men as we generally find them, a fortnight is a fair average. . . . Those who begin to clear early in the summer, and are any way industrious, may easily have two or three acres ready for fall wheat, which is sown about the end of September or the beginning of October. The seed is . . . sown at the rate of one bushel and a quarter to an acre, and is harrowed in with a triangular drag, or where oxen or horses cannot be had in new settlements, it is hoed in; new land needs no other preparation.

After this, till spring commences, they should employ the most of their time in chopping land for spring crop. It can be burnt off in spring soon enough for planting. Except during a few very cold days, chopping wood is a comfortable employment in winter, as the weather is always dry in that season. . . .

The stumps are left standing till they rot. Hardwood stumps become so rotten in the course of seven or eight years that they can easily be taken out, but the stumps of pines, hemlock, and all the other species of fir, stand quite fresh for thirty or forty years.

Nothing was more common in new settlements, Bell writes, than getting lost in the woods. Here he describes his own experience:

On the evening of the 23d of December, 1818, which was one of the coldest days in that winter, being on my way home from a distant part of the settlement, I wished to come by a line I had never before travelled. I walked along a creek, about two miles; but the ice at one place being bad, I broke through, and got wet to the knees. In less than half a minute, my clothes were as hard as boards, the frost being intense. It is in a case of this kind that freezing is most to be dreaded. As long as one is dry, the frost makes less impression. Knowing that I was now in great danger, I travelled with the utmost expedition; but I had not proceeded half a mile farther when I again broke through at a spring. The sun was just setting, and I was still three miles from home. I turned from the creek, and struck into the wood. My trowsers, stockings, and shoes were now as hard as stone, which greatly retarded

Rev. Jacques Frédéric Doudiet, *Sainte Thérèse, 1844*.

Rev. Jacques Frédéric Doudiet, Mr. *McKillican's, Breadalbane, Upper Canada*.

Rev. Jacques Frédéric Doudiet, *Vankleek Hill, 1845.*

Rev. Jacques Frédéric Doudiet, *House and Log Fences, 1845.*

my progress. My situation at this time was somewhat hazardous, my body being in a state of perspiration, and my extremities freezing. But, in a case of this kind, strange as it may appear, it is a pleasure to feel pain; for whenever a hand or a foot is frozen, it becomes insensible. On leaving the creek, I had to pass through about half a mile of cedar swamp, and here I lost my way. The snow was about a foot deep at an average; but while I climbed over fallen timber, and struggled through thickets, if I had firm footing at one step, the next I plunged in some hole up to the middle; but the exertions I made were the means of saving me. Had I stood still but a few minutes, I would have been frozen to death. After exerting myself for some time, and seeing no prospect of getting out of the swamp, I began to suspect that I was travelling in a wrong direction. The sun, which had been my only guide, was now sunk below the horizon, and there was a prospect of being benighted in the wood, with certain death as the consequence. I sprung forward with redoubled vigour; and, for near an hour, made the most strenuous exertions; but seeing no prospect of getting out, the shades of darkness falling around me, and my strength beginning to fail, I was about to sit down on a fallen tree, and resign myself to my fate; when, looking to my right, I observed that the darkness in that direction was less dense than in the others. A ray of hope sprung up, and I again set forward. I had not proceeded far, when I came to a clearing with a hut in the middle; but what was my disappointment, on reaching the door, to find it uninhabited. Now, however, the danger was at an end; for by following a tract which I found in the snow, I knew I would soon reach some inhabited house. After travelling some time, I got into a well-beaten path, in which I had not proceeded far when I met two men, from whom I learned that the road led to Perth, which was distant about three miles. I now discovered where my error lay. After losing sight of the sun, I had travelled to the north-east, instead of the south-east. In little more than half an hour I reached home, for I lost no time on the road. I found my family somewhat uneasy, being alarmed at my stay. After getting the clothes on my lower extremities thawed and taken off, I found that no part of my feet was frozen. My shirt was drenched with perspiration, and that which had descended from my head, hung in icicles round the ends of my hair. Since that time I have never ventured into the woods without a compass; and I would advice every one else to use the same precaution. Rev. William Bell. *Hints to Emigrants, in a series of letters from Upper Canada*. Edinburgh, 1824.

Edward Allen Talbot was a schoolteacher and, apparently, no relation to Col. Thomas Talbot, founder in 1802 of the Talbot Settlement on Lake Erie. The author notes in passing that Colonel Talbot of choice lived a cheerless, celibate life and refused to hire a female servant with the result that he milked his own cows, made his own butter, and performed every other function of kitchenmaid, housemaid, cook, and dairy woman.

Talbot makes the most astonishing remarks about the sex life of early Upper Canadians. As for the Lower Canadians, there were more bastards than legitimate children in the province.

Talbot's description of courtship — or "sparking" — must have verged on pornography in its day:

> Until tea, he [the suitor] seldom has an opportunity of enjoying any conversation with his fair intended, as she is busily employed in preparing the innumerable articles which compose a Canadian banquet. Soon after tea, or — as they call the afternoon repast — "supper" is over, the family retire to rest, leaving the hero and heroine in full possession of the supper-room in which, for the convenience of such visitors, a bed invariably occupies one corner. In this apartment they continue till morning. . . .
>
> An adjournment for a short time always takes place; and our hero goes home to pursue his usual avocations, promising to return at a particular time, provided they have been mutually satisfied with each other's conduct during the preceding night. . . .
>
> If there is a mutual agreement between them, they have two or three further meetings of this kind; after which, if their love increases, he acquaints a neighbouring magistrate with his intention of leading his beloved to the altar. . . .
>
> In Ireland, female virtue is estimated above every earthly consideration. It is valued above the world's worth, above all dignity and rank, and all extrinsic excellence. . . .
>
> Here [in Canada] we find females who are destitute of virtue as much respected, and as likely to make respectable alliances, as if they were not merely its proud possessors, but its chaste and attentive guardians.

Talbot quoted Alexander Pope's couplet as applicable to Canadian women:

> *Men some to business, some to pleasure take,*
> *But every woman is at heart a rake.*

The violation of chastity was not considered a crime in Canada, Talbot wrote. On the contrary, an unmarried woman with a baby in her arms was as respected "as she would be had she preserved her virtue with a Vestal's fidelity."

He added:

> You will be inclined to doubt it, but it is nevertheless an indubitable fact, that a Canadian female, particularly in the New Settlements,

with two or three young ones, ready reared, is much more likely to form an advantageous alliance than she who has had but one. . . . This, I believe, is principally owing to the high price of labour. A man who has the good fortune to meet with a wife who, on the morning of her marriage, presents him with a pair of thumping boys, considers that in a few years' time they will amply compensate him by their labours for the sacrifice which he makes of "a few mistaken and absurd notions imported from some European Nunnery."

Talbot didn't have a high opinion of Canadian husbands:

The women of Upper Canada pride themselves on being good housewives; and as few servants are to be met with in the country, they have ample opportunity for the exercise of their talents in the performance of domestic duties. But they are so particularly careful of themselves, that they compel their poor hen-pecked husbands to do the greatest part of their work. A Canadian is, in fact, a slave to his wife in the most extensive sense of that term. He is obliged to answer all her calls, to obey all her commands, and to execute all her commissions, without a murmur. No West-Indian slave-driver issues his mandates to the sable sons of Africa in a more authoritative tone than a Canadian fair one to him who is at once her Lord and Servant. Edward Allen Talbot. *Five Years' Residence in the Canadas.* 2 vols. London, 1824.

Henry John Boulton, an immigrant who had become solicitor-general of Upper Canada, urged newcomers to start by share-cropping so that they could gain valuable experience on the land while providing for their families. Share-cropping, not widely practised at the time, entitled the laborer to half the produce of the arable land while the farmer landlord supplied farm stock, seed, utensils and a house.

The emigrant, if not so habituated to idleness as to neglect the advantages the country holds out to him, can in two or three years earn sufficient money to purchase fifty acres of freehold land. He then becomes a juror, an elector of his own representative in Parliament, whose vote is canvassed with as much care as that of the squire in the parish he left behind him; and finds himself respected and looked up to, as one of the yeomanry.

Boulton warned emigrants away from the United States where

people very commonly wear dirks and other secret weapons to protect themselves from personal violence, and sometimes, I fear, to inflict it upon the unwary; and instances are not wanting of atrocious murders and robberies going unpunished, from the political influence of the offender. Henry John Boulton. A *Short Sketch of the Province of Upper Canada for the Information of the Labouring Poor throughout England.* London, 1826.

The British took a cold-blooded approach to emigration: get people off relief and into a colony where they could find work and thus be able to buy British manufactured goods.

The select committee of the British House of Commons began a long and detailed three-volume report by saying that there was a "superabundant agricultural pauper population":

> The labourer for whose services no real demand exists consumes more than he produces and consequently adds nothing to the general annual production, but so far tends to diminish the national wealth.

In districts of Ireland, England and Scotland (especially Ireland) the farming population was "redundant," living in destitution, misery bordering on famine, and "permanent pauperism." The cotton trade's transition from the hand loom to power-loom weaving had thrown thousands out of work. Meanwhile, there was lots of fertile land in the Canadas, New Brunswick, Nova Scotia, Prince Edward Island, Cape of Good Hope and Australia. Emigration was the "cheapest and most effectual relief which can be afforded." It was also a "voluntary, unexpensive and beneficial extraction from the population of the mother country."

Many weavers were also small farmers and particularly hard hit because their now idle hand looms left them unable to pay the rent for their small acreages. Their "agricultural habits" would render them more eligible for emigration. "Those removed will be placed in a situation of comfort and of ultimate independence . . . and by their success excite a strong feeling in favour of emigration as a general measure."

In 1823, 568 emigrants had been sent to the Bathurst district of Upper Canada, some thirty miles west of present-day Ottawa, at a cost to the national treasury of £12,593. This small exodus drew official "observations," which were published in the select committee's report. They were even more cold-blooded than the original report:

> The inconvenient excess of population could always be carried off imperceptibly; and . . . the pauper, for whose labour no remuneration can be afforded at home, will be transmuted by this process into an independent proprietor, and at no distant period will become a consumer of the manufactured articles of his native country. . . .
>
> It is calculated that three hundred thousand heads of families, which averaging three to each family, might be estimated at nine hundred thousand individuals, could be absorbed by Upper Canada alone.

Emigration should continue "until all the colonies of the British Empire are saturated and hundreds of millions added to those who speak the English language, and carry with them the liberty and the laws, and the sympathies of their native country." Farmers and others on parish relief would accept emigration with "eagerness and gratitude."

The committee called as witnesses eleven Canadians, including Peter Robinson, who had conducted the settlers to Bathurst and, in 1825, another 2,024 to the Newcastle-Peterborough district, and Alexander Buchanan of Yamaska River, Lower Canada, who had helped settle 3,000 destitute Irish in Cavan township in Upper Canada in 1817. The committee mainly wanted to know whether emigrants would be likely to repay loans for assisted passages to British North America (the answer was yes).

Buchanan put on the record the cost of establishing a pauper emigrant family of five (man, wife and three children) in Upper Canada for 450 days: £25 for provisions on a daily family ration of four pounds of flour, Indian meal and oatmeal, or potatoes, one-eighth pound of molasses or maple sugar, one pound of pork, and two herrings or other fish. Other costs came to a total of £40, for transportation, log house, one pair of blankets, two hoes, two axes, one auger, one iron wedge, seed grain and potatoes, a grindstone, medical attendance, a young pig and incidentals.

Buchanan said he presumed the emigrant already had a spade, a kettle and at least one pair of blankets. A cow was not included because the pioneer in his first year had no means of feeding it. A stove was excluded because paupers were ignorant of such an amenity. Instead, an additional pair of blankets, some flannel and shoes should be included. There was plenty of material for bricks in Canada.

Robinson reported to the committee that

> In the emigration of 1823, the widow Margaret Clahane was taken from Churchtown, in the county of Cork, with 2 boys and 3 girls above 14, and one girl under 14: they were located in Pakenham, in the Bathurst district, in the autumn of 1823; and on the 14th March, 1826, they had cleared 15 1/2 acres of land, raised 65 bushels of grain, 220 bushels potatoes, 150 bushels turnips and had acquired by their labour 6 head of cattle.

Roswell Mount, a land surveyor and resident of the Talbot Settlement in Upper Canada, told the committee:

> In the part of the country where I live a man is not considered much of a farmer who does not raise 15 to 20 acres of wheat in a year, and spring grain in proportion, say 10 acres, and many exceed that quantity.
> Britain. Reports from the Select Committee on Emigration from the United Kingdom. London, 1826 and 1827.

Peter Robinson was not the type to point settlers in the direction of their land and hurriedly decamp for easy urban life. He built one of the first five houses in Peterborough and settled in during the winter of 1825-26 to oversee apportionment of land and other needs of the pioneers.

Robinson had political influence. His brother, John Beverley Robinson, was attorney-general of Upper Canada and in December 1825, he accompanied the governor-general, Sir Peregrine Maitland, on a visit to the new settlement. Peterborough was named after Peter Robinson in 1826.

Thomas W. Poole informs us in *A Sketch of the Early Settlement and Subsequent Progress of the Town of Peterborough, and of each Township in the County of Peterborough*, published in Peterborough in 1867, that Maitland held a levee at which one settler, Jacob Bromwell, pleaded for a grist mill because "I have to get up at night to chew corn for the children." The mill was built in the spring of 1827.

Charles Rubidge, a Royal Navy officer, had settled even earlier – in 1820 — in Otonabee Township near Peterborough and became immigration agent in 1831. He supervised arrival of an Irish group of immigrants in 1839 and reported in a letter Oct. 26, 1840:

> I regret to say that very few of those who arrived have remained in this District, and also that some of the party reported by me last winter have removed elsewhere. . . . None have left for want of work, but from a desire to obtain higher wages. Public works have been going on near Peterboro' for some time, labourers receiving 3s a day; yet they were unable to get as many hands as they required at that rate.

Another observer, Charles Shirreff, held that public works should precede settlement. Shirreff, who lived at Fitzroy Harbour on the Ottawa River just west of Ottawa, then Bytown, held that the majority of immigrants should not go into farming but should be hired for vast public works: roads, bridges, canals, fortifications, court-houses, jails and churches. Such projects should precede settlers, not follow them. Shirreff did not have a high opinion of immigrants as farmers:

> Thousands of the million which it is proposed to collect from the dregs in England and Ireland, so far from being capable of managing a farm, will be unable to regulate their own conduct. How can it be expected that men who have never been accustomed to look beyond the wants of the present moment, brought direct from the haunts of idleness and dissipation, and whose very title to enrolment is that vagrancy to which they have been habituated, should all at once become a body of peaceable, prudent, industrious, and persevering husbandmen. . . .

They [settlers] cannot be driven into the woods, and allowed to range at will, like cattle. The country must be prepared for them. Charles Shirreff. *Thoughts on Emigration and on the Canadas as an Opening for it.* Quebec, 1831.

Things were so dead in Kingston, Upper Canada, after the war of 1812-14 that grass was growing in the streets. But Sir James Alexander put it this way in his account of his visit to Kingston: "In the high street a person may feed a horse."

A considerable pauper population could be turned into Upper Canada, provided they could be employed for one year on public works. The Rideau Canal, since 1826, has annually employed two thousand labourers, and has been of incalculable benefit to the pauper emigrant. If taken care of for one year, the emigrant gains a knowledge of the country, learns how to handle the axe, and is then able to occupy land. Road-making is the natural way of employing the emigrants, though many of them arrive with such extravagant notions of their own consequence, that though in absolute want, they will not condescend to be thus employed. Sir James E. Alexander. *Transatlantic Sketches.* Philadelphia, 1833.

Settlers were warned against American hustlers:

Many have suffered by want of caution, and by listening to the opinions of interested and designing characters, who frequently offer their advice unsolicitated, and are met generally about wharves and landing places frequented by strangers.

At New York, and on your route to your destination, you will find many plans and schemes offered to your consideration by persons assuming the character of Land and Emigrant Agents, without any responsibility or authority, (whose object is their own gain,) frequently misleading the credulous stranger, but turn away from all such persons, unless you are well satisfed of the purity of their statements. When you require advice at New York, apply at the office of His Britannic Majesty's Consul, between the hours of ten and two o'clock, daily (Sundays excepted), Law Buildings, Nassau Street. *Official Information for Emigrants, arriving at New York, and who are desirous of Settling in the Canadas,* as issued by A.C. Buchanan, Esq., His Britannic Majesty's Chief Agent for Emigration to the Canadas. Montreal, 1834.

G. Poulett Scrope was the brother of Sydenham, governor-general of Canada when Upper and Lower Canada were united as one province in 1841. Sydenham opposed bringing British paupers to Canada as immigrants. In a letter from Montreal, April 12, 1841, to the government, he wrote:

Neither is it in my opinion just or expedient that mere paupers should be transported, to be landed under the rock of Quebec, without means to transport themselves to where labour is in demand, and utterly unfit, both from want of capital and of necessary knowledge of the mode of clearing heavy-timbered land, to become settlers.

To be of service to the colony, and to succeed themselves, emigrants should consist of two classes — either of hardy, well-disposed labouring men, with or without their families, possessed of sufficient means either of their own, or provided by others, to enable them to reach the interior of the province, and subsist themselves tolerably until work can be obtained, that is, perhaps, for a few weeks, without claiming any pecuniary assistance here, or being exposed to the demoralisation and disease which are produced by loitering about the towns or sheds near them; or else of industrious families, possessed of moderate capital, and accustomed to farming pursuits, who can either purchase and clear a new settlement, or, what is far more advantageous to them, buy out the old settler, who is generally inclined to emigrate further into the forest, and who performs the work of pioneer at half the expense and labour which it would cost the others. G. Poulett Scrope. *Memoir of the Life of the Rt. Hon. Charles Lord Sydenham, with a narrative of his Administration in Canada*. London, 1843.

No frontier district in Canada was better or more fully described than Peterborough. The residents included authors such as Samuel Strickland, his two more famous immigrant sisters, Catharine Parr Traill and Susanna Moodie, Thomas Need, John Langton and Frances Stewart, and visiting writers like Capt. Basil Hall and Charles Richard Weld. Extracts of their works follow, but first it must be recorded that the Peterborough settler who had by far the widest impact on Canadian life was David Fife, one of the six sons of John Fife who arrived in Otonabee in 1820. David Fife developed Red Fife (or Scotch Fife) wheat, the most famous strain of wheat in Canada until it was crossed to produce Marquis at the turn of the century. Red Fife was *the* wheat of the prairies as well as of Ontario, other parts of Canada and many U.S. states. The most reliable account of the origin of Red Fife was given by George Essen (or Esson, Poole's spelling in *The Early Settlement of Peterborough*) in a letter to *The Canadian Agriculturist* in March 1861. Essen was Fife's neighbor in Otonabee Township.

About the year 1842 David Fife of the township of Otonabee, Canada West (now Ontario), procured through a friend in Glasgow, Scotland, a quantity of wheat which had been obtained from a cargo direct from Danzig. As it came to hand just before the spring seed-time, and not knowing whether it was a fall or spring variety, Mr.

Fife concluded to sow part of it that spring and wait for the result. It proved to be a fall wheat as it never ripened, except three ears which grew apparently from a single grain.

These were preserved, and although sown the next year under very unfavorable circumstances, being quite late and in a shady place, it proved at harvest entirely free from rust, when all the wheat in the neighborhood was badly rusted. The produce of this was carefully preserved, and from it sprang the variety of wheat known over Canada and the Northern States by the different names of Fife, Scotch, and Glasgow.

As the facts occurred in my immediate neighborhood and being intimately acquainted not only with the introducer, but with the circumstances, I can vouch for the correctness of the statement and, if necessary, produce incontestable proof.

Some forty years later, it was shown that Fife's sample had come through the port of Danzig from the central European district of Galicia. Red Fife was the male parent of the cross — the female was Hard Red Calcutta of India — which produced Marquis in 1903 at the Central Experimental Farm in Ottawa.

John Langton arrived in Upper Canada in 1833 and struck north from Cobourg for Peterborough:

I started by the stage or rather waggon, and after jolting over thirteen miles of mud and stumps arrived to dinner on the Rice Lake, which, as its name would denote, is a low, muddy, swampy, aguish looking place, covered over with Canadian rice and other aquatic weeds. . . .

It is astonishing what an immense quantity of work has to be expended even upon a small log-house before it is habitable. I have kept an exact account of our labours, and do not find, on review, that much time has been lost; but in looking back at the whole I can hardly comprehend how three men can have been kept constantly at work for two months and a half in fitting up a house and a shanty. . . .

The ground has to be cleared, the logs have to be cut here and there, to be carried on men's shoulders and raised to their places by mere human force; trees have to be split and hollowed out into troughs to form the roof; boards have to be fetched from a saw mill sixteen miles off and then carried a quarter of a mile on your shoulders; the cellar has to be dug; the stones for the chimney must be collected, and carried by hand sometimes a considerable distance, and, if you are unfortunately late in the season, the clay which is to cement and plaster your walls must be mixed with boiling water and worked before a fire, and you must keep a fire in the chimney whilst building to keep your cement from freezing. [Cuts and] wounds in frost will hardly ever heal, so that the scratches which in an ordinary way one would never think of, by accumulating sometimes make one's hands almost useless; we were once obliged to give up bread, none having a hand fit to knead with. . . .

Langton describes an 1834 incident in a letter to his father:

In the afternoon I went home in my boat with a most unruly cargo, consisting of a pig and six fowls together with some more manageable bags of flour, oats, etc. In the middle of the lake the pig got her legs loose and dire was the scuffle before I could get her down again and get her manacles adjusted. In her struggles she had kicked out some rags with which a leak had been temporarily stopped up till I can get a supply of oakum and pitch, and I had to stop every ten minutes to bale out, until by shifting my cargo to one side as to bring one gunwale almost to the water, I contrived to keep the leak above water, not however without imminent danger of drowning my pig in the water which still filled the bottom of the boat.

The pig, though a bad sailor, is nevertheless a good pig, a very tractable animal except for a great fondness for coming into the house. As . . . I have not yet been able to fence in my garden, I cannot fairly object against her rooting up my onion bed. The hens might as well have remained at Peterborough, for the brush heaps afford so many convenient hiding places that I have not found an egg. W. A. Langton, ed. *Early Days in Upper Canada: Letters of John Langton.* Toronto, 1926.

Thomas Need was a neighbor of John Langton's:

The distance from Peterboro' to the [Pigeon] Lake shore was about six miles, over which a friend kindly offered to transport my effects in his waggon. We started about nine o'clock in the morning; I, in my inexperience, believing that though the road through the forest was notoriously bad, a couple of hours at most would suffice for the traject; at the end of that time, however, we had accomplished scarcely half the distance, when the wheels sunk so deep in a slough that two hours more were taken up in extricating them. The next two miles were accomplished with still more difficulty, for we were obliged repeatedly to make a corduroy, or in other words, to cut stakes, and lay them horizontally for the waggon to pass over; but even this scheme failed at last, and a mile distant from the lake, our teamster declared the waggon inextricably fixed; our only chance was then to loosen the horses, and load them with the goods, which was done; and in this manner we reached the lake, at six o'clock in the evening, covered with mud, hungry, and exhausted. On regaining the waggon, we made some ineffectual efforts to draw it out backwards, but in the end were compelled to abandon it for the night, and make the best of our way back to the town. . . .

My [four] men having now chopped down a considerable quantity of trees, I helped them to log, that is, to draw them together in lengths for burning. It is a most dirty and disagreeable business, and especially in wet weather; but as it requires great strength both of men and oxen, all hands are put in requisition — I assisted at this work for some days, but a dip in the clear lake at sunset removed all external impurities; and when I sat down to my supper and book at the close of the day I felt myself again a gentleman. Thomas Need. *Six Years in the Bush; or Extracts from the Journal of a Settler in Upper Canada.* London, 1838.

Best known of the stable of writers of the Peterborough district, Susanna Moodie describes her arrival in the back settlement:

I gazed upon the place in perfect dismay, for I had never seen such a shed called a house before. . . . I was perfectly bewildered — I could only stare at the place, with my eyes swimming in tears; but as the horses plunged down into the broken hollow, my attention was drawn from my new residence to the perils which endangered life and limb at every step. The driver, however, was well used to such roads, and, steering us dexterously between the black stumps, at length drove up, not to the door, for there was none to the house, but to the open space from which that absent but very necessary appendage had been removed. Three young steers and two heifers, which the driver proceeded to drive out, were quietly reposing upon the floor. A few strokes of his whip, and a loud burst of gratuitous curses, soon effected an ejectment; and I dismounted, and took possession of this untenable tenement. Moodie [her husband] was not yet in sight with the teams. I begged the man to stay until he arrived, as I felt terrified at being left alone in this wild, strange-looking place. He laughed, as well he might, at our fears, and said that he had a long way to go, and must be off; then, cracking his whip, and nodding to the girl, who was crying aloud, he went his way, and Hannah and myself were left standing in the middle of the dirty floor.

The prospect was indeed dreary. Without, pouring rain; within, a fireless hearth; a room with but one window, and that containing only one whole pane of glass; not an article of furniture to be seen, save an old painted pine-wood cradle, which had been left there by some freak of fortune. This, turned upon its side, served us for a seat. . . .

The rain poured in at the open door, beat in the shattered window, and dropped upon our heads from the holes in the roof. The wind blew keenly through a thousand apertures in the log walls.

Years later, Mrs. Moodie tells us, she used to laugh about this unhappy beginning to roughing it in the bush.

The banks of the little streams abounded with wild strawberries, which, although small, were of a delicious flavour. Thither Bell and I, and the baby, daily repaired to gather the bright red berries of Nature's own providing. Katie, young as she was, was very expert at helping herself, and we used to seat her in the middle of a fine bed whilst we gathered farther on. Hearing her talking very lovingly to something in the grass, which she tried to clutch between her white hands, calling it "Pitty, pitty," I ran to the spot, and found that it was a large garter-snake that she was so affectionately courting to her embrace. Not then aware that this formidable-looking reptile was perfectly harmless, I snatched the child up in my arms, and ran with her home, never stopping until I gained the house, and saw her safely in her cradle. . . .

The Canadian women, while they retain the bloom and freshness of youth, are exceedingly pretty; but these charms soon fade, owing, perhaps, to the fierce extremes of their climate, or the withering effect of the dry, metallic air of stoves, and their going too early into company and being exposed, while yet children, to the noxious influence of late hours, and the sudden change from heated rooms to the cold, biting, bitter winter blast. . . .

I threw aside some of the [dandelion] roots, and when we left work collecting a sufficient quantity for the experiment, I carefully washed the roots quite clean, without depriving them of the fine brown skin which covers them, and which contains the aromatic flavour which so nearly resembles coffee that it is difficult to distinguish it from it while roasting.

I cut my roots into small pieces, the size of a kidney-bean, and roasted them on an iron baking-pan in the stove-oven, until they were as brown and crisp as coffee. I then ground and transferred a small cupful of the powder to the coffee-pot, pouring upon it scalding water, and boiling it for a few minutes briskly over the fire. The result was beyond my expectations. The coffee proved excellent — far superior to the common coffee we procured at the stores.

Mrs. Moodie says the logging bee was much praised as an indispensable co-operative effort to get rid of unwanted felled trees. The laudatory voices didn't include hers:

To me, they [logging bees] present the most disgusting picture of a bush life. They are noisy, riotous, drunken meetings, often terminating in violent quarrels, sometimes even in bloodshed. Accidents of the most serious nature often occur, and very little work is done, when we consider the number of hands employed, and the great consumption of food and liquor. . . . In these odious gatherings, the sober, moral and industrious man is more likely to suffer than the drunken and profane, as during the delirium of drink these men expose others to danger as well as themselves.

Her husband was twice seriously hurt at bees and her brother, Samuel Strickland, a teetotaller too, usually ended up doing most of the work. Mrs. Moodie says the family was obliged to endure three logging bees before sixteen acres of land were cleared for fall wheat. Her husband, J. W. D. Moodie, wrote one chapter in her book. It included this:

The early settlers were wretched farmers; they never ploughed deep enough, and never thought of manuring the land. After working the land for several years, they would let it lie waste for three or four years without sowing grass-seeds, and then plough it up again for wheat. The greater part of the hay raised on these farms was sold in the towns, and the cattle were fed during the long severe winter on wheat-straw. The natural result of this poor nourishment was that their cattle continually degenerated, and great numbers died every spring of a disease called the "hollow horn." Susanna Moodie. *Roughing it in the Bush; or, Life in Canada*. New York, 1852.

Samuel Strickland arrived in Upper Canada in 1825 at age twenty-one, preceding his two sisters by seven years. His book, edited by a third writing sister, Agnes Strickland, teems with anecdotes illustrating his sound advice for other settlers in the bush.

Soon after my arrival at Darlington [in 1825], one of my neighbours residing on the lake-shore invited me to a mowing and cradling "Bee." What the Canadian settlers call a "Bee" is a neighbourly gathering for any industrious purpose — a friendly clubbing of labour, assisted by an abundance of good cheer. As I had never seen anything of the kind, I accepted the invitation. On my arrival at the farm on the appointed day, I found assembled about forty men and boys. A man with a pail of spring water with a wooden cup floating on the surface in one hand, and a bottle of whiskey and glass in the other, now approached the swarm, every one helping himself as he pleased. This man is the most important personage at the "Bee," and is known by the appellation of the "Grog-bos." On this occasion his office was anything but a sinecure. The heat of the weather, I suppose, had made our party very thirsty. There were thirty-five bees cutting hay, among whom I was a rather awkward volunteer, and ten cradlers employed in cutting rye.

At eleven o'clock, cakes and pailfuls of tea were served round. At one, we were summoned by the sound of a tin bugle to dinner, which we found laid out in the barn. Some long pine-boards resting on tressels served for a table, which almost groaned with the good things of this earth, in the shape of roast lamb and green peas, roast sucking-pig, shoulder of mutton, apple-sauce, and pies, puddings, and preserves in abundance, with plenty of beer and Canadian whiskey. Our bees proved so industrious, that before six o'clock all Mr. Burke's hay and rye were finished cutting. Supper was then served on the same scale of profusion, with the addition of tea. After supper a variety of games and gymnastics were introduced, various trials of strength, wrestling, running, jumping, putting the stone, throwing the hammer, etc. . . .

I confess I do not like the system. I acknowledge, that in raising a log-house or barn it is absolutely necessary, especially in the Bush, but the general practice is bad. Some people can do nothing without a bee, and as the work has to be returned in the same manner, it causes a continual round of dissipation — if not of something worse. I have known several cases of manslaughter arising out of quarrels produced by intoxication at these every-day gatherings. . . .

The best and cheapest method of barn-building is as follows: In the winter season cut and square with the broad axe all the frame timber you require, and draw it home to the place you have fixed on for the building, and from the saw-mill all the lumber you require. As soon as the weather is warm enough hire a framer, whose business is to mark out all the tenons and mortices, and to make or superintend the making of them. When ready, the building is put together in what is called bents, each bent consisting of two posts, one on each side of the building, connected together by a strong beam running across the building. The foundation is composed of twelve cedar blocks, three feet long, sunk two-thirds of their depth into the ground, one under each corner of the barn, and under the foot of each post. These blocks support the sills, which are firmly united at the corner to the cross-sills. The bents, four in number, are then laid on this foundation, and are ready for raising, which is done by calling a "bee." Thirty-five men are ample for this service — more are only in the way. Every two persons should be provided with a light balsam or cedar pole, fifteen feet in length, shod at the end with a ring and strong spike. These pike-poles are laid in order in front of the bent to be raised, one between each person. All being ready, the framer gives the word "attention," when each man lays hold of the bent, one man being stationed at the foot of each post with a hand-spike, which he presses against it to prevent its slipping. "Yeo heave!" is then shouted by the framer, at which every man lifts, waiting always for the word, and lifting together. As soon as the bent is lifted as high as they can reach the pike, poles are driven into the beam, and the bent is soon in a perpendicular position. Several pikes are then stuck into the opposite side to keep the bent from being swayed over, until the tenons on the foot of the post is entered into the mortice on the sill: it is then secured by stays, until the next bent is raised, when the girts connect them together. In this manner all the bents are raised; the wall-plates are then lifted upon the building, which connect all the bents. The tenon on each post goes through the plate, and is firmly pinned; the putting up the rafters completes the frame. The raising of a building of this size should not occupy more than three-quarters of a day. No liquor should be served out to the swarm of working bees till the raising is over, as many serious accidents have occurred for want of this precaution.

Most fatal accidents occurred at logging bees, the mass burning of felled trees. Collapsing wells under construction were the second most usual cause of accidents among pioneers. Drunkenness became so prevalent at some types of bees that it was a leading factor in establishment of the temperance movement, Quakers and Methodists being the first to ban liquor at bees. Co-operative bees covered nearly every aspect of rural life, a few of which exist to this day. Strickland describes one:

Among the home productions of Canada, the counterpane, or quilt, holds a conspicuous place, not so much in regard to its actual usefulness, as to the species of frolic 'yclept a Quilting-bee, in which young gentlemen take their places with the Queen-bees, whose labours they aid by threading the needles, while cheering their spirits by talking nonsense.

The quilts are generally made of patchwork, and the quilting, with down or wool, is done in a frame. Some of the gentlemen are not mere drones on these occasions, but make very good assistants under the superintendence of the Queen-bees.

The quilting bee usually concludes with a regular evening party. The young people have a dance. The old ones look on. After supper the youthful visitors sing or guess charades. Mirth, good humour, and pleasant company generally abound at these quilting-bees, which are not liable to the serious objections which may be made against other bees in Canada.

Strickland advised immigrants to set out orchards, particularly apple orchards, as soon as they had made their first clearing. He had raised Ribstone pippins, Newtown pippins, Pearmains and the pomme-de-gris and pomme-de-neige, as well as other varieties equally good.

> The young trees should be washed with hot-lime wash, or scrubbed with strong wood-ash lye, or soft-soap, every two or three years, which will prevent canker, and keep the bark bright and clean. Instead of clay for grafting, it is better to use a composition of bee's-wax, rosin, and grease, put on hot with a brush. The farmer must remember, that whilst he is sleeping his trees are growing, and that, by paying proper attention to his orchard, in a few years he will have an abundance of fruit and cider, which will not only pay him better than any other portion of his farm, but add greatly to its ornament. I do not know anything that gives a greater air of comfort to a farm than a well-loaded orchard.

Both Strickland's wives died in childbirth, the first with her first child, the other with her fourteenth. Strickland describes the funeral of a neighbor named Copping:

> We had no clergyman near us then; so the neighbours collected on the Sabbath afternoon, and we buried the poor [Copping] in a secluded spot under the shade of the sugar maple on his own woodland. I read our beautiful church service over the remains of my humble friend. A rude fence of logs was placed round the grave, but they have long since decayed. Nothing now marks the spot but the more luxuriant growth of the wild flowers which wave above his tomb. Samuel Strickland. *Twenty-Seven Years in Canada West; or, The Experience of an Early Settler.* 2 vols. London, 1853.

Strickland's sister, Mrs. C. P. Traill, also produced widely read books on Upper Canada. In *The Canadian Settler's Guide,* she wrote:

> Whatever may be the destination of the intending emigrant, let him not exclude from his entire confidence the wife of his bosom, the natural sharer of his fortunes, be the path which leads to them rough or smooth. She ought not to be dragged as an unwilling sacrifice at the shrine of duty, from home, kindred and friends, without her full consent. . . .
>
> Woman, whose nature is to love home and to cling to all home ties and associations, cannot be torn from that spot that is the little centre of joy, peace and comfort to her, without many painful regrets. . . .
>
> Her thoughts wander back to it across the broad waters of the ocean that are bearing her far from it. In the new land it is still present to her mental eye, and years after she has formed another

home for herself she can still recall the bowery lane, the daisied meadow, the moss-grown well, the simple hawthorn hedge that bound the garden porch, the woodbine plot, the thatched roof and narrow casement window of her early home. She hears the singing of the birds, the murmuring of the bees, the tinkling of the rill, and busy hum of cheerful labour from the village and the farm, when those beside her can hear only the deep cadence of the wind among the lofty forest trees, the jingling of the cattle-bells, or strokes of the chopper's axe in the woods. As the seasons return she thinks of the flowers that she loved in childhood; the pale primrose, the cowslip and the bluebell, with the humble daisy and heath-flowers; and what would she not give for one, *just one* of those familiar flowers!

In *Lady Mary and Her Nurse; or, a peep into the Canadian Forest*, there is a discussion of wild fruits:

They [gooseberries] cannot be eaten without first being scalded. The settlers' wives contrive to make good pies and preserves with them by first scalding the fruit and then rubbing it between coarse linen cloths; I have heard these tarts called thornberry pies which, I think, was a good name for them.

When emigrants first come to Canada, and clear the backwoods, they have little time to make nice fruit-gardens for themselves, and they are glad to gather the wild berries that grow in the woods and swamps to make tarts and preserves, so that they do not even despise the thorny gooseberries or the wild black currants. Some swamp-gooseberries, however, are quite smooth, of a dark red colour, but small, and they are very nice when ripe. . . .

The red raspberry is one of the most common and the most useful to us of the wild fruits. It grows in abundance all over the country, by the roadside, in the half-opened woods, on upturned roots, or in old neglected clearings; there is no place so wild but it will grow, wherever its roots can find a crevice. . . . The poor Irish emigrants' children go out and gather pailsful, which they carry to the towns and villages to sell. The birds, too, live upon the fruit, and flying away with it to distant places, help to sow the seed. A great many small animals eat the ripe raspberry, for even the raccoon and great black bear come in for their share. Mrs. C. P. Traill. *The Canadian Settler's Guide*. Toronto, 1855; *Lady Mary and Her Nurse; or, a peep into the Canadian Forest*. London, 1856.

Basil Hall, an early traveller, came across "farms cut out of the wilderness, as stones are hewn out of quarries, insignificant indentures into the apparently boundless forest, but the inevitable forerunners of extensive, and real improvements."

Hall did not confine himself to the usual quick tour of Niagara Falls, Montreal and Quebec. He ventured deep into the bush to talk with settlers and took his wife with him. His advice to would-be British emigrants, after a visit to the Peterborough settlements, was aimed at a particular class:

> During the first few years after the arrival of any considerable body of emigrants, which of late years has frequently occurred, and before they have acquired any independence, all those members of each family who can be spared from field work go off to the neighbouring towns, villages or even to the better class of farm houses, and engage themselves as servants. Most of the young women are thus employed at first, and frequently also the boys. During certain periods of the first year, even the father and his grown-up sons cast about for employment as labourers, at some public works, such as the Erie or Welland canals, or wherever high wages may be offered. By one or other of these means, or all combined, the family manage ere long — in a country where labour is almost exclusively the capital — to acquire a little ready money. With this they buy oxen, cows, pigs, clothes, implements of husbandry, and other things useful for their own farms. The progress towards independence, it may be observed, is very rapid when industry is applied to the untouched soil of that country, and the parents are enabled gradually to withdraw their girls and boys from a description of service, which, in all transatlantic regions, is considered more or less disreputable, however lucrative it may be — a feeling arising, in some degree, from the great facility of acquiring landed property. Besides which, the children, even at a young age, can be rendered useful about the farm in many ways, as soon as the first heavy labour of clearing is over. . . .

The inconvenience to which even the wealthiest residents are put in all those countries from their attendants being called home and from there being absolutely no distinct order of persons bred in that line of life, is greater than can well be conceived in England. . . . In Canada . . . there is a deep-rooted, but surely very idle, prejudice against this description of labour, caused, probably, by some associations connected with the existence of negro slavery over so great a portion of the United States. Be this as it may, the fact is one which goes farther to make a residence on the western side of the Atlantic inconvenient, than people can easily comprehend who have never been subjected to the absolute want of servants; or, what is often worse, to the necessity of submitting in patience to the ungracious, capricious, sluggish, disrespectful, and, at the very best, ill qualified nature of attendance. Capt. Basil Hall, RN. *Travels in North America, in the Years 1827 and 1828*. 3 vols. Edinburgh, 1829.

Mrs. Frances Browne Stewart went directly to the backwoods from Dublin society. The following is from a letter dated February 10, 1823, describing her arrival in Douro Township:

The snow was about two feet deep, and late in the night when we were in the dark forests it began to snow again. The progress was much more difficult than I ever expected; the sleigh being heavily loaded I was obliged to walk. Our lantern, unfortunately, became filled with snow and the candle so wet that it could not be re-lit with the tinder-box. At last a light appeared and we soon reached our log house. The light proceeded from a large wood-fire which rejoiced our hearts. We found our house in a very unfinished state; the door had not yet been hung nor any partitions erected. Where the chimney was to be was a large opening in the roof; the intense frost had stopped the mason-work when about half completed. Finding things thus rather puzzled us, not knowing where to lay our children at this late hour of a weary day, the floor being coated with ice and mortar. However, we soon discovered some shavings in a corner, these we spread on the ice, on them laid our mattresses and cheerfully and thankfully lay down to rest after a supper of tea, bread and butter, and pork. Being very weary we slept soundly and on waking up in the morning I saw the stars looking down through the aperture left for the chimney. Frances Stewart. *Our Forest Home, being extracts from the correspondence of the late Frances Stewart, compiled and edited by her daughter, E. S. Dunlop*. Montreal, 1889.

The Society for the Relief of Strangers included these items in its 1827 report:

Lieut. Col. McGregor, commanding the 70th Regiment, having in his Regimental Store a number [16] of cast off Great Coats, in the kindest manner sent them to the officers of the society for distribution, and they were disposed of to the most needy applicants. . . .

Sickness prevailed among the poor, more especially the Emigrants, to a greater extent during last summer, than at any period since the existence of the Society; and the claims made upon the Medical Gentlemen of the Town for medicines and attendance were consequently great beyond all former years.

Expenditures for the year were £117, leaving a balance of £84. The number of persons "relieved" was 290 and 11,232 rations were issued. Each case was reported. Here are two of them:

Charles M'Guire came from Ireland three years ago — was at work on a farm in the woods, where a tree fell upon him, broke his thigh and collar bone, and bruised him greatly — this happened in March last. About eight weeks ago he was attempting to get on horse-back, but his foot slipping, he fell and again broke his thigh — he is now lame, unable to work, and quite destitute. . . .

Patrick Gannon, from Ireland, has been six years in Canada, purchased two hundred acres of land, went to live upon it, but being unaccustomed to work, has expended all his means, and is now destitute, with a wife and eight children, the eldest a girl of about 15 years, the youngest 15 months old — came to Town last Fall, in hopes of being employed, in which he failed, and wishing to go as a labourer to the Welland Canal for the support of his family — [given] a ration ticket for 14 days for 9 individuals, the oldest girl being left in the country. Society for the Relief of Strangers in Distress at York. *Annual Report of the Proceedings*. York, Upper Canada, 1827.

John MacTaggart, a surveyor and engineer on the Rideau Canal, then under construction, took a much different view of squatters than most:

Squatters are those who come to the country for the purpose of becoming settlers; but, not having wherewithal to come by a grant of land in a regular way, set themselves down, on unlocated lands, or those not in a state of cultivation. I have frequently thought that the squatters go to work the best of any: they deprive the clerks of the Land-office of all fees, — a thing they deserve; and, instead of being pointed out farms on *diagrams*, where, probably, no such things exist, or, if they do, are not worth the cultivating, they go forth their own surveyor into the wilds, and where they meet with a fine river, a fertile valley, and cool spring well, squat in contentment. Years may roll over before they have a chance of being molested by anyone; and should they be, they always obtain their farm at a fair value, possession being nine points of the law.

On winter taverns:

The winter roads are not those followed in summer: those of winter are along the edges of frozen rivers. When the snow falls deep, before the ice has had time to freeze to any considerable thickness, the river roads remain dangerous all the season; because, after they have got their covering of snow, say three feet deep, the ice below cannot continue to thicken by the frost. Sometimes the weight of the superincumbent snows breaks down the river ice; the water will then rise, and be frozen, while the lumps of snow, and projecting boards of ice, appear like a sea under the influence of a squall: the river roads are then forsaken, and new ones sought for through the country.

All farmers, generally, who have their dwelling houses by the way-side, keep taverns, the licence not being very expensive. When the way is changed to the rivers in winter, they follow with a temporary inn, and there form an establishment on the ice. Sometimes they will remain too long in these inns after the thaw comes on, being greedy, and not removing their quarters so long as they are catching a farthing; floods will therefore come on, sometimes during the night, and sweep all to desolation. It is vain for them to anchor the house, as the flakes of ice are sure to cut away the cable, even were it chain. Whole families have thus been hurried away and drowned, and others brought out of their floating houses alive, after drifting many miles down the rivers.

MacTaggart was an early conservationist:

We cut down the beautiful umbrellas that Nature has prepared to hinder the sun from glowing upon us; we frighten and extirpate the game which breed and thrive so plentifully in the woods. Where are the herds of deer, and flocks of turkeys now? — they are retired with their friend the Indian to the remote territories. And where are the fish that gambolled in the shady pools? — why, the pools are dried up in the summer's drought, and the trout are no more. Where, then, are our boasted improvements? — for my own part, I do not know where to find them.

He praised the woodpecker for its assistance in clearing land:

The woodpecker knows the trees that are likely to produce food even when on the wing — an excellent judge of timber infected with the dry-rot. Now this bird not only selects trees infected by the worms, but by doing so promotes their decomposition, and so succeeds sooner in clearing the forest of incumbrances. Without this bird, the trees running to decay would not moulder so soon, for the rain gets into the holes made by the bird.

MacTaggart didn't think much of Canada for farm settlement — "I have seen more distress in Canada than ever I saw out of it" — but saw advantages in part of it, the valley of the Gatineau, a tributary of the Ottawa, being used as a convict colony:

It seems to me it would be much to the benefit of Great Britain to transport a part of her convicts to this Vale of the Gatineau; they would here be quite apart from the rest of the inhabitants of the colony, and it would be perfectly impossible for them to escape. . . .

Convicts could be transported to the vale at about one-fourth of the expense that they now are to New Holland. They would find it, when cleared, extremely fertile, fit to produce roots and fruits in abundance. John MacTaggart. *Three Years in Canada: An Account of the Actual State of the Country in 1826-7-8. 2 vols.* London, 1829.

MacTaggart wasn't the only proponent of a convict colony in Canada.

Alexander Isbister was a Métis (his maternal grandmother was Indian) born at Cumberland House in what is now Saskatchewan in 1822. He worked for the Hudson's Bay Company from 1838 to 1842, explored the Mackenzie basin and wrote a treatise on Arctic geology. He went to Britain in 1842 and became a schoolmaster and lawyer. He championed Métis rights and development of the Canadian northwest. When he died in 1883 in London, he left a considerable fortune — and 5,000 books — to the University of Manitoba. Isbister in this twenty-two-page pamphlet suggested two "readily accessible" districts in Canada for penal settlement: James Bay, the southern extension of Hudson Bay, and the sixty-mile valley of the Kaministiquia River, which empties into Lake Superior at Thunder Bay. The Kaministiquia had become the main Canadian fur-trading route to the northwest after the Americans barred the preferred (and shorter) Pigeon River passage in 1804.

Isbister hoped that his proposal would "induce a revision of our present cumbrous and expensive system of transportation to Australia." He offered these advantages of the two districts he was recommending:

They appear to us to combine every requisite that can be desired — proximity to this country [Britain] and readiness of access, being, as compared with Australia and Van Diemen's Land, at our very door; a healthy climate; no means of escape; no population with whose interests and occupations the advent of the convicts would interfere; and lastly, a territory fitted by its great natural advantages to become the home of a vigorous and enterprising race, and which being in great part deserted by its ancient inhabitants, is already left free to the civilizing influences of the axe and the plough. Alexander Kennedy Isbister. *A Proposal for a New Penal Settlement in Connexion with the Colonization of the Uninhabited Districts of British North America.* London, 1850.

Joseph Pickering described an auction he attended:

Attended a vendue, or auction sale of farming stock lately, for which a credit of ten months was given, all the payment to be in wheat at the market price of the time of payment. The sale was conducted in much the same manner as an English country auction, with this peculiarity, that every time a person gives a bidding, he is offered the bottle of whisky to drink, besides its free and constant circulation through the whole company. A neighbour acts as auctioneer, paying for a license 4s. 6d. for a year. On account of credit being given,

things went off much higher than they otherwise would have done.
Joseph Pickering. *Inquiries of An Emigrant: being the Narrative of an English Farmer from the year 1824 to 1830; during which period he traversed the United States and Canada.* 3rd ed. London, 1832.

The sale realized £108, and the 50 acres, settled for seven years, £124.

Thomas Fowler wrote of his visit to Upper Canada:

> When new cleared land is sown, the oxen are yoked into small break-harrows, which they drag through the roots of the trees; and this is a work which oxen are more qualified for by nature than horses, as they stop when the harrows stick fast, but the horses are apt to start and break the harness. After the first year, the land gets a kind of ploughing, and the oxen will be preferable for this purpose till the roots be wasted away. They also use oxen for driving home firewood, and for dragging the logs off new cleared land; so that a farmer can make out four or six years without horses. . . .
>
> The wages of female servants are from three to four dollars per month. . . . Females engaged by the day in harvest generally get half a dollar each, besides board and lodging. . . . The very lowest [servants] here stand up briskly for equality, and, in general, they insist on being admitted to table with every master they serve. Although servants may be had without this privilege, yet it must be acknowledged that some would not serve a master on any other terms. . . . But they are so rude and impudent that a stranger would almost fancy that, being natives of the forest, they had got wooden heads. Thomas Fowler. *The Journal of a Tour through British America to the Falls of Niagara.* Aberdeen, 1832.

William Dunlop didn't think much of the prevailing farming practices.

> Of Agriculture, as practised in this province, I have very little to say, except that were the same slovenly system pursued in any country less favoured by nature, it would not pay for the seed that is used. . . .
>
> It is only in some parts of the province that manure is used at all; and it is not an uncommon occurrence, when the stable-litter has accumulated in front of the building called the barn to such a degree as to have become a nuisance, that a man invites his neighbours to assist him in removing the barn, which is always a frame building, away from the dunghill, instead of transporting the dunghill to the wheat field.

Dunlop pioneered near Goderich in the Huron Tract, opened in 1827, and warned following emigrants to beware of buying land already cleared of stumps: it had probably never been manured and was worn out. He also had this piece of advice:

It cannot be too strongly impressed upon emigrants the inexpediency of carrying to the woods of Upper Canada heavy lumbering articles of wooden furniture. All these can be procured here for far less than the cost of transport from Quebec and Montreal. . . . Mahogany furniture is not in keeping with the rest of the Canadian establishment; and our own black walnut makes, in my opinion, more handsome furniture than mahogany, and possesses this great advantage over its more costly and exotic neighbours, that it does not so easily stain — a property which saves much scrubbing and not a little scolding in families. William Dunlop. *Statistical Sketches of Upper Canada, for the Use of Emigrants: by a Backwoodsman.* London, 1832.

In 1832, the Dorking, Surrey, Emigration Society "fitted out and sent off" from Dorking to Upper Canada seventy-five persons, nearly all of whom were on parish relief, at a total cost of £742. On July 19, 1842, James Tewsley wrote from "Goderich on Lake Huron" to his friend, Richard Attlee, in Dorking, to let him know how he was doing. In summary, very well.

Tewsley had first settled in the Niagara district on a rented farm, but it later proved too small for his growing family (nine children). In January 1841, he drove his horse and sleigh to Goderich, a distance of some 152 miles, rented a 100-acre farm from William Dunlop, returned home, sold off everything and, with wife and family, returned to Goderich in February. By his five-year lease with Dunlop, he and his landlord shared equally in the produce of the farm, which had a large quantity of stock and "very superior outbuildings."

James Tewsley's *Letters from Goderich,* a manuscript in the National Archives of Canada (MG 40T1) is probably more interesting for what it says about William Dunlop than about farming. He got into a lawsuit with Dunlop because of the latter's "termagent" sister-in-law. Dunlop's lawyer was Colonel John Prince, who "shot some of his prisoners in the last [1837-38] rebellion."

Dunlop, elected to Parliament in 1841, was a man of "great talent but has lately become besotted with drinking." Tewsley described Dunlop's book, *A Statistical Account of Upper Canada by a backwoodsman,* as the "funniest, cleverest work on Canada ever published."

Tewsley was forced to vacate Dunlop's farm but landed on his feet, buying instead of renting. He purchased 100 acres on a good road seven miles from Goderich, "as fine land as I ever saw." Eight acres were cleared and well fenced; there was a good log house but "an apology for a barn." The previous owner had bought the land from the Canada Land Company for $250 but had been able to pay only interest. Tewsley took over the payments, paid the seller $75 for improvements in the property, and rejoiced in his "bargain."

Tewsley reported that Goderich had 800 inhabitants, a handsome jail and courthouse, which had cost £5,500, a bridge, which cost £2,500, a brewery, tannery, stores and taverns. Spring had been cold.

"I have only done mowing hay today," Tewsley wrote. "The crop of hay very light. Wheat looking remarkably fine. Other crops looking well."

A group of Sussex emigrants bound for the Huron Tract received careful instructions before leaving England: take a fur cap, warm great coat, three pairs of shoes and "a Bible and a prayer book." The settlers escaped the cholera epidemic at the port of Quebec by only a few days, but it pursued them. John Capelain wrote to his brother in England from the Huron Tract August 28, 1832:

> In a few days after we arrived at our intended place of settlement, I lost my poor little Mary for the first; then my poor dearest wife; then my two youngest, and little Edmund; all in the space of eight days. But, dear brother, I am not the only one the Almighty was pleased to send the affliction upon: poor Joseph Kinshott was the first; and his sister, Nathan Morley's wife, were next; and, I am very sorry to inform you, my poor brother-in-law, poor Bob, is gone; likewise the two young Landers. There were 32 of us came up into the woods together, and there is 12 of the 32 dead. The complaint was the cholera morbus; they all died in the space of a fortnight, none laid ill but a few days. . . .
>
> If my brother William could take heart to come, there shall be a home for him, for I have got a comfortable house up, and 100 acres of land, full of timber. . . . Let him bring a few onesided oats, a little barley, gooseberry and currant cuttings. *Emigration: Letters from Sussex Emigrants who sailed from Portsmouth in April 1832 on board the ships Lord Melville and Eveline for Upper Canada.* Petworth, England, 1833.

Cornelius Cosins, twenty years old, wrote on October 7, 1832:

> I live in a Dutch settlement in the township of Waterloo, 700 miles up the country. I can earn plenty of money here at any work. Sometimes I can earn a dollar a day and my board. I like this country very much; it's a far better place than Old England. There is fine land here full of timber, the finest I ever saw. Some of the trees is 250 feet in length. This country is improving very fast. . . . We were nine weeks on the seas but we all got safe to land at last. The Cholera has been very bad here. There is thousands died but it's got better now. Charles Barclay, ed. *Letters from the Dorking Emigrants, who went to Upper Canada in the spring of 1832.* London, 1833.

Francis Fairplay had words of advice for the transatlantic voyage:

> Some of the British vessels have an intermediate cabin separated from the steerage, by which persons of respectability, though of small

means, may avoid the indiscriminate mixture in the steerage of the American ships. . . .

If you have a desire to avoid sea-sickness, the experience of one who has tried its efficacy is subjoined. A few days previous to embarkation, by two or more doses of medicine, at proper intervals, make sure of a clear stomach, which is of the greatest importance. Be provided with some medicine, to remedy any confinement or relaxation which may occur during the voyage, and do not neglect to use them should there be occasion. Be as much on deck as you can when the weather will permit, and be frequently on the move: accommodate yourself to the motion of the ship, laying hold of the ropes, etc., as you would in a swing; and by no means resist the motion, as some will attempt to do, and always to their cost. Cheerfulness and gaiety, with cleanliness added to the above, will very likely secure you from illness, but will be quite sure to mitigate any that may arise; and, after, all, a voyage across the Atlantic is not so formidable an affair as some imagine it to be — if the vessel be not too much crowded. . . .

The great salubrity of Upper Canada is not questioned. There are no swamps of any considerable size; and if the workmen on the Rideau Canal were attacked by fever and ague, it is too much to attribute such attacks to the climate, when, perhaps, it was chiefly induced by their intemperate habits — great numbers of them being the lower class of Irish, who find spiritous liquors so abundant and cheap that they know not where to fix bounds to their indulgence.

Fairplay was keen on transportation:

In all parts of America the attention must be directed to the situation of the land rather than its quality. . . . Good land, remote from water carriage, is scarce worth cultivating as roads capable of bearing heavy loads do not, nor cannot be supposed to, exist. . . .

By the consolidation of the snow, the worst roads are converted into the best for the transport of heavy goods, with great ease to the cattle, while the lighter carriages spin along with a rapidity perfectly unattainable at other times. Indeed, a mild winter is regarded by the Canadians as a great calamity, especially by those situate at a distance from the navigable waters, who at this season convey their produce to market, and bring back their supplies of heavy goods, as potash kettles, liquors, etc., with the most trifling labour compared with what would be required without the snow. Francis Fairplay. *The Canadas As They Now Are.* London, 1833

Isaac Fidler wrote of wandering livestock:

Whether gregarious animals have any instinct which induces them to reciprocate the visits of other cattle, I will not take upon me to decide, but of this I am certain, that the cattle and sheep of others were as frequently in our landlady's grounds as hers were in those of others. Almost every week the landlady mounted her pony, and rode in the forests in quest of her livestock. Sometimes she continued seeking them for two or three days together before she found them. It occasionally happened, in consequence, that we passed a day without cream to our tea. This wandering of her cows and sheep arose from neglect in travellers and neighbours. These, in passing through her groves, omitted frequently to replace the rails of her fences and her cattle found their way through the opening. There are in Canada, as in the States, few fences of stone or earth — scarcely any thing but loose rails are used for fencing. Isaac Fidler. *Observations of Professions, Literature, Manners and Emigration in the United States and Canada made during a residence there in 1832.* New York, 1833.

Francis Evans had lived in the Canadas for eighteen years before he wrote his guide.

The planter having the [corn] seed in a small bag tied round his waist, commences the process of planting by striking his hoe into the ground, raising the earth a little by lowering the handle, and dropping in three or four grains; then withdrawing the hoe he takes a step forward, treading down the earth on the seed, and striking it in again about three feet from the former incision, so proceeds; the corn . . . will require no other attendance but weeding, until ripe. . . . About a gallon of Indian corn is sufficient to plant an acre, and if soaked in warm water it will sprout the quicker. Francis A. Evans. *The Emigrant's Directory and Guide.* Dublin, 1833.

On a farm west of Guelph in Upper Canada, Adam Fergusson encountered a bachelor who was contemplating marriage:

But I'll have her from Auld Scotland, for these Yankee lasses are good for nought; they'll blaw the horn and tak a man frae the plough to fetch a skeel o' water. Adam Fergusson. *Practical Notes made during a Tour in Canada, and a portion of the United States, in 1831.* Edinburgh and London, 1833.

This might have been ungallant, Fergusson said, but "it is nevertheless true that American females almost exclusively confine their attention to duties within doors." Their houses were immaculate, but they did not work in the turnip field or help fill the dung cart.

T.W. Magrath favored matrimony at all costs.

I do not recommend single gentlemen to come here, where, (I speak of the retirements in the bush) the only comforts they can expect are cigars, sour cider, the eternal annoyance of an ugly old housekeeper (one of the greatest plagues on earth,) and the glorious irregularity of a bachelor's house. . . . If a smart and pretty widow, under thirty-five, with a snug jointure or disposable fortune, with three or four ready made sons and daughters (the riches of the Canadian colonist) be inclined to migrate hither, I pledge myself to provide a mate for her. T. W. Magrath. *Authentic Letters from Upper Canada.* Dublin, 1833.

Alfred Domett worked on a farm near Woodstock.

Driving oxen is no joke. You take a twig, put yourself before their heads beckoning them towards the direction you wish them to take by waving the twig backwards and forwards, slightly touching their heads each time. All the while you bellow "haw! haw then!" most vehemently, using all sorts of gestures violent enough to inspire them by a sort of natural magic, I suppose, with a knowledge that you wish them to make a vigorous effort. The poor beasts are personifications of patience and strength, and the coarse heavy wooden yoke would move compassion even in a nature not gifted with sensibility. At the last deep hole, where the road crossed a stream, the 2 hind wheels of the waggon seemed determined to stick in the soft comfortable seat they had settled down into, nor could all the struggling of the oxen move them a peg. So . . . we all set to and unloaded the waggon of a vast many bags of grain. Then each of us with a big stick planted himself beside an ox, and at a preconcerted signal, began to beat and bellow with simultaneous discord. Luckily the waggon quitted its hold and came up like a fat plethoric dame rising from her easy chair. We reloaded and started afresh. Alfred Domett. *The Canadian Journal of Alfred Domett, 1833-1835,* edited by E. A. Horsman and Lillian Rea Benson. London, Ontario, 1955.

Walter Riddell gives a detailed account of everyday farm life:

The farmer of 1833 had to rise early in the morning; he would have been thought indolent if he had not his breakfast and "chores" done before daylight. His chores in the morning were not many. His horses (if he had any) were the only stock stabled; his other stock, cattle, sheep and pigs took the leeside of the barn or fence, or straw-stack, if there was one. This, in cold winters or late Springs, caused great losses in cattle; especially was it the case in the Springs of 1836 and 1843, when from want of shelter, the lateness of the season and scarcity of fodder, the cattle died by hundreds all over the County.

After his chores were done, he went either to the barn to thresh, or to the woods to chop, for firewood, cordwood, or fallow. The threshing at that time had all to be done with the flail, or else trodden out by horses; and providing the firewood for the house was no small job; there was no stove used in farmers' houses then — these houses were all well *ventilated* — and a good back log [in the fireplace] would have contained as much wood as would now keep a stove burning all day. These chores kept him busy during the winter; as spring drew on, sap troughs had to be provided, and tapping trees, sap-gathering and sugar-making had to be attended to — to prove his season's stock of sugar and molasses, and perhaps some to sell or trade.

Then rails had to be split, and fences made and mended, and, as soon as spring opened, ploughing, sowing, and harrowing had to be done. At that time, fall wheat was the only kind grown, and was the principal crop, and hardly any fall ploughing was done. Many of the farmers during seed time had to start early in the morning, throw some feed to their horses or oxen, and other stock — carry out seed and sow till breakfast time, and then harrow till dinner-time — and at the noon spell, again go out and sow enough of the ground to keep harrowing till sundown. Then they had the planting of Corn and Potatoes to attend to, no other roots were grown then. If one got his crops all sown, and his planting done by the 4th June he thought he was well forward with his work. After planting, etc., was done, his summer fallow, which was then generally rough and stumpy, had to be attended to — old logs drawn off — as many stumps pulled up and drawn off or burnt as possible. This fallow was mostly ploughed the first thing in the Spring; and by the time the planting was done it was ready for the second ploughing — when all the old logs, stumps, or other rubbish were burnt off — the land ploughed and well dragged so that nothing need be done at fall-wheat seeding but rig up and sow. . . .

Along with this work, he had to attend to his haying and harvest; he had to be early on the fields, swinging the scythe or rocking his [grain] cradle as the case might be till breakfast time (say 7 o'clock); then with a short breathing spell, he was again at work till noon, then dinner, and another short rest and he wrought till sundown. . . . After the first or second day's mowing he had to stop mowing after the dew was off and turn or shake out his hay, if need be, and then begin and gather and rake his hay, putting it up into cocks — this all had to be done with the hand-rake and pitch-fork; if the farmer had any children that could help, they all helped in hay and harvest time, to gather up the hay — sometimes his wife helped also —

especially to draw the hay to stack or barn, when no other help could be got.

In harvest the work was done much the same way, his own family helped all they could; if a man could be got, the farmer either cradled and the man bound, or the man cradled and the farmer bound himself; in any case, the binder was expected to keep up with the cradler. . . . As soon as the wheat was got into the barn, some had to be threshed by the flail for seed and enough to keep them in bread — the rest of the wheat was left until hard frost set in, when it threshed out better, cleaner and easier. . . . As frosty weather came on, before snow fell, if he was clearing up land, he brushed out as much as he intended to chop during the winter — to clear up the following summer for wheat.

While the husband was thus toiling without, his wife was just as busy labouring within; besides the never-ending care of her family, she often carded, spun and wove cloth to clothe herself, husband and family, thus providing the good "Canadian Grey" cloth in which every farmer was then clothed — with flannels or lighter cloth for herself and family, besides woollen cloth — many grew flax for summer wear — this flax had to be pulled, steeped, dried, broken and scutched, as well as spun and woven. . . .

[In 1895], when hay time comes round, instead of the scythe, he gets out his "mower," sitting on it as easy as if driving on the road, and cuts, in little more than an hour, as much as he could cut with the scythe in a whole day, with a great deal more sweat of the brow. Then he mounts his horse-rake and rakes up his hay as fast as eight or ten men could formerly do with hand-rakes. Some have hay-loaders that rake and load the hay on the waggon at one operation. When cocked, it has still to be done by hand, also pitched onto the waggon in the field; and though many have horse-forks for unloading at the barn, much is still pitched in there in the old way. Then when harvest time comes round, he takes out his Self-binder, riding round the field at his ease, leaving the sheaves all bound behind him ready for stooking up, harvesting as much in a day as ten men could formerly have done with the cradle or rake, and so much easier, even more than could be done with a reaper, when it had to be bound by hand. . . .

The farmer of old had laboriously to pound out his crops with the flail or tread them out with horses or oxen, but now calls in to his aid the Steam Thresher that will thrash six or seven hundred bushels of grain in a day, leaving the grain nearly ready for market.

Riddell traced the introduction of farm machinery in Northumberland County: the first thresher in 1832, which couldn't thresh more than 100 bushels a day;

the wooden horse-rake in 1841, cheap at seven or eight dollars; the first reaping machine in 1843; the McCormick reaper in 1847; the self-binder, about 1870, which first bound sheaves by wire, later by twine; the mowing machine about 1850; the two-horse cultivator about 1854. And there were all the improvements in tools:

> At first all our hoes and dung and hay forks were made of iron by the blacksmith; they were heavy and clumsy, very unlike the fine light hoes and forks we now have in use. Walter Riddell. *Farming in Northumberland County: 1833 to 1895.* Ontario Historical Society Papers and Records, Vol. XXX, 1934.

Martin Doyle said Irish peasants should give up "the old wig or stocking in the broken window" and emigrate to Upper Canada "where bodily strength will earn you bodily nourishment." He advised emigrants to press on to the western districts of Upper Canada, but warned that there would be no physicians within visiting distance, or any dispensaries:

> You should therefore provide yourselves with such simple medicines as may preserve the bowels from irregularity, by which many disorders, proceeding from neglect of those important organs, may be prevented; after the long voyage in particular, medicine is necessary — many persons have had bilious fevers and agues from not making use of it. Martin Doyle [William Hickey]. *Hints on Emigration to Upper Canada.* 3d ed., Dublin, 1834.

James Inches' 204-page book *Letters on Emigration to Canada* was an out-and-out condemnation of the Canadas as a settlement home for British emigrants. It was no diatribe, but a detailed and reasoned account of the colony's disadvantages. It meticulously picked apart books by Joseph Pickering, Adam Fergusson, William Dunlop and Martin Doyle which favored emigration to Canada. It dismissed them as "puffs" of Canada, "complete quackery," "pure invention," "gross deception," and "written for the express purpose of entrapping the unwary."

Inches described the Canadas as

> A country which has not yet been found capable of providing a sufficiency of the first necessaries of life for the subsistence of its own inhabitants. . . .
> Indeed, there is no such thing as the work ever being *finished* — it is always, in every case, *behind.*

Inches' work runs counter to nearly all the written views of the period and is therefore, perhaps, worth quoting extensively:

> The settlement of Canada with profit or advantage, in any respect, to Agricultural Emigrants from Great Britain, is not only as yet a

mere experiment, but an experiment which every day's better acquaintance with the subject, and a more extended knowledge of the true state of the country, shows is by no means likely to succeed. The public at large now begin to see the fallacy of the great proportion of the books which have been published upon Canada, and to know that the great majority of them have been written merely to serve the purposes of the Stock Exchange, and the interests of private individuals, who, by various means, have become owners of lands in Canada. These publications were so industriously and so successfully disseminated, and had for a moment such an effect upon the minds of many, that an immense influx of Emigrants rushed into Canada, and immediate advantage was taken of that circumstance, by a combination of the parties who had most influence and control over the prices and disposal of the lands, to effect a rise in price for their own immediate benefit. . . .

Thousands would gladly dispose of their property if they could get it done, for they have now found that the laying out of their money there has been ruinous, that they have had all their prospects of plenty, comfort, and permanent success completely blasted. . . .

He [the British agriculturist] is at once not only deprived of all those assistants and resources which he had at home, and to which, from early and habitual use, he had been accustomed to apply upon all occasions, but he is among strange people of many nations, without whose assistance, and even without whose direction, he is altogether unable to perform operations so different from what he had ever been accustomed to before. If in a thinly inhabited part of the country, he finds himself completely in a desert — in a wilderness which, for a while, strikes him with awe. What is called a farm is in such a state of roughness that to make the fields fit even for receiving the seed seems almost hopeless.

He must, however, set to work; but even this he cannot do without observing how others get such work done: he must ask of his neighbours — he must procure their assistance — he must, in great measure, conform to their habits — and he must repay that assistance with his own labour, at such time as called for, or at whatever distance — a payment which is lightly spoken of as another "frolic," but which is ruinous to his own arrangements.

Inches was committing heresy in attacking the co-operative "frolic" or "bee." He then discussed land-clearing.

Many persons, when they read at home in the publications, or rather advertisements, about Canada (in which this operation is always glossed over as a very light matter), consider it to be very easily done. They say —"Oh! it is only cutting down a parcel of trees and putting fire to them!" Very different, indeed, is the case when it has to be set about on the spot. Not only unaccustomed to wield the axe, but not even able to keep it in proper order without considerable practice, the Emigrant finds he has to cut down the majestic giants of the forest, which have withstood the storms and flourished for ages, until they have attained a growth and strength which makes it no easy matter to overcome, and of which, even when they have been levelled, it is no easy matter to clear away the very wreck. Indeed, although the trunk and branches have been at last destroyed with fire, before even a partial benefit can be derived from the ground, yet the roots, even when the young shoots are destroyed annually, and themselves much decayed, are of such immense size that in many cases the clearance (a partially cleared farm) has been abandoned without their ever having been removed. Of all the lands which have been "cleared" (as it is erroneously expressed) in Britsh America for the last twenty years, not one-tenth part has been brought into a state of regualr aration.

The clearance of the forest, therefore, is a most Herculean labour, and will never be spoken of lightly by any person who has ever wrought at it or seen the work done and will without partiality write upon the subject. . . .

They [other writers] say the stumps die, rot away, and then the land is made up into ridges as the farmer pleases; thus speaking of the roots as if they almost disappeared like snow.

So far from this being the case, the after part of the work is much more expensive than the previous clearing: with this difference, that there is not only a loss of several years in the clearing, but that the crops are necessarily inferior from the quantity of burnt and half-burnt remains of wood.

In the last seven pages of his book, Inches summarized the major disadvantages of trying to farm in the Canadas: length and "dreadful severity" of the winter; consequent shortness of spring, summer and fall; the necessity of keeping a double stock of horses to do the work in a shortened growing season; distance to markets over roads "invariably bad"; requirement for large amounts of hay to feed stock in winter; a consequent small proportion of cleared land for other crops; low prices of produce; high prices of labor, clothing and groceries; unhealthiness of the climate; frequency of fires; and the near impossibility of getting children educated. This last, said Inches, was the greatest disadvantage of all:

Young men, who have left Britain in high hopes, will not long toil among stumps, stones, and snow; and, after doing so for a few years, they break off, go to the southward, and leave the old people in helplessness and misery. James Inches. *Letters on Emigration to Canada.* 2nd ed. Perth, 1836.

James Marr Brydone, a Royal Navy surgeon, was in charge of a group that left Hamilton June 20, 1834, in fourteen wagons, four of them carrying women and children and the others baggage.

At 8 P.M. we arrived at Vanorman's Inn, where we stopped for the night.

I procured bread and milk for the children; tea and beds for the women; and a barn, with plenty of straw, for the men and boys; at a price agreed on with the Landlord.

The landlady (an American) as soon as the boys had retired to rest, in the barn, carried out eight or ten counterpanes and covered them, as they lay on the straw, in order to charge us, so many additional beds; but, as this was objected to, and she found, on reference to her husband, the device would not answer, she immediately carried off the counterpanes.

West's wife being taken in labour in the night, I was obliged to leave her here, with a daughter of Voice's, as her nurse, and we started at an early hour, in order that the house might be quiet, and proper accommodations afforded to the woman, but not before I had ascertained that all was right: that a midwife was at hand and a medical gentleman near. . . .

Into whatever township or district the emigrant passes, he will find many persons who will represent to him that the land in their particular neighbourhood is the best in the country; who will point out to him the great comfort and advantage of purchasing cleared land; how much expense of cutting down trees; burning them; rooting out stumps; and fencing the fields; he will thereby save: how much the land has been increased in value by these labours; but without once alluding to the number of crops that have, in the meantime, been taken from the ground; or hinting, that hitherto, no system of agriculture has been adopted in the country by which the land can be kept in proper heart.

I have observed land in Canada that had been cropped until, apparently, it could be cropped no longer; covered with weeds; and totally neglected.

I believe it to be an everyday occurrence in the Canadas, as well as in the United States, for persons to dispose of lands in this condition and remove further into the bush, (or woods) where they can purchase at a lower price. James Marr Brydone. *Narrative of a Voyage, with a party of emigrants sent out from Sussex in 1834, . . . also of the journey from Hamilton to the township of Blandford.* Petworth, 1834.

An anonymous emigrant had this advice:

> Let every man who has a wife and who intends to settle in Canada,
> bring her with him; and let him who has not the article and can get
> it good, and of a suitable temper, etc., provide himself before he
> starts; but mind, she must neither be a fine lady, nor one who cannot
> help, or has no resources within herself. . . .
>
> I have heard of numerous instances of Bachelor Settlers, who
> have discovered the want of the "one thing needful," and some have
> either returned for that one thing, or contemplate doing so. . . .
>
> I should certainly not advise the expense of bringing out female
> domestics; girls all have the opportunity of marrying here, and few
> can resist this first law of nature; and thus, however well suited you
> may be, you can never tell how soon you may be deserted. The best
> chance is, by taking them either before their marrying days are
> come, or when past, if you are clever enough to tell when that
> period is. . . . The older and uglier they are, the better perhaps is
> your chance, although I would in no case ensure you for so long a
> period as six months certain after landing. *A Cheering Voice from Upper
> Canada; addressed to all whom it may concern, in a Letter from an Emigrant.* London,
> 1834.

A Scottish farmer, Patrick Shirreff, was meticulous in his description and
assessment of the soil in nearly every township he visited, particularly in
western Upper Canada. His favorite adjective was "mean," and he applied it to
farm fields, animals, barns and houses. Many settlers were "encrusted with
sloth" and had a "sallow, dried and sickly appearance." But his cardinal sin in
Canadian eyes was his preference for Illinois over Upper Canada as a home for
British immigrants:

> The settler of Upper Canada has to struggle with the forest before he
> obtains a site for his house. If he ventures to keep a cow, she must
> browse on weeds and leaves of trees in summer, and in winter on the
> boughs of felled trees; the milk and butter which she yields is of the
> worst quality, and scarcely repays the trouble of roaming after her in
> the woods. A pig and poultry cannot be maintained at first, and
> many years must pass away before the farm can furnish mutton and
> wool for family use. Trees must be cut down, chopped into logs, and
> burned before even a garden can be formed. The first crops suffer
> both from the effects of frost and the want of circulation of air. The
> plough cannot be profitably used until eight years after the forest is
> cut down; during the greater part of this period the harrow and
> scythe move amongst blackened stumps, and there is difficulty in
> growing sufficient food for a family.

The settler of Illinois places his house on the skirts of the forest or on the open field, as fancy may dictate. The prairie furnishes summer and winter food for any number of cattle and sheep, and poultry and pigs shift for themselves until the crops ripen. With the preliminary of fencing, the plough enters the virgin soil, which in a few months afterwards yields a most abundant crop of Indian corn, and on its removal every agricultural operation may be executed with facility. The first crops are excellent, and seldom suffer from atmospheric effects. Pastoral, arable, or mixed husbandry, may be at once adopted, and produce of all kinds obtained in the utmost profusion.

In Upper Canada the settler is immersed in the forest with roads that are passable for heavy carriages only when frozen. The Illinois settler enjoys a prospect of wood and plain, and the open prairie affords good roads at all times when the weather is dry. In Upper Canada no part of the surface is productive which has not been cleared. In Illinois the whole of the prairie farm is productive without being cultivated. In Upper Canada the forest settler cannot at first produce his own food, and lives for a time on flour and salt provisions. In Illinois the settler at once raises on his farm almost every thing he can consume. In Upper Canada the farmer is not fully repaid for his first operations until the end of six or seven years. In Illinois the farmer is repaid for his first operations in course of a few months.

And so on. Shirreff described Canada as an "interminable forest" and said that in many Upper Canadian farmhouses fried salt pork imported from the U.S. was served twenty-one times a week.

Shirreff said that during his wide travels in Upper Canada he couldn't conceal his disappointment with Canadians:

The old settlers are evidently the least enterprising class. Having come to the country uncultivated themselves, and ever since living without intercourse with the world, they seem content with the necessaries of life, which are easily obtained. Their descendants imbibe the same sentiments and habits; and before the first settled portions of Upper Canada can be further improved, the present farmers must either sell to others of more enterprise, or another generation arise with new opinions. . . . Ardent spirits were too frequently used. . . . Eighty gallons of spirits were consumed at a bee which lasted two days. . . . People frequently speak of the danger of drinking cold water and recommend a mixture of spirits as a safeguard, a convenient doctrine for such as delight in stimulants.

But Shirreff also had compassion for the immigrants:

At Coteau de Lac our steamer took seven bateaux, or open boats, in tow, in one of which I counted 110 emigrants, of all ages, who were doomed to pass the night on board. Men, women, and children were huddled together as close as captives in a slave-trader, exposed to the sun's rays by day, and river damp by night, without protection. . . . The day had been so intensely hot, that the stoutest amongst them looked fatigued, while the females seemed ready to expire with exhaustion. Conversation was carried on in whispers, and a heaviness of heart seemed to pervade the whole assemblage. Patrick Shirreff. *A Tour through North America; together with A Comprehensive View of the Canadas and United States, as adapted for agricultural emigration.* Edinburgh, 1835.

Even bouncing in a wagon on a corduroy road of logs, or crossway, Shirreff recorded everything he saw and heard, including the soothing words of his driver for the horses: "Jim and Jerry, go-a-long; bid you both; what-you-about? wheel-away."

Sixty-five emigrants left the parish of Corsley, Wiltshire, England, in the spring of 1830 for Upper Canada. Picken quotes this letter from one of them, W. Clements, a laborer, dated October 10, 1830, from Port Talbot, Upper Canada:

My dear Father — I thank God I am got to the land of liberty and plenty. I arrived here on the 9th July. I had not a single shilling left when I got here. But I met with good friends that took me in; and I went to work at 6s. per day and my board, on to this day. And now I am going to work on my own Farm of 50 acres, which I bought at 55£., and I have 5 years to pay it in. I have bought me a Cow and 5 pigs. And I have sowed 4 1/2 acres of wheat, and I have 2 more to sow. I am going to build me a house this fall, if I live. And if I had staid in Corsley, I never should have had nothing. I like the country very much. I am at liberty to shoot turkeys, quail, pigeon, and all kinds of game which I have in my back wood. I have also a sugar bush which will make me a ton of sugar yearly. The timber is very fine. We sow but one bushel of wheat to an acre, and the increase is about 50. The land in general is black peat and sandy loam. My wife and two sons are all well and happy, and thankful that they have arrived over safe. Cows are worth from 50s. Sheep, large and fat, are worth 10s. 6d. No poor-rate, no taxes, no overseer, no beggars. The wheat that is left in the field would keep a whole parish. Andrew Picken. *The Canadas.* 2d ed., London, 1836.

En route from St. Catharines to York (Toronto), Richard Weston noted:

The houses are meaner than those in the States; the country low-lying, sandy, wet, foggy, the fever and ague raging. . . . Every emigrant is suspected to have the plague-spot of poverty about him.

Weston dismissed Niagara Falls:

> I visited the celebrated Falls of Niagara, but really could not see any
> thing so very imposing about them as I had been led to believe. The
> great breadth takes away from the height; and I must say I have seen
> as striking an effect produced by the fall from a common mill-dam at
> home. Richard Weston. *A Visit to the United States and Canada in 1833.*
> Edinburgh, 1836.

David Wilkie was among a "little flock of worshippers" in a backwoods
settlement in Upper Canada:

> The temple we occupied stood in a recess cut out of the forest on the
> way side, and was used during the week as a humble school-house. It
> was a log-hut, constructed after the most homely fashion; the seams
> between the trees (which were piled horizontally above each other),
> forming the four sides, were stuffed with a mixture of moss and clay;
> and the simple benches we rested on were put together with the
> utmost economy of nails and iron. The farmers as they arrived, some
> from many miles distance, threw the bridles of their horses over a
> convenient stump or branch at the door, quaffed a bowl of water
> from a pailful placed at the roadside, on the root of a fallen tree, and
> then, Bible in hand, slipped into their places with all the
> unobtrusive simplicity of the Covenanters of old.
>
> On our way back, we had tea at the house of one of the squires,
> who entertained us with much kindness. About sunset we started for
> home again, and had a most arduous task, having to plod through
> nearly five miles of forest road. In many places the rough and rugged
> stumps studded the way to such a degree that we were often in
> danger, as the night closed in, of breaking our noses on these black
> and unpleasant stumbling blocks. David Wilkie. *Sketches of a Summer Trip
> to New York and the Canadas.* Edinburgh, 1837.

W. B. Wells's treatise showed uncommon compassion for Indians:

> Their situation is melancholy and foreboding. Their pride and
> chivalry have passed away, and they are gradually following their
> fathers to the "great village under ground." Consumption, small-pox,
> and cholera, have thinned their ranks of thousands, and civilization
> seems also to affect them like a disease. . . . Their hunting grounds
> are trodden by others, and not much is left but misery and
> dependence. . . . Grief and care can be read in their swarthy visages
> and downcast eye. In the dead of winter they may be found going
> from house to house, with a few baskets or other handiwork, glad to
> get in exchange a morsel of bread. Many perish by their partiality to

the "fire waters," in the enjoyment of which they seek a cessation of trouble. All are passing away, and the places which know them will soon know them no more. W. B. Wells. *Canadiana: containing Sketches of Upper Canada*. London, 1837.

A farmer for many years in Nissouri Township, Oxford County, Upper Canada, Robert Davis visited Michigan, Ohio and Indiana in 1836 to scout out not so much better land as better political conditions. Speaking of himself in the third person, Davis gave these reasons for his visit:

The greater part of his time has been spent in close confinement in the wilderness of Nissouri Township. Indeed it has been confinement enough, to watch over and provide for a tender and increasing family. He had in most instances to make his own roads and bridges, clear his own farm, educate himself and children, be his own mechanic, and, except now and then, has had no society but his own family. Has had his bones broken by the fall of trees, his feet lacerated by the axe, and suffered almost everything except death.

He waited year after year in hopes of better days, expecting that the government would care less for themselves and more for the people. But every year he has been disappointed and instead of things getting better, in many instances they have been getting worse. The Church ascendancy has been getting worse and worse, till they have at least got fifty-seven rectories established, and what next, who can tell. The Orange mob is worse every election, so that it is impossible for any honest peaceable reformer to give his vote for a member of Parliament without the fear or realization of having his head broken. Also, honest reform magistrates are almost daily getting their discharge from the commission of the peace, and Court of requests, while the most ignorant and worthless of the tories are becoming magistrates. . . .

The curse of Canada is an unprincipled aristocracy, whose pretensions to superiority above other settlers would disgust a dog. Many of these would-be aristocrats came out from the old country under the title of half-pay officers, who, in fact, had commuted their pensions before they left home to help to convey them across the Atlantic; and then getting possession of a few hundred acres of wild land, thought themselves the Lords of Canada. Many of them have been Ensigns in the old country, but when they arrived in Canada they called themselves Captains. . . . They are slaves and sycophants to the Governor. Robert Davis. *The Canadian Farmer's Travels in the United States of America*. Buffalo, 1837.

Joseph Neilson warned:

> Gentlemen who cannot endure privations, and perform labours for a time for the sake of a certain reward, nor sacrifice the refinement of polished life for a more substantial equivalent, will find little to encourage them here. . . . The sickly, the shiftless, the idle, the timid, should never be encouraged to come to Upper Canada. . . . The idle need scarcely expect to be tolerated, and are ever sure of being despised. Joseph Neilson. *Observations Upon Emigration to Upper Canada.* Kingston, 1837.

A manual by Thomas Duncumb is one of the least known but most informative immigrant guides. Despite what one might think of him based on the first selection given here, Duncumb went into the back settlements and settlers' huts to see conditions first hand.

> Another great cause [of undutiful servants] is the present inconvenient mode of building log and frame houses, which compels such a hateful system of familiarity in the whole household, that it is next to an impossibility to keep the servants in their proper sphere. . . .
>
> The medical practitioners, particularly in the new and remotely settled districts, have difficulties to encounter which are not only unknown but scarcely credible to a British practitioner. Indeed such are the rides through forest and swamp, over huge logs and stumps, and on the most wretched roads intersected often with corduroy bridges of some miles in length, and to patients living perhaps fifty miles distant, if not much further. Besides it often happens that the remote settler cannot afford the usual fee of half a dollar per mile, therefore, sometimes patients through necessity, with fractured limbs are brought to the doctor in a light waggon over these natural roads perhaps above fifty miles, to their serious sufferings and injury.
>
> In such distant settlements it is quite out of the question the possibility of the settler being able to send for required medicines, and to remedy this inconvenience the doctor is provided with immense saddle-bags charged nearly to repletion with drugs of every kind which may be compounded at the bedside of the patient. Thomas Duncumb: *The British Emigrant's Advocate: Being a Manual for the use of emigrants and travellers in British America and the United States.* London, 1837.

Duncumb adds that it was not at all uncommon for doctors immediately after tending a patient to start selling to other members of the family small wares, such as needle and thread, which they carried with them as a sideline.

James Logan was one of the very few travellers who pitched into the farm work so that he could better write about it. In the Newcastle district of Upper Canada, he attended a logging bee:

There were about six acres to log, and Mr. F. had collected about twenty of his neighbours, or their servants. . . . There were five yokes of oxen, and generally four, but sometimes only three, men to a yoke, with a boy to drive. To the yoke over the necks of the oxen is fastened a long chain, with a hook at the end, and this chain is put round a log, which is thus dragged to the pile. Two of my friends, myself, and a servant, were attached to one of the yokes, which was driven by a boy. When the logs, which vary from ten to fifteen feet in length, and from one to two and a half feet in diameter, were brought to the pile, we laid them on in a proper manner. After the first layer was arranged, the rest of the logs were hoisted on with handspikes; the heaps vary from four to five feet in height, and are not made too large, so as to burn with facility. This is a very laborious part of the operation, especially when the logs are heavy; and if they should slip, you are in danger of getting your leg broken, or even of losing your life. We worked hard all day from nine and logged about three acres. At one we had dinner in the barn, masters and servants together, without distinction. . . . In the evening we had a dance, and were otherwise agreeably entertained until one in the morning, when we walked home, but were entangled in a wood, where we groped about for two hours, although the distance we had to go was only half a mile.

Logan spent sixteen days with his brother Vivian on the latter's farm (sixty acres cleared, eighteen of them in wheat) twelve miles from Dundas on the road to Guelph. He arrived at harvest time:

The crops are cut with the cradle or scythe. A man in this manner can cut an acre and a half in a day, and keep another fully occupied in raking and binding. I remained sixteen days with my brother, and assisted in stooking and forking, as well as in cutting the oats with a sickle.

The wheat being ripe, he commenced cutting on the 24th August, when two of his neighbours came with cradles. We all turned out at six o'clock, a.m., there being three cradlers and three binders. My brother and I undertook to put up the corn into stooks. My brother's two bondmen, one of whom was an Englishman, could not keep up with their cradlers, so that he was obliged to assist them in binding; but the other binder, being more active, and having been several years in Canada, kept pace with his cradler. The large thistles, some of them seven feet high, caused us great annoyance. We went home to breakfast at eight, returned in an hour, worked until one, when we had dinner, resumed our labour at two, and continued until six. It is customary to give to every two men a bottle of whisky to mix with the water. The food for breakfast is porridge and milk, for dinner pork and potatoes. . . . Most of the farm-servants become addicted to drinking, and when sent any distance are sure to come home in a state of intoxication. The three cradlers cut five acres daily, so that the eighteen acres of wheat were all reaped in less than four days. Much corn is wasted, both because the cradler scatters it about too much, and because the binder is too much hurried to keep up with him. What is left in the field, however, is used for fattening pigs. In three or four days more, we had it all in the stack-yard. The loading was a very tedious operation. . . . Even an empty cart has much difficulty in steering among the stumps. . . . Almost every load was twice overturned before it got out of the field. Sometimes the waggon would stick fast between two stumps and much time was lost in extracting it. . . . The eighteen acres of wheat would yield about 360 bushels, which would fetch a dollar the bushel. James Logan. *Notes of a Journey through Canada, the United States of America and the West Indies.* Edinburgh, 1838.

Patrick Matthew found practically nothing good to say about any of the British colonies in North America.

Winter in the Maritime provinces was "insupportable" and autumn-sown wheat usually rotted under the snow "from the very long period, sometimes six months, which the snow remains on the ground." In northern Nova Scotia and Newfoundland, the climate was "exceedingly rough" and "but for the vicinity of the fisheries (the most productive in the world) would be considered uninhabitable." The "prodigious quantity" of floating ice from Davis and Hudson Strait neutralized the sun's heat during the first half of the summer, producing fog, sleet and rain, sometimes chilling the season so much "as to ruin the prospects of the grain farmer."

The Canadians of Lower Canada were "indolent husbandmen" who were sometimes forced to vacate their land because of weeds, especially the Canadian thistle, "which appears to be possessed of considerably more constitutional energy than the *habitans.*" However, the habitans contrived to turn their "starved stock" on the weeds and eventually recover lost territory and resume cultivation.

Both Lower and Upper Canada were the most slovenly cultivated regions in the world, very far behind the neighboring farmlands of the United States. The British were a "mixed assortment of adventurers" ill suited to subduing the wilderness and who allowed the weeds to take over "complete occupation" of the soil. Matthew wrote of Upper Canada:

Nothing can exceed the sensation of loneliness which is experienced in the interminable forests where, for hundreds of miles, no object is recognisable beyond the tops of the trees. . . . The settler is as silent and sombre as the gloomy woods among which he is lost — nothing seeming to be alive and in a state of active noisy enjoyment in these interminable swampy forests but the myriad of frogs.

The "Arctic" winter of six or seven months meant that no agricultural work could be done until nearly the end of May. The intense heat of summer followed immediately upon dissolving of the snow, and consequently almost all ploughing, sowing, planting, haymaking and harvesting had to be performed in temperatures equal to those of the West Indies, ninety degrees in the shade. Animals lucky enough to survive the winter required the entire summer and fall "to repair their extreme emaciation." As for the settlers:

> The heat of summer and the cold of winter are intense and the great and sudden transition enfeebles the constitution of those who have sojourned for a number of years in the country. The universal paleness of the countenance indicates the prevalence of bilious affections, and the derangement of the digestive functions. Patrick Matthew. *Emigration Fields*. Edinburgh and London, 1839.

A select committee from the Upper Canada House of Assembly took sharp issue, in its report, with Lord Durham's characterization of the rural population as "poor and apparently unenterprising . . . living in mean houses, drawing little more than a rude subsistence from ill cultivated land, and seemingly incapable of improving their condition." This was, said the committee, a "degrading account" by a man who had "grossly misstated" conditions. Along the St. Lawrence and Niagara Frontier were

> farms of unsurpassing beauty and fertility, occupied and excellently worked by Yeomanry, who enjoyed every comfort, and whose wealth and independence placed within their reach almost every luxury that could be desired by man. Upper Canada. House of Assembly of Upper Canada. *Report from the Select Committee on the State of the Province*. Toronto, 1839.

T. R. Preston was overwhelmed by space in Upper Canada:

> If you traverse its vast lakes, if you penetrate its deep pine-forests, if you cross its wide-extending plains, nay, if you wander by the way-side in the outskirts of its towns, you are alike struck with a sense of surpassing loneliness, with a sort of melancholy at finding yourself an isolated unit, as it were, in the midst of a space so large. T. R. Preston. *Three Years' Residence in Canada from 1837 to 1839*. London, 1840.

Henry C. Todd advised emigrants not to put on airs.

> Emigrants should be mindful to get rid of self-esteem, and all such unsaleable commodities, in a new country, before entering it, as they

will find them not only very troublesome companions, but a sure means of annoyance and vexation. . . .

The class of persons principally wanted here are small capitalists, farmers, agricultural laborers, with most, if not all, the useful trades; lawyers abound. . . . At Goderich, a small sea-port in this state, 300 ship carpenters have entered into a compact to tar and feather the first lawyer who attempts to settle among them. . . .

Canadians and Americans indulge in overheated rooms, which not only enfeeble the body, but originate many diseases charged upon the country. Henry C. Todd. *Notes upon Canada and the United States from 1832 to 1840.* 2d ed., Toronto, 1840.

Richard Bonnycastle had a cure for the ague:

I never had the ague during the many [fifteen] years I resided in Upper Canada, excepting for about two hours; and, I believe, it is more confined to that class of settlers and labourers who have not the means of obtaining flannel and suitable clothing for the climate, as well as generous, but not stimulating, diet. I should advise every adult about to dwell in Upper Canada to wear a flannel waistcoat summer and winter, and flannel drawers as soon as autumn begins to wane. Rheumatic and aguish complaints may thus be avoided. Richard H. Bonnycastle. *The Canadas in 1841.* 2 vols. London, 1841.

Joseph John Gurney makes one of the few references in the literature of the time to the trapping of passenger pigeons. He was travelling along the Bay of Quinte near Bath:

A blinded decoy pigeon, called the "stool pigeon," is compelled to fly down from a lofty stool to the ground. The wild ones, seeing it flutter, immediately gather round it, and the net is so constructed as to spring over them. They are larger than our pigeons, and their flesh is tender and well-flavoured. . . . One of our friends had netted 700 in a few hours. Joseph John Gurney. *A Journey in North America.* Norwich, 1841.

Robert Barclay-Allardice found Upper Canada an unappealing place.

On entering Canada I had been impressed with a marked difference between it and the United States. In the latter the people were everywhere distinguished by that cheerfulness and appearance of contentment which attend activity and exertion in peaceful pursuits. In Canada there prevailed an almost universal gloom, the consequence of recent internal commotion; of the still existing conflict and rancour of political feeling; or of the withered hopes of many who, having speculated largely in land, have received little or no return for their money. . . . Of the two countries, the States hold out for agricultural pursuits by far the greater advantages to persons possessed of any capital. With the exception of portions of cleared land varying from fifty acres in some situations, to several hundred in others, Upper Canada is an immense and trackless forest, forlorn and forbidding at best, and in many places rendered more gloomy and repulsive by the trees having been burnt preparatory to being cut down, and consequently now presenting to the eye nothing but bare and blackened poles. And with regard to what is called cleared land, it consists of no more than a patch here and there, on which the huge pines that for ages had been tenants of the soil have by the application of fire and axe been reduced to stumps four feet in height, so thick set as in many places to preclude any mode of cultivation except sowing and hand-raking the seed. Robert Barclay-Allardice. *Agricultural Tour of the United States and Upper Canada.* Edinburgh and London, 1842.

William Thomson was another who didn't appreciate the "bee."

Good rich forest land can be bought within a day's journey of Toronto, the capital of Upper Canada, with a population of 16,000, for twelve dollars per acre. . . .

The next house I came to [where Dundas Street crossed the Humber River] was nothing more than a few logs, built up in the roughest manner, and covered over with brushwood. But I heard the sound of the settler's axe before I came near his dwelling. This was an active young man, with his neck bare and his shirt-sleeves folded up to his shoulders, chopping the logs into lengths for the purpose of burning; with a little boy beside him riding on a log.

This man told me he had only commenced four weeks before — that he rented fifty acres of land for ten years, at a mere nominal rent, only he had agreed to clear one half of it, and already had two acres chopped, piled and ready for burning. He laid down his axe, invited me into his shanty, and bade me sit down upon the stump of a tree that had been left for a seat. . . . He told me they were to put up a log house and would have everything snug and comfortable before winter, in the course of which he would be able to earn enough to keep them and buy a cow; and after that they would get on first-rate.

In the township of Vaughan, Thomson met farmer John William, a settler of sixteen years' standing:

He had a very simple mode of preventing his chickens from scraping and scratching up his garden seeds. Each foot has three toes; the two outside ones were taken up and tied over the middle one — thus they could not scrape with the foot that was tied nor stand upon the tied one to scrape with the other.

Also in Vaughan township, he attended a house-raising:

I was on the ground early, and found the settler and his wife busy cooking at a large fire, surrounded by fallen trees and brushwood. The neighbours came by twos and threes, from different quarters, with axes over their shoulders; and as they came up each got a drink of whisky out of a tin can. The stuff smelled most horribly, yet none of them made a wry face at it. Some had straw hats, some Scotch bonnets; some had wincey coats, some had none; all had strong boots. Those who did not smoke tobacco, and some of those who did, masticated it with the most untiring industry.

Four blocks of wood, about a foot and a half above the ground, marked out the corners of the dwelling that was to be erected before night. On these blocks were laid the first tier of logs, dove-tailed in a very rough way. Four of the most experienced hands took their station, one at each corner, whose duty it was to make the joints and carry up the angles perpendicular. I observed that they took particular care not to let the logs touch each other, except at the corners where they rested. After the walls got so high that they could not lift up the logs, two saplings were cut, and the bark being stripped off to make them smooth, they were placed against the wall in a slanting position. This answered for a slide on which the people below pushed up the logs with crutches, or long poles with forked ends.

At first they went to work moderately and with quietness, but after the whisky had been handed about several times they got very uproarious — swearing, shouting, tumbling down, and sometimes like to fight. . . .

I was sick of it, for most of them were drunk and all of them excited. The manner in which they use their axes was a "caution." Many accidents happen, and lives are frequently lost on these occasions, both from accidents and quarrels. In all there were about twenty-four men, one half Irish; on the whole about the roughest specimen of humanity I have ever seen. So much was I disgusted at their conduct, that, even if paid for it, I would not live amongst them.

The walls of a house, 15 by 26, and 12 feet high, were up before night; and some of the nearest neighbours were to return next day and cut out the doors and windows. When all was done they sat down, all about, eating bread and meat, and drinking whisky (I believe of the same quality as that known in Aberdeen by the name of "*Kill the carter*"). . . . I then left them, thinking I would not like the foundation of my house laid with so many oaths to consecrate it as I had heard that day. William Thomson. A *Tradesman's Travels, in the United States and Canada, in the years 1840, 41, & 42.* Edinburgh, 1842.

Samuel Butler draws a strange comparison to denote agricultural prosperity:

It appears that Upper Canada now owns as many horses as were to be found in England in the reign of Queen Elizabeth, who ordered a census to be taken on the prospect of invasion by the Spanish Armada, when all that could be mustered were stated at 56,000, a number much less than Upper Canada can now furnish . . . and Upper Canada scarcely can lay claim to half a century's existence. So that in the short space of fifty years, that important province, a very giant in its cradle, has an accumulation of agricultural wealth equal if not surpassing that of our ancestors after the toil of some four hundred years, without either famine, pestilence, or murrain amongst cattle. Samuel Butler. *The Emigrant's Hand-Book of Facts.* Glasgow, 1843.

The Canada Company, which sold land to immigrants, in 1843 issued a four-page brochure on light blue paper designed to answer questions most often put to it by prospective buyers. At the time, the company's principal block of land was one million acres with a sixty-mile frontage on Lake Huron intersected by two "grand leading roads on which more pains and labour have been bestowed than on any other roads of the same extent and magnitude in the Province."

The twenty-one questions dealt with the price of clearing land, rotation of crops, rate of yield, the cost of farm buildings, prices of livestock, farm implements, clothing and provisions, dates of arrival and departure of frost and so on. The replies were not intended to detract from the company's lands. Here are some of them:

A settler "very seldom spends *money* in erecting his buildings, they being generally built by himself, with the assistance of his neighbours." But a two-storey log house measuring twenty-four feet by sixteen with a shingled roof would cost $36, a log barn twenty-four by forty, $40. Wages of male servants were $8 a month with board, female servants $4 a month with board; carpenters made $1 to $2 a day. Taxes were "extremely trifling" (about one per cent.) There were no wild beasts and plenty of game, but "a new settler can earn a quarter of beef in the time which it takes him to hunt for a quarter of venison."

Question number ten asked what a farmer did during the winter. The reply: "Generally confined to taking care of his cattle and chopping." This referred not to chopping fodder but to felling and cutting up trees ready for spring burning. The Canada Company. *Question and Answer sheet.* Toronto, 1843.

A letter by Dr. Robert Alling to the commissioners of the Canada Company, dated Guelph, December 16, 1840, praised the company's settlement in and around Guelph, but added:

> Generally speaking, English families do not hold together long enough to ensure success; the sons of poor English emigrants leave their parents and become servants at the usual high wages, and instead of saving money to purchase land, the same is squandered away in fine clothes and at numerous country balls, etc. This course is followed up by taking a wife, becoming a common labourer, and hiring a smart house *in the town*, where he is determined his wife shall wear as rich a silk dress on a Sunday as any lady in the place. The lowest characters we have in Guelph, and pests they are, turn out to be English drunkards. From the brochure *A Statement of the Satisfactory Results which have attended Emigration to Upper Canada, from the establishment of the Canada Company.* 5th ed. London, 1846.

The Canadian Agricultural Reader, designed mainly as a school text, was compiled by officers of the Niagara District Agricultural Society.

> Farmers often suffer much at this season [March] from wet feet; we therefore request leave to recommend them to the following India rubber application:
>
> Melt one pound of tallow in an iron kettle, add from four to six ounces of India rubber cut small, and heat the melted tallow until the India rubber in it is dissolved. It will then be fit for greasing boots and shoes, and will render them perfectly impervious to water, though in it all day. During the preparation of this mixture it will boil up in foam, and send off copious pungent fumes, but this does not injure it. One-twentieth part of beeswax improves it. Old worn out India rubber over-shoes may be used in the manufacture. . . .
>
> Mowing is one of the most laborious parts of the husbandman's calling, and the more fatiguing as it must be performed in the hottest season of the year. The mower [should] rise very early, and be at his work before the rising of the sun. He may easily perform half the usual day's work before nine in the morning. His work will not only be made easier by the coolness of the morning air, but also by the dew on the grass, which is cut the more easily for being wet. By this means he will lie and rest himself during all the hottest of the day, while others who began late are sweating themselves excessively, and hurting their health,

probably, by taking down large draughts of cold drink to slake their raging thirst. The other half of the work may be performed after three or four o'clock, and at night he will find himself free from fatigue. If the mower would husband his strength to advantage, he should take care to have his scythe, and all the apparatus for mowing, in the best order. . . .

To prevent horses being teased with flies, take two or three handfuls of walnut leaves, upon which pour two or three pints of soft and cold water — let it infuse one night, and let it boil a quarter of an hour — when cold it will be fit to use. No more is required than to moisten a sponge, and before the horse goes out of the stable let those parts which are most irritable be smeared over with the liquor, viz: between and upon the ears, the flank, etc. *The Canadian Agricultural Reader.* Niagara, 1845.

About an isolated farm in the Niagara district R. G. A. Levine wrote:

It would have astonished an inhabitant of the old world not a little to see a door open every evening at sun-down, and a pair of oxen yoked to a huge piece of magnificent oak timber, which would square between three and four feet, and drag it bodily into the middle of the habitation; when, detaching it from the chains, our host and his brother rolled the log into the back of the grate with hand-spikes (the said grate comprising the whole length of one end of the hut), where it would burn for four-and-twenty hours, when the same operation would again be repeated. Our host had no means of getting any sale for his timber, and therefore the sooner it was got rid of (by fire) the sooner his land would be cleared. R. G. A. Levigne. *Echoes from the Backwoods; or Sketches of Transatlantic Life.* 2 vols. London, 1846.

Thomas H. James regarded Americans as drunken criminals and advised emigrants from England and Scotland to avoid the United States where taxes were high, clothing dear, produce very low and nothing to welcome the settler but fever and ague and the "constant nuisance of Yankee swindling and Yankee swagger." James added, "No, no, Canada is the place; a thousand times preferable to the United States for the farming emigrant." But, he warned, there were already in Canada too many Irish "fond of lingering about the towns and taking their chance of picking up a living round the taverns and drinking-houses."

James recommended Upper Canada:

Although the cold is severe, and the winter long they consider it Italy itself as compared with the Quebec country, where a pail of water, in less than an hour, is converted into a solid lump of ice the shape of the pail, without a drop of moisture remaining; and the milk is brought to market in bags and sacks, every separate block of milk being scribed with a knife or a nail to mark the price; whilst the half-finished tumblers of brandy and water, left on the tavern tables overnight, are all solid ice the following morning!

A great many rich people in Toronto were living on their fortunes

and in the winter season the military and better classes of the inhabitants keep up a constant round of visits and festivities. Everything is English, whilst the spacious streets, substantial houses, and handsome stores, make it preferable to even Rochester or Albany. Thomas H. James. *Rambles in the United States and Canada during the year 1845*. London, 1846.

Sir Francis B. Head was lieutenant-governor of Upper Canada for three turbulent years, 1836 to 1838.

In riding through the forest I often passed deserted log-huts, standing in the middle of what is called "cleared land" — that is to say, the enormous pine trees of the surrounding forest had been chopped down to stumps about a yard high, around which there had rushed up a luxurious growth of hard brushwood, the height of which denoted that several years must have elapsed since the tenants had retired.

There was something which I always felt to be deeply affecting in passing these little monuments of the failure of human expectations — of the blight of human hopes.

The courage that had been evinced in settling in the heart of the wilderness, and the amount of labour that had been expended in cutting down so many large trees, had all ended in disappointment, and occasionally in sorrows of the severest description. The arm that had wielded the axe had perhaps become gradually enervated by ague (which always ungratefully rises out of cleared ground), until death had slowly terminated the existence of the poor emigrant, leaving a broken-hearted woman and a helpless family with nothing to look to for support but the clear bright blue heavens above them.

In many of the spots I passed, I ascertained that these dispensations of Providence had been as sudden as they were awful. The emigrant had arisen in robust health — surrounded by his numerous and happy family, had partaken of a homely breakfast — had left his log-hut with a firm step, and with manly pride had again resumed his attack upon the wilderness, through which every blow of his axe, like the tick of a clock, recorded the steady progress of the hand that belonged to it. But at the hour of dinner he did not return. The wife waited — bid her rosy-faced children be patient — waited — felt anxious — alarmed — stepped beyond the threshhold of her log-hut — listened: the axe was not at work. Excepting that indescribable aeolian murmur which the air makes in passing through the stems and branches of the forest, not a sound was to be heard. Her heart misgives her; she walks — runs towards the spot where she knew her husband to have been at work. She finds him, without his jacket or neckcloth, lying, with extended arms, on his back, cold, and crushed to death by the last tree he had felled, which in falling, jumping from its stump, had knocked him down, and which is now resting with its whole weight upon his bared breast. Sir Francis B. Head. *The Emigrant.* 2d ed. London, 1846.

Wheat was really the only cash crop.

During the winter months innumerable visits and distant excursions are made to the most remote of the Canadian settlements; and, as the people are exceedingly hospitable, this may be termed quite "the season" in Canada. . . . As the rivers and small lakes of Canada are all frozen over during the winter months, by far the best roads are made upon their surfaces; and, considering the vast number of persons and vehicles that are continually running, it is astonishing that more accidents do not occur.

As a matter of course all agricultural pursuits are suspended during the continuance of the frost; and yet the farmer is by no means idle: this is his time for cleaving, chopping, and drawing home his firewood, thrashing out his grain and bringing his produce to market, and, over and above this, his cattle require great attention during the cold weather. . . .

Wheat is really the only crop upon which the farmer calculates as a means of bringing in cash — in all other articles of produce barter is resorted to; but in wheat nobody ever thinks of buying or selling except for ready money, so that a farm incapable of producing this grain is almost valueless. . . .

The Lower Canadian horse is a remarkable animal — thick, short, and amazingly strong; whilst little more than half the ordinary food is required to keep him in excellent condition.

No animal, however, is so indispensably necessary as the ox; the driver obtains the most perfect mastery over them, stubborn and stupid though they be; and the very slowness of their motion constitutes their excellence. When ploughing is required on newly-cleared land, a yoke of oxen can be driven round the stumps without sustaining the slightest injury, while horses would be maimed and become perfectly useless. . . .

As for the pigs, they are not only of a wretched appearance, but of a very ferocious nature. The author can well remember the fear of a beautiful dog in traversing the woods in constant danger from troops of these half-wild animals. Rev. G. W. Warr. *Canada As It Is; or, the Emigrant's Friend and Guide to Upper Canada*. 2d ed. London, 1847.

William Brown was a Leeds clothier who wrote in greater detail about backwoods life than about town society:

In the back woods the settlers breed large quantities of hogs, which they turn out into the woods as soon as the snow is gone, and there they wander many miles from home in the forest during the whole summer; but as soon as the snow again covers the land they find their way back to the place where they were bred, or at least as many of them as are left, for many casualties arise by disease and the wolves; but generally a fair proportion comes back, and a good many more than the farmer calculated upon, as many of the sows will have had young ones; so that a settler never knows to a certainty the number of hogs he is possessed of. The hogs of one year old will, when they return home, have become quite fat with eating the nuts, acorns, and beechmast, as well as the roots found in the ground; and the farmer will immediately commence killing some for present use, and also for barrelling; but the greater part he will put up and commence feeding them with milk and Indian corn, or any other grain he may have produced, till near Christmas, and then commences slaughtering. Some he barrels, and the remainder he takes in carcases to market. . . .

At night, in travelling through the bush, you are much amused by the various sounds you hear; the forest and the swamp seem to be all alive; and the singing of the tree toads, whistling of the frogs, with the chirping of the locusts, and the thorough bass of the bull frog, is a concert which once heard a man does not soon forget. Then there is the whip-poor-will, a night bird flying about you and pronouncing its name as plainly as you can do it yourself. . . . A low swampy tract seems at first sight to be filled with small shooting stars: these are the fire flies which are so numerous that you may see thousands at any moment, and if you take a few and keep them under a tumbler glass, they will give as much light as a small candle. . . .

The saw mill which I occupied was situated in the township of Scarborough upon the creek called the Rouge River, and being the last waterfall nearest the lake, the situation was very subject to summer and autumn complaints; that is, to diarrhoea and fever ague. The first we kept down by a medicine composed of tincture of rhubarb and tincture of cinnamon, each half an ounce, and about sixteen drops of laudanum to each adult person, given all in one dose. . . . For the fever ague I prescribed a strong dose of horse radish, fermented for one night in cider, a tumbler full at one dose. . . . We never had a case so bad that we had occasion to call in any medical man. William Brown. *America: A Four Years' Residence in the United States and Canada*. Leeds, 1849.

The original snake-oil:

> My respectable old friend, T. MacConnell, the trapper, told me, that he was in the habit of visiting Niagara for the purpose of killing the rattle-snakes for the sake of their fat, and that he has sometimes killed three hundred in a season, and thus: — he watched beside a ledge of rocks where their holes were, and stood behind a tree, club in hand, and with his legs cased in sheep skins with the wool on, to guard against bites. The snakes would come out cautiously to seek on account of food or to sun themselves, fearing to go far for their enemies, the pigs. The trapper would then rush forward and lay about him with his club, those which escaped to their holes he seized by the tail, and if they turned round and bit him in the hand, he would spit some snake-root (which he kept chewing in his mouth) on the wound, it frothed up and danger would cease. The dead snakes were then roasted, hung up by the tail, over a slow fire, and their fat collected, taking care there was no blood in it. The fat would sell for twelve dollars a bottle, and was considered of great value by the country people in cases of rheumatism and stiff joints.
> Sir James E. Alexander. *L'Acadie; or, Seven Years' Exploration in British America*. 2 vols. London, 1849.

Few people saw more of Canada in his day than John Bigsby. He was secretary of the British section of the International Boundary Commission, which surveyed the Canada-U.S. border from the St. Lawrence near Cornwall to Lake of the Woods. Here he reports on a rattlesnake hunt near Amherstburg:

> We put on strong boots, reaching nearly to the knees, and thick pantaloons. We therefore did not fear a bite. As to our weapon of offence, we had a long elastic switch.
> We landed on a field of long grass, twenty or thirty acres in extent, and found mowers at work, defended by pieces of blanket tied round their legs. They said they had seen several rattlesnakes in the course of the morning, and we were not long in finding six — three among the long grass, and three among some fallen timber. We had the pleasure (such as it was) of several runs, and of hearing the dread rattle in full force. We killed two, each more than a yard long.
> Amherstburgh is famous for rattlesnakes. Dr. N. told me that a few months before, one of the children (aged six years) of an officer was bitten. The usual symptoms set in with severity. He used all the known remedies assiduously, external and internal, but the child only grew

worse. As its life was now despaired of, the parents sent for an old Indian woman with the medical man's full concurrence. After having looked upon the child she hastened into the woods, and returned with some rattlesnake root (*Goodyera pubescens*). Of part of the leaves she made an infusion, of which she caused the child to swallow doses at certain intervals, and of part she made a poultice, which she applied to the wound. The child soon began to improve; one by one the symptoms disappeared, and in forty-eight hours the little sufferer was out of danger. This is a well-authenticated case, and very remarkable. John J. Bigsby, M.D. *The Shoe and Canoe or Pictures of Travel in the Canadas*. 2 vols. London, 1850.

W. H. Smith liked French pears.

In the year 1752, two ships laden with Canadian wheat arrived at Marseilles; this was probably the first grain sent from the Colony. . . .

About two miles below Windsor, after a pleasant walk or drive, you reach the pretty little town of Sandwich [which] is one of the oldest settlements in Canada, the neighbourhood having been originally settled by disbanded French soldiers. The immense pear trees in the orchards about the town give sufficient evidence of its antiquity (for a new country). . . .

On the first discovery of Canada, by the French, the only vegetable cultivated by the natives was maize or Indian corn, a plant indigenous to the south-western portion of the continent. The conquerors brought with them, from the old world, such of the cereal and other vegetables as were in use in those days, with fruit trees. The French have always been celebrated for the excellent quality of their pears, and, even in the present day, trees of large size, descendants of those originally conveyed across the Atlantic, ornament the banks of the Detroit River, from Windsor to Amherstburg. W. H. Smith. *Canada: Past, Present and Future*. 2 vols. Toronto, 1852.

The *Canadian Journal's* review of the provincial agricultural exhibition at Toronto from September 21 to 24, 1852, included a look at new farm machinery. But the paint seemed more important than the gears:

A Threshing Machine and Horse-power by Medcalf of Toronto appears to leave but little to desire in this class of implements; the arrangement and character of workmanship is equal to anything we have seen. We much regretted the bad taste which induced the attempt at ornamental (daubing?) painting displayed on this excellent piece of mechanism; the real wood or plain white colours always look appropriate, while the wretched attempts which are sometimes made at imitating a mahogany panel on a Fanning Mill, with perhaps satinwood framing and rosewood mouldings, are truly distressing; in equally bad taste we noticed some Farm Waggons bedaubed with all the colours of the rainbow. Commend to us the mechanic whose work will bear inspection without such wretched aid. How well the natural grain of the tough ash, hickory, and oak, of some of the American machines contrasted with the gaudy colours of our own. *The Canadian Journal, a Repertory of Industry, Science, and Art.* Toronto, Upper Canada, October, 1852.

Anna Brownell Jameson was in Canada only nine months and complained frequently about the ignorance and vulgarity of backwoods life.

I have not often in my life met with contented and cheerful-minded women, but I never met with so many repining and discontented women as in Canada. I never met with *one* woman recently settled here who considered herself happy in her new home and country. . . . I find the women of the better class lamenting over the want of all society, except of the lowest grade in manners and morals. For those who have recently emigrated, and are settled more in the interior, there is absolutely no social intercourse whatever; it is quite out of the question. They seem to me to be perishing of ennui . . . for being in general unfitted for out-door occupations, unable to comprehend or enter into the interests around them, and all their earliest prejudices and ideas of the fitness of things continually outraged in a manner exceedingly unpleasant, they may be said to live in a perpetual state of inward passive discord and fretful endurance.

Mrs. Jameson grasped the pioneer's attitude toward the forest:

A Canadian settler *hates* a tree, regards it as his natural enemy, as something to be destroyed, eradicated, annihilated by all and any means. The idea of useful or ornamental is seldom associated here even with the most magnificent timber trees. Anna Brownell Jameson. *Sketches in Canada, and Rambles among the Red Men.* New ed. London, 1852.

Robert McVicar, a farmer at Norval, near Toronto, spent a lot of time and effort trying to persuade the authorities to relax immigration laws and provide poor immigrants with credit to buy land. The poor were compelled to seek daily labour "at such wages as any one chooses to give them on the absence of the land which was their sole object before leaving home." McVicar said in a submission to Governor-General Sir Charles Metcalfe on April 29, 1843:

Heads of Families with their tender babes flocking around, enquiring of their parents, at every post they arrive, where was their future home, or how far was it yet away? What must be the feelings of the poor parents when unable to reply, post after post is passed and yet perhaps no employment, night after night passes away during which they sleep on the decks of crowded steamboats or in the hold of crowded barges without changing clothes for weeks and are finally landed somewhere to take up their lodgings generally in immigration sheds, much crowded and full of disease, where they remain until employment is found for them. Robert McVicar. *Letters on Emigration from the British Isles and the Settlement of Waste Lands in the Province of Canada*. Hamilton, 1853.

What a difference seven years makes!

Those who have been in the habit of passing early clearings in Upper Canada must have been struck with the cheerless and lonely, even desolate, appearance of the first settler's little log hut.

In the midst of a dense forest, and with a "patch of clearing" scarcely large enough to let the sun shine in upon him, he looks not unlike a person struggling for existence on a single plank in the middle of an ocean. For weeks, often months, he sees not the face of a stranger. The same still, wild and boundless forest every morning rises up to his view; and his only hope against its shutting him in for life rests in the axe upon his shoulder. A few blades of corn peeping up between stumps whose very roots interlace, they are so close together, are his sole safeguards against want; whilst the few potato plants, in the little far-between "hills," and which struggle for existence against the briar bush and luxuriant underwood, are to form the seeds of his future plenty. Tall pine trees, girdled and blackened by the fires, stand out as grim monuments of the prevailing loneliness, whilst the forest itself, like an immense wall round a fortress, seems to say to the settler, "how can poverty ever expect to escape from such a prison house. . . ."

Seven years afterwards I passed that same settler's cottage — it was in the valley of the Grand River in Upper Canada, not far from the present Village of Caledonia. The little log hut was used as a back kitchen to a neat two-storey frame house, painted white. A large barn stood near by, with stock of every description within its yard. The stumps, round which the blades of corn, when I last saw the place, had so much difficulty in springing up, had nearly all disappeared. Luxuriant Indian corn had sole possession of the place where the potatoes had so hard a struggle against the briar bushes and the underwood. The forest — dense, impenetrable though it seemed — had been pushed far back by the energetic arm of man. A garden, bright with flowers, and enclosed in a neat picket fence, fronted the house; a young orchard spread out in rear. . . .

Were I asked what is the leading characteristic of the Upper Canadian farmer, I should unquestionably answer: plenty. Plenty reigns in his granary, plenty is exhibited in his farm yard, plenty gleams from his corn fields, and plenty smiles in the faces of his children. But let it not be imagined that this plenty is gained without continuous labour, and the exercise of judgment and intelligence.

The author made a comparison between farmers of Upper and Lower Canada:

No persons can contrast more strongly than the habitant of Lower Canada and the farmer of Upper. The latter is enterprising, adventurous, and cosmopolitan in his feelings. He is always ready to change his neighbourhood for a better one; and his homestead of a hundred acres of cleared land is never more dear to him than five hundred acres of wilderness, if he can satisfy himself that the latter would be better for his children.

The habitant, on the contrary, knows no love stronger than that for the place where he was born, though giving him, in many cases, but a slender livelihood. In vain for him has the magnificent West been opened up, in vain for him have America and Europe been filled with accounts of prosperity in it. His dreams hover around his own fireside. His imagination is bounded by the fences round his farm. He asks no better lot than to live where his father lived, and to die where his father died. . . . There is not a more cheerful, happy and contented being in existence than the Lower Canadian habitant. His little farm — for, as a general rule, on account of frequent subdivisions, the farms in Lower Canada are small — supplies him with enough to live upon; and he never by any chance invokes the cares of tomorrow. He has five or six cows, and he knows they should give milk enough for himself and his family, and he never gives himself anxiety about the economy of increasing their number or improving their quality. He has six or eight pigs, and instead of fattening two or three for market — as an [Upper Canadian] would be sure to do — he takes the blessings of Heaven as they are sent to him, and eats the whole of them. He copies no man's improvement, and imitates no person's mode of living. J. Sheridan Hogan. *Canada: An Essay*. Montreal, 1855.

John Lynch, a Brampton farmer, won Board of Agriculture prizes for his essays on farming in Peel, Simcoe, Grey and Bruce Counties. His report on Grey County contained an admirable summary of how to carve out a farm in the bush. He advised, first, a £50 expenditure for a yoke of oxen, yoke, logging chain, drag, two cows, a couple of pigs and one year's provisions. A similar amount should be on hand for building of house and sheds, hiring help for chopping and logging and "contingencies."

The best time for entering upon new land is in the latter part of the winter. Your attention must of course first be directed to building a house; but you must not neglect to chop and clear at least two or three acres, by or before the first of June, for potatoes, Indian corn, and turnips — though the turnip ground will do a month or six weeks later; these are the crops that thrive best on new ground, and make the quickest return. They will also be found very useful, not only for yourself and family, but for feeding your cattle the following winter. Plant pumpkins with the corn. You should also prepare a good vegetable garden, which will be found of great service. Many kinds of garden vegetables, as cucumbers, melons, etc., thrive best on new ground. To plant your potatoes, you should get a strong heavy hoe, made for the purpose; with this hoe, which should be kept almost as sharp as your axe, you can cut most of the surface roots, and cover your potatoes in large hills; they will then need no hoeing, or any more care or trouble until they are ready to dig. As soon as your spring crop is in the ground, you must proceed to chop a "fallow" for fall wheat. Consider well the number of acres you will be able to prepare in time for seeding. Do not undertake more than you can see your way clear to complete in due time, and in good order; and having resolved on the quantity, and measured, and marked it out, let nothing divert you from completing it. This chopping should be completed by the first, or at the latest, the second week in July. It will then have four or five weeks of hot sun to dry the brush, and prepare it for burning. June is the best month for chopping for fall wheat. The roots in land, chopped in June, rot sooner, and do not sprout nearly so much as when the chopping is done in the winter. You should take this opportunity, while your brush is drying, to finish off your dwelling house. The description of your house, will, of course, depend much on the state of your finances; but if you have from fifteen to twenty pounds to appropriate for that purpose, besides your own labor, you can build a very good log-house, in which you can live comfortably for many years.

Towards the latter end of July, you should look out for a dry time to burn your brush. Getting a "good burn" will much facilitate the after clearing of your land, and also leave it in a much better condition for receiving the seed. I hope you have been careful, when chopping, to heap your brush properly, for on that, in a great measure, will depend your prospect of a good burn. If you have no boys, or other constant assistants, you must hire a couple of men for "logging," or else change work with some of your neighbors, for you cannot log with advantage alone. You should have your ground logged and burned, and fully cleared so as to have your seed sown and harrowed by the 10th of September. Sow timothy and clover seed, and dray it in with the last stroke of the harrow. You have not neglected to sow grass seeds with your turnips? If you do not sell your ashes, you should spread them over the ground, before sowing. If your land is clay soil, and generally level or low, there is one thing you should particularly attend to, which is too often neglected, that is to drain it well. Many people think new land does not need draining, and cannot be drained for the roots, but this is a mistake. There will be slight swails, and troughs or hollow places in your land, which may appear quite dry in seed time, but which the next spring will be covered with water, and will completely destroy, not only your wheat, but your grass. Immediately after seeding, before the wheat has time to sprout, you should cut drains along the deepest part of all those hollows, with branches, or lateral drains, where they may be required; about one foot in depth, and as much in breadth, at the top, cutting through roots and everything. This will be no trifling job, if there is much length of those hollows; but you will find it to pay you well for your labor. With a spade, an old axe, and your big potato hoe, you will go over a considerable distance in a day. Spread the earth you take from the ditch, as far as possible, over the ground on each side, and you will probably have the best wheat along that ditch, where, without it, you would have nothing but weeds.

After your wheat is sown and fenced, you will attend to harvesting your corn, potatoes, and turnips, and also make preparations for building a log-barn, and stables, or sheds, for your cattle. Your cattle will have to depend for food, the first winter, chiefly on "brouse," and they will do very well on it, with care, and an occasional feed of corn-stalks and turnips. The next winter, you will have plenty of straw for them, and a little hay from the turnip ground.

The last thing you have to do before the snow falls, is to "under-brush" as much ground as you intend to chop during the winter; as when there is much snow on the ground, you cannot cut the under-brush close to the ground. As you will not have much other work the first winter, you should not only chop what will be required for your spring crop, but something towards your summer fallow for fall wheat. If you have a good "sugar-bush," you should prepare a sufficient number of sap-troughs, of pine timber, if you can get it; but failing that, black ash is the next best. In the second spring, in addition to your potatoes, turnips, and corn, you should clear and sow a few acres of oats, not forgetting to sow grass seeds with it. You can also sow oats, or barley and grass, on the ground which was last year in potatoes, and plant potatoes on your corn ground of the last year.

You will then proceed, as in the preceding year, except that your time will not be so much occupied with building, and in consequence you will be able to put in a larger quantity of fall wheat. John Lynch. "Report of the State of Agriculture in the County of Grey — 1853," *Journal and Transactions of the Board of Agriculture of Upper Canada.* Vol. 1. Toronto, 1856.

Jacob Bingham was the author of an essay on ploughs in 1856. Bingham not only wrote about ploughs. He developed improvements, and his plough was one of three selected to represent Canada in the 1855 Paris Exposition.

Some ploughmen are in the habit of leaning the plough over to the left, the plough thereby cutting less land than when made to run on the flat of the sole; and to overcome this, the draught is shifted to the right, in order to make the plough cut its proper width. Leaning the plough much to the left is a bad custom, because it makes the lowest edge of the furrow slice, when turned over, thinner than the upper edge, which is exposed to view, thereby inducing the delusion that the land has all been ploughed of equal depth. Old ploughmen are too apt to practice this deceptive mode of ploughing. Jacob Bingham: *A Practical Essay on the Plough.* Toronto, 1856.

Writing from a farm near St. Thomas, John Shaw said:

From the great influx of uneducated immigrants, English and foreign, the well-bred settler has frequently the hard task of submitting to the humiliating contact of these would-be great people, who, having suddenly left potatoe diet, and naturally finding themselves rapidly elevated to the dignity of "Lords of the Soil," with a carriage and pair to boot (for all appear to ride in that vehicle, inasmuch as it carries corn to the market at the same time, and possesses also some of the qualities of the light waggon, drawn by an active pair of horses), fancy it is now their turn to play the part of Lord and Esquire; and, unfortunately, having neither education nor manners, the contact, conversation, and demeanour of these gentlemen cannot fail in rendering them not very agreeable to persons of good breeding.

Of the bar room of his London, Canada West, hotel:

I am sorry to say that occasionally the sons of gentlemen are to be seen drinking with those who, in the Old Country, would be keeping at a respectful distance, or probably grooming their horses, or blacking the boots of those who have to submit to the humiliation of being taken by the hand and forced, by the democratic spirit that prevails here, to submit to be treated as equals, who, from their manner and bearing, would look much better in the stable or behind a table in the capacity of groom or waiter. John Shaw, M. D. *A Ramble through the United States, Canada, and the West Indies.* London, 1856.

Professor George Buckland, secretary of the Board of Agriculture, was struck by "live fences" (hedges) in the Beaver Dam settlement in Thorold Township:

Mr. Ash has an English thorn hedge, which appeared to be thriving. Mr. Russel has also a hedge of considerable extent, a portion consisting of American thorn in a very growing state, the rest is made of locust, which is inferior. These hedges did not appear to have suffered from the depredations of mice which have proved so disastrous to young fruit trees in particular during the peculiarly inclement season of last winter. The subject of live hedges is beginning to engage the attention of farmers in this country, as well as in others of early settlement. As yet experience . . . has not been sufficiently extended to lead to positive conclusions as to what particular materials are the best for making live fences. Although I have seen a few instances of the ordinary English hawthorn looking healthy and promising, yet I am strongly inclined to the opinion, from all that I have observed and heard, that our own native thorn, when properly treated, will answer better. Hedges, like fruit trees or the ordinary crops of the farm, require, and will amply repay, all the rational treatment and care that can be bestowed on them. George Buckland. "An Agricultural Tour of Welland County," *The Canadian Agriculturist.* Toronto, October 1856.

Robert Russell, a Scottish farmer, didn't think much of most Canadian cities: "Traffic in some of the wide streets [of Kingston] is not sufficient to prevent the grasses from springing up"; and Bytown (Ottawa) was "dirty and disagreeable" and its hotel bar rooms "full of rude drunken fellows."

But he found it different at London, where he attended the Upper Canada agricultural exhibition on September 27, 1854:

This was the chief day of the show and about 40,000 persons were on the grounds. I was quite surprised to see so many fine specimens of cattle, sheep, horses, and pigs. . . . Among the implements, that were in great variety, the machines for mowing grass attracted considerable attention, and many parties who had used them spoke favourably of them. Indeed, several of the makers said the demand was greater than could in the meantime be supplied. Two different machines were on the ground for cutting, and at the same time planting, potatoes. A machine for paring apples did its work amazingly well. There was an endless variety of ploughs and scarifiers.

The display of fruit and vegetables was particularly fine, while the apples and peaches were truly splendid. Carrots and parsnips were of large size, the former especially thriving well in Canada. There were a large number of pumpkins, which were curious specimens of the vegetable tribe. Four of them shown by one exhibitor weighed 180, 150, 148, and 112 pounds. The pumpkin is used for feeding cattle in autumn and early winter, but it does not keep long, and its seeds have an injurious action on the kidneys when cattle are fed long upon them. . . .

Besides the articles which have been enumerated, everything that enters into the domestic economy of the Canadian farmer has a premium awarded to it if the judges think it worthy of one. Numbers of booths were erected over the grounds — in some were pictures, pianos, and needle-work in great variety; in others, dogs, rabbits, and poultry. About £2000 were expended in prizes; of this sum the provincial government gave about one half, and the other half was subscribed by the local societies. Nothing can be better calculated to stimulate agricultural improvement than the provincial shows. The best breeds of cattle are brought together, and all who attend have an opportunity of seeing first-class animals, which stirs up emulation.

Robert Russell. *North America: Its Agriculture and Climate*. Edinburgh, 1857.

The ninety-nine-mile Opeongo Road in the upper Ottawa Valley was built to encourage colonization:

One hundred acres will be given FREE to any settler, 18 years of age, who shall take possession of the Lot within one month from the date of his application, erect on it a house, 18 by 20 feet, put in a state of cultivation at least 12 acres in the course of four years, and live on the Lot during that period. . . . As the Canadian Government do not wish to lay claim to more liberality than they actually possess, or to have their generosity undeservedly extolled, and have, moreover, no desire to encourage emigration to this Colony by sanctioning fancy sketches of rural felicity, or by permitting hopes of prosperity that cannot be completely realized to be held out, he [the writer] deems it incumbent on him to remind all who may be disposed to emigrate to this country, that they must not estimate the value of land here by the standard that obtains in the parent kingdom. . . .

The soil in this part of the Province is a sandy loam, in some places light, but in others deep and rich. . . . Few of the very highest hills are incapable of cultivation, and it is strange that the best soil is not unfrequently found on their summits. A good deal of rock and loose surface-stone is also met with, and while it must not be denied that they often prove a source of much annoyance to the farmer, yet they do not prevent the proper cultivation of the land, nor form any great obstacles to the raising of excellent crops. T. P. French. *Information for Intending Settlers on the Ottawa and Opeongo Road, And its Vicinity.* Ottawa, 1857.

Albert Smallfield, editor of *The Renfrew Mercury*, was one of the few writers of brochures who did not describe his district as a garden of Eden. He starts out by saying that the farms of his Ottawa Valley county are cut-over remains of the lumber barons:

> Lumbering until recent years was the principal industry in the County. As the forests, bordering on the rivers, have gradually receded further northward and westward before the lumberman's axe, the townships "in the front" have been converted into farms: and the lumbermen's principal "limits" are mostly from 50 to 100 miles back into the interior.

Immigrants from Britain had gone mainly to western Upper Canada where the land was more level and freer from rock, and the climate milder. By 1850, settlement had extended scarcely more than twenty miles north of Lake Ontario and, westerly from the Ottawa River, even less. Government agents had attracted immigrants with glowing but largely untrue accounts of Ottawa Valley lands: there was the "greatest possible difference between promises and prospects held out and the reality." Roads were bad, work hard and markets far away. Many settlers had abandoned their clearings and gone on relief.

However, Smallfield said, there had been recent improvements in the Opeongo colonization road crossing Renfrew County, and crops in 1880 had been splendid. Why go west? he asked. Many Renfrew County farmers had visited the west and

> they return home satisfied that this is just as good a country, with an equally good climate and a settled state of society: and they are not disposed to break up all their present associations, and fly to the West — perhaps to be blown away in a whirlwind — not knowing where to locate to the best advantage — or to pitch down haphazard on the prairies where, as far as the eye can reach, nothing can be seen but the vast broad, level plain touching the horizon. Albert Smallfield. *Lands and Resources of Renfrew County, Province of Ontario.* Renfrew, 1881.

Joshua Fraser's *Shanty, Forest and River Life* is best known for its vivid description of life in the lumber camps of the Ottawa Valley. But it is also highly critical of the Canadian government for inducing settlers to try to farm rocky and sterile land, known as rock farming. Not only were thousands of acres of timber cut down and burned in land clearing, but the settlers inadvertently caused forest fires, which resulted in enormous losses.

> Not one-fourth of even the cleared land of the Ottawa valley is fit for cultivation, and many put it at a much lower proportion. . . . It is pitiful to think of the incalculable amount of capital of every kind, intelligence, labor and money, both public and private, that have been absolutely wasted in this region. No greater mistake was ever made in political economy than the attempt to open up and colonize this country with the view of developing its agricultural resources. . . .
>
> There are some of the saddest histories in connection with experiences of this kind that have ever been written. Histories of long years of patient waiting, of hard toiling, of menial drudging, of privation, sickness and absolute want; and after all was done and endured, to find that they might as well have thrown their money and labor into the Ottawa [River] as far as any substantial fruit or return was realized. Joshua Fraser. *Shanty, Forest and River Life in the Backwoods of Canada*. Montreal, 1883.

James Anderson was editor of *The Canadian Farmers' Journal* and had been imperial drainage commissioner in Scotland. Like John Young in Nova Scotia and William Evans in Lower Canada, he was prone to preaching as well as teaching:

> There are some — the foolish and unthinking — who hold many pursuits more honourable than Agriculture — but he who is daily and hourly cheered with lights and life flowing from the fountain of true happiness, can well afford to disregard such disparaging opinions and forget their babbling — whilst he listens with native rapture to the merry songsters around him — making the hills to rejoice, and gladdening the valleys with their melody.
>
> The farmer is placed beyond the vulgar temptations of the city. He lives frugally — it may be — but comfortably, and in independence . . . and when called on to bid adieu to the fields and scenes he so fondly loved, he rejoices in the prospect of rejoining his departed neighbours, who valued him while they lived as a friend and a brother.

Anderson is at pains to outline ways of getting an agricultural education and gives the curriculum for the two-year Bachelor of Agriculture course at University College, Toronto, under Professor George Buckland.

Subjects of Lectures:

I — History of the Art.

(a) Agriculture, as understood and practised by the ancients.

(b) Agriculture during the Middle Ages.

(c) Modern Agriculture.

II — The Science of Agriculture

(a) Soils: their origin, composition, distribution, classification, etc.

(b) Plants: their structure, composition, growth, etc. Manures theory, action and relative value of; modes of preparing, applying, and economizing.

(c) The domesticated animals of the farm; history and description of varieties or breeds; the principles of breeding; diseases and treatment.

(d) Influence of climate on agricultural productions, both animal and vegetable.

III — The Practice of Agriculture

(a) Methods of acquiring a practical knowledge of farming. Importance of an agricultural literature.

(b) Principles of cultivation; instruments of tillage.

(c) Draining; subsoil ploughing; fallowing; rotation of crops.

(d) History, cultivation, and economic uses of the various grains, roots, etc., raised on the farm; weeds; blights and their remedies; harvesting and securing crops.

(e) The practice of manuring, and the means of restoring exhausted land; management of pasture, irrigation, etc.

(f) The management of stock, and the construction and arrangement of farm buildings.

(g) Dairy management; butter and cheese-making, etc.

(h) Management of landed property; principles of the lease theory of rent; relations of Political Economy to rural affairs.

(i) Agriculture as a pursuit; economic importance of; its place in a system of general education; tendency to foster feelings of patriotism, etc.

N.B. Instructions are regularly given on the Experimental Grounds attached to the College, illustrating the principles of practice with science.

(Books of reference — Stephens' Farmer's Guide; London Encyclopedia of Agriculture; Morton's ditto; Johnston's Elements of Agriculture Chemistry and Geology; Boussingault's Rural Economy; Low's Practical Agriculture, and Domesticated Animals.

James Anderson. *The Improvement of Agriculture and the Elevation in the Social Scale of Both Husbandman and Operative.* Montreal, 1858.

Anderson said the student body numbered between ten and twenty.

The first agricultural college in Canada was founded by Bishop Laval at Cap Tourmente, near Quebec City, in 1668.

The view from a train window could be deceptive, according to Philip Kelland.

> The truth must be told, that hundreds of miles of railway travelling present the same uniform look-out of a foreground of blackened stump, backed by a dense forest at a few feet distance, with here and there a log hut and a clearing. . . . In many places, you do find a crop struggling with the charred remains of the forest, which stand in thick array, with their blackened arms, like a giant army of scarecrows, to protect the grain. And even where cultivation is of old standing, as between Toronto and Hamilton . . . the soil, if not naturally thin, gets little manure, and you encounter everywhere armies of the great mullein, and they, too, weeds as they are, look half starved. . . .
>
> Yet there is abundance of everything. Agriculture is improving, at any rate, in one essential particular — the substitution of machinery for manual labour. Reaping-machines are in great abundance, as are all kinds of agricultural implements. In such places as London, C. W., you see vast stores of them. Philip Kelland. *Transatlantic Sketches.* Edinburgh, 1858.

James Caird's book was not particularly harsh on Canadian agriculture; it rather praised highly the virtues and benefits of farming in Illinois. But it was enough to raise Canadian hackles because it was a Briton taking sides with an American state in the tug-of-war for British emigrants between the British North American colonies and the United States. Caird criss-crossed Illinois and his Canadian detractors accused him of being a bond-holder in, or at least a paid agent for, the Illinois Central Railroad.

Caird, a noted agriculturalist, had some favorable words about the Canadas. But, he said, the tide of British emigration was steadily westward to the open prairies because of the time and cost of clearing land in the Canadas. Cutting down the forest was "one of the most pleasing of out-of-door occupations" for a strong, healthy, young man, but the most you could expect after a year of hard work was "hog and hominy" (bacon and cornmeal). It was this last remark which infuriated Canadians and the 36-page pamphlet, published, apparently by the Canadian government (only the printer's name is given), in rebuttal to Caird, went to great lengths to show how well off a settler could be with only a few acres cleared.

The pamphlet said Caird was directly interested in selling in Illinois "wretched lands—tree-less, water-less, the very nursery of ague and fever." Canada presented a "wonderful contrast" to Caird's "arid wilderness" in Illinois.

Caird's book was "ungenerous," "untrue," and full of "gross errors" and "inconsistencies, exaggerations and falsehoods." His views on Canada had been based on two or three days of looking out train windows. James Caird. *Prairie Farming in America, with notes by the way on Canada and the United States*. New York, 1859; *Caird's Slanders on Canada Answered & Refuted!* Toronto, 1859.

Mrs. Edward Copleston favored thatching.

> A great and general defect in Canadian farming is in the art of securing the grain in mows or stacks, as well as hay, after the large barns are filled. Occasionally, as during the autumn of 1860, deluging rains fall, which would severely test the best thatching in the world. The straw here used for thatching has all been passed through the machine, and is therefore ill fitted for thatching purposes. Few farmers ever reserve any hand-threshed straw, and comb it into a reed, as at home, but those few are amply rewarded. . . .

> The American horse-rake is a most useful, ingenious, and economical machine, as patented in Canada West; it is made almost entirely of wood — consisting of a frame some twelve feet in width, mounted on wheels, with shafts; to this frame are attached twenty-four teeth, three feet or so in length, made of the hardest and toughest ash, strung upon an iron rod, so as to rise over any obstruction, and fall again immediately. The driver stands on the platform, and by the aid of a lever, on which he merely plants his foot and leans his weight, he raises the teeth off the ground, and they immediately drop the hay or grain, whenever he does so. About eight acres can be gone over with this rake in about half a day. After this, the land is so clean that when the hay waggon has left the field no litter is visible anywhere. This machine alone saves the labour of three or four hands in haying time . . . and it is quite light work for the horse that draws it. Mrs. Edward Copleston. *Canada: Why we Live in it, and Why we Like it*. London, 1861.

Mrs. Copleston adds that the horse-rake costs £4.

James Croil quotes a Scottish settler who came to Canada in 1845 with his wife and family and began share-cropping in eastern Upper Canada. After laying in provisions for the summer, he had five shillings left. The next year he rented a farm at £20 a year and stayed there three years, acquiring stock and implements. He then bought a 100-acre farm for £300, paying for it over six years. Forty acres had been cleared, and he and his sons cleared the other sixty in ten years. The farmer tells Croil:

> My farm is worth today in cash £1,000 and I am out of debt. The older boys have left home and are doing well for themselves; the two

are with me, and work the farm. We manage every thing ourselves" and employ no hired labor. My farm is the best lot I know of . . . 28 acres among the stumps are devoted to pasture, the remaining 72 are fenced off in 12 fields of six acres apiece. I adhere to a regular course of cropping and I attribute much of my success to my system of rotation. My crops of grain have been excellent.

I sow yearly 24 bushels of wheat upon 12 acres, and my average return has been 240 bushels. Of oats, I sow 12 acres, with three bushels per acre, which average me 30 bushels per acre. Of barley, 12 acres, which I sow at the rate of 2 1/4 bushels per acre. My returns vary from 35 to 50 bushels per acre. I sow three acres of peas, three bushels seed per acre, average 20 to 25 bushels per acre. Of corn and potatoes I plant six acres. The remaining 24 acres are in grass. . . .

The whole of the hay and straw, oats, peas, corn, and potatoes, are consumed on the premises, which secures me a large pile of manure. My wheat straw is all used for bedding, and I am thus enabled to manure 12 acres each year. I keep ten cows, four horses and a few sheep; I sell yearly about 140 bushels wheat, 360 of barley, and $100 worth of pork.

In summer time, we live upon bacon, beef, and pork hams, nicely cured and smoked, and fried with eggs, supplemented with cheese, bread, and butter, all home made, and of the best. In October we kill a beast. The blacksmith takes a quarter, the shoemaker another, the tailor or the carpenter a third, and ourselves the remaining one. In December, we kill a second, cut it up, freeze it, and pack it away in barrels in straw, where it will keep till the first of April. The hides go to the tanner, who takes one half of each, and gives me the other when tanned; the shoemaker comes to the house once a year and makes out of it boots and shoes for young and old. The tallow is rendered and made into candles, and all the refuse scraps at "killing time" are boiled up with lye, and converted into barrels of soap. And then the women folk spin the wool and weave the stockings, sew the quilts and counterpanes, and make the featherbeds, so that come what may we are always sure of a living. When a son or daughter is to be married, I sell a span of horses and a cow or two, give them a decent outfit and am none the poorer, as there are always young ones coming on to take their places.

Croil himself adds:

The greater part of the labor of the farm in Canada is performed by the farmer himself, his sons and his daughters, the former managing all the out of door operations, and the latter the dairy and domestic departments.

Herein lies the secret of the farmer's success. Whatever qualifications a farmer should have, mental or physical, all are agreed upon this point, that a good wife is indispensable. What it is the aim of the husband to accumulate, it becomes the province of the wife to manage, and wherever we hear of a managing wife, we are sure to find a money-making farmer. James Croil. *Dundas; or, A Sketch of Canadian History, and more particularly of the County of Dundas*. Montreal, 1861.

Formal religion often suffered in the backwoods.

Many of the Presbyterian settlers in the forest that I visited had not heard a sermon preached, some of them for nine years, others for seven, and many for five years. Their highest joy was when they were visited once and again with a Herald of the Gospel, who found his way through the forest, and over roads almost impassable, and collected a few families for the public worship of God, either in open log barns, log school houses, or dwelling houses, and instructed them in Gospel truth. J. Carruthers. *Retrospect of Thirty-Six Years' Residence in Canada West: being a Christian Journal and Narrative*. Hamilton, 1861.

Agricultural fairs were popular:

Collectively, the exhibitors [at the provincial agricultural fair] amounted to three hundred and eighty-two, and the entries to about two thousand. The aggregated total of prizes was one thousand five hundred and twenty pounds sterling, distributed in sums varying from one to sixty dollars. Of this sum thirteen hundred and ninety-six dollars were offered for horses; two thousand seven hundred and sixty-three dollars for cattle; twelve hundred and sixteen dollars for sheep; five hundred and four dollars for pigs; and two hundred dollars for poultry. . . . The number of prizes for paintings and water-colour drawings were reduced, although such an arrangement had not the effect of precluding rubbish from being obtruded upon public observation. . . . I trust such an execrable display of wry, graceless figures, hideous colouring, abominable grouping, and the entire absence of perspective will never again be permitted to the public eye. . . . I was informed that at antecedent exhibitions numerous works of Art — as they have been styled out of courtesy — received prizes that were utterly unworthy either of recognition or reward. . . .

[There were] drinking booths innumerable, where "cock-tails," "brandy-smashes," "Lager-beer," "John Collinses," and other potations were imbibed in immeasurable quantities. Samuel Phillips Day. *English America: or Pictures of Canadian Places and People*. 2 vols. London, 1864.

The Canada Farmer magazine, published by the estimable George Brown and edited by W.F. Clarke, was the successor to *The Canadian Agriculturist*, put out by George Buckland and William McDougall. The monthly *Agriculturist*, itself a successor to the *British-American Cultivator*, labored for a dozen years; the November, 1852, issue, for example, bore this announcement:

> To Our Subscribers: the delay in the publication of the present number of the *Agriculturist* has been occasioned by unavoidable circumstances; among them may be mentioned our having to wait for the paper being manufactured.

The 24-page *Agriculturist* started up in 1849 but the next year it had to discard advertisements as costing more to put into type than they brought in. Tighter typesetting saved space and the subscription price of $1 a year was cut by half for agricultural societies ordering copies in bulk. *The Canada Farmer* went to a larger format, which became the norm for most large-circulation magazines until well into the second half of the 20th century. In its lead article in its first issue, *The Canada Farmer* said:

> Settlers in a new country very generally wage a war of extermination against the "trees of the wood." They come to look upon them as natural enemies and cumberers of the ground, whose inevitable doom is to be cut down and cast into the fire. Since their removal is the first step toward making a farm out of the wilderness, they sweep them away as rapidly as possible. The consequence is, that many stretches of country have come to be nearly as bare as a Western prairie, on which no plant or shrub knee-high can be seen. A monotonous belt of woodland stretches away in the rear of the cleared portions of the farms through which the highways run, but beside that, scarcely a single tree or grove diversifies the scene. The wholesale destruction of the forests of Canada is an evil that begins, at least in many localities, to demand a check. Firewood grows scarce and dear, the landscape is becoming naked, it is difficult to procure timber suitable for various mechanical uses, the shelter needed by many crops in exposed situations is removed, and unfavorable climatic changes are taking place which can be clearly traced to the wholesale and indiscriminate destruction of timber. A little exercise of judgement, forethought and taste would mend matters very much. For example, why cannot some of the young wood be preserved when land is cleared, to form groups which shall at once ornament the landscape, furnish shade for stock when the scorching summer sun pours down its almost tropical rays, and act as a wind-break when cold and biting blasts sweep over the fields? *The Canada Farmer, a Fortnightly Journal of Agriculture, Horticulture and Rural Affairs.* Vol. 1, no. 1. Toronto, January 15, 1864.

W. F. Munro blessed the tavern keeper:

> One of the first institutions of a new country undergoing anything like rapid settlement is the tavern. The inference, however, is not that settlers as a class are more addicted to the use of drink than others. The tavern in Canada, especially in the backwoods, still bears something of its old English signification — it is a place of hospitable entertainment for man and beast and, as such, is one of the prime necessities of a new country, particularly in that season of the year when an hour's ride often reduces the caloric in the human system to a degree which renders the sight of a roaring fire, with a glass of "hot stuff," an almost indispensable condition of travelling. The man who has the courage to move into a new country in the course of settlement, taking with him a span of horses, or a yoke of oxen, with the material to set up a tavern — say some whiskey, brandy, flour and pork, is considered a sort of public benefactor, and if he keeps sober and minds his business there is no fear of his future. Let no one, therefore, judge rashly of the tavern, or imagine that the tavernkeeper is ex officio a publican and a sinner. Nor needs the traveller scruple to sit down to his meal, or lie down to rest, if it should only be on the soft side of a plank, he will find mine host do the fair thing by him; for he is generally a sturdy honest fellow, and has the credit of the settlement to maintain. W.F. Munro. *The Backwoods' Life*. Toronto, 1869.

As with a wand, the pamphlet *Emigration to Canada* waved away the back-breaking work that went into the making of a pioneer farm:

> Gradually but surely the work of improving a new farm goes forward, until it is astonishing what a change is brought about in a few short years. The wilderness is transformed into a fruitful field. One by one the stumps have rotted out, and given the plough free scope to work. Inequalities in the surface of the land have become smoothed down, and almost the only evidence that the country is new is furnished by the rail fences. The log buildings have given place to structures of frame or stone. A garden has been laid out and stocked. The small fruits and fresh vegetables plentifully supply the family table. An orchard has been planted, and brought into bearing. Apples, pears, plums, cherries, and, in some parts of the country, peaches are grown abundantly. . . . The front fences have ceased to be of rails. A neat, ornamental paling or hedge skirts the public road, and a tasteful bit of shrubbery environs the house and out-buildings. Altogether, there is an air of beauty and attractiveness about the scene, but recently so wild. Ontario. *Emigration to Canada. The Province of Ontario; its soil, climate, resources, institutions, free grant lands, etc., etc.* Toronto, 1869.

Veterinary knowledge was a practical necessity.

> The Veterinary School [in Toronto] has now been in existence about six years. It has been attended so far with decidedly satisfactory progress, considering the small means with which it commenced, the almost total absence at that time of a demand for, or indeed of the possibility of, obtaining veterinary skill in the treatment of the diseases of domestic animals, and the little inducement then supposed to be held out to young men to acquire the profession. But with the establishment of the school, which is indeed still comparatively in the stage of a new undertaking, more correct ideas have gradually obtained currency in regard to the treatment of farm stock or other domestic animals. Many young men have attended the lectures, a considerable proportion of them with the view of studying the veterinary art as a profession, and, up to the present time, some fifteen of them have received the Diploma certifying that they are competent to practise. It is satisfactory to be able to state that where these young men have settled, they have, as a general rule, been able to realize reasonable incomes from the practice of their business, and have proved valuable acquisitions in their respective neighbourhoods. If persevered in, as there is every reason to believe will be the case, the Veterinary School promises to be one of our most valuable institutions, and of increasing importance, as the country becomes more thickly settled, and more largely filled with improved breeds of live stock. Ontario. *Supplement to the Report of the Commissioner of Agriculture and Arts for the year 1868.* Toronto, 1869.

Edward Mitchell was the author of *Five Thousand A Year and How I Made It in Five Years' Time*. How he made it was with a market garden and flower greenhouse near the city. By the fifth year, when he was clearing more than $5,000 annually, Mitchell concentrated on onions in summer and verbenas in winter. Tilling the soil, he wrote, was one of the most useful, honest, pure, noble and elevating callings man could undertake.

> When I first entered this business, as an experiment, my weight stood at 127 lbs. At present I average 182 lbs, and am fleshy enough to be an alderman. Edward Mitchell. *Five Thousand A Year and How I Made It in Five Years' Time, Starting without Capital.* Toronto, 1870.

A surgeon in the Crimean War, Harvey Philpot was a country doctor in Canada for seven years before writing this common-sense guidebook.

One luxury he [the British immigrant] will sadly miss at first is his beer, of which very little is drunk in the Colony, the substitute for it being a good wholesome whisky, distilled from Indian corn and rye.

Dr. Philpot advised planting tobacco as well as wheat with the very first crop. Canada was an exceptionally healthy country

The most common complaint among the settlers is simple functional derangement of the digestive organs, mainly attributable to the habit of eating in too great a hurry, and occupying themselves with severe manual labour immediately after meals. Canadians, as a rule, live very well, meats, vegetables, puddings, tarts, dried fruits, plenty of cheese, milk, eggs, and butter being supplied at all their meals.

Here is the good doctor's description of a corduroy road:

Large quantities of brush and underwood are cut and flung down upon the swampy ground. Upon the top of this are placed, side by side, trunks of trees about 14 or 20 feet in length, and nearly of a size as possible. Over these again, if the traffic is expected to be pretty brisk, earth and sods are thrown and left to be compacted by the waggons and teams which will eventually pass over it. Should any of my readers be desirous of forming some idea of the sensation produced through their organism by travelling over a "corduroy road," I would suggest to them to get into a Bath-chair and allow themselves to be dragged for a mile or two over the sleepers of a neighbouring railway. . . .

I shall not forget, in a hurry, my first experience of a journey over one of these timber pontoons. I hung on with my hands to the wooden seat of our waggon, my feet played vigorously like castanets the "devil's tattoo" upon the floor of the springless conveyance, whilst my teeth rattled one against another like dice in a box; my hat was soon shaken off, and my body jarred and strained in every joint and ligament. . . . My driver kept conversing with me all the time quite unconcernedly. Harvey J. Philpot. *Guide Book to the Canadian Dominion*. London, 1871.

C. C. James was deputy minister of agriculture for Ontario and a former professor of chemistry at Ontario Agricultural College. He wrote voluminously on every aspect of agriculture to the great benefit of Ontario farmers. The following is part of his chapter on roads:

When the settlers first came into the forest to make their homes, the first thing required was a road by which to get in to and on to the lot. This road was made as quickly and as cheaply as possible. The trees were cleared away, making the "road allowance," some of the stumps were removed, and the road was thus used in its first stage. It was found, however, that such a road was impassable and useless in the spring and fall or during heavy rains — it needed drainage. Then followed the next improvement, namely, the cutting of a ditch on each side, the dirt from which was thrown upon the road, thereby raising the centre a little above the sides. This second stage was a great improvement; the water drained off into the side ditches, and the roadway was kept fairly dry. The wheels of carts and the feet of horses and of oxen do not cut into the dry earth so easily as into the mud. Such a road as this we call a dirt or earth road. Many are still found, and they are the only kind of road possible in certain places, but in order to be useful they must be kept well rounded up and well drained on the sides. The greatest enemy of all roads is water, whether it is water *in* the material of the road or on the surface of the road. The frost can do no damage unless there is water in the road. You know that water expands when it freezes, so that when a wet road freezes it heaves, and becomes broken up. This, then, is the first principle of road-making — keep it dry by open drains on the side, or by covered tile drains on the side, or by tile drains below the road.

The next principle in road-making is to get a fairly hard surface. In early days the settlers sometimes cut down small trees, and, after trimming them, laid them side by side across the dirt road. By this means there was made a surface that was hard but a little rough. Such a road, from its ribbed nature, was called a "corduroy" road. Later on, when saw-mills became common, sawn-planks were sometimes laid down, forming a plank road. The object in both cases was to get a hard, level surface. A horse can pull but a light load through loose sand or deep miry mud; he can draw much more on a hard, level road. C. C. James. *Agriculture*. Toronto, 1898.

Canadian Fruit, Flower, and Kitchen Gardener (Toronto, 1872), by the famous Ontario horticulturist and secretary of the Fruit Growers' Association, D. W. Beadle, was the first extensive work of its kind in Canada.

It is interesting now to note the main varieties of apples listed by Beadle and his assessment of the best of them: Alexander (exceedingly hardy), Baldwin (deserves its high popularity), Benoni, Duchess of Oldenburgh (vigorous, endures cold), Early Harvest (excellent), Early Joe (most delightfully flavored), Esopus Spitzenburgh (abundant tree), Fameuse (very tender and juicy), Golden Russet (flourishes in all soils), Gravenstein (commands highest price of any apple), Grimes' Golden Pippin, Hubbardston Nonsuch, Jersey Sweeting, King of Tompkins County, Keswick Codlin, Large Yellow Bough (best early sweet apple), Late Strawberry (very handsome), Monmouth Pippin, Mother (hardy and durable), Northern Spy (succeeds even in Ottawa area), Pomme Grise (favorite dessert apple), Red Astrachan (crisp and juicy, with rich acid flavor), Ribston Pippin (truly splendid), Roxbury Russet (long-keeping), Saint Lawrence, Swaar, Talman's Sweet (best sweet winter apple), Tetofsky (beautifully striped with red), Twenty Ounce (large), Wagener, and four varieties that originated in Nova Scotia, Sutton's Early, Bishop's Bourne, Marquis of Lorne, and Morton's Red.

Beadle not only told how to grow and graft apple trees, he gave advice on how to market apples and, even, how to pack them:

> Apples should be so put up that they will be perfectly tight, and not shake about in the barrel. A little practice will enable any one to pack apples securely. Pave the bottom of the barrel with apples, placing the stem down, as closely as they can be packed without bruising; then put in a market basketful at a time, introducing the basket into the barrel and pouring the fruit out gently, not allowing the apples to fall, but roll out and on to those already in the barrel. As each basketful is emptied, the barrel is gently shaken so that the apples shall be well settled to their places. The barrel is filled full, even with the top, the head placed on, and by means of a screw packer pressed down into its place. If this is not roughly done, the apples will be pressed just enough to keep them tight, so that when the barrel is rolled about, the apples will not be shaken in the barrel. As soon as the head is in place, the hoops should be put on, driven home, and securely nailed, and the heading at both ends secured by nailing cleats on the inside of the chime. Mark the barrel on the end which was the bottom when putting the apples in so that it may be opened and the fruit taken out from that end. After the barrel has been fully secured and marked, it should be laid on the side and kept in a cool place, under cover from sun and rain, until sent to market or removed to the cellar. A dry cellar that can be kept at a temperature just above freezing is an excellent place in which to keep apples in a fresh and sound condition.

David Gardiner, a farmer in Clarence, Ontario, had been fifteen years in Canada after emigrating from Scotland and living for two years in the United States. Shaller's comments, sent to him by a friend in Perthshire, apparently infuriated Gardiner, who found a ready publisher for his reply in a twenty-five-page pamphlet, printed by *The Times* of Ottawa.

Gardiner said a frame house in Nebraska cost an outrageous $1,000 because of expensive lumber:

> Poor Emigrants have not this sum to lay out on a house, or anything else. Therefore they have to do as one half the settlers in Nebraska

have done — build a hut of prairie sod or mud and in courtesy call it a cabin. . . .

One advantage the Emigrant has in Nebraska over Canada is, there is plenty of pasturage for his horses. He may work them all day and let them loose at night to find their supper where they may, and he will have the pleasure of walking perhaps twenty miles over the "beautiful prairie" next morning in search of them, and may thank his stars should he find them by the end of seed-time. . . . Keep away from the "beautiful prairie" until you have riches.

To Shaller's comment that Canada was very heavily wooded and clearing land very difficult:

True, plenty of fine ash, elm, linden, larch, birch, beech, spruce, maple and many other kinds [are] all at hand to be cut down and turned into houses, barns, stables, fences, ships, boats, carts, ploughs, harrows, tables, chairs, bedsteads, or cradles for young Canadians.

But many farmers probably shot up their eyebrows at Gardiner's remark about the ease of clearing land. This was in reply to Shaller's comment on the prevalence of stumps. After a "few" years, said Gardiner,

We kick over the most of the stumps with our foot, or watch for a dry spell, apply the match, and they are gone in half an hour.

Comparing eastern Ontario and Nebraska, Gardiner said the counties of Prescott and Russell had a population of 3,600 with only one jail, twelve years old, while Nebraska had "lynch law, mob law, gambling, divorce, murder, bowie-knives, revolvers, and free love." David Gardiner. Canada Vs. Nebraska. A Refutation of attacks made on Canada by C. R. Shaller, Commissioner of the Missouri Railroad Company, in the "People's Journal," of Dundee, Scotland. Ottawa, 1873.

Seven years after Confederation, the agriculture department conducted a detailed survey of how many persons could be employed in farming across Canada. Manitoba and British Columbia had only recently become provinces, and it would be another thirty-two years before Saskatchewan and Alberta achieved that status.

The overall figure was 175,550 employables, including farm "servants," male and female, dairy maids, "ordinary" laborers, blacksmiths, gardeners, harness-, wagon- and plough-makers, and wheelwrights. By far the largest number were in the first three categories. For example, in the county of Middlesex, Ontario, there were jobs for 2,255 persons, including 1,884 farm servants, 213 dairy maids and eighty-nine country laborers. Canada. Department of Agriculture. Labour Needs of Canada. Ottawa, 1873.

Advice on horse breaking:

> If you want to break a horse that has long been in the habit of balking,
> you ought to set apart a half day for it. Put him by the side of a steady
> horse, have check lines on them, tie up all the traces and straps so that
> there will be nothing to excite them. Do not rein them up, but let them
> have their heads loose; walk them about as slow as possible; stop often,
> and go to your balky horse and gentle him; do not take any whips about
> him, or do anything to excite him, but keep him just as quiet as you can;
> he will soon start off at the word, and stop whenever you tell him. As
> soon as he performs right, hitch him to an empty waggon and have it
> stand in a favourable place for starting. It would be well to shorten the
> stay chain behind the steady horse, so that if it is necessary he can take
> the weight of the waggon. The first time you start them do not drive
> more than two rods at first; watch your balky horse closely, and if you
> see he is getting a little excited, stop him before he stops of his own
> accord, caress him a little, and start again; drive them over a small hill a
> few times, and then over a larger one, all the while adding a light load.
> This process will make any horse pull true. Charles Edward Whitcombe: *The
> Canadian Farmer's Manual of Agriculture*. Toronto, 1874.

The federal agriculture department said chopping down trees was "unfettered
freedom."

> Though they have to face hard work, and though oftentimes compelled to
> deny themselves many a little comfort, the social condition of the Canadian
> people is generally a happy one. Prof. Goldwin Smith [of Toronto; British-
> born historian and essayist], who has resided in Canada for many [six] years,
> and who is well known as a close observer of men and things, expresses the
> opinion that "there are no happier nor more contented people in the world
> than the agricultural population of Canada." This remark applies to the
> French of Quebec as well as to the English, Irish, Scotch, German and
> native Canadians of the other provinces.
>
> Most undoubtedly, during the first few years of his life in the back-
> woods, the settler has to put up with many privations, to face great
> difficulties, and to endure not a few hardships; yet even in this state,
> while hewing out a home for himself in the forest, he is blessed with
> a feeling of independence and of unfettered freedom which the
> labouring classes of older countries seldom enjoy and can hardly
> understand. Though his home may be poor and lowly, he has the
> proud consciousness that it is his own, and that the hills and plains
> around it are his and his alone. He fears no landlord, and as for the
> tax gatherer his visits are few and far between, and his demands are
> easily supplied. With gun in hand the settler may roam the forests

over; game keepers are unknown; the beasts and the birds are common property; he is free to shoot what he will without begging anybody's permission; and to keep his gun he pays no licence. . . .

There's more, much more: the fertile farm with golden grain, substantial mansion, great frame barns, fat herds, all bespeaking comfort, prosperity and contentment.

This edition of the handbook included an appendix listing some farms for sale in Ontario:

Two farms in County of Halton, south half of Lot 11 in the 1st concession, and south half of 12 in 1st concession, south of Dundas street, about a mile and half from Oakville Station. Comfortable dwellings on each, barns, stables, driving sheds, orchards, etc. These farms adjoin, and are not only delightfully situated but first-class land. Price $50 per acre. . . .

Lot 16 on 2nd and 3rd concession, township of Sarawack, 3 1/2 miles from Owen Sound, containing 150 acres, 100 cleared, balance in good hardwood. Beautifully situated on lakeshore, and known as Bay View. There are on the premises three good dwellings, one calculated for an hotel, large barns, stablings, etc. There is also a saw mill in good running order, which will cut 10 thousand feet of lumber in 24 hours. Three good mill sites on premises, and a beautiful fall of 44 feet, known as the Indian Falls. Well watered and fenced, and a most desirable property. Price $14,000 on easy terms of payment, with mortgage at 6 per cent interest. . . .

The east half of lot 13 in the 1st concession of Uxbridge, county of Ontario, 100 acres, 90 cleared, balance good pine and hardwood bush. Soil, a clay loam. Two good houses on it with stone cellars, two good barns with driving houses, stables and other outbuildings. Good orchard. Price $6,000. Canada. Department of Agriculture. *Canada: A Handbook of Information for Intending Emigrants.* Ottawa, 1877.

Ellen Agnes Bilbrough wrote *British Children in Canadian Homes,* one of the first accounts of British slum children settled in Canada, mainly on farms, by Annie McPherson and her friends and backers, who operated homes in Belleville, Galt, Ont., and Knowlton, Que. The first hundred children sailed from England on May 12, 1870, and were accompanied by McPherson herself, L.W. Thorn, and the author of this little book.

Among the many efforts made in the present day for the benefit of the human race and the alleviation of their sufferings, none we think has met with more success, or more blessed results, than the transplanting of young children from the haunts of sin, misery, and want in the old land, to homes of comfort and plenty in the new.

For eight or nine years this work had been steadily carried on by various instrumentalities, so that now upwards of 4000 children have been settled in Canada. . . .

Notwithstanding the hardships and want of care which many of the children experienced in early days, taken as a whole they are remarkably healthy. Fresh air and exercise, nourishing food, and proper clothing soon tell favourably upon them. In eight years we have only had six deaths in the Home [Marchmont House, Belleville], and these mostly from consumption inherited from parents. Some have died in their places, receiving loving care and attention from those around. Ellen Agnes Bilbrough. *British Children in Canadian Homes*. Belleville, Ont., 1879.

The author does not mention that some of the children were treated like slaves except to say that "some returned, complaining of hard work."

Thomas Moore attended the Dominion Agricultural Exhibition at Ottawa in September:

The collection of Potatoes was quite an interesting feature, not only on account of its extent, but of the exceptionally fine quality of the tubers. Early Rose seems to be a favourite variety throughout the country; this with Snowflake and Breese's Prolific are the principal kinds grown. Any person who has grown Early Rose here [Ireland] knows it is a very heavy cropper, but, so far as I am aware, it has never proved itself to be a Potato of good quality; in Canada the reverse is the case; whilst the crop it produces is exceedingly large, the size and quality of the tubers leave nothing to be desired. Thomas Moore. *A Tour through Canada in 1879*. Dublin, 1880.

The 432-page book *Canadian Farming* is a summary of a five-volume commission report and says in its concluding remarks:

Very satisfactory is the almost universal use of labour-saving machinery. If the average all over be taken, it would appear that 71 per cent of the farmers of Ontario use machinery in their ordinary operations. But as a matter of fact, if the area still encumbered with stumps, where machinery cannot be successfully employed, be eliminated from the calculation, the use of machinery may be said to be all but universal. The exceptions to its use in well-settled counties are very few indeed. The supply, too, of ingenious inventions keep pace with the demand. It was informally stated in the course of the inquiry that only two wants in this respect needed to be supplied: the one a machine for sowing gypsum; the other, one for distributing liquid manure to the roots of plants. It is believed that the first-mentioned desideratum has been provided; the other will not be long behind. So far as the purchase of machines is concerned, the danger is rather in the direction of a too ready yielding to the persuasiveness of the agent introducing some novelty which is not invariably an improvement, backed by the beguilements of offers of long credit. But the reasonable desire to lessen manual labour, and abridge the time needed in particular operations when time is very precious, is the best ally of the agricultural implement and machine maker.

The commission had this to say about tobacco:

The cultivation of tobacco was only met with by the Commissioners in Kent and Essex. It was formerly carried on in those counties to a considerable extent, but present prices give it no encouragement, and the tendency has been, for some time, to limit the growth to very small proportions. . . . It costs a large amount to cultivate it. It requires the richest soil, and it is susceptible to the frost. The market is also very fluctuating. Ontario Agricultural Commission. *Canadian Farming: an Encyclopedia of Agriculture.* Toronto, 1881.

Edward Harris was an early advocate of game conservation.

In Canada, instead of taking advantage of our northern location, the destructiveness of our neighbours and the circumstances which would give us the monopoly of a great and profitable trade, by legislating to encourage game preservation as a business, we prohibit "export and sale," leaving with camping-out parties, professional sports, and a few people in the backwoods, the power to continue the extermination of game.

The question arises whether it will not pay to encourage the preservation of game on lands fitted for it by nature, and even to discourage entire dependence upon farming in unfitted localities where farming and starvation are synonyms. Edward Harris. *Is Game of any Value to The Farmer?* Toronto, 1881.

The Society for Promoting Christian Knowledge provided advice on both godliness and cleanliness:

Prayer on first settling in a new country:
Give me courage, cheerfulness, patience and hope. In every time of loneliness, and discouragement, and anxiety, may my trust be in Thee. Keep me from murmuring and unbelief and forgetfulness of Thee. Though far removed from the restraints that may have been

about me in my former home, yet may I be on my guard against everything that would dishonour or displease Thee. . . .

Closets — one of the best kinds of closet is an earth-closet. As good an earth-closet for a cottage as any, is simply a zinc bucket coming up close to the wood of the seat, and with a handle to enable it to be lifted out. The wooden top of the seat should be made with a hinge, so that it can be lifted up and the bucket removed and emptied from time to time. Very little earth is necessary if no slops are thrown into the bucket, and the earth can be thrown in with a shovel. It should be quite dry. In the winter time it should be dried under the fire before it is used. The material from an earth-closet may be put into a hole in the garden, and afterwards dug in as manure. All places of this kind, as well as water-closets, require attention and give a little trouble; but he must be the most careless of mortals who, in a matter so important for health, will not give half an hour's work every week to preserve cleanliness, and really no more time is demanded than this. Society for Promoting Christian Knowledge. *Colonists' Handbooks, No. 1: Canada, containing statistical and other information from government sources, and useful counsels to emigrants.* London, 1882.

Samuel Thompson was living in a shanty about halfway between Barrie and Georgian Bay.

We were annoyed by flies, and I noticed an old toad creep stealthily from under the house logs, wait patiently near a patch of sunshine on the floor, and as soon as two or three flies, attracted by the sun's warmth, drew near its post, dart out its long slender tongue, and so catch them all one after another.

Improving upon the hint, we afterwards regularly scattered a few grains of sugar to attract more flies within the old fellow's reach, and thus kept the shanty comparatively clear of those winged nuisances, and secured quiet repose for ourselves in the early mornings. Another toad soon joined the first one, and they became so much at home as to allow us to scratch their backs gently with a stick, when they would heave up their puffed sides to be scrubbed. These toads swallow mice and young ducks, and in their turn fall victims to garter and other snakes. Samuel Thompson. *Reminiscences of a Canadian Pioneer for the last fifty years.* Toronto, 1884.

Canniff Haight had almost total recall of his youth in the Bay of Quinte area of Upper Canada, making his reminiscences particularly valuable for their descriptions of early farming methods and tools.

The only way known to produce fire was the primitive one of rubbing two sticks together and producing fire by friction — a somewhat tedious process — or with a flint, a heavy jack-knife, and a bit of punk, a fungous growth, the best of which for this purpose is obtained from the beech. Gun flints were most generally used. One of these was placed on a bit of dry punk, and held firmly in the left hand, while the back of the closed blade of the knife thus brought into contact with the flint by a quick downward stroke of the right hand produced a shower of sparks, some of which, falling on the punk, would ignite. . . .

It was necessary to carefully cover up the live coals on the hearth before going to bed, so that there would be something to start the fire with in the morning. This precaution rarely failed with good hard-wood coals. But sometimes they died out, and then some one would have to go to a neighbour's house for fire, a thing which I have done sometimes, and it was not nice to have to crawl out of my warm nest and run through the keen cold air for a half mile or more to fetch some live coals, before the morning light had broken in the east. . . .

The great barn filled with grain [which] had to be threshed, for the cattle needed the straw, and the grain had to be got out for the market. So day after day he [the farmer] and his men hammered away with the flail, or spread the sheaves on the barn floor to be trampled out by horses. Threshing machines were unknown then [and] his muscular arm was the only machine he then had to rely upon. . . .

Cooking was done in the oven, and over the kitchen fire, and the utensils were a dinner pot, teakettle, frying pan and skillet. There were no cooking stoves. The only washing machines were the ordinary wash tubs, soft soap, and the brawny arms and hands of the girls; and the only wringers were the strong wrists and firm grip that could give a vigorous twist to what passed through the hands. Water was drawn from the wells with a bucket fastened to a long slender pole attached to a sweep suspended to a crotch. Butter was made in upright churns and many an hour have I stood, with mother's apron pinned around me to keep my clothes from getting spattered, pounding at the stubborn cream, when every minute seemed an hour, thinking the butter would never come. When evening set in, we were wont to draw around the cheerful fire on the hearth, or perhaps up to the kitchen table, and read and work by the dim light of "tallow dips" placed in tin candlesticks. Now, we sit by the brilliant light of the coal oil lamp. . . .

Carriages were not kept, for the simple reason that the farmer seldom had occasion to use them. He rarely went from home, and when he did he mounted his horse or drove in his lumber-waggon to market or to meeting. He usually had one or two waggon-chairs, as they were called, which would hold two persons very comfortably.

These were put in the waggon and a buffalo skin thrown over them, and then the vehicle was equipped for the Sunday drive. There was a light waggon kept for the old people to drive about in, the box of which rested on the axles. The seat, however, was secured to wooden springs, which made it somewhat more comfortable to ride in. Canniff Haight. *Country Life in Canada Fifty Years Ago*. Toronto, 1885.

Arthur S. Hardy was the commissioner and David Spence the secretary of the Ontario immigration department. They wrote:

From the beginning of April till the end of October there is always a steady demand for farm labourers, especially for single men. More than double the number arriving could easily find employment by the year at fair wages. It must, however, be understood that only experienced men are wanted by the year. A single man who can plough well, and who has had some experience in taking care of stock, can readily obtain employment at about $150 per annum with maintenance, with a prospect of considerable increase if he should be found to be a good trustworthy man. Should thirty or forty come together and advise the Immigration Department on their arrival at Quebec, farmers would certainly be in waiting at Toronto to employ them.

Families of farm labourers can find ready employment if they are experienced and have the means of providing a little furniture and provisions. If there are young women in the family, able and willing to take places as servants, so much the better.

The demand for female domestic servants is constant everywhere throughout the Province at all seasons of the year. Wages of experienced servants were higher in 1885 than in the preceding year. Good general servants can readily find employment at from $8 to $10 per month. Young women, however, who are not able or willing to work will not succeed in the Province. Arthur S. Hardy and David Spence. *Ontario as a Home for the British Tenant Farmer who desires to become his own Landlord*. Toronto, 1886.

William Saunders, director of the Central Experimental Farm, gives this background in the first of the thousands of pamphlets published since by federal experimental farms across the country:

In November, 1885, shortly after the present Minister of Agriculture [John Carling] took office, the writer [Saunders] was instructed to visit as many of the Experimental Farms and Stations in the United States as might be necessary in order to gain information as to the benefits such institutions were conferring on practical agriculture, including stock raising, dairying, etc., and on horticulture, with special reference to the production of fruit. Also to enquire into the subject of forestry and all other useful phases of this work.

A report was prepared and submitted to the Minister of Agriculture on the 20th of February, 1886, containing the results of this enquiry, accompanied by an outline of a proposed system of experimental work, embracing those features which it was thought would be most particularly beneficial to the great agricultural interests of Canada.

During the session of Parliament for 1886 the Minister of Agriculture introduced "An Act respecting Experimental Farm Stations," which after a brief discussion was passed without opposition. This Act provided for the establishment of an experimental farm for the Provinces of Ontario and Quebec jointly, to be known as the principal or central farm, one for the Maritime Provinces jointly, one for the Province of Manitoba, one for the North-West Territories, and one for the Province of British Columbia. Provision was also made for the setting apart of several sections of land in Manitoba, and North-West Territories and British Columbia for the special purpose of tree planting and timber growing. . . .

The Central Experimental Farm has been located near the Capital, within three miles of the Parliament Buildings. Four hundred and sixty acres of land have been secured in a commanding position overlooking the city of Ottawa, possessing every desirable variety of soil and aspect to meet the varied requirements of the experimental work to be conducted there. Although possession was had but a few days before winter set in, some work has been accomplished, unnecessary internal fences have been removed, the loose stone cleared over a large area, some grading done and about twenty acres of land ploughed. During the winter a large amount of stable manure has been obtained, between fifty and sixty acres of undergrowth chopped and piled, an office and store room erected, and a glass structure built for the purpose of testing the vitality and germinating power of seeds. . . .

Purchases of seed-grain in great variety, including wheat, barley, oats and rye, also grass seeds for meadows and permanent pastures have been made in Northern Russia, Germany, England, Canada and United States with the view of testing their comparative merits when grown side by side. A collection of many varieties of potatoes has also been secured for a similar purpose. A large number of standard fruit trees and vines are being obtained; also a collection of hardy Russian sorts, comprising nearly two hundred varieties, some of which it is hoped will succeed in colder sections of the Dominion where the more tender kinds cannot be successfully grown. Canada. Department of Agriculture. Central Experimental Farm, Ottawa, Canada, *Bulletin No. 1*. February 12th, 1887.

Only fifteen months went by from the time Saunders received his instructions to prepare a report until the report had been researched and written, an act of Parliament presented and passed, land acquired, clearing and ploughing started, seeds bought and construction under way on the necessary buildings. Today, it would take at least that long to achieve the first draft of the initial report.

The first twenty bulletins from the central farm, many of them written by Saunders himself, covered subjects such as: smuts affecting wheat, Russian Ladoga wheat, strawberry culture, two-rowed and six-rowed barley, treatment of apple scab, prevention of insect damage, chemical composition of Indian corn, the cattle horn-fly, fattening swine, analyses of grasses.

Saunders, in charge of all experimental farms, did not neglect any aspect of his wide field, but his passion was to breed an earlier-ripening wheat. He and his son, Charles, brought fame to Canada and money to Canadian farmers with their development of Marquis wheat in the first decade of this century. By 1920, it was estimated that ninety per cent of the 17,100,000 acres of wheat in Canada were Marquis. Charles Saunders was so fluent in French that a book of his French poems and essays was published in 1928.

P.J. Bainbrigge, *A Bush Road, Upper Canada, 1842*.

THE WEST

MANITOBA

WHEN THEY [the Indians] kill any [buffalo] cows, the young calves follow them and lick their hands. They bring them to their children, who eat them, after having for some time played with them. They keep the hoofs of those little creatures, and when they are very dry, they tie them to some wand, and move them according to the various postures of those who sing and dance. This is the most ridiculous musical instrument that I ever met with. These young calves might be easily tamed, and made use of to plow the land, which would be very advantageous to the Savages. These bulls find in all seasons forage to subsist by; for if they are surprised in the northern countries by the snow, before they can reach the southern parts, they have the dexterity to remove the snow, and eat the grass under it. Louis Hennepin. *A New Discovery of a Vast Country in America.* Reprinted at Chicago in 1903 from the second London issue of 1698.

Capt. Ernest J. Chambers compiled from official accounts a profile of the resources of the north. Among them:

Robson, a civil engineer who constructed Fort Churchill [and] who was there at various periods from 1733 onwards . . . spoke of the vegetables which he had raised there, and also of the horses which had been employed for several years, and also the cattle at the fort. He said that in spite of the cold winds on Esquimaux Point he was able to produce excellent vegetables. He dug down in the soil — it was in the month of July — and found that he had to dig down a depth of three feet six inches before he came to the frost, represented by a sheet of eight inches of ice, and he makes the note that this thin stratum of ice below does not in any way affect the vegetation. He went on to speak of the horses that were used in drawing stones and other material for the fort, and the fine butter that was made, and spoke of it generally as a good agricultural country round about there. That was in 1733 to 1747. . . .

The Indians, constantly in hunting, plant little patches of potatoes here and there in the spring and leave them all summer and go back in the fall and dig them up when they go back to their hunting grounds, and use them for their winter supply. The witness [mining engineer Joseph Burr Tyrrell] had gone out and dug a pail of beautiful potatoes on several occasions out of these little Indian patches buried in the woods. They had never been hoed or cultivated in any way. They are not looked after from the time they are planted in the spring until they are dug up in the fall. The potatoes seem to be able to grow sufficiently to keep down the weeds. As a protection against wild animals these potato patches are usually planted on islands. Capt. Ernest J. Chambers, ed. *Canada's Fertile Northland: A Glimpse of the Enormous Resources of Part of the Unexplored Regions of the Dominion.* Ottawa, 1907.

Alexander Mackenzie describes Grand Portage, the great rendezvous on Lake Superior for the canoe traffic into and out of the western interior:

The proprietors, clerks, guides, and interpreters, mess together, to the number of sometimes an hundred, at several tables, in one large hall, the provision consisting of bread, salt pork, beef, hams, fish, and venison, butter, peas, Indian corn, potatoes, tea, spirits, wine, and plenty of milk, for which purpose several milch cows are constantly kept. Alexander Mackenzie. *Voyages from Montreal, on the River St. Laurence, through the Continent of North-America, to the Frozen and Pacific Oceans; In the Years 1789 and 1793.* London, 1801.

The canoemen, or voyageurs, who did the heavy labor, were allowed only "Indian corn and melted fat." Mackenzie in 1787 met fur trader Peter Pond at Fort Chipewyan in the Athabasca country (Mackenzie's headquarters for eight years) where Pond had "formed as fine a kitchen garden as I ever saw in Canada," with turnips, carrots, parsnips, and potatoes. The cabbages failed, however.

Jonathan Carver came upon Lake Winnipeg during his travels:

Lake Winnipeck, or as the French write it, Lac Ouinipique, has on the north-east some mountains, and on the east many barren plains. The maple or sugar tree grows here in great plenty, and there is likewise gathered an amazing quantity of rice, which proves that grain will flourish in these northern climates as well as in warmer. Jonathan Carver. *Three Years Travels through the Interior Parts of North America.* Philadelphia, 1796.

Alexander Henry "the Younger" kept a journal while he was a trader for the North-West Company and makes several references to his garden at the company fort just west of the Forks, the confluence of the Assiniboine and Red Rivers (today's Winnipeg).

Oct. 1, 1801. My fort and buildings finished. Sent men to make hay on the E. side of Red River.

Oct. 6. A heavy fall of snow. I took my potatoes out of the ground, 1 1/2 bushels; the horses had destroyed my other vegetables.

May 21, 1802. A small canoe arrived from Portage la Prairie, bringing nearly a bushel of potatoes for seed.

May 6, 7, 1803. Indians arrive daily and drink continually. I planted potatoes, turnips, carrots, beets, parsnips, onions. Sowed cabbage seed. Elliott Coues, ed. *The Manuscript Journals of Alexander Henry and of David Thompson 1799-1814.* 3 vols. New York, 1897.

Daniel Williams Harmon, another Nor'wester, noted in his journal at Stuart Lake in northern British Columbia that in early September, 1818, he had cut and threshed his barley; five quarts sown in May had yielded as many bushels. In earlier years, he commented on the success or failure of his kitchen gardens at Fort Alexandria on the Assiniboine, Cumberland House, Fort Dunvegan on the Peace River, and Île à la Crosse. The gardens were enclosed by palisades, just like the forts.

In the Saskatechewan correspondence of the Hudson's Bay Company are references to such gardens preventing starvation. For instance, William Tomison wrote from Edmonton House Nov. 25, 1798, that "we have been in a starving condition ever since our arrival at this place . . . and had it not been for the garden stuff it would have been much worse."

In his *Narrative of a Journey to Manitoba*, published by the agriculture department in 1873, J.Y. Shantz informs us that the Hudson's Bay Company station White Horse Post, near Pigeon Lake, carried on farming extensively. In 1871 it had raised 9,870 bushels of grain on 299 acres and maintained 500 head of cattle.

A. J. Russell cites George Gladman, born in 1802 at a Hudson's Bay Company post and in company service for thirty-one years, about East Main Old Factory on the eastern shore of James Bay:

He raised good potatoes, turnips and other vegetables. East Main Factory is 60 miles north of Rupert's River. He says further that a large herd of cattle was kept there as a resource in case of the company's ships wintering in the bay, an abundant supply of hay being made in the salt marshes on the shores of the bay. A. J. Russell. *The Red River Country, Hudson's Bay & North-West Territories, considered in relation to Canada.* 3d ed. Montreal, 1870.

J. L. Scripps saw through the misconceptions many held about the north:

It is the popular idea concerning this vast region of country that it is "a waste howling wilderness" abounding in sandy plains, and everywhere unadapted to cultivation, both on account of its poor soil and its high latitude. But this is a mistake. . . . The fur companies that have occupied it have always been opposed to its settlement. The presence of civilization in any portion of it would put an immediate end to the business of these companies within the district thus occupied. It was essential, therefore, to maintain the undisturbed possession of it to the Indian tribes which were found within it. There were two ways by which this might be done. The first was to maintain a constant silence respecting it; the other, to spread reports prejudicial to it.

Scripps, editor of the *Daily Democratic Press* of Chicago, quotes explorer Gabriel Franchère on his visit to a North-West Company post on Lake Winnipeg in 1814:

This trading post had more the appearance of a large and well-cultivated farm than of a fur trader's factory; a neat and elegant mansion built on a slight eminence and surrounded with bars, stables, storehouses, etc., and by fields of barley, peas, oats and potatoes, reminded us of the civilized countries which we had left so long ago. J. L. Scripps. *The Undeveloped Northern Region of the American Continent.* Chicago, 1856.

Miles Macdonnell was the leader of the Red River settlers in 1812 and reported to Selkirk, founder of the settlement:

Our crops from bad culture and the seed being old do not promise great returns; the winter wheat being late sown has totally failed, as also the summer wheat, Pease and English Barley; of all these there must be fresh seed sent us. The appearance of the Potatoes promises good returns. The Indian Corn has almost totally failed from a great drowth after planting, grubs, etc. The sowing was chiefly done with the hoe, as well as the planting; only one imperfect plough was got agoing late in the season, there being no man here capable of making a good one. I feel the want of handy workmen in everything I attempt. A wheel-wright and a constructor of windmills would be great acquisitions to us. The Country exceeds any idea I had formed of its goodness. I am only astonished it has lain so long unsettled with good management. The Buffaloe in winter and fish in summer are sufficient to subsist any number of people until more certain supplies are got out of the ground; the river has amply fed us and about 200 people in the neighbourhood since the beginning of June. The land is most fertile and the climate most extraordinarily healthy. Miles Macdonnell. *Letter to the Earl of Selkirk*, July 17, 1813. The Selkirk Papers, National Archives of Canada..

John West noted in his journal:

> We get a few raspberries in the woods, and strawberries from the plains in summer; and on the route to York Factory, we meet with black and red currants, gooseberries, and cranberries. There is a root which is found in large quantities, and generally called by settlers, the Indian potatoe. It strongly resembles the Jerusalem artichoke, and is eaten by the natives in a raw state; but when boiled it is not badly flavoured. The characteristic improvidence of the Indians, and their precarious means of subsistence, will often reduce them to extreme want, and I have seen them collecting small roots in the swamps, and eating the inner rind of the poplar tree. John West. *The Substance of a Journal during a Residence at the Red River Colony.* London, 1824.

White Dog, between Lake Superior and Red River, was an oasis surrounded by granite:

> Islington Mission, or the White Dog, or Chien Blanc, for by these names it is known to the voyageurs, occupies an area of what seems to be drift clay, extending over 250 acres, surrounded by granite hills. The soil of this small oasis is very fertile, and all kinds of farm and garden crops succeed well. Wheat sown on the 20th of May was reaped 26th August in general; it requires but ninety-three days to mature. Potatoes have never been attacked by spring or fall frosts (five years); Indian corn ripens well; spring opens and vegetation commences about the 10th of May; and winter sets in generally about the 1st of November. . . .
>
> Some distance from the [Great Winnipeg] river there are extensive rice grounds covering many thousand acres, and continuing for many miles on either bank. Here the game congregates, and revelling in the midst of such an abundant supply of nutritious food, vast flocks of ducks, geese and all kinds of aquatic birds are to be found. The Indians, too, assemble at stated periods, and visit the rice grounds, procuring without any difficulty, in favourable seasons, a large supply for winter consumption. Province of Canada. *Report of the Exploration of the Country between Lake Superior and the Red River Settlement.* Toronto, 1858.

A four-page newspaper, *The Nor'-Wester,* was published every two weeks by William Buckingham and William Coldwell:

> We refer to [the farmers'] determination to raise little more than enough of produce for home consumption; and so strictly did they carry out their resolves — so nicely did they gauge the needed home supplies — that last year the temporary presence in the Settlement of a couple of exploring parties and a few batches of fortune-hunters, on their way to the Fraser River, almost created a famine. Produce

W.G.R. Hind, *Camping on Plains*.

Edward Roper, *Sulky Plow Near Carberry, Manitoba*.

(NAC# C-13965)

(NAC# C-13975)

W.G.R. Hind, *Settler's House and Red River Cart, Manitoba.*

W.G.R. Hind, *Wheat Field with Ox-Cart.*

(NAC# C-13977)

W.G.R. Hind, *Breaking a Road in Manitoba.*

was scarce, at enormous rates. Wheat rose from 3s 6d to 9s per bushel, flour from 11s 6d to 30s per 112 pounds, pease from 3s to 6s per bushel. *The Nor'-Wester*, Vol. 1, no. 1. Red River Settlement, December 28, 1859.

Charles Bass wrote of the crushing weight of the work:

Many hardy emigrants, especially those of the Scandinavian races, annually pass through Canada to seek new homes in the far Western settlements of the United States, simply from the belief that Canada is a thickly wooded country, presenting great difficulties in clearing, while the open prairies of the Western States of the Union have a world-wide renown, giving promise of a quick return for labor.

Now, in a thickly wooded country, the labor of years is necessary to clear away the timber before prosperous farming is attainable. . . . The immigrant from Europe who, though skilled in other labor, is wholly unaccustomed to the use of the woodman's axe. Thus for a clearing of an hundred acres, a loss of time and labor is incurred to the amount of between two and three thousand dollars, and the best years of life sacrificed in toilsome struggle to prepare a farm in an equal state for cultivation to that a prairie settler finds when he first sets foot upon it. Often such years of crushing toil will destroy a man's best energies, deprive him of all muscular power, and bring him to a premature grave in the wilderness; or, he may more painfully survive, to linger out his remaining years in disease and penury. Charles Bass. *Lectures on Canada, illustrating its present position, and shewing forth its onward progress, and predictive of its future destiny.* Hamilton, 1863.

Bass maintained that the route from Lake Superior to Red River would require construction of "but" 130 miles of road at a cost of £50,000. The rest of the route was navigable water, enabling the immigrant to reach the Red River settlement in sixty-three hours after leaving Lake Superior. Bass recommended construction of an Atlantic-to-Pacific railway and annexation by Canada of all Hudson's Bay Company territory. Both were achieved after his death.

Henry Youle Hind was an explorer who observed early farming methods:

On the morning of the 16th [September, 1858] we paid a visit to Mr. Gowler, whose farm is situated on the immediate banks of the Assiniboine, about nine miles from Fort Garry [Winnipeg]. A small stack-yard was filled with stacks of wheat and hay; his barn, which was very roomy, was crammed with wheat, barley, potatoes, pumpkins, turnips and carrots. The root crops were shortly to be transferred to root houses, which he had constructed by excavating chambers near the high bank of the Assiniboine, and draining them into the river. The drain was supplied with a close and tightly fitting trap, which was closed when the water rose during the spring above its mouth, at that time eight feet above the level of the river. The chambers were about nine feet high, and their ceilings three feet below the prairie level. Access was obtained through a hole in the ceiling, which was covered with a neat little movable roof. There were three of these cellars or root-houses before the dwelling-house, and between it and the river. Frost never entered them, and he found no difficulty in preserving a large stock of potatoes and turnips through the severe winters of this region. . . .

I had been previously informed of the extraordinary success of Mr. Gowler in growing wheat, but I found upon inquiry that the practice he employed was simply not to grow wheat after wheat; he had grown fifty-six measured bushels to the acre. . . .

His turnips (Swedes) were magnificent; four of them weighed 70 lbs., two weighing 39 lbs., and two others 31 lbs. . . .

Mr. Gowler insisted on my tasting his wife's cheese, and smoking his tobacco, before I departed. The cheese was tolerable; the tobacco, which was grown in the neighbourhood and highly prized by Mr. Gowler, was dreadfully strong, and would involve long training in order to acquire a taste for its qualities. Nevertheless, Mr. Gowler preferred it to some excellent fig-leaf which I offered him; he remarked that he had grown and prepared it himself, and knew what it was.

Hind took a poor view of farming methods on the Red River:

Weeds abound in most of the fields appropriated to grain; some fields are seen here and there to be altogether abandoned, and the out-houses wear a neglected aspect, or one of ruinous decay.

On grasshoppers:

During the month of September, 1857, I saw the females engaged in laying their eggs. They did not limit themselves to the prairie soil in forming a nest, but riddled the decayed trunks of trees, the thatch of houses and barns, the wood of which they were built, everything, indeed, which they could penetrate with the little blades provided for that purpose. . . .

Their power of sustaining long flights is also very remarkable. They generally rose from the prairie about nine in the morning and alighted about four in the afternoon. During the intermediate hours I do not recollect one instance in which they were observed to alight, except in anticipation of a thunder-storm, when they would descend perpendicularly from a great altitude. Assuming their speed to have been twenty miles an hour, the distance they would fly in one day probably amounted to one hundred and twenty miles. They have been seen hurrying swiftly to the north at an elevation of 14,500 to 15,000 feet above the sea. . . .

Their principal food is the prairie grass and the leaves of shrubs, but they will attack any substances presented to them, even such indigestible articles as leather, travelling bags, woollen garments, saddle girths, and harness. In a few minutes they ate the varnish from the leather case of a telescope I left on the ground in 1858, and so disfigured a valise that the owner who had seen it sound and untouched a few minutes before we stopped to camp, could not recognize if after it had lain ten minutes on the grass. Blankets became instantly covered with them and eaten into holes. Henry Youle Hind. *Narrative of The Canadian Red River Exploring Expedition of 1857 and of the Assiniboine and Saskatchewan Exploring Expedition of 1858. 2 vols.* London, 1860.

The Synod of the Diocese of Rupert's Land, held February 24, 1869, at Fort Garry (Winnipeg), heard the Bishop of Rupert's Land, Rt. Rev. Robert Machray:

No one can think of the frightful plague of the past summer without a degree of misgiving and anxiety as regards the remaining years of our isolation. The description of it is appalling. The ground was riddled with the eggs of the grasshopper. When spring opened the young grasshoppers came out and filled the land. Some weeks passed before they reached their full growth and were able to fly. During that period they crawled on in one unceasing march. The whole country for a great distance was alive with them. They devoured every green thing — the young crops, weeds, grass. They filled the trees till they were covered with them, as when bees are swarming. They covered every piece of fence or wall. They crowded on each other, when any obstacle came in their way, till they formed masses feet deep. Having no more food in the fields, or crowding each other, they devoured each other — till the whole country was filled with masses of their corrupting bodies. In many places the air was filled with a noisome stench from them. It was a merciful providence that no pestilence broke out. At length they took wing and in a short time all disappeared. The country in many places never recovered all the season. The trees and grass seemed poisoned. The land remained black and bare. There have been previous trials of the same kind, but by common consent this last has exceeded in severity every previous one. It shows what God can do by an apparently very feeble instrument. Oh, may we be moved by a sense of our dependence on Him and . . . devote ourselves more heartily and unselfishly to His glory and service. *Report of the Synod of the Diocese of Rupert's Land*. Cambridge, 1869.

An appendix in an early official Manitoba report dealt with grasshoppers:

These destructive creatures made their first appearance in the colony in the latter end of July, in the year 1818, six years after the commencement of the Settlement [Red River]. The crops were ripe when they came, and they did not injure the wheat to any serious degree, but it was otherwise with the barley, which they attacked by cutting off the ears; but, with all their voracity, they could not eat the ears, and the settlers secured as much as they were able by gleaning. This great swarm, after accomplishing the work of reproduction, disappeared. . . .

In the spring of 1819 . . . the young grasshoppers made their appearance in immense numbers. During the first eight or ten days of their existence they are feeble, inactive, and innoxious, but as they became strong enough to travel, they seemed to have moved in one direction, devouring every green thing that they found in their way, leaving in the evening bare and black what they found in the morning green and flourishing. And thus, they destroyed the unfortunate settler's expectations of realizing what, otherwise, would have been the reward of his industry.

The grasshopper plague was repeated in 1820 and 1821 but then the dreaded swarm did not reappear until 1857. There was another lull until 1867 when the grasshoppers "literally covered the whole face of the country":

The potatoes had their stalks eaten into the ground, but after the grasshoppers had left, so far recovered as to produce a small quantity of very small potatoes. Manitoba. *Report of the Joint Committee of Both Houses on Agriculture, Immigration, and Colonization, during the First Session of the First Legislature of Manitoba*. Winnipeg, 1871.

J. C. Hamilton reported that some Manitoba farmers always reckoned their crops at so many bushels to the acre — after feeding the grasshoppers. One had told him this grasshopper story:

When I saw them travelling on the road I took occasion to count a few of them, and found that there were at least twenty to the square foot on an average. That would give sixteen hundred and two millions to the square mile. Now, allowing that they were placed, one behind the other in a row, and each to occupy one inch of space (and allowing that at present they cover say twenty miles in width north and south, and one hundred miles east and west), there would be twelve hundred and sixty-seven thousand three hundred and sixty millions of hoppers in the Province; placed as aforesaid, they would encircle the earth seven hundred and ninety-one times, and have one hundred and eighty-two millions to spare; or, in other words, they would form a band around the earth sixty-six feet wide. J. C. Hamilton. *The Prairie Province: Sketches of Travel from Lake Ontario to Lake Winnipeg*. Toronto, 1876.

Charles Mair, the Canadian poet, was the paymaster on a relief project cutting a winter road from Oak Point, thirty miles east of Winnipeg, to Lake of the Woods. Joseph James Hargrave quotes from letters by Mair on the subject of the Red River cart:

There are the Red River half-breeds with their oxen and carts in strings of fifty, one hundred and sometimes two hundred carts together. The creaking of the wheels is indescribable; it is like no sound you ever heard in all your life, and makes your blood run cold. These all camp out in the prairie together without blankets or any other covering than their capotes. Their load is about one thousand pounds, and it takes them two months to make the trip from Red River to St. Paul [Minnesota] and back, travelling at the rate of twenty miles per day. . . .

Continually we either met or overtook the Red River cart train. To hear a thousand of those wheels all groaning and creaking on at one time is a sound never to be forgotten; it is simply hellish. Joseph James Hargrave. *Red River*. Montreal, 1871.

Peter O'Leary had this to say about the carts:

Red River carts are made entirely of wood, without a morsel of iron, even a nail, and every half-breed makes his own. Fifteen or twenty carts may be seen drawn in one train by bullocks or small hardy horses, a breed peculiar to the country and known as Red River horses. The surveying parties, explorers, hunters, fur traders, etc., all have to be supplied from Winnipeg with nearly everything they require, and as they are generally two or three hundred miles away and often more, the importance of the business will be at once understood.

The reason that the carts have no iron is because the clay is very sticky and clogs on the tires; secondly, on the prairies iron would be an attraction to lightning; thirdly, they are better able to ford rivers without it; and fourthly, until recently there was but very little of it in the country, and the natives scarcely yet understand its use, and as necessity is the mother of invention they managed to do without it.

These carts will take three quarters of a ton for a thousand miles over the plains, but of course they would not last long on our hard roads. Peter O'Leary. *Travels and Experiences in Canada, The Red River Territory, and the United States.* London, [1877].

Jean d'Artigue was a member of the North West Mounted Police when it marched west in 1874. Many of the force's supplies were carried in Red River carts.

> I would here like to describe the noise made by the carts, but words fail me. It must be heard to be understood. A den of wild beasts cannot be compared with it in hideousness. Combine all the discordant sounds ever heard in Ontario and they cannot produce anything so horrid as a train of Red River carts. At each turn of the wheel, they run up and down all the notes of the scale in one continuous screech, without sounding distinctly any note or giving one harmonious sound. And this unearthly discord is so loud, that a train of carts, coming towards you, can be heard long before they are seen. Jean d'Artigue. *Six Years in the Canadian North-West.* Toronto, 1882.

George H. Wyatt was impressed by the carts' versatility:

> A poor man can adopt the mode of farming on a small scale for the commencement, as practised by the half-breeds. They have carts made of two wheels and a straight axle, with two poles fastened on the axle to form shafts, and a rack or box thereon. To a cart so made is hitched one ox. The cart costs about ten dollars, and the ox and harness 50 to 60 dollars. With such a vehicle a man can do all the teaming that is required on a small farm — and after the first ploughing one ox can plough all that is required. George H. Wyatt. *Manitoba, the Canadian North-West, and Ontario.* Toronto, 1880.

James Trow was an Ontario MP and chairman of the Commons committee on immigration and colonization. In 1877 he undertook a trip west to see for himself the possibilities for increased settlement and his detailed report appeared as a series of letters to the *Stratford Beacon.* They were reprinted in 1878 by the federal government as a booklet. Trow liked most of what he saw, but set out what he disliked as well. He wrote that many would-be settlers who had set out from Winnipeg in 1877 had been forced to return because of impassable roads or extortionate sums demanded for conveyances. Very few had made it outside the city limits and their doleful, but false, tales that the prairie was flooded, crops destroyed and the inhabitants starving were widely circulated in the United States by "interested parties," i.e., land speculators and railway agents. James Trow. *Manitoba and North West Territories.* Ottawa, 1878.

In 1879, Agriculture Minister J. H. Pope embarked on a scheme to bring British farmers to Canada to check out the land to determine whether it might be suitable for settlement by them and farming colleagues back home. These delegates reported verbally to their farm associations or wrote reports, which the Canadian government published and circulated.

Among the first group of fourteen delegates was James Biggar of Grange Farm, Kirkcudbright, Scotland, and after a three-months visit to Canada, he reported to a meeting of the stewardry of Kirkcudbright December 22, 1879:

> You are no doubt aware that of late agents of the various Land and Railway Companies in the United States have been making extraordinary efforts to induce settlers to purchase and take up the large extent of unoccupied lands which they possess.
>
> Canada has lately discovered that she possesses in her North-West an immense extent of fertile country fit for settlement, and consequently invites a share of emigration, more especially from this country — partly to settle these new lands and partly to take the places of those farmers in Ontario and other older settled Provinces who are moving to the North-West.
>
> So many people have been deceived by overdrawn and highly coloured pictures of the Western States, published by land companies, railway companies, speculators, and others, that much suspicion and distrust of these agents generally has arisen. The Canadian Government therefore decided on asking the farmers of this country to send delegates from amongst themselves whose reports would be received at home with more confidence than the statements, however true, of their agents who were strangers. Canada. Department of Agriculture. *Reports of Tenant Farmers' Delegates.* Ottawa, 1880.

Biggar proceeded to give Canadian farming — and Mr. Pope — a very good mark.

R. H. Anderson, a tenant farmer delegate from Ireland, dismissed South Africa, New Zealand and Australia as suitable for settlers: the Basutos of South Africa were murdering farmers; as for New Zealand, "I would remind mothers of young families that the Maoris were cannibals, and they still show that the old nature is not quite dead in them." Australia had droughts and some of the deadliest snakes in the world. But Canada!

> Manitoba and the North-West are free from venomous reptiles and they seldom suffer from drought. There are snakes in the North-West but they are harmless. . . .
>
> Canada is a land of sunshine, sunshine the whole year round, and never more brilliant than in the depth of winter. Canada is a land of peace, plenty and contentment; a land of liberty, civil and religious. She is a rising country. She is bound to be the country of the future. . . . Canada can support eighty millions.

Do you wish to raise wheat? No wheat in the world is better than that grown in Manitoba, and there is nothing to limit the quantity but the ability to cultivate the soil. Do you wish to raise cattle? The largest herds of pure bred cattle in the world are in Quebec and Ontario, and there is land enough to rear cattle to supply all Europe. Do you wish to become a wine producer? Go to the valley of the Ottawa, it can be turned into one vast vineyard. Do you wish for fruit culture? Why, half Ontario is an orchard. Dominion of Canada. *Views of Members of the British Association and others. Information for Intending Settlers.* Ottawa, 1884.

William Edwards, Ruthin, Wales:

Grain elevators are erected on the railroads at convenient distances, which are of great value to settlers. The farmers cart their grain in bushel bags and empty them into the hopper. The grain is then passed through the machinery and deposited in large receptacles, perfectly clean and ready for transit. These large grain stores belong to private individuals, corn merchants, or millers, who have practical men in charge sorting or grading and pricing the wheat, which is divided into four different samples — Nos. 1 and 2 hard, Nos. 1 and 2 Northern. . . .

In crossing the stubbles in all these places [Brandon, Neepawa, Indian Head, etc.] I noticed the softness of the earth, the surface yielding under the foot like snow. Canada. Department of Agriculture. *The Visit of The Tenant-Farmer Delegates to Canada in 1890.* London, 1891.

Travel was easy on the prairie:

I arrived at Portage la Prairie [from Winnipeg] by horse teams in the short space of seven hours — a distance of 65 miles as the crow flies, but as travelled with all the prairie turnings and twistings increased by at least six or eight miles. That was only about one hour longer than it took us to travel on the Pembina Branch Railway, a distance of 62 miles — rather a humiliating commentary on the railway system of the country. . . . The roads were simply perfection, the surface was smooth and you could select your own track. When the beaten track did not suit you, you could take the grass of the Prairie, and you could drive anywhere except where, as occasionally happened, it was swampy. Peter Mitchell. *The West and North-West.* Montreal, 1880.

Mary Fitzgibbon, on roughing it:

Manitoba mosquitoes are larger than those of any other part of Canada, and nothing but smoke will drive them away. Many people who live on the prairies, instead of going for their cattle at milking time, build a smudge (a fire of chips mulched with wet hay or green twigs when well started, to create smoke) near the milk-house, and the cattle will come to the fire to obtain relief from the mosquitoes. The black-flies are smaller, and the first intimation one has of their attack is a small stream of blood trickling down one's neck from behind the ear. They bite and die, but there are myriads to take their place. The black-flies are most troublesome during the day, the mosquitoes at night. Sand-flies, as their name implies, resemble a grain of sand, and their bites are like a thousand red-hot needles piercing the skin at once; they are attracted by a light, and no netting will keep them out. Last, but by no means least, are the deer-flies, great big brutes, larger than the largest blue-bottle fly. They generally devote their attention to cattle, and I have seen the poor cows rushing madly down the clearing, the bells round their necks jangling wildly, lashing their tails and tossing their heads, never stopping until safe from their tormentors in the shelter of the dark stable. The dogs, too, are often so covered with these wretched pests, that nothing but dragging themselves through the thick underbrush will set them free.

Mary Fitzgibbon. *A Trip to Manitoba; or, Roughing It On The Line.* Toronto, 1880.

Acton Burrows was a land seller and placed an advertisement in his own pamphlet for "valuable farm lands, town lots and water privileges." He did not heavily criticize the west:

Humidity is absent; the air is bracing and dry; stagnant waters and their poisonous exhalations are unknown; fogs and mists do not occur. No epidemic has ever visited any portion of the region, with a single exception, when small-pox, first contracted in Montreal, broke out among the Icelandic settlers on the shores of Lake Winnipeg. . . .

The results of explorations leave no doubt that a large proportion of the land is of the richest possible character, ready for cultivation and for the immediate growth of crops. The enormous area occupied by this description, and the sufficiency of estate it offers for millions, places in the far future the time when it will be necessary to locate on lands whose soil is of a secondary quality. . . . No deserts similar to the arid wastes in many of the United States exist in Canadian territory.

Acton Burrows. *North Western Canada, Its Climate, Soil and Productions with a Sketch of its Natural Features and Social Condition. Land for the Landless, Homes for the Homeless, Offered in the future Wheat Field of the World.* Winnipeg, 1880.

In 1883, the Canadian agriculture department became incensed over one paragraph in an American settlers' guide that said, "The climate of Manitoba consists of seven months of Arctic winter and five months of cold weather." The department, to refute this one paragraph, issued a thirty-two-page pamphlet entitled *Canadian North-West, Climate and Productions. A Misrepresentation Exposed.* Its object, said the pamphlet, was to prevent intending immigrants from Britain being "grossly deceived."

Local puffery was also common; for example, this article, "Growth and Progress," appeared in *The Morris Herald*, Morris, Manitoba, 1882:

> The land on all sides of Morris cannot be surpassed, if indeed it can be equalled in any part of the continent. . . . The land in this section is classed A1 on Government reports, and there is nothing to prevent every acre of it from being put under cultivation. The growth is simply astonishing and the yield per acre unequalled; wheat, barley, oats, etc., growing in abundance year after year without the aid of fertilizers — no such article being heard of or used in the country. Root crops cannot be approached either as to size, quantity or quality; regardless of size, the quality is sure to be the best — solid to the core and dry.

L. O. Armstrong and several colleagues scouted the land in winter by fitting a large box on runners and using it as a mobile horse-drawn home. It bogged down in blizzards but, as Armstrong observed, so did everything else. But in his chapter on "Winter in Manitoba," he did not refer to blizzards:

> The telegrams that appear in Eastern papers, and that are copied into English papers and most industriously used against the country by the Americans, in regard to the great cold of the North-west, do us great injustice, and are to a great extent untrue. In the course of the winter we may have fifteen or twenty days when, at the coldest hour — the hour before dawn — the thermometer may fall to 40, 44, 46 and very rarely 50 below zero, but very likely the same day at noon the thermometer will rise to zero, which state of temperature, with a strong sun which always shines with us, and the stillness that always accompanies these cold snaps, gives us a delightful day. . . .
>
> The writer drove his horse on Xmas eve some distance, when it was 50 degrees below zero, and on Xmas day drove six miles with a large pleasure party of ten or twelve sleighs. It was a few degrees warmer, but not a single person of the many who went got the least frost-bitten; some of the party were dressed in furs, but many had none. . . .
>
> We have had only one heavy snowfall, and at present we have not more than six or eight inches of snow on the ground. Our climate is fascinating. The longer a man has lived in the country the fonder he is of it; there is no country under the sun that he

would exchange for it. L. O. Armstrong. *Southern Manitoba and Turtle Mountain Country*. N.p., 1880.

W. B. Macdougall wrote a useful guide that included an eight-page gazeteer of Manitoba and the Northwest Territories. It is particularly interesting today for the locations not included in 1880: Regina and Calgary, for two. It listed thirty-four separate Mennonite villages and

> Mennonite Settlements, Pembina Mountain — The first settlement of Mennonites in the Pembina Mountain Reserve took place in July, 1870, when about 300 families arrived. At the present time there are thirty-four villages, with populations of 70 to 200 each, making a total of about seven hundred families, or over four thousand souls. The only church in the reserve is in their land, and there is no post office, the mail being taken from Emerson. There is a school in every village, and also a grocer, blacksmith, shoemaker, carpenter, and saddler. There are several grist and saw mills; and the people, who are nearly all farmers, are well supplied with farm stock and implements.
> W. B. Macdougall. *Guide to Manitoba and the North-West*. N.p., 1880.

A Winnipeg firm of barristers, in its thirty-two-page land sale catalogue, quoted Alexander Begg's 1877 *Guide to Manitoba*:

> It is our opinion that an immigrant would be unwise to go far beyond the line of settlement, or to undertake to go to the Saskatchewan in advance of civilization, for the following reasons:
> 1. The heavy cost of getting to his claim.
> 2. His isolation until settlements reach him.
> 3. The high cost for procuring the necessaries of life.
> 4. The distance from a market.
> 5. His isolation from churches and schools.

This advice went hand in glove with Ross, Ross & Killam's attempt to sell land near Winnipeg, Portage La Prairie, Emerson, West Lynne, Morris, Palestine, Westbourne and Selkirk. The company said it had no desire to belittle Saskatchewan, which was equal to Manitoba in soil, climate and other advantages

> But our desire is not to mislead people for the mere purpose of advancing immigration, and the development of the country will be sufficiently promoted by allowing the progress of settlements to be gradual rather than scattered in its character.

The lawyers' brochure listed these prices for farm machinery at Winnipeg: breaking ploughs, $25 to $29; reapers, $140 to $160; mowers, $80 to $120; horse rakes, $35 to $45; wagons, $80 to $95; fanning mills, $30 to $45; spades, $1; hay forks, 75 cents; manure forks, $1; harrows, $15 to $35. A span of horses

n $200 and $300, a yoke of oxen between $140 and $175, and cows
5 and $35.

:llent is the prairie grass that cattle driven for hundreds of miles
__ the plains, towards a market, improve steadily in weight and
condition as they proceed on their journey. Ross, Ross & Killam. *Canada,
Manitoba. Sixty Thousand Acres of Select Farming Lands in the vicinity of Winnipeg and
the various Settlements of the Province of Manitoba, for sale by. . .* Toronto, 1880.

Capt. C. W. Allen recommended that land hunters travel in small parties of no
more than three or four. Otherwise, disputes arose over choice of locations:

The small parties should travel as light as possible with a small wagon or Red
River cart drawn by oxen or a pair of native ponies. The ponies were hardy,
thrived on prairie grass and there was no need to carry oats for them. An extra
horse was recommended, with saddle and bridle, because a man on horse could
cover more ground and see farther than a man on foot. The harness should
include a breast band so that the extra horse could help pull the wagon out of
swamps or coulees.

Allen advised a party to equip itself with a map of the desired district; a
telescope or field glasses; pocket compass; measuring tape or chain, with cross-
staff and rods and calico (the last to be used as flags); kettle; frying pan; teapot;
axe; auger; butcher's knife; lantern; scythe and whetstone (to cut grass for the
ponies, which would not stray from mosquito smudges to forage for
themselves); halter and pair of hobbles for each animal; fifty feet of rope; spade;
strong cord; nails and screws; coal-oil stove for woodless areas; bacon; potatoes
or beans; biscuits and flour; tea or coffee; sugar; molasses; dried apples; coal oil;
matches; soap; baking powder; candles; pencils (black, red and blue to sketch
trails, rivers and lakes, and woods); knife, fork and spoon each; one-pint
drinking cup; change of shirt, drawers and socks; towels; blankets; mosquito
bars; waterproof coats; long boots and one or two guns for game. Capt. C. W.
Allen. *The Land Prospector's Manual and Field-Book, for the use of immigrants and capitalists
taking up lands in Manitoba and the North-West Territories of Canada.* Ottawa, 1881.

Allen's manual received high praise from an experienced prairie traveller,
John Macoun, in his 1882 book, *Manitoba and the Great North-West*: "Should
any person be travelling in the surveyed districts, Captain Allen's Prospector's
Manual will be found invaluable, as it is superior to a whole army of unlettered
guides, and will never lead any one astray."

Thomas Spence was the clerk of the legislative council of Manitoba and put
out at least five pamphlets on the resources of the Northwest, that is, all
Canadian territory west of Lake Superior, excepting British Columbia.

Agriculture implements of all kinds should be brought by the
immigrant, as they are yet both scarce and dear. The most

indispensable would be a good steel plough for breaking land, harrow, etc., and as many of the necessaries required by an emigrant as can be conveniently carried. . . .

For fencing, poplar will generally be found in small groves on the prairie, or on the banks of streams, and, if the bark is peeled off, makes a good and lasting fence, small ash or oak being used for the pickets, when it can be conveniently found. A good tent is indispensable for the comfort of the immigrant and his family, both for the journey and for summer accommodation till a house is built. Thomas Spence. *Manitoba and the North-West of the Dominion, Its Resources and Advantages to the Emigrant and Capitalist. Toronto, 1871; Useful and Practical Hints for the Settler on Canadian Prairie Lands*. Ottawa, 1881.

W. Fraser Rae, a British newspaperman, noted in Winnipeg that the common catfish sold very well under the name "Red River salmon" and that vegetables at the market were "gigantic."

It is a common thing for potatoes to weigh two pounds each and turnips 20 pounds and for them to be as good as they are heavy. A squash has been produced weighing 138 pounds and a vegetable marrow 26. Cabbages measuring four feet eight inches and five feet one inch in circumference have excited the astonishment of other visitors as well as my own, while a cucumber, grown in open air and measuring six feet three inches in length, was rightly considered a curiosity. The display of fruit was not equal to that of vegetables, the culture of fruit having been neglected owing to the supply of wild fruit being so varied and abundant.

Rae found in the Red River Valley the same disinterest in manure noted by writers in Newfoundland and Lower Canada:

I visited farms in the parish of Kildonan where wheat had been sown and where crops had been reaped for sixty years in succession without manure being applied. Indeed, the Red River farmers have long regarded the natural fertilizers of the soil as an incumbrance of which they try to rid themselves with the least possible trouble. Their habit was to cast manure into the river. . . . One of the earliest legislative enactments [in 1870] provided that the farmer who polluted a river with manure should pay a fine of $25 or else be imprisoned for two months. W. Fraser Rae. *Newfoundland to Manitoba*. New York, 1881.

Settlers were in for rude surprises:

The question of a suitable settlement for the sons of naval and military officers, clergymen, professional men, etc., has long been an anxious one, the system of competitive examinations having practically excluded all but the talented and studious from the prizes in the civil and military services, and professional life generally.

Although the English have been termed "a nation of shopkeepers," trade seldom commends itself to the classes above referred to, and Colonial Life seems the only 'refuge for the destitute' that in most cases offers itself.

The first rule of settlement had been ignored and purchase made sight unseen on a piece of land near Headingly:

> It would be difficult to describe our dismay when we contemplated one of the dirtiest and most delapitated-looking sheds called a dwelling-house we had ever entered. Certainly I had never kept my horses in a stable half so bad. . . . Down came the rain in drenching storms that lasted, on and off, the whole night through. All was dirt and rubbish within, aggravated by some evident attempts at whitewashing that had left the floors with spots of lime all over. . . . Rain came right through the roof and bedroom floor, down into the room we occupied, in such quantity as almost to rival a shower-bath. Mosquitoes were worrying us the night through. W. & R. Chambers. *A Year in Manitoba 1880-1881 being the Experience of a Retired Officer in Settling his Sons.* 2d ed. London and Edinburgh, 1882.

John Macoun's *Manitoba and The Great North-West*, at 692 pages, is encyclopedic. Macoun was an agriculturalist, botanist, geologist, geographer, surveyor, climatologist, railway enthusiast, bird watcher and what have you, all rolled into one sturdy traveller who criss-crossed the prairies year after year. In two summers alone, 1879 and 1880, he covered 4,300 miles, chiefly by compass. His journeyings produced a wealth of practical advice:

> I consider a prairie thunder storm as one of the most appalling occurrences which a traveller on the plain has to encounter, and one which he has no means to escape. There are few days in June and July when thunder is not heard from some point of the compass. . . .
>
> All travellers should have a strong cover for each waggon or cart, and see that it is securely fastened every night before retiring to his tent. Very frequently, the traveller may retire to rest with not a speck of cloud anywhere above the horizon, and wake up a little after midnight with the incessant roll of thunder in his ears, and his eyes blinded with the vivid lightning. It is now that the unwary traveller pays the penalty for being ignorant. Carelessly pitched tents are blown down, or the rain pours through, and everything is thoroughly soaked. Morning breaks and the goods are found injured by the rain, and to complete the disaster, the horses have stampeded and are nowhere to be found.

When seeking a camping place for the night, any time during the summer, an elevated spot, near a pool of water, should be chosen, so that comparative freedom from mosquitoes may be secured if there should be a little wind. All the conveyances should be placed west of the tents, and each tent securely tied to a cart by a guy rope passing over the end of the ridge-pole. The rear of the tents should be next to the carts, so that should a storm arise during the night, there would be no danger of the tents being blown down. . . .

Horses will not face a severe rain and wind storm on the prairie, so that it is absolutely necessary to stop if the storm is meeting you. On the approach of a thunder storm in the day time, which may be of short duration, it is only necessary to turn the horses' heads away from the storm, and they will stand perfectly quiet. All through the summer, mosquitoes are very troublesome at night, and often put the horses almost wild. Every evening it is necessary to make a "smudge" to keep off the flies and enable the horses to eat a little during the night. It is made by lighting a fire with a little dry wood, and then putting on green sticks and covering all up with sods, so as to make a continuous smoke. When flies are troublesome and a little wind stirring, horses always feed head to wind, and it is necessary to note the direction of the wind before retiring to rest, as it is nothing unusual to find that the horses have gone off miles during the night. By noting how the wind blows in the evening and how it is in the morning, a man of some experience will always go straight to the horses, even if they are miles away. Many parties think it cruel to hobble horses every night after having been in harness all day, but experience proves that horses eat more and wander less by adopting this practice. . . .

The chief trouble of the North-West is the mosquito. I have seen men so punished by them that their eyes were closed, their necks swollen, and they suffered great agony. There is no use in disguising the fact of their constant presence, and of their being a real plague. Settlers on the prairie must expect them for years to come. Tents can be kept clear of mosquitoes only by closing every aperture by which they can enter, as one small hole will often admit more flies than two men can dispose of. They enter tents just in the same way that bees enter a hive, and should one make its way in, it will be followed by hundreds in a short time. After closing the tent so that none could enter, a man with a lighted candle soon singed the wings of those within.

In the depth of winter, tents are not used by travellers except they are supplied with a small stove. A winter camping place is chosen in a thicket or grove where wood is abundant. One section of the party gets wood while the other clears away the snow from where the sleeping place and fire are to be. Brush is strewn thickly for a bed and in the direction of the wind it is piled up to make a wind-break. The fire is built in front and along the back a piece of canvas is stretched which keeps out the wind and reflects the heat. Buffalo robes and blankets are now spread on the boughs, and although the temperature of the air may be far below zero, comfort and genuine pleasure reign in the bivouac. John Macoun. *Manitoba and The Great North-West.* Guelph, 1882.

Thomas Stephenson, a Yorkshire farmer, paid his own way to check on Canada's agricultural prospects for himself and his neighbors. In Ottawa, he met Agriculture Minister Pope, who told him:

Go through the country, form your own conclusions as to its advantages and disadvantages and when you get back to England state them to the people, give them the dark side as well as the bright side, and let them decide for themselves.

Near Oakville, Ontario, on Mr. White's 427-acre farm,

I saw, to me, a most remarkable sight, six miles of fencing made with the roots of the pine trees which had been drawn out of the ground by a stump extractor, and then placed on their edges around the fields, making a very formidable fence.

In Manitoba,

last spring's floods did a large amount of mischief, yet the reports which reached the lower provinces of Canada and England were very much exaggerated, and I fear that it was done intentionally by parties who wished to turn the stream of emigration towards the States rather than Canada.

In Brandon, Stephenson noted a primitive rural post office — "a three-legged stool, and underneath a tin pail to put the letters in" — and of his ride "by stage waggon" over the open prairie to Rapid City and Oak River, he wrote:

There are no fences, and one of the laws of Manitoba compels all the people in each township who have cattle to send them all in a flock, attended by a boy or man on horseback. They are pastured by the sides of the rivers and creeks during the day, are taken home at night and shut up in large pens till the morning, when they are again taken in charge, so that there is no danger to the farmers' crops. Thomas Stephenson. *Notes of a Tour through the provinces of Quebec, Ontario, Manitoba and the North-West Territory.* Liverpool, N.d. [ca. 1882].

Mrs. Mary Georgina Caroline Hall wrote of a farm eight miles from Headingly, Manitoba:

> All the winter the four men were what is called in this country "baching it" (from bachelor), namely, having to do everything for themselves; it is, perhaps, not surprising that the floors are rather dirty and that there is a little dust. The weather is much against our cleaning, as the mud sticks to the boots and, do what you will, it is almost impossible to get off; not that the men seem to have thought much about it, as, until we arrived and suggested it, there was no scraper to either door. Poor Mr. B expressing some lament . . . that all his cabbages would be killed [by frost], we said that it was a pity he had sown them out of doors, as he might almost have grown them on the dining-room carpet. . . .
>
> At half-past 1 when the men turn out again, we generally go out with them, and some out-door occupation is found for us; either driving the waggons or any other odd jobs. There is a lot of hay littered about, and that has to be stacked; also the waste straw or rubbish which is burnt, and the fires have to be made up. . . . The [horses] are hard, plucky little beasts, and curiously quiet. The long winter makes them, as well as all the other animals, feel a dependence upon man, and they become unusually tame. The cows, cats, and everything follow the men about everywhere. They used to have to keep the kitchen door shut to prevent one of the cows walking in. . . .
>
> [On Sunday] the men lie stetched on the straw-heaps in the yard, basking and snoozing in the sun. We generally have some stray man out from Winnipeg, and are much struck with the coolness of their ways. Colonial manners, somehow, jar a good deal on one; they take it quite as a matter of course that we ladies should wait on them at table, and attend to their bodily comforts. Mrs. Cecil Hall. *A Lady's Life on a Farm in Manitoba*. London, 1884.

W. Henry Barneby wrote of a prairie field:

> Of 1,200 acres, two miles long, being ploughed, the team having to traverse that distance before turning. Two trips are made in the morning and two in the evening (feeding-time coming between), so that the horses have to make good time in order to reach the feeding trough at the proper hour. They plough seventy acres a day, using no steam power, only horses. We saw a stable for waggon-horses built to hold no less than 105.

In southern Manitoba, he visited the Mennonite farming village of Rosenfeld:

The homesteads are very picturesque, being, as nearly as possible, exact copies of the inhabitants' old Russian homes; a very few are built entirely of wood, but most of them had wood-framing, plastered and whitewashed at the base, the two gable ends being of wood, and surmounted by a thatched roof. The living-room, stable, cow-house, and waggon-house all join, communicating throughout with doors, but the pigs have, as a rule, a separate establishment to themselves outside. Over the whole building (living-house, stable, etc.) there is one large open loft which forms a kind of granary, and serves every sort of purpose, being not only a store-room, but a general receptacle for everything, whether because not wanted downstairs or as requiring shelter.

At the first house . . . we found the owner, with his mother-in-law, wife, and child, all seated at a table with a tin dish of milk and sour-krout before them; this constituted their dinner; they were all eating out of the common dish, though, happily, with separate spoons.

The floor of the room was partly of earth, and partly neatly boarded, and a ladder communicated with the loft above. The earthen floor formed, as it were, the parlour of the establishment, the boarded portion being used as the dairy, and for the various utensils not in immediate use, which were arranged here on little wooden forms, or small square tables. The buckets were generally placed in threes, and many of the other utensils appeared to have special forms allotted to them, and were placed three or four in a row. All was clean and perfectly neat; indeed, it was more like a show-house at an exhibition than an ordinary dwelling-room. . . . In the windows stood neat little pots of flowers and prairie roses.

Opening out of this combined room (in which the difference in the flooring was the only distinction) were two bedrooms, separated by a boarded partition with a curtain drawn across. The family treasures, consisting of china, glass, spoons, etc., were kept in one of the bedrooms, on shelves in a window opening into the sitting-room. Thus the contents of the room could be seen on both sides.

There were two wooden beds, a crib, a very large oak case, a table with a pile of winter blankets, and what we would call eider-down quilts, and a couple of stools. The oven opened out of the bedroom; from the sitting-room passed an open chimney, which acted partly as an escape for the smoke from the stove below, and partly as a ventilator.

Under the same roof, and communicating by a door, were the stable, cow-house, etc.; and I think it is very possibly owing to this arrangement that the report has been spread that these Mennonites are such a dirty people, living under the same roof as their animals.

For my part, I must say I do not think it is at all a bad arrangement but, on the contrary, very suitable to the climate, for it enables the owners to get to the stock without having to go out-of-doors; and, as far as I could ascertain, the plan was not open to objection on the score of want of cleanliness.

Barneby had a useful tip for travellers not usually found in travel accounts of the time:

Let me here recommend future travellers in North America never to be without medicine of some description in case of a sudden attack of diarrhoea, which is very prevalent, partly on account of the climate, and more often by reason of drinking bad water or too much iced water. From personal experience I can strongly recommend the diarrhoea and cholera tablets of Messrs. Savory and Moore, of New Bond Street, which may be carried without inconvenience. Another remedy is a few drops of chlorodyne in water; this I have found the stronger and perhaps the more efficacious of the two. W. Henry Barneby. *Life and Labour in the Far, Far West.* London, 1884.

The CPR published many pamphlets to attract settlers to the prairies and, more specifically, to the farmland it had for sale adjacent to its tracks. Prices started at $2.50 an acre, one-tenth down and nine more years to pay, interest six per cent a year. The pamphlets included such titles as *Dairy Farming and Ranching, A Scotch Farmer's Success, 100 Farmers Testify, The Manitoba Land Folder, British Columbia,* and *The North-West Farmer in Manitoba, Assiniboia, Alberta.*

This was probably the most unusual pamphlet issued by any agency, government or private. The railway company had sought the views of women through a questionnaire in September, 1885, and here set them out — at least the favorable ones. The general tone of the replies was that things were pretty tough at the start, but hard work brought good crops and comfort.

The chief question concerned advice for newcomers, and here are some of the replies:

Mrs. F. Robbie, Birtle P.O., Man. — "Keep your eyes open. Live within your means. Take no notice of grumblers. Make ready for winter. Let the children wear woollen underclothing. Take in the *Nor'West Farmer* [magazine], and a weekly newspaper. Settle near a railroad if possible. Go in for mixed farming. Never blame the country for any misfortune you may have. Have a good garden. Exhibit all you can at the Fall Shows. Determine that the North-West is to be your home."

Mrs. A.B. Harris of Beulah, Manitoba — "A man should spend his first summer putting up buildings, digging a well, and getting everything into shape for his wife and family. He will save time in the long run. A cold house and no water when it is wanted will make a smiling face look sour and make her a grumbler."

Mrs. G. Butcher, of Russell P.O., Shell River, Man. — "Every housekeeper here learns to be baker, laundress, tailoress, soap and candle maker, and dairywoman."

Mrs. C.C. Clitten, of Bird's Hill — "Make a point of setting out raspberries, currants, and strawberries as soon as possible."

Mrs. W. Cooper, of Treherne — "Lend a helping hand to the men, not supposing it is out of a woman's sphere, as the first year brings lots of extra work on the men."

Mrs. J.N. Davidson, Rapid City — "Bring plain, comfortable clothing, and sufficient good sense to avoid all romantic ideas of accepting the first offer of marriage on arriving here; also frivolous notions about dress, reading novels, and the like."

By design or accident, one male reply made its way into the 50-page pamphlet:

Mr. John Pollock, of Wolf Creek — "If you have any young girls in your country who would like to start housekeeping, this is the place to come. There are lots of young men who want housekeepers. I would like to give over the job of washing the dishes myself." Canadian Pacific Railway: *What Women Say of the Canadian North West*. Montreal, 1886.

Prairie life created rich hospitality:

Hospitality is a right, not a virtue, in these far off climes. When you have driven perhaps 30 miles, and mid-day with its corresponding hunger has come, you simply make for the first house that you see, unhitch your horses and make them comfortable in the stable, and then walk into the kitchen and ask for dinner without so much as "by your leave." Whatever the house affords is spread out before you, and if you are a stranger you offer to pay, and the offer is generally accepted, especially if the house is on a frequented trail and half way between two towns. *The Montreal Star. The Prairies of Manitoba and Who Live on Them*. Montreal, N.d. [ca. 1888].

W. A. Webster, a Leeds county farmer in Ontario, made what he called a "personal examination" of the regions of his title to judge their worth as settlement lands. The Canadian side of the border came out far ahead. Webster's trip was one of the many devices backed by the Canadian government — though *The Ottawa Citizen* and not the government printed his highly detailed report — to counter American immigration agents operating throughout Ontario. Webster's report is impressive because he covered so much territory by train, buggy, horseback, and on foot, talking to farmers and not to land agents.

Webster quickly dismissed Minnesota: farmers were leaving that state for Dakota because of drought and lack of desirable land except for that held by grasping speculators and syndicates. In Dakota, many areas were subject to fearful cyclones that blew seed right out of the ground and caused hailstones as big as hens' eggs. Rail freight rates on wheat were exorbitant and taxes too high on farmland. Remains of homestead cabins littered the Dakota prairie, and on the door of one abandoned hut he found this notice:

Four miles from a nayber
Sixty miles from a post ofis
Twenty miles from a ralerode
A Hundred and Atey from timber
250 feet from water. God bless our Home.
We have gone east to spend the winter with my wife's relations.

By contrast, southern Manitoba was fine, rolling prairie with a promising wheat crop. Webster, who had had to clear land in Ontario, was fascinated by the treeless prairie. The land, he wrote, is

a fine black mould, no stones, no ditching required after the sod is once broke. The farmer sits on the gang plough and ploughs the ground; a boy sits on the seeder and sows the grain; another boy sits on the harrow and harrows in the seed. When the wheat is ripe, a man sits on the binder, cuts and binds the grain; up to this point all the work has been done sitting on a spring seat. Such are some of the agricultural possibilities of the alluvial prairie in Manitoba and the North-West. W. A. Webster. *A Canadian Farmer's Report. Minnesota and Dakota compared with Manitoba and the Canadian North-West.* Ottawa, 1888.

H. A. McGusty worked his way on farms and ranches (he learned to plough and break a bronco) but was mainly in Canada, like a lot of other young Englishmen at the time, for hunting and fishing. His small book was printed originally for relatives and friends.

I should not recommend you to waste any time, but just start out, you can learn what is necessary to run a ranch best on the ranch. For instance, I myself learnt to shoe horses before going out. When I got there, I found that it is very seldom a horse is shod on the prairie. . . .

You must address people whom in England you would probably consider your inferiors as equals, as it is no uncommon circumstances to find that the boots in the hotel, or the ostler in a livery stable, is a gentleman and public school man. . . .

The shanty of Manitoba is small, usually built of lumber, and has rather the appearance of a toy house; but it is a palace compared to the "shack" which the inhabitants of the North-West territories live in. . . .

It takes the "tenderfoot" some time to get used to sleeping on the floor, though in Manitoba the majority of settlers manage to get a bedstead and a mattress, which in the North-West are usually deemed superfluous. People think they are well fixed if they can afford to lay in a stock of the following articles: flour, tea, sugar, bacon, salt, potatoes, syrup. Milk and butter are usually considered luxuries. Of course we have to make our own bread, and the first few attempts would kill an ostrich. . . .

The only difficult part of driving oxen is the swearing. You must swear: they refuse to move if you do not, and it must be genuine profanity, no half and half swear words. However, if a chap is industrious and really sets his mind to it, he will be able to swear pretty well in a month or two. . . .

The farmers have very large pieces of ploughing, some as much as 400 or 500 acres; still, they do not seem to make money; in fact, I never saw people so universally hard up in my life. This is chiefly due to the mortgages which almost every farmer has upon his place, also to the great cost of machinery. H. A. McGusty. *Two Years in Manitoba and the North-West Territory.* Frome, N.d., [ca. 1890].

John Pritchard describes being lost on the prairie:

I suffered greatly by a kind of grass very common in the plains, called by the Canadians and very justly, the thorn grass. Even your shoes and leather breeches it finds its way through. At night when I encamped my legs had the appearance of a porcupine. I durst not take them out in the day, as others would immediately enter, and at night you may suppose the blood flowed. John Pritchard. *Glimpses of the Past in the Red River Settlement.* Middle Church, Manitoba, 1892.

R. G. MacBeth's four-page pamphlet, from a series produced by the Historical and Scientific Society of Manitoba, reminds one of what nearly all early travellers along the St. Lawrence River also remarked on: the narrow, deep farms that made the shore a "continuous village."

The colonists brought out from Scotland by Lord Selkirk chose to settle along the banks of the Red River on narrow farms (the general width being ten chains frontage on the river) running back at right angles from it on the prairie. These farms extended back two miles as a freehold with an additional two miles as a hay privilege. These ten chain lots owned by the head of the family were frequently subdivided amongst the sons, so that when the Ontario people, accustomed to square farms, began to come amongst us, they were greatly amused at "our farming on lanes," and pointed out the disadvantages of having to go a distance of two miles or more to the cultivated plots at the outlying ends of these river strips. But there was much method in the madness of long, narrow farms; or, to be plainer, there were many good reasons to justify that plan of settlement. To begin with, the settlers built along the river banks for convenience in obtaining water. Outside the swamps and sloughs, the river was practically the only source of water supply. . . . Settlement by the river bank had food as well as water supply in view, for fish, from "gold eyes" to sturgeon, were then plentiful in the unpolluted stream, and afforded a provision by no means to be despised. As to the narrow lots, it can be readily seen that the colonists settled together for mutual defence and the advantages of social life as well as for church and school facilities. . . .

Besides the raising of grain and root crops the settlers, as the years advanced, went into stock raising, and had horses, cattle, sheep and swine on their farms. In the days before the incoming of machinery they raised horses principally for the buffalo hunters from famous running stock imported originally from England. The "plain hunters" came in at certain seasons around Fort Garry, when the settlers would take to them such horses as they had to sell. Trials of speed followed, and the winning horses brought good prices in cash from the hunters who had just disposed of their buffalo meat, robes and furs to the Hudson's Bay Company. R. G. MacBeth. *Farm Life in the Selkirk Colony*. Winnipeg, 1897.

Settler John Hardy outlined early prairie life:

When the required number of acres is broken up attention should be given to the building of the house. If of logs, they should be stripped of the bark and got in readiness for placing in position. The house should face south, on the highest point possible, to command a good view of the farm and surrounding district. This would ensure a dry cellar — an absolute necessity in Manitoba — for it is here that potatoes and other such perishables are stored during winter. . . .

A mower and rake costs from 70 to 80 dollars. By paying cash for all implements, one is in a better position for making bargains, and should obtain a substantial rebate. I should like to point out the curse of getting machinery and implements on the credit system, this being the keynote of many failures. Dealers are only too ready to let you have what you require at an enhanced price plus 10 per cent for accommodation. Many farmers have paid twice over for their binders, etc., under this system, and I know of several cases where the machinery has been quite worn out before the last payment has been made. Make sure you really require the implement before buying it, and then, if possible, pay cash. . . .

When stacked [hay] should be fenced with barbed wire to keep out stray horses and cattle that may be roaming the prairie. A fire-guard should also be ploughed round it. A very safe guard can be made by ploughing a strip of land, ten yards wide, then leave a space of ten yards unploughed in the centre, and then plough another strip of ten yards on the outside of this. Proceed either to burn or cut down any tall grasses that remain on the unploughed strip in the centre. . . . A good plan is to grow root crops, especially potatoes, on the guard, as constant hoeing keeps it free of weeds and so serves a double purpose. . . .

The threshing gang proper consists of about 12 or 14 men who are paid by the owner of the machine at the rate of 1 1/4 dollars for pitchers, and 2 dollars per day for feeders. They work from daylight to dark, and very often by the light of the burning straw if there is a prospect of finishing up the job. Most engines burn straw for fuel and it is one man's work firing. The gang is supposed to do all the pitching, band-cutting, feeding, and bagging, and cart their own water. . . .

Great activity prevails at the house. Special long tables are provided, placed on trestles, which are laden with steaming hot potatoes, roast beef, and other such commodities, all placed on dishes for everyone to help themselves. To help yourself is one of the customs of the country, for they do not stand on ceremony.

The whistle is blown for supper, and the men rush to the house. . . . After supper the kitchen is cleared of tables and merry-making is indulged in. This goes on until about 10 o'clock, when the men retire to their caboose for the night. The caboose is a house on wheels, fitted with berths similar to those met with on board ship. . . .

Canadian boys take to farmwork at an early age. They learn to ride and herd cattle when quite young, and are accustomed to look after their own horse during school days, for in numbers of cases they have to drive to school owing to the long distances they have to go. There is usually a stable at each school and each boy attends to his own horse. From this period onwards he makes steady progress and will be found with a plough and a team of horses at the age of fourteen.

The girls learn to milk when quite young and soon become useful, so it will be seen, indeed, that lucky is the man with a large family.

Canadian girls seldom or never go out to service as there is always plenty for them to do at home. Domestic servants are very scarce. . . . If one is fortunate enough to obtain a girl, she seldom stays long, and, considering the dearth of women in the country, it is in no way surprising to find a number of bachelor farmers calling at the homestead offering to drive the girl out to look around. It invariably ends in her becoming the mistress of a farm and making some bachelor happy. An Old Settler [John Hardy]: *Farming in the Canadian North-West*. London, N.d.. [ca. 1903].

E. Way Elkington was able to laugh about hunting for his property.

When in Winnipeg you are shown a map of the country cut up into sections and on certain squares is written the word "School." You are told how to get to the place you choose, and away you go smiling. You take your ticket to the nearest railway station and arrive at a tumble-down village with two or three wooden shacks, an hotel, a general store and perhaps a barber's shop; then your troubles begin.

The place you want may be up at the North Pole for all the inhabitants of the shack-town care or know, but if you pay a big enough price, one of the enterprising farmers in the district may lend you a rig (four-wheeled buggy) so that you can look for it yourself. You pay by the day for the rig anything from £2 to £5. At the end of three weeks you return and say you have not found it and have had almost nothing to eat and seen no one from whom you could get anything, you will greatly amuse your listeners and they will then offer to sell you some land quite close to the "city" — don't pass any remarks about the use of the word "city" or look round in the direction of the five shacks or you will hurt their feelings and they might even refuse to sell land to you.

If you are still persistent and want your one hundred and sixty free acres, they will probably offer to send out a search-party for it, but it will cost you at least fifty dollars, and then they might not be able to locate it.

If you are wise you will stand them all drinks and wait till the next train comes and then return to civilisation. You will save yourself endless disappointment and much worry and misery. The chief duty of the Royal North-West Mounted Police is fetching in maniacs from these free quarter-sections — the loneliness gets on their nerves and then they get what the Canadians call "bug-house." E. Way Elkington. *Canada The Land of Hope*. London, 1910.

There was no end to chores:

Mr. Gregory calls everyone at 5 o'clock when he gets up and lights the fire. Little Ben and I go out first to the stables, and feed the cows and clean out the cows' stalls, while Mr. Gregory attends to the horses. By this time Mrs. Gregory is out, and she and Little Ben milk the cows between them. As soon as I can milk properly, Little Ben and I are to do all the milking. At present I am learning to milk on what they call a "stripper," that is, a cow which only gives a little milk, and which they will stop milking altogether soon. . . .

For breakfast the chief item is the oatmeal porridge, of which everyone has a large soup-plate full, with milk and sugar. There are bread and butter and coffee, and sometimes cold meat — pork — but the porridge is the "stand by". . . .

Mr. Gregory and Little Ben go to the stables, and are soon out in the fields. Big Ben with the seeder, sowing the corn, and Little Ben with the harrows, covering it over and smoothing the ground.

Mrs. Gregory and I attend to the milk. All the new milk is put through a thing called a "separator," which separates the cream from the milk — it is worked with a big wheel and a handle, and I turn the handle while Mrs. Gregory attends to the milk and the cream. It takes about half-an-hour, but it is hard work while it lasts. When that is done I feed the calves and the pigs with the milk and some other stuff that is put in the milk (some kind of crushed corn) they call it "chop" — nothing to do with mutton!

My next chore is to feed the hens, of which there are nearly a hundred. We get about fifty eggs a day, but there are not many of them that appear on the table as they fetch a good price in town. When they get down to fifteen cents a dozen, Mrs. Gregory says we can eat all we like.

This finishes my regular morning round; the rest of the chores are incidental, and vary from day to day — getting water for the house from the well at the back of the bluff, a hundred yards away; cutting long poles into fire-wood for the stove with a "buck" saw; splitting the wood with an axe and filling the wood box in the shed; and the last few days I have been doing some gardening and putting in some seeds. This, from my old fondness for gardening, is more in my line, and I find I know more about it then they do here. It was a treat to find something I could do without having to have a woman or a "kid" to show me how.

At twelve o'clock Mr. Gregory and Little Ben come in with their horses and we have dinner, usually "pig" in some shape (roasted, boiled or fried), plenty of very good potatoes, rice pudding also, usually, with an occasional "pie" (so called), of dried apples, or prunes, or raisins. Then there is bread and butter and tea again. I am always as hungry as a hunter, or it would be a pretty monotonous diet. After dinner, Mr. Gregory goes back to his seeding, and Little Ben and I . . . let the cattle out and drive them to a slough (a big pond) for water, and back again to a big yard where there were some straw stacks, but now the weather is warmer we let them out in the morning and they wander about on the prairie till evening, when we put them back in the stable, and give them some hay before we have supper.

In the afternoon I get out with Little Ben and work with him at the harrowing. He has a quiet pair of horses and I can drive them pretty well now, and can put their harness on, and "hitch" onto the harrows quite farmer-like. It seems generally to be windy here, and the ground is very dry and dusty; when we come in from the fields we are as black as sweeps.

We come in from work at about five o'clock, and by supper time, at six, we have the cattle fed and all the chores done, except milking. For supper we have bread and butter, fried potatoes and cold meat — still pig — and tea. Supper over, the milking and its attendant chores of separating the cream and feeding the pigs and calves brings the day to an end. Mr. Gregory helps at these at night, and they do not take long. Then bed, and it's a pretty tired "chore boy" that lays his head on the pillow. E. A. Wharton Gill. *A Manitoba Chore Boy. The Experiences of a Young Emigrant Told from his Letters.* London, 1912.

From a report prepared for the Manitoba government when John Bracken was premier. Multiculturalism decades ahead of its time?

The total population of this area [southeastern Manitoba] is about 20,000, of whom only 8.2 per cent are of British origin, 42 per cent are Slav, chiefly Ukranian, 22.2 per cent are French, 21.3 per cent are German or Mennonite, and about 4 per cent are Scandinavian.

The settlement of the western half of this area began at quite an early date, but the southern portion was settled in the first decade of this century, while the extreme southeast is somewhat newer still.

While the population is mixed as to its origin, it would be wrong to assume that the mixture was leading rapidly to assimilation. There is a decided tendency to segregate and with very few exceptions the customs, language and in some respects the farming methods are reproductions of their European prototypes and, however undesirable it may appear to the sociologist to have these types persist without modification, it would seem expedient from the point of view of immediate establishment of new settlers to direct members of the different nationalities to settle amongst their own people. R. W. Murchie and H. C. Grant. *Unused Lands of Manitoba.* Winnipeg, 1926.

In a similar vein, here's a short extract from testimony given April 25, 1870, to the Senate committee on Rupert's Land, Red River and the North-West Territory. The witness is a schoolteacher, John James Setter of Portage la Prairie, then a settlement of 300:

Q: The settlement where you reside is entirely Protestant?

A: Entirely so.

Q: Is there a higher school belonging to the Protestants?

A: Yes, Bishop M'Crae's, at St. John's [Winnipeg], where they teach classics, mathematics, theology. There are several Divinity students there. There are no Protestants at St. Boniface. The Protestants and Catholics do not mix as a rule.

Agricultural technology advanced quickly:

At the beginning of our grain growing era all grain had to be bagged at the threshing machine, handled in bags by the farmers in delivering to the railway and carried into the cars. This laborious method of handling was carried right through to the ultimate consumer.

Sometime in the later 1880s someone conceived the brilliant idea that threshed grain had a good deal of fluidity, that it would flow almost like a liquid and that this characteristic could be taken advantage of in its transportation and storage.

So we find a whole series of mechanical changes coming in to make possible the bulk handling of grain. First in the threshing machine the grain is raised so that it will flow into a waggon, then the farmer uses a tight waggon box and hauls his grain as a liquid, then the country elevator arises at every shipping point, followed by the big terminal elevator and the tank-like grain boat. So in every move that wheat makes it is raised by mechanical power and flows into the appointed place. And thus from the time the unthreshed sheaf enters the threshing machine until the flour emerges from the mill, the strength of man is never used to move the wheat. This is such a commonplace to us in Manitoba now that it is hard to believe that it has all come about in forty-five years and that some of the world's greatest wheat growing countries are still handling it in bags.
W. C. McKillican. *An Outline of the History of Agriculture in Manitoba. Given before the Historical and Scientific Society of Manitoba, Winnipeg, Nov. 6, 1929.* [Manuscript] *Provincial Library Manitoba.*

Alexander Ross retired from Hudson's Bay Company service so that he could settle in one place that would provide a "Christian education" for his children. As a gift, HBC Governor George Simpson presented him with a 100-acre farm on the Red River.

What a hundred acres! The farm was, as usual in the Red River Settlement, long and narrow. It ran back two miles from the Red — between, it turned out, William Avenue on the south and Logan Avenue on the north in the City of Winnipeg. Alexander Ross. *Letters of a Pioneer*. Winnipeg: The Historical and Scientific Society of Manitoba, 1903.

SASKATCHEWAN

THE LAND AROUND CUMBERLAND HOUSE is low, but the soil, from having a considerable intermixture of limestone, is good, and capable of producing abundance of corn, and vegetables of every description. Many kinds of pot-herbs have already been brought to some perfection, and the potatoes bid fair to equal those of England. The spontaneous productions of nature would afford ample nourishment for all the European animals. Horses feed extremely well even during the winter, and so would oxen if provided with hay, which might be easily done.

"The wild buffalo [Franklin here quotes Dr. John Richardson, expedition naturalist] scrapes away the snow with its feet to get at the herbage beneath, and the horse, which was introduced by the Spanish invaders of Mexico, and may be said to have become naturalized, does the same; but it is worthy of remark that the ox, more lately brought from Europe, has not yet acquired an art so necessary for procuring its food."

Pigs also improve, but require to be kept warm in winter. Hence it appears that the residents might easily render themselves far less dependant on the Indians for support and be relieved from the great anxiety which they too often suffer when the hunters are unsuccessful. . . .

The land is fertile [at Carlton House] and produces, with little trouble, ample returns of wheat, barley, oats and potatoes. The ground is prepared for the reception of these vegetables about the middle of April, and . . . on May 10th the blade of wheat looked strong and healthy. There were only five acres in cultivation at the period of my visit. Capt. John Franklin. *Journey to the Shores of the Polar Sea, In 1819-20-21-22; with a Brief Account of the Second Journey In 1825-26-27.* 4 vols. London, 1829.

John Palliser's name became attached to the dry belt (Palliser's triangle) that he found across the southern prairies, mainly in today's Saskatchewan. Indeed, the word *triangle* is in the original report:

The fertile savannahs and valuable woodlands of the Atlantic United States are succeeded . . . on the west by a more or less arid desert, occupying a region on both sides of the Rocky Mountains, which presents a barrier to the continuous growth of settlement between the Mississippi Valley and the States on the Pacific coast. This central desert extends, however, but a short way into the British territory, forming a triangle, having for its base the 49th parallel from longitude 100 degrees to 114 degrees W., with its apex reaching to the 52nd parallel of latitude. . . .

The South Saskatchewan flows in a deep and narrow valley, through a region of arid plains, devoid of timber or pasture of good quality. Even on the alluvial points in the bottom of the valley trees and shrubs only occur in a few isolated patches. The steep and lofty sides of the valley are composed of calcareous marls and clays that are baked into a compact mass under the heat of the parching sun. The sage and the cactus abound, and the whole of the scanty vegetation bespeaks an arid climate. John Palliser. *Journals, Detailed Reports and Observations relative to Captain Palliser's Exploration of a portion of British North America.* London, 1862.

But the land in the triangle was not as bleak as Palliser made out.

The Commons Immigration and Colonization Committee in 1876 quoted testimony given it March 24 that year by geologist George Dawson and published by the federal Department of Agriculture in a brochure entitled *Province of Manitoba and North West Territory of the Dominion of Canada:*

In July of 1873 I saw a band of cattle in the vicinity of the Line, south of Wood Mountain, which had strayed from one of the United States forts to the south. They were quite wild, and almost as difficult of approach as the buffalo; and notwithstanding the fact that they had come originally from Texas, and were unaccustomed to frost and snow, they had passed through the winter and were in capital condition.

John Macoun, a botanist who had travelled extensively across the prairies from Winnipeg to the Rockies and north to Athabasca, testified at the same time about the Palliser Triangle:

Our part of the "Desert," besides being first-class pasture land, contains many depressions well suited for raising all kinds of grain.

A book by the widely travelled bishop of St. Boniface, Msgr Taché, was translated from the French by Capt. D. R. Cameron, himself to be equally well travelled in the west as Canadian commissioner of the Canada - U.S. agency that mapped the border along the forty-ninth parallel from Lake of the Woods to the Rocky Mountains in 1872-74. Taché wrote of the southern prairie desert, that is, the Palliser Triangle:

> The prairie hay supplies pasturage of the best kind: not only the buffalo delights in it, but horses and other draught animals are very fond of it. This herb, barely six inches high, of which the plants grow so sparsely as to leave the sand or gravel on which it grows everywhere visible, preserves its flavor and nourishing power, even in the midst of the rigors of winter, to such an extent that a few days grazing on one of these remarkable pasturages suffices to restore horses worn out by work to good condition. . . .
>
> The wearied eye seeks in vain for a shore to this ocean of short hay. The weakened traveller sighs in vain for a stream or spring at which to quench his thirst. The heavens, dry as the earth, hardly ever grant their dews and beneficent showers. . . . One travels across this desert for days and weeks without seeing the smallest shrub. The only fuel procurable by the traveller or hunter is buffalo dung, which our Half-breeds call bois de prairie (prairie wood). Msgr Taché. *Sketch of the North-West of America*. Montreal, 1870.

Saskatchewan and the Rocky Mountains is mainly a diary of a trip in 1859 and 1860 from Fort Garry (Winnipeg) to what today is Jasper, Alberta, and the return. It is lively because the Earl of Southesk, at the end of every day, jotted down notes on everything he'd seen. He was a huntsman but more an adventurer, and he travelled in January as well as June.

> We were not altogether wanting in fuel, [the prairie] being thickly strewn with dry buffalo dung — "bois de prairie" I believe the French voyageurs call it; it is sometimes also spoken of as buffalo chips. We frequently used it in our camp fires. I rather liked to burn it, as it throws out a very pleasant strongly aromatic smell redolent of wild thyme and other herbs of the prairie. . . .
>
> As we were travelling along, we came upon a new-born buffalo calf: we merely looked at it and went our way, leaving it quietly crouching in the grass. The mother cow, however, seeing us so near its resting-place, came running from the herd, and full of the notion that her little one was being carried off, the poor foolish creature never went to see if it were still where she had hidden it, but kept following on and on, watching all our movements with an air of most pitiable anxiety. In vain we tried to drive her back; she would not be driven; she seemed incapable of fear. But after a long time she quitted us of her own accord, and slowly retraced her steps. We hoped that she found the little calf alive and well, but most probably the wolves had devoured it while she was far away. . . .
>
> My people made a set of [Red River] cart harness in a very singular manner. They carved it out in its proper shape on the very

body of a [buffalo] bull as he lay back upwards, and then lifted it up complete in a single piece. The sun quickly dried the raw hide, and it turned into the toughest of leather. They also made some of the long lines that are used for so many purposes. These they carved out in the same fashion from the hind quarters of a bull, by forming a series of spirally-enlarging circular cuts, passing the knife under them, and lifting off the hide exactly like the skin of a well-peeled apple or orange. The ends were then attached to two stakes, between which the strip, being tightly stretched, soon became a straight and perfect line.

When running buffalo, the hunter generally carries a line of this sort coiled up and tucked under his belt, one end being fastened to the horse's head. Should a fall take place, as it frequently does when badger-holes are numerous, the line uncoils itself from the rider's belt as he is quitting the saddle, and trails upon the ground, making it easier for him to recover his horse. Earl of Southesk. *Saskatchewan and the Rocky Mountains*. Edinburgh, 1875.

The gopher proved a hardy survivor:

Shortly after leaving Swift Current we drew into a siding to await the train going east. As usual, upon the stoppage of the train, a large number of passengers alighted. Suddenly a gopher appeared in sight. Twenty-five construction men, for the most part carrying revolvers, hastened in pursuit of the little fellow, and commenced firing as fast as they could; others from the party fired from the car. Happily the gopher made its escape unharmed. Presently, others emerged from their burrows, and were pursued with the same relentless determination to secure the tail as a trophy. Those who had no pistols armed themselves as best they could with any lethal weapon at hand. In the end the earth squirrel proved victorious, to the delight of those of us who were not animated by a desire for its destruction. Alfred Pegler. *A Visit to Canada and the United States*. Southampton, 1884.

New settlers required instruction.

An especial interest naturally attaches to the Jews located here by the London Mansion House Committee. Like the Mennonites, they have found a new and happy home in Canada, and a freedom from all persecution and injustice. They consist of various nationalities, for the settlement contains the families of 10 Polish and Hungarian Jews, 10 Austrian Jews, 9 German and Russian Jews.

They are located from 18 to 30 miles south of the Canadian Pacific Railway between Pipestone Creek and Moose Mountain. The successful organization of this settlement is largely due to the kind and active care of Mr. Wurtheim of Winnipeg, who has very prudently expended the funds provided for these emigrants. They have had practical instruction in farm work given to them by Mr. Thompson, and right well has he discharged his duty. A breadth of 320 acres of thoroughly good land has been secured for each of these 29 families, and various kinds of houses have been fitted up for them, some being properly framed houses, whilst others are turf or log huts. About 5 acres were put under crop for each family during the present season, and preparations have been made for sowing more land next spring. In this settlement we have another instance of the great importance of rendering help and guidance to settlers who have no practical knowledge of farm work. Henry Tanner. *Successful Emigration to Canada.* London and New York, 1884.

William Fream, a professor of natural history at the College of Agriculture in Salisbury, England, was one of many visitors at the Bell farm at Indian Head, 310 miles west of Winnipeg. This showplace farm was founded by the Qu'Appelle Valley Farming Company in 1882 on 56,000 acres. In 1884, during Fream's visit, 7,000 acres were under wheat, and wheat acreage was to be doubled the following year.

The harvest is usually over by the middle of August, but this year the season was somewhat backward, and harvest operations were in full swing in the middle of September. Thirty-eight reaping machines were at work simultaneously at the ingathering of the crop, and the sheaves as they come from the self-binders are left in the field for a day or two, and then carried to the threshing machines, so that the wheat never goes into stack. The grain is delivered from the threshing machines into large wooden granaries erected in the fields, whence in winter it is sleighed across the snow to the elevators adjacent to the railway.

It was found practicable, with the machines already mentioned, to cut as much as 800 acres of wheat per day, so at this rate the entire 7,000 acres could be cut in nine working days. The yield this year was expected to be 25 bushels an acre, and, on this estimate, it would not cost more than 33 cents per bushel to grow. The manager of the farm, Major Bell, believes he can grow wheat and place it on the wharves at Liverpool at 69 cents per bushel, this price including 8 per cent interest on the working capital involved. . . .

About 300 horses were found necessary this year, and through the summer they are occupied in breaking new land or in ploughing fallow land for the next spring's sowings. As soon as harvest is finished they would be all engaged in ploughing till the winter's frosts closed the ploughing season. A good heavy carthorse weighing, say, 1,400 pounds, costs from 180 to 190 dollars. In summer, 135 men are employed, and about half this number in winter. The summer labourers are paid at the rate of 30 dollars a month and all found. The resident labourers get a cottage and one acre of land free, with 35 dollars a month in summer and 30 dollars a month in winter. The first foreman gets 50 dollars a month, and the four head foremen 40 dollars a month each and all found. The farm is worked in five divisions and Major Bell telephones instructions to each division from his residence every evening. The hours of work are from 7 a.m. to 6 p.m. with one hour out. . . .

Only one variety of wheat was grown, that known as Fyfe, or No. 1 Hard, and it yielded a dry, bright, marketable sample. No "docking" or weeding of any sort has yet been found necessary. William Fream. *Across Canada: A Report on its Agricultural Resources.* Ottawa, 1886.

Mr. Neil Martin of Wascana, twelve miles north-west of Regina, made the following statement for the Regina Board of Trade:

I struck "Pile o' Bones" [Regina] on the 24th day of May, 1882, after travelling over 400 miles with oxen. The land here suited me better than anything I saw, and I pitched my tent. I am from the county of Northumberland [Ontario] and to all farmers in my old county who are struggling with expensive farms under mortgages, and to all who can hardly make ends meet, or to any one who wants to get along quickly in the world, I say to come to this new country. I had 140 acres of crop this year. I have not threshed yet, but I put my wheat down at 35 bushels to the acre and oats at 60. . . . I have always grown splendid vegetables here, and I consider the country No. 1 for dairying. Potatoes always a sure crop. Trees can be grown successfully. Climate first-class and healthy, paid less doctor bills here than any other place I ever lived. School and church within easy distance. One big advantage in this country, there is no taxes, except a trifle for school purposes. Regina Board of Trade. *An Unvarnished Tale of Regina and its Agricultural and Ranching District, in the Great Province of Assiniboia, N. W. T., Canada.* Regina, 1891.

An 1892 pamphlet, published by a Winnipeg newspaper, quoted William Miller, the first Canadian settler in the district. He had moved from Ontario to Saskatchewan in 1873 and taken up land close to where Prince Albert now stands.

[Miller] has farmed seventeen seasons and states that his wheat will average about 40 bushels per acre eight years out of the seventeen.

The remaining nine years he estimates that his wheat crop would average one year with another 25 bushels per acre. The poorest wheat crop he has had was in 1889, owing to the drought, when the yield was 18 to 20 bushels per acre. This was the first year he had suffered from drought to any extent. The crops of 1890 were later with him than he ever had before, and he had about eight acres of wheat damaged by frost. The balance of his crop escaped serious injury. Mr. Miller has kept a diary since he came to the country, so that his statements are not made from memory. *The Commercial. The Advantages of the Prince Albert District, Saskatchewan, Are Unsurpassed.* Winnipeg, 1892.

Near Whitewood, Assiniboia, Julian Ralph came across a small settlement of European nobility: "the most distinguished and aristocratic little band of immigrants and farmers in the New World."

Dr. Rudolph Meyer of Berlin, Prussia, and three Frenchmen, Comte de Cazes, Comte de Raffignac, and M. le Bideau de St. Mars "till the soil, strive for prizes at the provincial fairs, fish, hunt, read the current literature of two continents, and are happy."

Dr. Meyer, fifty-three, was a political exile for opposition to Bismarck but managed to employ "servants imported from Paris." Comte de Raffignac had had a fine house built to command a view of the Pipestone Valley but vacationed in Paris now and then. Comte de Cazes usually won all the vegetable prizes.

> Out-of-doors one saw what untold good it does to the present and future settlers to have such men among them. The hot-houses, glazed vegetable beds, the plots of cultivated ground, the nurseries of young trees — all show at what cost of money and patience the Herr Doctor is experimenting with every tree and flower and vegetable and cereal to discover what can be grown with profit in that region of rich soil and short summers, and what cannot. He is in communication with the seedsmen, to say nothing of the savants of Europe and this country, and whatever he plants is of the best. Near his quaint dwelling he has a house for his gardener, a smithy, tool-house, a barn, and a cheese-factory, for he makes gruyere cheese in great quantities. Julian Ralph. *On Canada's Frontier.* New York, 1892.

"Canada" in W. M. Elkington's *Five Years in Canada* refers almost entirely to Saskatchewan, and the book is probably the best of its period for describing the life of a prairie farmhand. In this account, four men conduct a five-day cattle drive of forty head in winter:

> It was a bitterly cold morning, with the wind blowing straight in our faces, and as we had some trouble in driving the cattle, we only

travelled about twelve miles, to where the bush began, before night came on, and we had to camp in an old shanty. Each man took two hours' watch to look after the cattle, and, with his rifle ready, to keep the wolves at a distance, and some nights this proved to be a nasty job. We had good skin coats and buffalo robes, so that we made ourselves fairly comfortable when our turn came to sleep.

The second day we travelled slower than ever, the cattle continually running into the bush; but that night we found a favourable camping place where some hay had been cut, and on which the cattle made a good meal. There was no shanty near, and as we had no tent we were obliged to sleep under the stars. . . . The thermometer was constantly as low as twenty degrees below zero; every night we milked some of the cows, and partook of a good pot of boiled bread and milk before turning in to sleep. There were three calves which gave us more trouble than the whole herd, and by day and night we were obliged to keep an eye on these, or they be off into the bush; one dinner time we left them for a few minutes, which cost us a three hours' search before we could recover them.

On the third day we made a little more headway, and at night reached the shanty . . . half burnt down by some careless person's camp fire. The bush was very thick here, and we found it almost impossible to look after the cattle. Early in the morning B. and I went out to round them up, and got lost, and the sky being clouded and no sights to be seen, were several hours before we came to a place which we recognized. . . .

The next day, the fourth, a beast ran between two large spruce trees, and stuck fast there, not being able to move either way; we had to cut one tree down, which occasioned some delay, and nearly killed the beast. . . .

We had twelve miles to go [the fifth day] to where B. had built a small shanty on the bank of the Wilson River, and it was an hour after dark before we got there. We found it a very small place; the logs had not been plastered in between; there was no door or window yet put in, and no flooring down. Across the frozen river, which was twenty yards wide, was a stable and yard for the cattle; we soon had them fed, and then, having fastened skins over the doorway and window, we made ourselves comfortable. . . . When we had got the door and window on, and the holes in the wall stopped up, we found the place a good deal warmer. . . .

In order to water the cattle we cut holes in the ice every morning; there was generally a good deal of crushing to get at these, and one day one of the calves got pushed in; we rescued him with great difficulty and carried him into the shanty, where we wrapped him in a buffalo robe in front of the fire; he seemed nearly dead for a time, but presently he showed his gratitude by getting up and upsetting the table, on which was spread our dinner, and finally taking a flying leap through the window; two days later he fell in again, but this time the stable was deemed quite good enough for him.

On a farm he rented:

The house on the place was but a poor attempt at a building; it was very low — so low that one had to bend nearly double to get in at the door; the roof was constructed with rough poles, plastered over with mud, and held up in the middle by a log made fast in the floor; it was eighteen feet long by fifteen wide, all one room, with a small cellar underneath. On one side was a small outhouse for keeping tools, etc.; the granary was at the back of the house and near the stackyard, and the stables, such as they were, were some little distance away; whilst in front of the house, sloping down to the creek, was a small piece of ploughing which I used as a garden. . . .

The seeding and fencing being finished, I began to break up some more land; my team was well suited for this work, and although the ground was dry and hard, we got on very well and ploughed up a nice piece of virgin prairie; the great drawback to the work was the quantity of stones, which had to be taken out and piled in heaps, ready to be hauled away at some future time.

Elkington describes a prairie fire:

Before the snow had been gone many days the settlement was alarmed by a prairie fire which had sprung up a few miles south; a strong wind was blowing at the time from that quarter, and we began to make preparations to fight it; barrels of water were brought up to the houses, and everyone was armed with bunches of willows and wet clothes to beat it out. It jumped over the township fireguard, and came right towards my place; before I knew what had happened my fence was blazing away and the fire was creeping slowly up the hill towards the buildings. Now was the time for it to be stopped, and after getting singed all over, I managed to beat it out in the most dangerous place, so that it divided and passed my place on both sides. Others escaped altogether, but one man, after fighting it for a long time, had to get in the well while the fire passed over him and burnt his house and buildings. My loss was about twenty fence-rails, and some lost all their fences. The prairie was quite black after this, and the cattle had to pick about in parts which the fire had missed till the young grass came up again. W. M. Elkington. *Five Years in Canada*. London and Rugby, 1895.

Septimus Field, whose laudatory book was published by the government printing bureau, quotes an immigrant farmer, C. Bonnycastle, of Katepwa, N.W.T.:

> I cut 200 acres and threshed 6000 bushels [of wheat] which, when sold, brought me a clear profit of 50 cents a bushel, the market price being 75 cents. . . .
>
> It is wonderful to see the changes on the prairie; good substantial stone and brick houses and stables are to be seen all over. I built and improved my own to the amount of $1,500 and bought half a section more land. This winter has been, so far, a very fine one. Most of the time has been a very little below freezing, and my cattle have never seen the inside of a shed, and all my horses that are not working are out on the prairie. I expect this summer to have between 300 and 400 acres ready for wheat. Septimus Field. *Western Canada*. Ottawa, 1898.

To Find the Daily Bread is an account of a Mennonite family's move to a homestead near Maymont, northwest of Saskatoon, in 1903.

> Having found the wood and located a place as near as we could get to it with our wagons, we placed them across the wind and shovelled snow under them to make something of a windbreak to get ourselves and the horses some protection from the storm that was developing. By the time all this was done and some fire wood brought and cut up and a fire started on a spot cleared of snow in the lee of our windbreak, the snow flakes became smaller and denser and looked and felt like winter.
>
> However, the fire cheered us somewhat. We tried melting snow to get water for the horses to drink but they flatly refused. They stood and later got so cold that their teeth at times chattered and the harness rings rattled as they shivered. Gerhard Andrew Fast and Jacob Fast. *To Find the Daily Bread*. N.p., n.d.

This brief account was written by George Larkey, of Radville, Saskatchewan, when he was seventy-nine years old:

> During the winter I rounded up some things that would be needed on the homestead: 5 horses, the cow and calf and some farm implements. Also some household things and some blacksmith tools. These were all loaded in a box car in Kenmare, N.D. My brother went with me and on the morning of March 17th, 1903, we landed in Weyburn, Northwest Territories, Canada. The weather was cold with about a foot of snow. Here we were on the same big prairie that was destined to be my home.
>
> The next day after putting the livestock in a livery stable we took a team and loaded such things as we would need and started out. For

the first six or seven miles there was a faint road but after that it was open country with snow all over. It must have been 3 o'clock when we arrived on the homestead. There was a little hill where the wind had blown the snow away and there we started to establish our residence by erecting a small tent. I well remember, after making several attempts to get a stovepipe connected and failing with hands that were almost frozen, I threw it down on the ground and tromped them. Thereafter, the smoke went out a hole in the top of the tent.
Geo. Larkey. *Days of the Past.* Lemon Grove, California, 1956.

ALBERTA

An ENTERPRISING NUN from Montreal wrote of a ten-day trip she made by dogsled from Lac la Biche to St. Albert in November 1872. The day she started out, the temperature was thirty-six degrees below zero.

> I would strongly dissuade anyone, through simple pleasure, from undertaking the same project, for, I promise, they would bitterly repent it, not alone on account of the cold they would be compelled to support, or on account of the many other inconveniences to which they would be subject, no, no, but for reason of the intense fear with which they would unavoidably be seized in hearing the howling of the wolves, whose recent foot-prints indicate them at no great distance from the unfortunate traveller. . . .
>
> We always manage to camp in or near the woods where, on arriving, the men set to work: one is breaking down trees, another preparing the requisites wherewith to build a fire, while you can see the third hurrying with the vessel in which he has gathered snow. In a short space of time, with a strong fire, the water is boiling; into this you throw a piece of *tora*, adding a handful of flour; thus is made the renowned, delicious dish called rabibon. A Sister of Charity of Montreal. *Notes and Sketches collected from a Voyage in the North-West*. Montreal, 1875.

Sandford Fleming, the engineer in chief for the Canadian Pacific Railway, also made a long report on the agricultural prospects of western Canada.

> At Little Slave Lake in 1872 I found barley in stack, which had been cut on the 12th August, while that at Edmonton, on the Saskatchewan, was not cut until the 26th of the same month. I was at Isle La Crosse on the 22nd September, 1875, and saw potatoes still as green as they were in July. I was told by Mr. Cummings that their potatoes are hardly ever killed by frost in September. Here there was a flour mill driven by horse power, and all kinds of grain are reported as ripening successfully. On the borders of Clearwater, Buffalo and Methy lakes, I saw numerous potato fields cultivated by Chipewyan Indians, who lived altogether on fish and potatoes.
>
> I was at the forks of the Athabasca and Clearwater Rivers on the 8th September, 1875, and found tomatoes, cucumbers, wheat and barley under cultivation together with all the vegetables found in kitchen gardens in Ontario. . . .

Mr. Hardisty, chief factor in charge of Fort Simpson, in lat. 61 degrees N., informed me that barley always ripened there, and that wheat was sure four times out of five. Melons, if started under glass, ripen well; frost seldom does them much damage. Sandford Fleming. *Report on Surveys and Preliminary Operations on the Canadian Pacific Railway up to January 1877. Ottawa, 1877.*

Alexander Sutherland, a clergyman, made a quick assessment of the land near the Milk River in southern Alberta: "The soil thrown up by the badgers seemed of excellent quality."

On Fish Creek near Calgary, he visited a government supply farm established to raise food and seed grain for Indians:

> The buffalo having disappeared from the country, the Indians will probably have to be fed at intervals for years to come, and supplies can be raised more cheaply in the country than they can be imported. The farm lies at the confluence of Fish Creek and Bow River, and comprises some 5,000 acres of splendid bottoms and rolling prairie. Nearly 200 acres are now under cultivation [and superintendent] Wright expects to have 500 acres broken up and under cultivation next year; but he labours under the disadvantage of unsuitable and insufficient farm machinery.

Sutherland returns to this subject later during an inspection of farm implements supplied to Indians by the government in its agricultural training scheme:

> Although I am by no means a good specimen of "muscular Christianity," I picked up one of the plows in my hands and carried it across the yard with the greatest ease. I next took up a whippletree, which some slight accident had broken in two, and found it to be a half-rotten stick, no stronger than a piece of black ash. The harrows, in weight and strength, were about suitable for a well-plowed garden. Other implements were very similar. Alexander Sutherland. *A Summer in Prairie-land. Notes of a Tour through the North-West Territory.* Toronto, 1881.

He blamed the government contractor for "ways dark" and "tricks vain."

Alexander Staveley Hill was afflicted with snowblindness during a horseback survey in the foothills of the Rockies in southern Alberta. Afterwards, he heard of two preventives:

> One plan suggested, which it is said gives some relief, and perhaps if taken at an early stage would prevent the blindness coming on, is to take the charred end of a stick and to blacken the cheek-bones and upper part of the face round the eyes and close up to the eyes themselves.

But the better plan by far is to cut out a thin piece of wood to the shape of a pair of spectacles, and in the round pieces which cover the eyes and take the place of the glasses, to cut a slit for each eye, and with a piece of string fastened to each end of the piece of wood passing round the head to wear it as spectacles: the small amount of light which is thus allowed to come in through the crevices will, it is said, entirely protect the eyes against the glare which produces the snow-blindness. . . .

It was as we were coming away from Snowy Camp, and during the time that my eyes were nearly closed when I was suffering from snow-blindness, that I felt a hot breath on my face from the southwest, as if it came from across some heated surface. I at once recognized the wind I had heard described and turning round called out to Mr. Craig that it was the "Chinook." Alex. Staveley Hill. *From Home To Home: Autumn Wanderings in the North-West, in the years 1881, 1882, 1883, 1884.* London, 1885.

The *Calgary Herald* made a buggy trip to visit several surrounding farms.

In order that we might give our readers a true and reliable account of the farming prospects, we determined to see for ourselves, and accordingly in company with some other gentlemen procured a rig and proceeded to visit some of the farms in the vicinity.

The first place we drew up at was Mr. Glen's on Fish Creek about eight miles south, on the Fort Macleod trail, and found a fine, well cultivated farm with a comfortable 1 1/2 storey house, out-buildings, and farm-yard which would compete favorably with many of the oldest settlements of Ontario. After inspecting the buildings, we repaired to the garden and were surprised and delighted with a view of the best vegetable garden it has ever been our privilege to inspect, of about 14 acres in extent, and containing potatoes, cabbage, cauliflower, turnips, carrots, beets, parsnips, and corn, all in the highest state of cultivation. . . . Although this was the second week of August, Mr. Glen had been using garden produce for nearly a month. We brought home some samples, and after trying them can testify as to their excellent qualities.

Mr. Glen has also about 32 acres of Oats, 2 acres of Wheat and 5 acres of Barley, all of which notwithstanding the dry season will compare favorably with the average crop of the best parts of Ontario. *The Calgary Herald, Mining and Ranche Advocate and General Advertiser.* Vol. 1, no. 1, August 31, 1883.

J. G. Fitzgerald, the secretary of the Calgary Agricultural Society, said the pamphlet was written by settlers and not by land speculators.

The stock interests of Alberta are much greater than may be imagined. Considerable capital is already invested in this industry. At the close of last season the number of cattle in the district aggregated about 37,500 head valued at $1,875,000. Since then about 12,000 head have been driven in from Montana by the different stockmen. Range cattle are neither sheltered nor in any way cared for during the winter. Many of the stockmen placed their losses during the winter of 1884 under 1 per cent. The warm spring weather proved very favourable for the calves and very few were lost. J. G. Fitzgerald. *Dominion of Canada. District of Alberta. Information for Intending Settlers, compiled by the Calgary District Agricultural Society.* Ottawa, 1884.

The complete annual report to the minister of agriculture by the Calgary immigration agent, J. Z. C. Miquelon, dated December 31, 1887 ran thus:

The total number of immigrants registered by me during the year is 309.

A few might have possibly arrived without my knowledge, from the fact that I was sick during the months of May and June, on account of having been seriously wounded by a bullet; but the number so omitted is small.

From the correspondence I have had to answer, I have reason to hope that the immigration during the following year will be pretty good.

I had the honour to report in the month of October last, that in spite of the seeding season having been very dry, and the drought having lasted until the first of June, the harvest has been tolerably good, and half of the wheat ripened.

The farmers cherish good hopes for the future of the District of Alberta as respects the cultivation of grain. As to the vegetable crop, it has been excellent.

From the information gathered, the 25,000 horses, 60,000 cattle and 30,000 sheep actually pasturing on the prairie in the District of Alberta are in very good condition, and the season has been very favourable to them. Canada. *Sessional Papers.* Vol. 4. Second Session of the Sixth Parliament. Ottawa, 1888.

There was no explanation for the bullet wound.

Farming always involved unpredictable hazards:

The only one [summer frost] we had was on the 11th of July, 1887, when the barley was just heading out. Frost in those localities goes in veins or streaks, something like a hail storm, and quite often you will find that while the grain on one half-section has been injured, that on the neighbouring half-section has not been touched at all. The frost was local. We have this to fear. It is one of the drawbacks that may come; I cannot guarantee that it will not. It is one of those occurrences, however, that may come to almost any country, and when it destroys the tobacco crop of Virginia, as it did last year, it will be very likely to strike out and reach the crops in northern parts of Canada. Leo Gaetz. *Alberta, N-W. T. Report of Six Years' Experience of a Farmer in the Red Deer District*. Ottawa, 1890.

Nicholas Flood Davin, M. P., described the improvement brought about in Alberta horse-breeding:

In the early days of the country's history the horses found on the ranges were divided into two classes of breeds if they may be so called, i.e., the broncho, or large bodied light limbed horse of mixed breed, brought over from Montana or Oregon, a horse with wonderful powers of endurance inherited from his Mexican ancestry, a horse with lots of "go," but little style or beauty; and the Cayuse or Indian pony, a mongrel of the first order, in-bred and mean looking, yet able at all seasons, with no care, or other food than prairie grass, to cover distances of from 50 to 80 miles a day for days at a stretch. These were the horses of Alberta a few years ago.

Today we find a different breed and kind of animal. The large and wealthy cattle owners and enterprising farmers saw in Alberta all that a horse breeder could ask or desire in a country. They went to the old country and the East and purchased the best stallions they could procure, thoroughbreds, standard trotters, Clydes, Percherons, Shires and Hackneys. They culled out the poorest of the native mares and shipped them East to Manitoba and kept the best for breeding purposes. They went further; they shipped in and continued to ship in from Ontario brood mares largely half and three-quarter bred Clydes; one company going further still, to secure a good foundation for its breeding stock and importing from Ireland some 250 splendid brood mares, which have thriven beyond expectation in the foot hills at the base of the Rockies. That such enterprise has brought its reward goes without saying. Today it is estimated that there are some 25,000 head of horses in Alberta the greater number of which are running at large in summer and winter with no shelter or food other than that which they find for themselves on the prairie and foot hills. Horsemen from the East gaze with wonder and admiration on the bands of horses which they see on the ranges in the Macleod and Calgary districts. With pardonable pride the rancher points out the breeding, symmetry and development of his young stock raised on native grass. Unsheltered though they be, their coats are as sleek and shining as the best groomed city animals. The clear light air, the pure water and the nutritious grasses of Alberta produce an animal full of stamina and health, free from lung or bone disease. Nicholas Flood Davin, M.P., ed. *Homes for Millions. The Great Canadian North-West, Its Resources Fully Described.* Ottawa, 1891.

There was a use of horses in Alberta not mentioned here: polo ponies. Polo is said to have been played for the first time in North America in 1886 near Pincher Creek when a rancher brought sticks and balls from England. There were soon clubs in almost every ranching centre, including Pincher Creek, Macleod, High River, Millarville, Calgary and Cochrane.

Not everyone took to the bald prairie as quickly as horses did, however.

The whole area [Peace River district] fit for cultivation only comprises a few small river-side flats in many thousands of square miles. There has lately been a great "boom" about the Peace River. . . . I have heard so many ignorant people aver that this is a great farming country, that I think these facts cannot be too often repeated. It is a dreadful thing to think of the wretched emigrants who toil to this promised land only to find a useless country, and who are often unable to return to civilization, but are forced to endure all the severities of the winter in a latitude where the temperature has often fallen to sixty degrees below zero. H. Somers Somerset. *The Land of the Muskeg.* London, 1895.

The seventy-two-page pamphlet *Ranching in the Canadian North West* must have been issued by the government or a land promoter:

The winter in the ranching section, Southern Alberta and Western Assiniboia, is a season of bright, cloudless days, infrequent and scanty snowfalls and frequent and prolonged breaks of warm weather, heralded by the chinook wind. Wagons are used during the entire year, and it is only in occasional seasons that sleighs are necessary for brief periods. In January and the early part of February there are sometimes short periods of cold, sharp weather. Heavy snowstorms have at times covered the prairie more than a foot deep, but this is exceptional. N.p., n.d. [ca. 1902].

When the Laurier government took power in Ottawa in 1896, Clifford Sifton became minister of the Interior with a forceful policy of increasing immigration to the prairies. First, he had to shake up his department. He said of it: "The crying complaint was that it was a Department of delay, a Department in which people could not get business done, a Department which tired men to death who undertook to get any business transacted with it." (Where is Sifton today when we need him?)

The Interior ministry soon was turning out a flood of books and pamphlets in several European languages besides English and French to try to attract settlers. One of these pamphlets was this 112-page collection of letters ostensibly written by immigrants. There was not a discouraging word among them. The letters about unrelieved farming success bore such headings:

Seven Years in Alberta — is healthy, happy and likes the country well.
Workers Get Along
Satisified Michigan Man
Likes It Better than Idaho
What a Plucky Pioneer Has Done
Had Nothing When He Started
Started Ten Years Ago, Now Well Fixed
Had $500; Now Has Buildings Worth $3000
Average 5,000 Bushels of Wheat for Ten Years

Canada: *Settlers' Experiences in Western Canada*. Ottawa, 1900.

Cattle could not recognize the Canada-U.S. border. A report of the North-West Territories said in 1900:

Some dissatisfaction has arisen in connection with the question of American "tramp cattle." It is alleged that, owing to the large number of Texas steers on the range in Montana, and the alarming prevalence of contagious diseases there, that the indiscriminate drifting backwards and forwards of Montana cattle may at any time be responsible for the introduction of such diseases into our range. It is even positively asserted that the contagious mange owes its origin to American tramp cattle. Be this, however, as it may, it certainly appears advisable that measures should be adopted to obviate this breach of the Dominion quarantine regulations. It is a notorious fact that the Territories, or at least that portion thereof lying along the Milk River in South-eastern Alberta and to the south of the Cypress Hills and Wood Mountain, furnish a convenient grazing ground for stock belonging to Montana ranchers. It is even stated that some of these gentlemen in order to avoid inconvenience have the same brands recorded on both sides of the line, and are not very particular as to whether or not stock on this side of the line are bred here, when they are driven south, ostensibly as strays, for shipment to the Chicago market. North-West Territories. *Annual Report of the Department of Agriculture of the North-West Territories 1899*. Regina, 1900.

The Customs department was made responsible for cattle quarantine and Customs collectors at Coutts and other Alberta points often spent long hours in the saddle driving Montana cattle back across the border.

A. B. Stock had useful hints for prairie settlers, from the proper measurements for a stable or machine shed to stringing fence wire tightly. He advised chinking the log cabin with gumbo, a sticky white clay, or "cow-dung, mixed into a thick paste with water." Cow-dung dried hard, but required more frequent renewal than gumbo. A shingled roof was preferable to turf, which was excellent in winter but leaked badly when the snow was melting. On the roundup:

> The party consists of from fifteen to thirty or forty men, as a rule, at the head of which a captain is elected, whose word is law on all matters concerning the conduct of the round-up. The balance of the company comprises the "riders" (cow-boys are practically extinct now), the horse-wrangler, one or more cooks, and the herders, all of whom are detailed to their individual duties by the captain. The camping outfit and everything necessary to the expedition are carried in a waggon, and accompanying them goes the herd of spare saddle-horses, under the charge of the wrangler during the daytime. At night they are herded by one (or sometimes two) of the cow-hands, in turns arranged by the captain, and for the first few days the horses are apt to give a deal of trouble in their efforts to break away and get to their respective homes. With the miles and miles of territory that the riders have to cover, it will be readily realized that the horses soon become exhausted, so that a frequent change is necessary. Each man, therefore, according to his weight and the amount of riding he expects to do, takes with him from his ranch a "string" of between six and nine of them for his use during the time he may be out. . . .
>
> The new hand is nearly always put on to horse-wrangling or cattle-herding to start with, as it is the simplest work, although the least congenial, the older and more experienced ones being sent round the country in twos (as a rule) to hunt up and bring in any horses or cattle which they may find on the circuit. At about 4:30 a.m. the herder takes the horses out on to the plain a little way from camp, staying with them and keeping them together by riding round and round them until noon, when he is relieved for half an hour for dinner. He then goes on again from 12:30 until six or seven, when the night-herder (or two herders, if the horses are fresh) undertakes the care of them until the early hours of the morning.
>
> Very early in the morning the cook prepares breakfast, which is despatched quickly, and the work of the day begins. The saddle-

horses are driven into an improvised corral, consisting of a long rope made fast to the waggon at each end, and the bight supported at the requisite height by pointed stakes driven into the ground, forming thereby a small enclosure. Each man who is about to beat round the country selects ropes (lassoes) and saddles up the horse he intends to use, getting away to his work as quickly as possible, leaving the camp to the care of the cook, the wrangler, and the man who has done the last shift at night-herding.

At the end of the first day's operations quite a respectable bunch of cattle or horses is driven into camp, and makes things busy for all concerned. The numbers gradually increase as the days go on, which necessitates more men being employed in herding, for it would never do to allow any beasts to escape after all the trouble entailed in gathering them.

After the round-up has completed its work, the cutting out of all cows and calves commences. The "cutters" ride at a walk through the bunch, select those animals that are required, and edge them gradually towards the outside, round which all the other available men keep moving (mounted) to prevent any beast breaking through. When the animals wanted approach sufficiently near the outer circle, they are quickly driven out and away to their own ranch-mates. As a rule the calves at a spring round-up are not branded until they and their mothers have arrived at their respective homes. Branding would naturally play no part in a fall round-up, which is usually devoted solely to the gathering in of cattle for beef. . . .

It is desirable to have the [branding] irons made as large as possible, on account of the growth of the beast's coat in winter-time, which would quite obliterate a brand of small proportions. A half or totally effaced marking is more productive of bad language than anything during a round-up, when it involves the roping and throwing of an animal to ascertain the brand while "cutting out" from a big herd. The brand marking grows with the animal, so the necessity seldom arises to apply the irons more than once during the beast's lifetime.

As the employment of several men is necessary to satisfactorily brand an animal, it is the usual custom in the ranching districts to form "bees" for the purpose. Your neighbours (often living five to twenty or more miles distant) will come over and give you a hand, on the understanding that you will do a like service for them when required.

The calves about to be branded should be driven into the corral, where a fire has already been made, and the irons placed therein in readiness for the ordeal. The animals are each in turn roped

Unknown Artist, *Cowboys' Camp near Quorn Ranch, Alberta, 1893.*

John Pedder, *Threshing Wheat on the Plains, Manitoba, 1887.*

W.G.R. Hind, *Caught in a Thunderstorm.*

R. Maynard, *Farming Land at Spillamacheen*, B.C.

HOW TO READ A BRAND

Brands are read from left to right (—76 is Bar Seventy-Six),
from top to bottom (JB is Half Diamond JB), or from
outside to inside (◇R is Diamond R). Besides letters and
numbers, a whole series of other symbols were used.
The most common were:

Ū	Bar U	⌒U	Running MU
LG	LG Bar	W	Flying W
Ⓙ	Circle J	R	Walking R
⊕	Half Circle Cross	A	Walking A
FA	Quarter Circle FA	К	Reverse K
P	Rocking P	ЛL	J Reverse J
◠	Lazy D	±	Cross Bar
N N	Lazy ZZ	⚕	Cross Bell
WR	WR Connected	32	Half Diamond 32
W	Running W	999	Three open 9's

*Horse and cattle brands date from 1880 in western Canada. The rancher
selected symbols which could be easily recognized and which were difficult
to change with the "running iron," used by rustlers to alter brands.*

(lassoed) by the hind-legs while on the run, and thrown by a man on horseback. The calf is then dragged by the rope (which is made fast to the horn of the Mexican saddle) to the fire, where a man should be ready to apply the irons to whatever part of the body is indicated on your brand certificate, while another man holds down the beast's head, and another one its flank.

The chief difficulty about the operation lies with him who manipulates the irons. It requires one with experience to know exactly how hard and how long to apply them so as to burn away the hair and make a slight impression in the hide without burning through it. If too deeply pressed, it blotches the brand, and in time a horny excrescence forms over it; and if done too lightly the hair is apt to cover the markings and obliterate them in winter-time.

Castration of the steers, and branding and ear-marking of both sexes, should all be done at the same time so that the calves are then free of any further attention of this kind until their death at maturity.

Newly-branded animals should be herded for a week or two and watched closely. Should flies cause the markings to fester, a weak solution of carbolic acid and water may be applied until the wounds heal, after which they may be turned loose on the prairie to roam "fancy free." A. B. Stock. *Ranching in the Canadian West*. London, 1912.

C. M. MacInnes's *In The Shadow of the Rockies*, along with L. V. Kelly's *The Range Men*, provides probably the best record of the development of cattle ranching in Alberta. Here MacInnes discusses the Cochrane ranch near Calgary, founded by Senator M. H. Cochrane of Compton, Quebec, on a lease of 109,000 acres with headquarters one mile west of the present town of Cochrane.

The Cochrane ranch, which was the oldest large concern in the country, had a very chequered history in its early years which illustrates the kind of difficulties with which many ranchers were confronted. Its founder . . . took great care to see that it was stocked with suitable cattle, and Colonel [James] Walker, his first manager, was a man with unequalled knowledge of the country and its ways.

The first Cochrane herd was purchased in Montana in the summer of 1881, and was received at the boundary line by one of I. G. Baker's foremen with thirty cowboys, who were to turn it over to Colonel Walker at the new ranch west of Calgary. This foreman and his cowboys treated the herd in a way which would make any decent cattleman blush with shame. Having separated the steers from the cows, the two herds were mercilessly moved forward, and it is said that the former averaged between fifteen and eighteen miles a day, while even the cows did fourteen. No time was given for grazing on the trail, and at night the tired animals were herded so closely that they had no room either to feed or even to lie down to rest. Wagons followed behind to pick up calves that had fallen on the trail, but there were not enough wagons to collect all of these, and so many were left to die on the prairie, while others were traded by the unscrupulous cowboys for tea, sugar or whisky. This brutal drive has the record for speed and also, it might be added, criminal stupidity, for those in charge neglected almost everything that common sense and humanity should have suggested.

When finally the herd reached the new Cochrane ranch, the cattle were thoroughly out of condition and unfit to face the winter. Thus hundreds more, which normally should have come through with comparative ease, died during that season. Further, as there was no time to brand the cattle properly when they arrived, it was decided to trust to the hair-brand until the winter was over. But when spring came the hair-brand had disappeared, owing to the growth of their new coats.

Colonel Walker therefore decided to place the Cochrane brand on all unbranded cattle he found on his range, a policy which at once landed him in a veritable hornet's nest, since there were other ranchers in the neighbourhood who also had unbranded cattle.

When their expostulations were not listened to, they determined to take a leaf out of Colonel Walker's book, and hastily put their irons on all the unbranded beasts they could find. As the Cochrane herds were far more numerous than those of the other ranchers, and these knew where to find the cattle better than many of the Cochrane cowboys, who were newcomers to the country, the result was that the Cochrane losses were proportionately greater.

Misfortune continued to afflict this ranch through the following winter, for while the land to the east and south was comparatively free of frost and snow, the Cochrane ranges were caught in the grip of a hard frost and covered in deep snow for months. This made it impossible for the animals to get through to the grasses, and when they attempted to break away to the open ranges they were at once driven back.

In consequence of all these misfortunes, when the spring of 1883 arrived, only a scant four thousand poorly conditioned animals remained of the twelve thousand splendid cattle that had been purchased some eighteen months before.

The Cochrane ranch was moved to other leases farther south, and twenty-five miles of fence was built around the new range between Oldman's River and the

Porcupine Hills. Fences were, however, an abomination to cowboys, and this one was demolished piecemeal: "The only good purpose it ever served was that the posts made excellent firewood for the ranchers and farmers of the neighbourhood."

MacInnes says there was always cattle stealing but that "the way of thieves was hard." As late as 1904, a thief had been imprisoned for ten years for falsifying brands.

> From time to time organized gangs appeared in the country, but they were invariably broken up by the [North West Mounted] Police and the majority of their members brought to justice. Always . . . the punishment of thieves remained in the hands of the authorities, and there were no usurpations of the functions of the state by such organizations as the Vigilantes or other lynching fraternities. C. M. MacInnes. *In The Shadow of the Rockies*. London, 1930.

Kelly wrote in his book:

> They [cowboys] might go on hilarious "busts" when in town, they might "shoot-up" a bar-room and smash every light in the place, they might ride into stores on the backs of frantic horses, but they were good men, the kind who worked for their employers. If a flooded river must be crossed to save some of the cattle carrying the brand of the outfit they worked for, they plunged in and braved the torrents with their driftwood and their deadly "drag." If a fifty-mile ride was necessary in order to save a horse they took it. If an all-night vigil beside a herd of freezing stock was necessary to save those animals the vigil was cheerfully undertaken. Many and many a night the cowboys sat on their horses, bundled to the ears, while the bitter winds of ten and twenty below zero swept across the prairies; and there are known instances where cowboys whose feet and legs were frozen remained by the herd and pulled it through until relief came. The employer's stock was their own; a theft was a personal loss and a mark against the character of the cowboys working for that outfit. . . .
>
> Slavery had been dead in the United States for nearly twenty years, but Alberta holds a record of having come near to this obsolete condition.
>
> In September [1884] a mulatto named Harrison was ordered to leave Calgary, which order he followed so strictly that he did not stop until Lethbridge was reached. At that thriving village he succeeded in running a debt amounting to seventy dollars to a barber named Charles Bryer, who decided to get his money back. Harrison had nothing but his body to realize any capital on, so Bryer put him up at auction, knocking him down to a restaurant keeper for

a hundred dollars, and the mulatto then set to work and earned his freedom. L. V. Kelly. *The Range Men.* Toronto, 1913.

John R. Craig relates that he was stopping the night at Jim Lamotte's stage station and bar in Arrow Creek when he saw a man lying on the floor, rolled up in blankets. He had been shot through the side by his landlady at a nearby ranch. She had apparently mistaken him for an intruder. Craig offered to go for the nearest doctor, seventy-five miles away. The wounded man declined:

> "I don't need a doctor for a thing like that. The bullet went right through, and I can do all the doctoring or surgery needed." He showed me the wound, and his method of treatment, which was a cottonwood stick he had smoothed down very fine, on which he rubbed bacon grease, and gently pushed through the hole by his own hand, squirming and swearing throughout the operation. The wound was about four inches in from the hip bone, and came out at the back. He wouldn't listen to my suggestion to send him in a surgeon when I got to Fort Benton, but said he would like to get a bottle of sweet oil as a change from the bacon grease. John R. Craig. *Ranching with Lords and Commons, or Twenty Years on the Range.* Toronto, 1903.

J. K. Sutherland, a Hanna, Alberta, farmer, talking of a dust storm:

> The morning is usually fine and clear, with maybe just a gentle breeze blowing. We farmers are all out in the fields ploughing, seeding, summer fallowing — doing any one of a score of jobs and duties that fall to the farmer's lot ere the soil will produce. The breeze comes on just a little stronger, and a few small particles of soil start to drift gently along the top of the cultivated land. These tiny soil particles soon loosen up other little particles. Very soon, with the increasing wind, the whole surface of the field is gently sifting along, always moving, always gathering fresh momentum by rapidly increasing volume. There is nothing spectacular yet. But wait — away off to the northwest a heavy black cloud is forming between sky and earth. Black, yes, black as night. It sweeps towards us rapidly at forty, fifty, sixty miles an hour. We turn, each individual one of us, looking for the nearest shelter. Teams are unhooked as quickly as possible, and if no stable room is near turned with their heads away from the storm. . . . The air gets colder. The huge black wall is now only a mile away. A minute, and with a blast like the roar of a thousand lions it is upon us. We are alone in a sightless mass of hurtling soil, stinging sand and thumping clods. We lose all sense of direction. Unless one happens to be within hand's reach of a fence progress in any calculated direction is almost impossible. We can

only stand buffeted by the blows of a thousand hammers, or drift helpless, choking, blinded. This is the black blizzard.

For hours the tortured soil is torn and ravished until the storm ceases. Then we look out on the fields which we have tilled. They are as smooth as if polished by a giant plane. Here and there a few wheat plants, stricken, stand on roots still remaining in the hard subsoil. With to-morrow's sun they will probably fade and die. Millions in rich top soil is gone forever. That is the black blizzard, the most appalling thing in nature. J. K. Sutherland. *The Black Blizzards and What We Must Do about Them.* "Next-Year Country," by Jean Burnet. Toronto, 1951.

These were some of the rules and regulations which, John Higinbotham wrote, Harry (Old Kamoose) Taylor posted in his Macleod Hotel in 1882:

> Spiked boots and spurs must be removed at night before retiring.
> Two or more persons must sleep in one bed when so requested by the proprietor.
> Dogs are not allowed in the Bunks, but may sleep underneath.
> Candles, hot water and other luxuries charged extra, also towels and soap.
> Towels changed weekly. Insect powder for sale at the bar.
> Crap, Chuck Luck, Stud Horse Poker and Black Jack games are run by the management. Indians and niggers charged double rates.
> Baths furnished free down at the river.
> Those who do not like the provender will get out, or be put out.
> All Day drinks, 50 cents each; Night drinks, $1.00 each. No Mixed Drinks will be served except in the case of death in the family.
> When boarders are leaving, a rebate will be made on all candles or parts of candles not burned or eaten.
> The proprietor will not be accountable for anything.
> No cheques cashed for anybody. Payment must be made in Cash, Gold Dust, or Blue Chips. Board $25 per month. Board and Lodging $60 per month.

John D. Higinbotham. *When The West Was Young: Historical Reminiscences of the Early Canadian West.* Toronto, 1933.

Higinbotham described a bad winter:

The winter of 1886-1887 was extraordinarily long and severe, the snow being very deep, and there were no Chinooks to remove sufficient snow to enable the cattle to reach the grass beneath it on the prairie. The ranchers had put up hay for emergencies but, not anticipating weeks of sub-zero weather, the supply was soon exhausted. The hungry cattle, driven by northern blizzards from their ranges, sought the shelter of the coulees and well-treed river bottoms where they browsed upon the alders, willows, and small shrubbery, many of them having their stomachs punctured by the twigs. The rivers, creeks and valleys throughout the country were strewn with the carcasses of starved and frozen animals. The bellowing, especially during still, frosty nights, was pitiable. . . .

Most of the ranch houses in the eighties were built of logs chinked with mud and had roofs of poles, brush and earth capped with sods to prevent the soil from being blown away in the wind. Houses so constructed were cool in summer and warm in winter and comfortable except in wet weather. After a prolonged period of rain, infrequent except in May or June, the water-soaked roof would drip liquid mud long after the rain outside had ceased, when it might be truthfully stated that there was "running water in every room." . . . Such experience must have given inspiration for this well-known western song:

Oh for life in the old-time shack, when the rain begins to fall;
Drip, drip through the mud in the roof and the winds blow through the wall.
The tenderfoot curses his luck, and sighs out feebly, "Ah,
"This bloomin' country's a fraud and I want to go home to my ma."

BRITISH COLUMBIA

THE AREA'S RICHES were catalogued, and found good, by Henry DeGroot in 1859:

In ascending Fraser river, the first fort arrived at is Langley, on the south bank of the river twenty-five miles from its mouth. It is an old and extensive establishment. The [Hudson's Bay] Company have a large farm at this place, with a considerable amount of stock. The land, cleared of heavy timber, is said to produce good crops, and in the garden attached to the fort vegetables grew last summer with the greatest luxuriance, while the apple trees were loaded down with fruit. There are many little prairies in the neighbourhood which, being covered with coarse grass, afford ample feed for stock as well as hay for winter use. . . . There are several hundred acres of land under cultivation near Fort Kamloops, a large proportion being planted to potatoes, which grow here with little culture, and of an excellent quality. Wheat and other cereals also thrive well, the yield being abundant and the crop quite certain. There is also a fine range for stock in the neighborhood, the cows and oxen, of which there are several hundred head, with a large number of horses, keeping fat through the summer, and in tolerable condition through the winter, though none except the working animals receive any fodder, unless, perhaps, it be a little straw. Henry DeGroot. *British Columbia; Its Condition and Prospects, Soil, Climate, and Mineral Resources, Considered*. San Francisco, 1859.

J. Despard Pemberton was surveyor-general of Vancouver Island when it was a separate colony and a promoter of colonization:

The fertility of the soil in the neighbourhood of the gold-bearing rocks is very remarkable, and is indicated rather by the production from ordinary seed of gigantic roots, and vegetables and fruits, than by crops of grain. Turnips as large as hassocks, radishes as large as beets or mangolds, and bushels of potatoes to a single stalk, are nothing astonishing. . . .

Indians everywhere grow potatoes and carrots as far north as Queen Charlotte's Island; their plan is to repeat the crop until the ground is exhausted, and then to clear some more. The potatoes are excellent; and potatoes and salmon their standing dish. . . .

With a market close at hand, and high prices for everything he can produce, the farmer's prospects are extremely promising; and in consequence of the dearness of labour in every department, the larger his family the wealthier he is. J. Despard Pemberton. *Facts and Figures relating to Vancouver Island and British Columbia*. London, 1860.

A sailor who helped survey the coastlines of British Columbia and Vancouver Island, R. C. Mayne took a boundless interest in all other aspects of the then separate colonies. He travelled extensively in the interior on horseback. Near Pavilion Lake in the upper Fraser Valley he saw a farmer ploughing — the first time, he says, he had seen such an instrument in use in British Columbia. The farmer raised vegetables to sell to gold seekers and miners. Mayne adds that irrigation in the interior would not be difficult,

> for so numerous are the streams all over the country, and in such a variety of directions do they run, that very little care will enable a man so to lay out his fields that he may always have plenty of water at his command. Cmdr. R. C. Mayne. *Four Years in British Columbia and Vancouver Island*. London, 1862.

Squatters were called pre-emptors in British Columbia:

> Vancouver Island is still [mostly] unsurveyed, and the emigrant who intends to farm may have land in almost any part of the island by "pre-emption." In British Columbia likewise, much of the land within a certain distance of its different townships and settlements is already surveyed and sold, but pre-empted land may be had anywhere else. Pre-emption enables the emigrant to hold and farm a limited amount of land, for which he is not required to pay until it be surveyed, when he becomes liable for the usual government price of 4s. 2d. per acre, payable by instalments. The pre-emptor must record his claim at the land-office on occupation, for which he has to pay a small fee. A single man can pre-empt 150 acres; a married man, whose wife is resident in the colony, 200 acres; and for each of his children under 18 years of age, and resident in the colony, an additional 10 acres. The emigrant has thus every facility for obtaining cheap land [with] a wide choice. Alexander Rattray. *Vancouver Island and British Columbia: Where They Are; What They Are; and What They May Become*. London, 1862.

Charles Forbes was stationed at the British base at Esquimalt as a Royal Navy surgeon and his pamphlet was published by the colonial government.

> Nowhere does the potato flourish more, or attain a better flavour; it is grown in great quantities by the natives on all parts of the coast. The Hydah [Haida] Indians of Queen Charlotte's Island hold an

annual potato fair, customers reaching them from Fort Simpson on the mainland. . . .

An Agricultural and Horticultural Society has been formed, and was very successfully inaugurated in the autumn of the present year. The first exhibition was held in October, prizes being awarded to the exhibitors of the best horned cattle, sheep, stallions, and brood mares (thoroughbred and for farming purposes) and also for pigs. . . . Large herds of cattle exist in the mountains in a wild state, having strayed from the different farms and settlements.

Charles Forbes. *Vancouver Island: Its Resources and Capabilities as a Colony.* Victoria, 1862.

D. G. F. MacDonald saw a great deal of the British Columbia interior as a surveyor with the International Boundary Commission. His comments are probably the most astringent on record:

Exaggerated accounts have been spread in Europe regarding the climate of British Columbia. It has not the clear skies and fine bracing atmosphere of Canada, as snow, sleet, rain and fog visit the settler in rapid succession, and the winter takes up eight months out of the twelve, commencing in September and lasting till May, while the temperature is severe, the thermometer at times falling 30 degrees below zero. . . .

At Stewart's Lake in the month of July, every possible change of weather was experienced within twelve hours — frost in the morning, scorching heat at noon, and then rain, hail, and snow. . . . During winter, a traveller in the highlands of British Columbia must envelope himself in furs to a most inconvenient degree. Horses have suffocated from ice forming in their nostrils, and their hoofs have burst from the effects of the cold. . . . In these dreary lands, consumption and inflammatory complaints are very common, and few escape rheumatism. A long sickness in the backwoods brings famine and utter ruin. . . .

Prairies are few, swampy, and of small extent, and are overhung in summer by clouds of insects; while pestilence exhales from the decaying vegetation, and reptiles sport in the stagnant pools, or crawl over piles of mouldering logs, brush and rushes. These low grounds, which indeed are little else than extended marshes, are also infested by legions of vicious mosquitoes, which destroy comfort by day and sleep by night, biting alike through socks and sheets, or settling upon the nose or forehead; and woe betide the sleeper who has a rent in his curtains. They have subjected cows and horses to the torture of a lingering death, and forced whole families to leave their homes for months together. . . .

Swampy lands are met with along all the rivers, which are not only unfit for cultivation, but are prejudicial to health. I have more than once been nearly thrown into a fever by the pestilential vapours which the summer heat had caused to float from the slimy sediment of these flats.

MacDonald takes this parting shot at Victoria:

There is no society for ladies, nor indeed for cultivated persons of any description. D. G. F. MacDonald. *Lecture on British Columbia and Vancouver's Island*. London, 1863.

Agriculture suffered in Newfoundland because of the greater economic attraction of the fishery, in New Brunswick because of the enticement of the lumber trade, and in Quebec and Red River because of the lure of quick riches from the beaver pelt. In British Columbia, Matthew MacFie found, farming lost favor because of the proximity of gold strikes. A gold rush, he wrote, was a serious hindrance to agricultural development because workers refused to stay on the farm.

But some did. MacFie describes what he termed probably the best farm in British Columbia, the Lake Valley ranch owned by a Mr. Davidson on the upper Fraser and not far from the Cariboo gold finds. It employed sixteen "servant men," the number being reduced in winter to four or five.

Davidson had established the ranch in June 1862 on 1,860 acres and had 175 acres under cultivation, principally barley and oats, by the next year. There were about fifteen acres of potatoes, two acres of cabbages, one of turnips, one of onions, and several of corn, beans, parsnips and carrots. The ranch also had some of the best livestock in the province, eight yoke of working oxen, six to eight horses, and a good selection of farm implements, including a reaper, mower and threshing machine, which could thresh 1,000 bushels a day.

MacFie concludes:

The country is pre-eminent for stock-raising. "Bunch grass," which is highly nutritious for cattle, is also abundant. On this fodder the Cayoosh nags or native horses so thrive that they surpass, in power of endurance, many an English hack fed on grain. One of those hardy animals can accomplish without injury a journey of 40 miles in a day. Mules that, in the upper country, have to carry 300 or 400 pounds, over long daily stages, have bunch grass for their only provender on the journey. Matthew MacFie. *Vancouver Island and British Columbia*. London, 1865.

A. C. Anderson was enthusiastic about British Columbia's agricultural possibilities:

> On the peninsula near Victoria, and I presume in other choice localities, the Musk-melon and the Water-melon attain perfect maturity in the open air, without artificial aid. . . .
>
> About Thompson's River the continuous summer heat is specially favorable for the production of such fruits as the Melon. . . . Approaching the Southern frontier, upon the Okanagan, the Grape, were it desirable, might be largely cultivated and, I do not hesitate to say, with success. . . .
>
> From 1843 to 1848, between 400 and 500 bushels of wheat were raised annually at the Hudson's Bay Company's Post [at Alexandria], and converted into flour by means of a mill, with stones eighteen inches in diameter, wrought [worked] by horses.

Anderson described the delta of the Fraser River as "teeming with fertility" and yielding "enormous products," for example, a twenty-eight-pound cauliflower. He adds:

> Portions only on the borders of this exuberant tract have hitherto been pre-empted; and before the whole can be rendered available for occupation a system of dyking must be resorted to, to exclude the overflow of the summer freshets. This process, I am informed, has already been entered upon a small scale by individual settlers; but a systematic prosecution of the work, whereby a wide expanse may at once be redeemed, is obviously necessary in an economic point of view. A. C. Anderson. *The Dominion At The West*. Victoria, 1872.

An elaborate, illustrated brochure, *Information for Emigrants*, was issued by the agent-general for British Columbia in Britain, G. M. Sproat.

> The great snow question. *British Columbia has not a snowy winter.* There is snow, but not much snow. . . . British Columbia has not a snowy winter such as Eastern Canada and the Northern States of the Union have. The British Columbia winter is the winter of England and of France. British Columbia. *Information for Emigrants*. London, 1875.

Newton H. Chittenden wrote of his travels:

> I have traversed hundreds of thousands of acres in the Nicola, Kamloops and Okanagan Valleys and Lake La Hache country, covered with a luxuriant growth of the nutricious bunch grass, and saw bands of thousands of cattle rolling fat. . . . Along the lower Fraser, including the delta, there are about 175,000 acres of unsurpassed fertility. There is a large tract of open arable land on the Queen Charlotte Islands without a white settler. Newton H. Chittenden. *Travels in British Columbia*. Victoria, 1882.

Even choosing a site for a farm involved a lot of work. The province of British Columbia tried to help:

It is difficult to say where the best district is for any kind of farming. In choosing a location, or a particular kind of farming, the settler of the present day should have regard to the effect of the making of the Canadian Pacific railway through the province, both in the markets its construction opens locally, and those which it will open permanently, east of the Rocky mountains, for various farm products — say, cattle, sheep, horses, mules, cheese, butter, fruit, etc. He will do well, also, not to forget that he is in a mineral country, with varied resources. Nothing gives farming such a lift as a mining camp within reach of the farmers. . . .

Most countries have peculiar names of their own for agricultural lands, and the immigrant, on arriving in British Columbia, will hear men talk of "prairies," "beaver-dam lands," "bottom lands," "tide lands," and "flats." A few words to explain these terms may assist him in selecting a proper location.

The term "prairie," on the Pacific slope, does not mean the treeless sea of grass which is called by that name in the centre of America, east from the Rocky range. The Pacific slope prairies may be classed, broadly, as "wet" and "dry" prairies. "Wet prairies" are level spaces at the meeting (forks) of rivers. They are often overflowed in early summer by "freshets." This kind of prairie is also found at the mouths of tidal rivers, where the land is overflowed in winter by high tides raised by wind. These prairies are generally free of timber, except perhaps some alder shrubs, and produce a coarse grass called "swamp hay." These prairies need dyking and draining in some parts. The soil generally is very rich, and they are considered desirable locations. In British Columbia they are free from malaria and ague.

The choice pieces of land scattered through forests, and known as "alder land" (or easily drained swamp), seem to be, in fact, "wet prairies" on which the alder bushes have grown to be trees. Another kind of "wet prairie" is "beaver-dam land," that is, flat land made marshy by beavers having dammed small streams which run through it. . . . We may also class as "wet prairies" the open marshes ("tide lands" or "flats") where the sea coast is low and shelves back.

"Dry prairies" are open spaces generally near rivers. They have fine grass, beautiful flowers, and often a dense crop of ferns not liked by farmers. The pine forest bounds them abruptly like a regiment of trees called to a halt.

"Bottom lands" are flat lands in river valleys dry enough to be classed as "dry prairie" land. . . .

The term "bench" is applied to the raised level spaces, or terraces, in some of the river valleys in the interior. These terraces run at intervals along both sides of the rivers for miles in length. They are objects of curiosity and speculation and, from the regularity and evenness of their structure, add much to the beauty of the rude scenes in which they occur. British Columbia. *Province of British Columbia, Canada. Its Climate and Resources; with Information for Emigrants.* Victoria, 1883.

Senator D. MacInnes followed the Columbia River from Golden to Fort Steele and the Moyie River from there to the B.C. - U.S. border.

We passed a small shack. Our driver knew the owner, an Englishman. We met him after passing his shack and had some talk with him. He evidently came from gentle stock, but he said he liked the life; he was quite alone, not a soul within miles of him.

"We go out occasionally," he said. I asked him what he meant by "going out." "Oh," he said, "when I save a certain amount from the sale of cattle (he had a small ranch) I go to England and remain as long as my money lasts, then I come in again." We were told that this was the case with many of the young men settled and living alone in these mountains. Hon. D. MacInnes. *A Trip Across British Columbia.* Hamilton, 1889.

William Shannon and C. McLachlan wrote optimistically of ranching:

In some portions of the province, cattle can remain out all winter, and even in the coldest years need only be sheltered for two or three months. . . . Cattle ranching is one of the healthiest occupations in the world, being particularly so in this district [Chilcotin], which is not subject to high winds or blizzards, but enjoys a clear, dry atmosphere, making the settler feel light-hearted and buoyant. William Shannon and C. McLachlan. *British Columbia and Its Resources.* London, 1889.

New settlers were urged, however, to recognize the hardships as well as the benefits that faced them:

The man who pre-empts land must understand that he acquires the right to a certain tract hitherto untouched by cultivation of any sort. In many instances dense forests await his attack, before he can grow even the amount produced upon the quarter acre of garden ground he left at home.

The choicest piece of his property is probably an alder bottom, upon which a rich deposit of alluvial soil and vegetable mould will reward the successful cultivator with phenomenal crops. But he has to clear, and to some extent drain, this land before he can hope for reward. The skilful pioneer from the Eastern Provinces is familiar with the aspect of "Nature unadorned," but the British labourer, who has been accustomed to look upon nothing but the plough lands of his own district, becomes terribly disheartened when he is brought face to face with the realities of the backwoods. Not that he need despair. His prospects of a free and happy life were never greater; but he must be prepared for the effort of becoming his own master by gaining the mastery over Nature. . . . [He] must be prepared to face a life of isolation and hard labour for some years. . . .

A comparatively new district, of great beauty, fertility and almost unlimited possibilities, is being placed within reach of a market by the new Shuswap and Okanagan railway and lake navigation. This district may be described as a belt of land extending from the shores of the great Shuswap lake, in a southerly direction, to the boundary line between British Columbia and the United States. For many years the value of the land has been recognized, and some large cattle ranches and grain farms have been carried on successfully by their enterprising owners. But the inaccessibility of the country and the absence of any available market discouraged settlers, and it is only quite recently that the capabilities of the district for mixed and fruit farming have been fully realized. British Columbia. *British Columbia as a field for Emigration and Investment.* Victoria, 1891.

THE YUKON

ALEXANDER HUNTER MURRAY ESTABLISHED THE THEN farthest-north Hudson's Bay Company post, Fort Yukon, on the Yukon River (he spelled it Youcon) in June 1847. It comprised six dwellings made of willow poles covered with pine bark, a log store, a cabin for dried fish, and a fenced garden measuring twelve feet by eight feet.

On the 1st of July a few potatoes were planted, and it was my peculiar care and pleasure to attend to it and have it duly watered in droughty weather, never expecting that at that advanced season the crop could be brought to maturity, but to try by every means in my power to preserve seed for the ensuing summer. . . .

I begin to fear the summer season is too short; the few potatoes were allowed to grow as long as the season permitted, and taken up on the 13th of September, after the rivers were blackened by the frost. Only ten potatoes were planted, but cut in pieces as usual and our whole crop was nearly a gallon, varying in size from a pea to a partridge egg. Only about half a dozen of the largest has kept over winter, although kept in the house in dry sand packed around with dry moss. . . .

Ground is now being prepared and in a day or two more they will be planted and some barley sown . . . and may God grant us a genial summer say I, though it should only be for the "tators," for I would fight with the pigs for them. Alexander Hunter Murray. *Journal of the Yukon 1847-48*. Canadian Archives, Ottawa, 1910.

Surveyor William Ogilvie a half-century later dismissed agricultural possibilities on the Yukon. Ogilvie built his camp on the Yukon near the Canada-Alaska border and found the permafrost only two feet down. In the woods, the frost was immediately below the covering moss.

The agricultural capabilities of the country along the river are not great, nor is the land which can be seen from the river of good quality.

When we consider further the unsuitable climatic conditions which prevail in the region it may be said that as an agricultural district this portion of the country will never be of value. William Ogilvie. *Information respecting the Yukon District*. Ottawa, 1897.

The Klondike gold rush began in 1897. Some vegetables were grown successfully (and remuneratively) at Dawson City.

The agricultural possibilities of the Yukon are greater than has been generally supposed, but the short summer probably will not allow the raising of cereals or fruits that require a long season to ripen, and it will hardly support an independent agricultural population. Several small vegetable gardens at Dawson were a source of large revenue to their owners. A bunch of about six radishes, each no larger than the end of one's thumb, readily brought $1 in the restaurants. Tappan Adney. *The Klondike Stampede*. New York and London, 1900.

EPILOGUE

IN THE FIRST HALF OF THE twentieth century, farm life didn't make great strides over what comforts there had been in the nineteenth.

The total living expenditures of the 115 families [visited in Lanark County] averaged $2,018 during the twelve-month period extending from July, 1947, to June, 1948. The goods and services such as food, fuel and shelter which the farm provided were valued at an average of $676 per family. One-third of their total living expenditures, therefore, did not involve a direct cash outlay. . . .

Thirty-one per cent of the homes had electric lighting and 37 per cent were lighted by gasoline or kerosene mantle lamps but wick lamps were still being used exclusively in 32 per cent of the homes.

The majority of the families pumped water from wells by hand; only four per cent of the families had running water in their homes. Sixty-nine per cent had kitchen sinks, only 12 per cent had a bathtub or shower and only three per cent had flush toilets. All but 11 per cent of the homes had a power or hand operated washing machine. The majority of the homes did not have any refrigeration facilities. . . . The average distance to a doctor was eight miles and to a hospital, 13 miles. . . .

Of the 75 families [visited in southeastern Saskatchewan] during the twelve-month period, June, 1947, to May, 1948, the total living expenditures average $2,277 per family. The farm-furnished goods and services such as food, fuel and housing used during the year were valued at an average of $777 per family. A direct cash outlay, therefore, was not required for one-third of their total living expenditures. . . . Only 24 per cent of the homes had a furnace or space heater in the basement but 72 per cent had storm windows. Although every home had a basement, only 60 per cent had full basements. . . . Only one family had running water in their home. Most of the families pumped water from a well by hand and carried it to the house. Sixty-one per cent of the homes had kitchen sinks and 12 per cent had bathtubs or showers; none of the homes had flush toilets. The majority of homes were lighted by gasoline or kerosene mantle lamps; only 12 per cent had electric lighting. . . .

Only two homes were more than 15 miles from a gravel road; the average distance of all homes from this facility was only 1.2 miles. The average distance to a grade school was 2.5 miles. . . . The average distance to a doctor was nine miles and to a hospital, 14 miles. . . .

Every family had entertained visitors and only one family had not visited away from home. M. A. MacNaughton, J. M. Mann and M. B. Blackwood. *Farm Family Living in Lanark County, Ontario, 1947-48; Farm Family Living in Southeastern Saskatchewan, 1947-48.* Economics Division, Department of Agriculture, Ottawa, 1950.

BIBLIOGRAPHY

ATLANTIC PROVINCES

Acadian Orchardist. Vol. 1, no. 12. Kentville, N.S., Tuesday, May 2, 1893.

Adams, A. Leith. *Field and Forest Rambles*. London, 1873.

Atkinson, C. W. *A Historical and Statistical Account of New-Brunswick*. 3d. ed., Edinburgh, 1844.

Bagster, C. Birch. *The Progress and Prospects of Prince Edward Island*. Charlottetown, 1861.

Baillie, Thomas. *An Account of the Province of New Brunswick; with Advice to Emigrants*. London, 1832.

Beavan, Mrs. F.. *Sketches and Tales Illustrative of Life in the Backwoods of New Brunswick*. London, 1845.

Bonnycastle, Sir Richard Henry. *Newfoundland in 1842*. 2 vols. London, 1842.

Brown, James. *New Brunswick as a Home for Emigrants*. Saint John, N.B., 1860.

Buckingham, James S.. *Canada, Nova Scotia, New Brunswick, and the other British Provinces in North America*. London, 1843.

Chambers, William. *Things as They Are in America*. London and Edinburgh, 1854.

Coke, E. T.. *A Subaltern's Furlough: Descriptive of Scene in Various Parts of the United States, Upper and Lower Canada, New-Brunswick, and Nova Scotia*. 2 vols. New York, 1833.

The Colonial Farmer, devoted to the agricultural interests of Nova-Scotia, New-Brunswick, and Prince Edward's Island. Vol. 1, no. 2. Halifax, Nova Scotia, August 1841.

A Colonist. *A Reply to the Report of the Earl of Durham*. London, 1839.

Crosskill, Herbert. *Nova Scotia: Its Climate, Resources, and Advantages*. Halifax, 1874.

Crosskill, J. H.. *Agricultural Exhibition of Nova Scotia*. Halifax, 1853.

Dashwood, Richard Lewes. *Chiploquorgan; or, Life by the Camp Fire*. Dublin, 1871.

Dawson, J. W.. *Contributions toward the Improvement of Agriculture in Nova-Scotia*. Halifax, 1856.

De Roos, Frederick Fitzgerald. *Personal Narrative of Travels in the United States and Canada in 1826*. London, 1827.

A Description of the Island of Cape Breton in North America . . . by a Gentleman who has Resided Many Years in the British Colonies. London, n.d. [ca. 1818].

Everest, Rev. Robert. *A Journey through the United States and part of Canada*. London, 1855.

Ferguson, Donald. *Agricultural Education*. Charlottetown, 1884.

Fergusson, James. *Notes of a Tour in North America in 1861*. Edinburgh, 1861.

[Fisher, Peter] An Inhabitant of the Province. *Sketches of New Brunswick*. Saint John, 1825.

Gardiner, Mr., of Charlottetown. *A History of early Prince Edward Island*. [Manuscript]. N.p., n.d. National Archives of Canada, MG 55/30 #139.

A Genuine Account of Nova Scotia. London, 1750.

Gesner, Abraham. *New Brunswick, with Notes for Emigrants*. London, 1847.

———— . *The Industrial Resources of Nova Scotia*. Halifax, 1849.

The Gleaner and Northumberland, Kent, Gloucester and Restigouche Commercial and Agricultural Journal. Vol. XIII. [Chatham-Miramichi, N.B.], Saturday Evening, February 4, 1854.

Gordon, Arthur Hamilton. *Wilderness Journeys in New Brunswick in 1862-63.* Saint John, 1864.

Haliburton, Thomas C.. *A General Description of Nova Scotia.* Halifax, 1825.

———— *The Old Judge, or Life in a Colony.* 2 vols. London, 1849.

Hamilton, John. *Experimental Dairy Station at New Perth.* Charlottetown, 1893.

Harvey, Moses. *Hand-Book of Newfoundland.* Boston, 1886.

Hatheway, C.L.. *The History of New Brunswick from its first Settlement.* Fredericton, 1846.

Hatton, Joseph, and Moses Harvey. *Newfoundland.* London, 1883.

Hill, S. S.. *A Short Account of Prince Edward Island.* London, 1839.

Hollingsworth, S.. *The Present State of Nova Scotia.* 2d ed. Edinburgh, 1787.

Johnston, James F. W.. *Report on the Agricultural Capabilities of the Province of New Brunswick.* Fredericton, 1850.

———— *Notes on North America.* 2 vols. London and Edinburgh, 1851.

Johnstone, Walter: *Travels in Prince Edward Island.* Edinburgh, 1823

Jukes, J. B.. *Excursions in and about Newfoundland during the years 1839 and 1840.* 2 vols. London, 1842.

Letters and Papers on Agriculture extracted from the correspondence of a Society instituted at Halifax for Promoting Agriculture in the Province of Nova-Scotia. Vol. I. Halifax, 1791.

Lewellin, J. L.. *Emigration. Prince Edward Island: A Brief But Faithful Account Of This Fine Colony.* Charlotte-Town, 1832.

London, M. C. S.. *Two Months on the Tobique, New Brunswick; An Emigrant's Journal, 1851.* London, 1866.

Mann, John. *Travels in North America: particularly in the Provinces of Upper & Lower Canada, and New Brunswick.* Glasgow, 1824.

Martin, R. Montgomery. *History of Nova Scotia, Cape Breton, The Sable Islands, New Brunswick, Prince Edward Island, the Bermudas, Newfoundland, etc.* London, 1837.

McGregor, John. *Historical and Descriptive Sketches of the Maritime Colonies of British America.* London, 1828.

The Mechanic and Farmer. Vol. IV, no. 2. Pictou, N.S., May 26, 1841.

Mitchell, John. *The Present State of Great Britain and North America, with regard to Agriculture, Population, Trade, and Manufactures.* London, 1767.

Monro, Alexander. *New Brunswick; with a brief outline of Nova Scotia, and Prince Edward Island.* Halifax, 1855.

Moorsom, Capt. W. *Letters from Nova Scotia.* London, 1830.

New Brunswick Agricultural and Emigrant Society: Young Cannon Ball. [Manuscript] Fredericton, 1825-1828. National Archives of Canada MG 24 L6 Vol. 3.

The New-Brunswick Agriculturist. Vol. 1, no. 1. Saint John, May 1841.

New Brunswick Society for the Encouragement of Agriculture, Home Manufactures, and Commerce. *For the Back Settlements. On General Management of a Farm.* Saint John, 1851.

———— *Journal.* Part II. Fredericton, N.B., 1851.

The Nova Scotian Farmer and Annapolis County Times. Vol. 7, no. 46. Annapolis Royal, Thursday, January 22, 1874.

The Nova Scotian Farmer and Bridgewater Times. Vol. 4, no. 46. Bridgewater, Nova Scotia, January 4, 1871.

Oldmixon, John. *The British Empire in America.* 2d ed. 2 vols. London, 1741.

Outram, Joseph. *Nova Scotia, Its Condition and Resources.* Edinburgh and London, 1850.

Perley, M. H.. *A Hand Book of Information for Emigrants to New-Brunswick.* Saint John, 1854.

Peters, James H.. *Hints to the Farmers of Prince Edward Island.* Charlottetown, 1851.

Pichon, Thomas. *Genuine Letters and Memoirs Relating to the Natural, Civil, and Commercial History of the Islands of Cape Breton and Saint John.* London, 1760.

Pope, A. M.. *In and Around the Magdalen Islands.* New York, 1884.

Prince Edward Island Royal Agricultural Society. *Annual Report for the Year 1845.* Charlottetown, 1846.

A Proprietor. *Remarks upon that Portion of the Earl of Durham's Report relating to Prince Edward Island.* London, 1839.

Pryor, Abraham. *An Interesting Description of British America, from personal knowledge and observation.* Providence, 1819.

Public Archives of Nova Scotia. *Holland's Description of Cape Breton Island.* Halifax, 1935.

Raynal, Abbé. *A Philosophical and Political History of the Settlements and Trade of the Europeans in the East and West Indies.* 8 vols. London, 1783.

Reid, H.. *Sketches in North America; with some account of Congress and of The Slavery Question.* London, 1861.

Rivington, Alex. *In The Track of Our Emigrants.* London, 1872.

Robb, James. *Agricultural Progress.* Fredericton, 1856.

Robertson, J. W.. *Lectures on Agriculture.* Fredericton, 1890.

Robinson, John, and Thomas Rispin. *Journey through Nova-Scotia, containing a particular Account of the Country and its Inhabitants.* York, 1774.

Rogers, Robert. *A Concise Account of North America.* London, 1765.

Selkirk, Earl of. *Observations on the Present State of the Highlands of Scotland, with a view of the Causes and Probable Consequences of Emigration.* London, 1805.

Sleigh, C. M.. *Pine Forests and Hacmatack Clearings; or, Travel, Life and Adventure in the British North American Provinces.* 2d ed. London, 1853.

Spedon, Andrew Learmont. *Rambles among the Blue-Noses; or Reminiscences of a Tour through New Brunswick and Nova Scotia during the summer of 1862.* Montreal, 1863.

Stewart, John. *An Account of Prince Edward Island in the Gulph of St. Laurence.* London, 1806.

Trueman, Howard. *The Chignecto Isthmus And Its First Settlers.* Toronto, 1902.

———— *Early Agriculture in the Atlantic Provinces.* Moncton, 1907.

Tucker, Ephraim W. *Five Months in Labrador and Newfoundland.* Concord, 1839.

Ward, Edmund. *An Account of the River St. John with its Tributary Rivers and Lakes.* Fredericton, 1841.

Watts, Samuel. *Facts for the Information of Intending Emmigrants about New Brunswick.* Woodstock, N.B., 1870.

Whitbourne, Richard. *A Discourse and Discovery of Newfoundland.* London, 1622.

Young, John. *The Letters of Agricola on the Principles of Vegetation and Tillage.* Halifax, 1822.

THE CANADAS

Abbott, Rev. Joseph. *Philip Musgrave; or Memoirs of a Church of England Missionary in the North American Colonies.* London, 1846.

Agricultural Society in Canada. *Papers and Letters on Agriculture, Recommended to the Attention of the Canadian Farmers.* Quebec, 1790.

Alexander, Sir James E. *Transatlantic Sketches.* Philadelphia, 1833.

———— *L'Acadie; or Seven Years' Exploration in British America.* 2 vols. London, 1849.

Anderson, James. *The Improvement of Agriculture and the Elevation in the Social Scale of Both Husbandman and Operative.* Montreal, 1858.

Barclay, Charles, ed.. *Letters from the Dorking Emigrants, who went to Upper Canada in the spring of 1832.* London, 1833.

Barclay-Allardice, Robert. *Agricultural Tour of the Untied States and Upper Canada.* Edinburgh and London, 1842.

Beadle, D. W.. *Canadian Fruit, Flower, and Kitchen Gardener.* Toronto, 1872.

Bell, Rev. William. *Hints to Emigrants, in a series of letters from Upper Canada.* Edinburgh, 1824.

Bigsby, John J., M.D. *The Shoe and Canoe or Pictures of Travel in The Canadas*. 2 vols. London, 1850.

Bilbrough, Ellen Agnes. *British Children in Canadian Homes*. Belleville, Ontario, 1879.

Bingham, Jacob. *A Practical Essay on the Plough*. Toronto, 1856.

Bonnycastle, Sir Richard H. *The Canadas in 1841*. 2 vols. London, 1841.

Boucher, Pierre. *True and Genuine Description of New France, commonly called Canada*. Paris, 1664 [trans.].

Bouchette, Joseph. *A Topographical Description of the Province of Lower Canada with Remarks upon Upper Canada*. London, 1815.

Boulton, D'Arcy. *Sketch of His Majesty's Province of Upper Canada*. London, 1805.

Boulton, Henry John. *A Short Sketch of the Province of Upper Canada for the Information of the Labouring Poor throughout England*. London, 1826.

Bowen, N. H. *An Historical Sketch of the Isle of Orleans*. Quebec, 1860.

Britain. *Reports from the Select Committee on Emigration from the United Kingdom*. London, 1826 and 1827.

Brown, William. *America: A Four Years' Residence in the United States and Canada*. Leeds, 1849.

Brydone, James Marr. *Narrative of a Voyage with a Party of Emigrants, sent out from Sussex, in 1834. . .* Petworth, 1834.

Buchan, William F. *Remarks on Emigration*. 2d ed. Devonport and London, n.d. [ca. 1835].

Buckland, George. "An Agricultural Tour of Welland County," *The Canadian Agriculturist*. Toronto, October 1856.

Butler, Samuel. *The Emigrant's Hand-Book of Facts*. Glasgow, 1843.

Caird, James. *Prairie Farming in America, with notes by the way on Canada and the United States*. New York, 1859.

—— *Caird's Slanders on Canada Answered & Refuted!* Toronto, 1859.

Canada. Department of Agriculture. *Canada: A Handbook of Information for Intending Emigrants*. Ottawa, 1877.

—— Central Experimental Farm, Ottawa, Canada, *Bulletin No. 1*. February 12th, 1887.

—— *Labour Needs of Canada*. Ottawa, 1873.

The Canada Company. *Question and Answer sheet*. Toronto, 1843.

The Canada Farmer. Vol. 1, no. 1. Toronto, January 15, 1864.

The Canadian Agricultural Reader. Niagara, 1845.

The Canadian Antiquarian and Numismatic Journal, Vol. IX, nos. 3 & 4. Montreal, 1912.

The Canadian Journal. A Repertory of Industry, Science, and Art. Toronto, Upper Canada, October, 1852.

Carruthers, J. *Retrospect of Thirty-Six Years Residence in Canada West: being a Christian Journal and Narrative*. Hamilton, 1861.

Champlain. *The Voyages of Samuel de Champlain*. C. P. Otis translation in the Prince Society edition. Boston, 1882.

Charlevoix, Pierre. *Journal of a Voyage to North-America*. London, 1761.

Copleston, Mrs. Edward. *Canada: Why we Live in it, and Why we Like it*. London, 1861.

Croil, James. *Dundas; or A Sketch of Canadian History and more particularly of the County of Dundas*. Montreal, 1861.

Dalton, William. *Travels in the United States of America and Part of Upper Canada*. Appleby, 1821.

Davenport, Mrs. *Journal of a Fourteen Days' Ride through the Bush from Quebec to Lake St. John*. Quebec, 1872.

Davis, Robert. *The Canadian Farmer's Travels in the United States of America*. Buffalo, 1837.

Day, Mrs. C.M. *History of the Eastern Townships*. Montreal, 1869.

Day, Samuel Phillips. *English America: or Pictures of Canadian Places and People*. 2 vols. London, 1864.

Domett, Alfred. *The Canadian Journal of Alfred Domett 1833-1835*. Edited by E. A. Horsman and Lillian Rea Benson. London, Ontario, 1955.

Dominion Grange. *History of the Grange in Canada*. Toronto, May, 1876.

Duncan, John M. *Travels through part of the United States and Canada in 1818 and 1819*. 2 vols. Glasgow, 1823.

Duncumb, Thomas. *The British Emigrant's Advocate: Being a Manual for the use of emigrants and travellers in British America and the United States*. London, 1837.

Dunlop, William. *Statistical Sketches of Upper Canada, for the Use of Emigrants: by a Backwoodsman*. London, 1832.

Durham, Earl of. *Report on the Affairs of British North America*. Montreal, 1839.

Emigration: Letters from Sussex Emigrants. Petworth, 1833.

Essen, George. Letter to *The Canadian Agriculturist*, March, 1861.

Evans, Francis A. *The Emigrant's Directory and Guide*. Dublin, 1833.

Evans, William. *A Treatise on the Theory and Practice of Agriculture, adapted to the cultivation and economy of the animal and vegetable productions of agriculture in Canada*. Montreal, 1835.

———. *Supplementary Volume to a Treatise on the Theory and Practice of Agriculture*. Montreal, 1836.

———. *Agricultural Improvement by the Education of those who are engaged in it as a profession; addressed very respectfully to the Farmers of Canada*. Montreal, 1837.

———, ed. *The Canadian Quarterly Agricultural & Industrial Magazine*. Vol. 1, no. 1. Montreal, 1838.

———, ed. *The British American Cultivator*. Vol. 1. Toronto, 1842.

———, ed. *Agricultural Journal and Transactions of the Lower Canada Agricultural Society*. Vol. 1, no. 1. Montreal, 1848.

Fairplay, Francis. *The Canadas As They Now Are*. London, 1833.

Fergusson, Adam. *Practical Notes made during a Tour in Canada, and a portion of the United States, in 1831*. Edinburgh and London, 1833.

Fidler, Isaac. *Observations on Professions, Literature, Manners and Emigration, in the United States and Canada*. New York, 1833.

Finan, P.. *Journal of a Voyage to Quebec in the Year 1825*. Newry, 1828.

Fowler, Thomas. *Journal of a Tour through British America to the Falls of Niagara*. Aberdeen, 1832.

Fraser, Joshua. *Shanty, Forest and River Life in the Backwoods of Canada*. Montreal, 1883.

French, T. P. *Information for Intending Settlers on the Ottawa and Opeongo Road, And its Vicinity*. Ottawa, 1857.

Gardiner, David. *Canada VS. Nebraska*. Ottawa, 1873.

Le Glaneur. Vol. 1, no. 1. St. Charles, Quebec, December, 1836.

Gourlay, Robert. *Statistical Account of Upper Canada Compiled With a View to a Grand System of Emigration*. 2 vols. London, 1822.

Grece, Charles Frederick. *Essays on Practical Husbandry addressed to the Canadian Farmers*. Montreal, 1817.

———. *Facts and Observations respecting Canada and the United States of America*. London, 1819.

Gurney, Joseph John. *A Journey in North America*. Norwich, 1841.

Haight, Canniff. *Country Life in Canada Fifty Years Ago*. Toronto, 1885.

Hall, Capt. Basil. *Travels in North America in the Years 1827 and 1828*. 3 vols. Edinburgh, 1829.

Hall, Francis. *Travels in Canada and the United States in 1816 and 1817*. 2d ed. London, 1819.

Hardy, Arthur S., and David Spence. *Ontario as a Home for the British Tenant Farmer who desires to become his own Landlord*. Toronto, 1886.

Harris, Edward. *Is Game of any Value to the Farmer?* Toronto, 1881.

Head, Sir Francis B. *The Emigrant*. 2d ed. London, 1846.

Henry, George. *The Emigrant's Guide, or, Canada As It Is*. Quebec, n.d. [ca. 1835].

Heriot, George. *Travels Through the Canadas*. London, 1807.

[Hickey, William] Martin Doyle. *Hints on Emigration to Upper Canada*. 3d ed. Dublin, 1834.

Hodgson, Adam. *Remarks during a Journey through North America in the years 1819, 1820, and 1821 in a Series of Letters*. New York, 1823.

Hogan, J. Sheridan. *Canada: An Essay*. Montreal, 1855.

Howison, John. *Sketches of Upper Canada*. London, 1821.

Inches, James. *Letters on Emigration to Canada*. 2d ed. Perth, 1836.

Isbister, Alexander K. *A Proposal for a New Penal Settlement in Connexion with the Colonization of the Uninhabited Districts of British North America*. London, 1850.

James, C. C. *Agriculture*. Toronto, 1898.

James, Thomas H. *Rambles in the United States and Canada during the year 1845*. London, 1846.

Jameson, Anna Brownell. *Sketches in Canada, and Rambles among the Red Men*. New ed. London, 1852.

Kelland, Philip. *Transatlantic Sketches*. Edinburgh, 1858.

Kingdom, William, Jun. *America and the British Colonies*. London, 1820.

Kingston, William H. G. *Western Wanderings, or a Pleasure Tour in the Canadas*. 2 vols. London, 1856.

Lahontan, Baron de. *New Voyages to North-America*. 2 vols. London, 1703.

Lambert, John. *Travels through Canada and the United States in North America in the Years 1806, 1807 and 1808*. London, 1816.

Langelier, J. C. *Notes on Gaspesia*. 3d ed. Ottawa, 1886.

Langton, W. A., ed. *Early Days in Upper Canada: Letter of John Langton*. Toronto, 1926.

Letters from Canada. 10th ed. Quebec, 1862.

Levigne, R. G. A. *Echoes from the Backwoods; or Sketches of Transatlantic Life*. 2 vols. London, 1846.

Logan, James. *Notes of a Journey through Canada, the United States of America and the West Indies*. Edinburgh, 1838.

Lower Canada Agricultural Society. *Prospectus*. Montreal, 1847.

Lower Canada Agriculturist. Montreal, October 1863.

Lynch, John. "Report of the State of Agriculture in the County of Grey — 1853," *Journal and Transactions of the Board of Agriculture of Upper Canada*. Vol. 1. Toronto, 1856.

MacTaggart, John. *Three Years in Canada: An Account of the Actual State of the Country in 1826-7-8*. 2 vols. London, 1829.

Magrath, T. W. *Authentic Letters from Upper Canada*. Dublin, 1833.

Matthew, Patrick. *Emigration Fields*. Edinburgh and London, 1839.

McGregor, John. *British America*. 2 vols. Edinburgh and London, 1832.

McVicar, Robert. *Letters on Emigration*. Hamilton, 1853.

Mitchell, Edward. *Five Thousand A Year and How I Made It*. Toronto, 1870.

Moodie, Susanna. *Roughing it in the Bush; or, Life in Canada*. New York, 1852.

Moore, Thomas. *A Tour through Canada in 1879*. Dublin, 1880.

Munro, W. F. *The Backwoods' Life*. Toronto, 1869.

Murray, Amelia M. *Letters from the United States, Cuba and Canada*. New York, 1856.

Need, Thomas. *Six Years in the Bush; or Extracts from the Journal of a Settler in Upper Canada*. London, 1838.

Neilson, Joseph. *Observations Upon Emigration to Upper Canada*. Kingston, 1837.

Official Information for Emigrants, arriving at New York, and who are desirous of Settling in the Canadas. Montreal, 1834.

Ogden, J. C. *A Tour through Upper and Lower Canada*. Litchfield, 1799.

Oliver, Andrew. *A View of Lower Canada, interspersed with Canadian Tales and Anecdotes, and Interesting Information to Intending Emigrants*. Edinburgh, 1821.

Ontario. *Emigration to Canada. The Province of Ontario*. Toronto, 1869.

———— . *Supplement to the Report of the Commissioner of Agriculture and Arts for the Year 1868*. Toronto, 1869.

Ontario Agricultural Commission. *Canadian Farming: An Encyclopedia of Agriculture*. Toronto, 1881.

Outline on Means to increase Cultivation and Production of lands in Canada and avoid famines without cost to King or Colony. [Manuscript]. National Archives of Canada, MG 18 H 62 Canada, 1753.

Perrault, J., ed. *Journal of the Transactions of the Board of Agriculture of Lower Canada.* Montreal, 1859.

Philpot, Harvey J. *Guide Book to the Canadian Dominion.* London, 1871.

Picken, Andrew. *The Canadas.* 2d ed. London, 1836.

Pickering, Joseph. *Inquiries of an Emigrant.* 3d ed. London, 1832.

Poole, Thomas W. *A Sketch of the Early Settlement and Subsequent Progress of the Town of Peterborough.* Peterborough, 1867.

Preston, T. R. *Three Years' Residence in Canada from 1837 to 1839.* London, 1840.

Province of Canada. Legislative Assembly of Lower Canada. *Report of the Select Committee into the Causes and Importance of the Emigration which has taken place annually from Lower Canada to the United States.* Montreal, 1849.

————. *Report of the Minister of Agriculture for the year 1864.* Quebec, 1865.

Quebec Gazette. *The Lower Canada Farmers' and Mechanics' Almanack for the year 1834.* Quebec, 1834.

Raynal, Abbé. *Philosophical and Political History of the British Settlements and Trade in North America.* Edinburgh, 1779.

Riddell, Walter. *Farming in Northumberland County: 1833 to 1895.* Ontario Historical Society Papers and Records. Vol. XXX. 1934.

Rubidge, Charles. *Letter from Woodlands, near Peterboro' 26th October, 1840.* N.p., n.d.

Russell, Robert. *North America: Its Agriculture and Climate.* Edinburgh, 1857.

Sansom, Joseph. *Sketches of Lower Canada.* New York, 1817.

Scrope, G. Poulett. *Memoir of the Life of the Rt. Hon. Charles Lord Sydenham, with a Narrative of his Administration in Canada.* London, 1843.

Shaw, John, M.D.. *A Ramble through the United States, Canada, and the West Indies.* London, 1856.

Shirreff, Charles. *Thoughts on Emigration and on the Canadas as an Opening for it.* Quebec, 1831.

Shirreff, Patrick. *A Tour through North America; together with a comprehensive view of the Canadas and United States, as adapted for agricultural emigration.* Edinburgh, 1835.

Silliman, Benjamin. *Remarks Made on a Short Tour between Hartford and Quebec in the Autumn of 1819.* New Haven, 1820.

Smallfield, Albert. *Lands and Resources of Renfrew County, Province of Ontario.* Renfrew, 1881.

Smith, Michael. *A Geographical View of the Province of Upper Canada.* 3d ed. Philadelphia, 1813.

Smith, W.H. *Canada: Past, Present and Future.* 2 vols. Toronto, 1852.

Smyth, David William. *A Short Topographical Description of His Majesty's Province of Upper Canada in North America.* 2d ed. London, 1813.

Society for Promoting Christian Knowledge. *Colonists' Handbooks: No. 1: Canada.* London, 1882.

Society for the Relief of Strangers in Distress at York. *Annual Report of the Proceedings.* York, Upper Canada, 1827.

A Statement of the Satisfactory Results which have attended Emigration to Upper Canada from the establishment of the Canada Company. 5th ed. London, 1846.

Stewart, Rev. Charles. *A Short View of the Present State of the Eastern Townships in the Province of Lower Canada.* London, 1817.

Stewart, Frances. *Our Forest Home.* Montreal, 1889.

Stratton, T., M.D. *Remarks on the Sickness and Mortality among the Emigrants to Canada in 1847.* Montreal, 1848.

Strickland, Samuel. *Twenty-Seven Years in Canada West; or, The Experience of an Early Settler.* 2 vols. London, 1853.

Stuart, Charles. *The Emigrant's Guide to Upper Canada.* London, 1820.

Sullivan, Edward. *Rambles and Scrambles in North and South America.* London, 1852.

Talbot, Edward Allen. *Five Years' Residence in the Canadas.* 2 vols. London, 1824.

Talbot, John. *History of North America.* 2 vols. Leeds, 1820.

Tewsley, James. *Letters from Goderich.* [Manuscript] 1842. National Archives of Canada, MG40T1

Thomas, Cyrus. *Contributions to the History of the Eastern Townships*. Montreal, 1866.

Thompson, Samuel. *Reminiscences of a Canadian Pioneer for the last fifty years*. Toronto, 1884.

Thomson, William. *A Tradesman's Travels, in the United States and Canada, in the years 1840, 41, &* *42*. Edinburgh, 1842.

Todd, Henry C. *Notes upon Canada and the United States from 1832 to 1840*. 2d ed. Toronto, 1840.

Traill, Mrs. C. P. *The Canadian Settler's Guide*. Toronto, 1855.

———. *Lady Mary and Her Nurse: or, a peep into the Canadian Forest*. London, 1856.

Tudor, Henry. *Narrative of a Tour in North America*. 2 vols. London, 1834.

Upper Canada. House of Assembly of Upper Canada. *Report from the Select Committee on the State of the Province*. Toronto, 1839.

Vigne, Godfrey T. *Six Months in America*. 2 vols. London, 1832.

Warr, Rev. G. W. *Canada As It Is; or, the Emigrant's Friend and Guide to Upper Canada*. 2d ed. London, 1847.

Weld, Isaac. *Travels through the States of North America and the Provinces of Upper and Lower Canada during the years 1795, 1796 and 1797*. London, 1799.

Wells, W. B.. *Canadiana: containing Sketches of Upper Canada*. London, 1837.

Weston, Richard. *A Visit to the United States and Canada in 1833*. Edinburgh, 1836.

Whitcombe, Charles Edward. *The Canadian Farmer's Manual of Agriculture*. Toronto, 1874.

Wilkie, David. *Sketches of a Summer Trip to New York and the Canadas*. Edinburgh, 1837.

Wright, Philemon. *An Account of the First Settlement of the Township of Hull, on the Ottawa River, Lower Canada*. Quebec, 1821.

THE WEST

Adney, Tappan. *The Klondike Stampede*. New York and London, 1900.

Allen, Capt. C. W. *The Land Prospector's Manual and Field-Book*. Ottawa, 1881.

Anderson, A. C. *The Dominion at the West*. Victoria, 1872.

Armstrong, L. O. *Southern Manitoba and Turtle Mountain Country*. N.p., 1880.

Barneby, W. Henry. *Life and Labour in the Far, Far West*. London, 1884.

Bass, Charles. *Lectures on Canada*. Hamilton, 1863.

British Columbia. *British Columbia as a Field for Emigration and Investment*. Victoria, 1891.

———. *Information for Emigrants*. London, 1875.

———. *Province of British Columbia, Canada. Its Climate and Resources; with Information for Emigrants*. Victoria, 1883.

Burrows, Acton. *North Western Canada, Its Climate, Soil and Productions*. Winnipeg. 1880.

The Calgary Herald. Vol. 1, no. 1. August 31, 1883.

Canada. Department of Agriculture. *Canadian North-West. Climate and Productions. A Misrepresentation Exposed*. Ottawa, 1883.

———. *Province of Manitoba and North West Territory*. Ottawa, 1876.

———. *Report of the Select Committee of the Senate on Rupert's Land, Red River . . . and the North-West Territory*. Ottawa, 1870.

———. *Reports of Tenant Farmers' Delegates*. Ottawa, 1880.

———. *Sessional Papers* Vol. 4. Second Session of the Sixth Parliament. Ottawa, 1888.

———. *Settlers' Experiences in Western Canada*. Ottawa, 1900.

———. *Views of Members of the British Association and others. Information for Intending Settlers*. Ottawa, 1884.

———. *The Visit of the Tenant-Farmer Delegates to Canada in 1890*. London, 1891.

Canadian Pacific Railway. *The North-West Farmer in Manitoba, Assiniboia, Alberta*. N.p., 1891.

———. *What Women Say of the Canadian North West*. Montreal, 1886.

Carver, Jonathan. *Three Years Travels through the Interior Parts of North America*. Philadelphia, 1796.

Chambers, Capt. Ernest J., ed. *Canada's Fertile Northland*. Ottawa, 1907.

Chambers, W. & R. *A Year in Manitoba 1880-1881*. 2d ed. London and Edinburgh, 1882.

Chittenden, Newton H. *Travels in British Columbia*. Victoria, 1882.

The Commercial. The Advantages of the Prince Albert District, Saskatchewan, Are Unsurpassed. Winnipeg, 1892.

Coues, Elliott, ed. *The Manuscript Journals of Alexander Henry and of David Thompson 1799-1814*. 3 vols. New York, 1897.

Craig, John R. *Ranching with Lords and Commons, or Twenty Years on the Range.* Toronto, 1903.

d'Artigue, Jean, *Six Years in the Canadian North-West.* Toronto, 1882.

Davin, Nicholas Flood, M.P., ed. *Homes for Millions. The Great Canadian North-West.* Ottawa, 1891.

DeGroot, Henry. *British Columbia; its Conditions and Prospects, Soil, Climate, and Mineral Resources Considered.* San Francisco, 1859.

Elkington, E. Way. *Canada The Land of Hope.* London, 1910.

Elkington, W. M. *Five Years in Canada.* London and Rugby, 1895.

England, Roberts. *The Colonization of Western Canada.* London, 1936.

Fast, Gerhard Andrew, and Jacob Fast. *To Find the Daily Bread.* N.p., n.d.

Field, Septimus. *Western Canada.* Ottawa, 1898.

Fitzgerald J. G. *Dominion of Canada. District of Alberta. Information for Intending Settlers.* Ottawa, 1884.

Fitzgibbon, Mary. *A Trip to Manitoba.* Toronto, 1880.

Fleming, Sandford. *Report on Surveys and Preliminary Operations on the Canadian Pacific Railway up to January 1877.* Ottawa, 1877.

Forbes, Charles. *Vancouver Island: Its Resources and Capabilities as a Colony.* Victoria, 1862.

Franklin, Capt. John. *Journey to the Shores of the Polar Sea, In 1819-20-21-22; with a Brief Account of the Second Journey In 1825-26-27.* 4 vols. London, 1829.

Fream, William. *Across Canada: A Report on Its Agricultural Resources.* Ottawa, 1886.

Gaetz, Leo. *Alberta, North-West Territory: Report of Six Years' Experience of a Farmer in the Red River District.* Ottawa, 1890.

Gill: E. A. Wharton. *A Manitoba Chore Boy. The Experiences of a Young Emigrant Told from his Letters.* London, 1912.

Glenbow Museum. *How to Read a Brand.* Calgary, n.d.

Hall, Mrs. Cecil. *A Lady's Life on a Farm in Manitoba.* London, 1884.

Hamilton, J. C. *The Prairie Province.* Toronto, 1876.

[Hardy, John] *An Old Settler. Farming in the Canadian North-West.* London, n.d. [ca. 1903].

Hargrave, Joseph James. *Red River.* Montreal, 1871.

Hennepin, Louis. *A New Discovery of a Vast Country in America.* 2d London issue, 1698.

Higinbotham, John D. *When the West Was Young.* Toronto, 1933.

Hill, Alex Stavely. *From Home to Home: Autumn Wanderings in the North-West, in the years 1881, 1882, 1883, 1884.* London, 1885.

Hind, Henry Youle. *Narrative of the Canadian Red River Exploring Expedition of 1857 and of the Assiniboine and Saskatchewan Exploring Expedition of 1858.* 2 vols. London, 1860.

Johnson, Alice M., ed. *Saskatchewan Journals and Correspondence.* Hudson's Bay Record Society. London, 1967.

Kelly, L. V. *The Range Men.* Toronto, 1913.

Lamb, W. Kaye, ed. *Sixteen Years in the Indian Country: The Journal of Daniel Williams Harmon.* Toronto, 1957.

Larkey, George. *Days of the Past.* Lemon Grove, California, 1956.

MacBeth, R. G. *Farm Life in the Selkirk Colony.* Winnipeg, 1897.

MacDonald, D. G. F. *Lecture on British Columbia and Vancouver's Island.* London, 1863.

Macdonnell, Miles. *Letter to the Earl of Selkirk, July 17, 1813.* The Selkirk Papers, National Archives of Canada.

Macdougall, W. B. *Guide to Manitoba and the North-West.* N.p., 1880.

MacFie, Matthew. *Vancouver Island and British Columbia*. London, 1865.

MacInnes, C. M. *In the Shadow of the Rockies*. London, 1930.

MacInnes, D. *A Trip Across British Columbia*. Hamilton, 1889.

Mackenzie, Alexander. *Voyages from Montreal, on the River St. Laurence, through the Continent of North-America, to the Frozen and Pacific Oceans; In the Years 1789 and 1793*. London, 1801.

Macoun, John. *Manitoba and The Great North-West*. Guelph, 1882.

Manitoba. *Report of the Joint Committee of Both Houses on Agriculture, Immigration and Colonization, during the First Session of the first legislature of Manitoba*. Winnipeg, 1871.

Mayne, Cmdr. R. C. *Four Years in British Columbia and Vancouver Island*. London, 1862.

McCaig, J. *Alberta*. Edmonton, 1919.

McGusty, H. A. *Two Years in Manitoba and the North-West Territory*. Frome, n.d. [c. 1890].

McKillican, W. C. *An Outline of the History of Agriculture in Manitoba*. [Manuscript] Provincial Library, Manitoba. Winnipeg, 1929.

Memorial of Settlers in the tract granted to the Saskatchewan Homestead Co. N.p., 1883.

Mitchell, Peter. *The West and North-West*. Montreal, 1880.

The Montreal Star. The Prairies of Manitoba and Who Live on Them. Montreal, n.d. [ca. 1888].

Morris Herald. Morris Manitoba. Growth and Progress. Morris, 1882.

Murchie, R. W., and H. C. Grant. *Unused Lands of Manitoba*. Winnipeg, 1926.

Murray, Alexander Hunter. *Journal of the Yukon 1847-48*. Ottawa, 1910.

North-West Territories. *Annual Report of the Department of Agriculture 1899*. Regina, 1900.

The Nor'-Wester. Vol. 1, no. 1. Red River Settlement, December 28, 1859.

Ogilvie, William. *Information respecting the Yukon District*. Ottawa, 1897.

O'Leary, Peter. *Travels and Experiences in Canada, the Red River Territory, and the United States*. London, [1877].

Palliser, John. *Journals, Detailed Reports and Observations relative to Captain Palliser's Exploration of a portion of British North America*. London, 1862.

Pegler, Alfred. *A Visit to Canada and the United States*. Southampton, 1884.

Pemberton, J. Despard. *Facts and Figures Relating to Vancouver Island and British Columbia*. London, 1860.

Pritchard, John. *Glimpses of the Past in the Red River Settlement*. Middle Church, Manitoba, 1892.

Province of Canada. *Report of the Exploration of the Country Between Lake Superior and the Red River Settlement*. Toronto, 1858.

Raw, W. Fraser. *Newfoundland to Manitoba*. New York, 1881.

Ralph, Julian. *On Canada's Frontier*. New York, 1892.

Ranching in the Canadian North West. N.p., n.d. [ca. 1902].

Rattray, Alexander. *Vancouver Island and British Columbia. Where They Are; What They Are; and What They May Become*. London, 1862.

Regina Board of Trade. *An Unvarnished Tale of Regina and its Agricultural and Ranching District*. Regina, 1891.

Report of the Synod of the Diocese of Rupert's Land. Cambridge, 1869.

Ross, Alexander. *Letters of a Pioneer*. Winnipeg: The Historical and Scientific Society of Manitoba, 1903.

Ross, Ross & Killam, Canada. *Manitoba, Sixty Thousand Acres of Select Farming Lands*. Toronto, 1880.

Russell, A. J. *The Red River Country, Hudson's Bay & North-West Territories considered in relation to Canada*. 3d ed. Montreal, 1870.

Scripps, J. L. *The Undeveloped Northern Region of the American Continent*. Chicago, 1856.

Shannon, William, and C. McLachlan. *British Columbia and Its Resources*. London, 1889.

Shantz, J. Y. *Narrative of a Journey to Manitoba*. Ottawa, 1873.

A Sister of Charity of Montreal: Notes and Sketches collected from a Voyage in the North-West. Montreal, 1875.

Somerset, H. Somers. *The Land of the Muskeg*. London, 1895.

Southesk, Earl of. *Saskatchewan and the Rocky Mountains*. Edinburgh, 1875.

Spence, Thomas. *Manitoba and the North-West of the Dominion*. Toronto, 1871.

———— . *Useful and Practical Hints for the Settler on Canadian Prairie Lands*. Ottawa, 1881.

Stephenson, Thomas. *Notes of a Tour through the Provinces of Quebec, Ontario, Manitoba and the North-West Territory*. Liverpool, n.d. [ca. 1882].

Stock, A. B. *Ranching in the Canadian West*. London, 1912.

Sutherland, Alexander. *A Summer in Prairie Land. Notes of a Tour through the North-West Territory*. Toronto, 1881.

Sutherland, J. K. *The Black Blizzards and What We Must Do about Them. "Next-Year Country,"* by Jean Burnet. Toronto, 1951.

Taché, Msgr, Bishop of St. Boniface. *Sketch of the North-West of America*. Montreal, 1870.

Tanner, Henry. *Successful Emigration to Canada*. London and New York, 1884.

Trow, James. *Manitoba and North West Territories*. Ottawa, 1878.

Webster, W. A. *A Canadian Farmer's Report. Minnesota and Dakota compared with Manitoba and the Canadian North-West*. Ottawa, 1888.

West, John. *The Substance of a Journal during a Residence at the Red River Colony*. London, 1824.

Wyatt, George H. *Manitoba, the Canadian North-West, and Ontario*. Toronto, 1880.